THE CHURCH
IN THE
NEW TESTAMENT

THE CHURCH
IN THE
NEW TESTAMENT

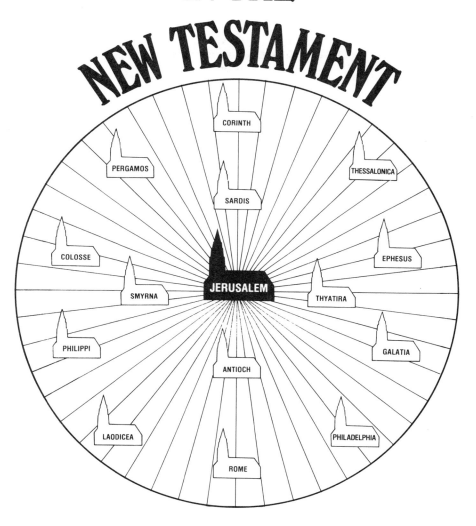

CORINTH

PERGAMOS

THESSALONICA

SARDIS

COLOSSE

EPHESUS

SMYRNA

JERUSALEM

THYATIRA

PHILIPPI

GALATIA

ANTIOCH

LAODICEA

PHILADELPHIA

ROME

by Kevin J. Conner

First Australian Edition 1983
Second Australian Edition 1987
Reprinted 1988

ISBN 0 949829 17 X

DISTRIBUTORS

Australia:
Waverley Book Store
P.O. Box 140, Vermont,
Victoria, 3133.

U.S.A.
Bible & Gift Shop
7545 N.E. Glisan Street,
Portland, Oregon, 97213.
(503) 253 9020

Typeset and printed in Australia by:
ACACIA PRESS PTY. LTD., BLACKBURN, VICTORIA.

THE CHURCH IN THE NEW TESTAMENT
TABLE OF CONTENTS

SUPPLEMENTAL CHAPTER

THE CHURCH IN THE NEW TESTAMENT

FOREWORD

In Matthew 16:15-20 and 18:15-20 we have the first distinct mentions of "The Church" in the New Testament. Both of these are mentioned by the Lord Jesus Christ Himself, the builder of the Church.

It is important to know and understand what God is saying to our generation, and what is God's purpose in the earth in these days. We need Biblical concepts in order to build according to God's purpose.

Important questions to which every minister should have clear answers are: What is our *vision*? What are our *goals*? What do we believe is the *central* thing in God's mind? What is the *hub* of God's will and purpose?

The answer to these crucial questions determine a minister's direction, preaching and teaching, his faith and spiritual endurance.

I. **The Ministry of Jeremiah** — Jeremiah 1:9, 10

    The Scriptures reveal that Jeremiah's ministry was twofold or in two stages.

    ★ Stage one — Jeremiah had "to root out, and to pull down, and to destroy, and to throw down".

    ★ Stage two — Jeremiah then was "to build and to plant".
       These two stages include the thought of architectural and agricultural ministries.

    So we say that there are various concepts of the Church that have to be "rooted out, pulled down, destroyed and thrown down" before God can "build and plant" the truth concerning His Church.

II. **The Great Shaking**

    In connection with the above "Jeremiah-ministry" the Scripture also shows us that everything is to be shaken that can be shaken. Nations, governments, philosophies, denominations, cultures, people, traditions of men, doctrines, concepts and values will be, and are being shaken as never before.

    ★ The earth is to be shaken — Isaiah 2:19-21.
    ★ The nation of Israel is to be shaken — Ezekiel 38:19, 20.
    ★ The heavens are to be shaken — Haggai 2:6, 7.
    ★ The nations are to be shaken — Haggai 2:6, 7.
    ★ Everything that can be shaken is to be shaken — Hebrews 12:26-29.

    We are living in that period of human history when many traditions and concepts are being shaken, things are being rooted out, torn down, plucked up and destroyed. This has to be before the Lord can build and plant the truth. The only unshakable thing is THE CHURCH in THE KINGDOM of God.

III. **Traditional Methods and Concepts**

    The Church today has built up so many things that are not necessarily THE CHURCH that Christ said He would build. They could be part of it and practical expressions of its ministry but these are necessarily THE Church. Some of these are noted here and all need to be considered in the light of the Divine intention.

    ★ Educational Institutions, Schools and Colleges.
    ★ Hospitals, Leprosariums, Medical Clinics, etc.
    ★ Orphanages.

★ Bible Colleges, Theological Seminaries.

★ Sunday School Programs, Children's Works.

★ Missionary Compounds, Communes, Evangelistic Centres.

★ Revival Centres, Charismatic Home Groups and Meetings, Clubs, etc.

★ Other Para-Church Groups.

These things may be good in themselves and the work they do, but they are not necessarily THE CHURCH of which Christ is the Head and the Builder! It is possible to have these things yet not have a New Testament Church!

There are also other concepts of the Church that are faulty and have to be rooted out before we can build and plant the Church which Christ had in mind. Some of these are listed here, and the writer had to experience this ''rooting out'' phase of ministry before he could understand the ''building and planting'' ministry.

★ The Church is a parenthetical plan and purpose of God.

★ The Church is a mystery and not to be seen or found in the Old Testament.

★ The Church is to end in Laodicean failure, with only ''the little flock'' saved.

★ The Church is to be replaced by Jewish ministry in the Last Days before Christ comes.

★ The Church is to be renewed as to its own wine skin denominational structures.

★ The Church is to be replaced by some ''new thing'' that the Lord will do.

★ The Church will be superseded by the restoration of the Old Mosaic Covenant economy.

WHAT IS YOUR CONCEPT OF THE CHURCH that Christ said He would build? These are things that this text grapples with. To know the truth is to be set free. To know the Christ of God is to be set free.

It is the writer's prayer that all who read will come into a greater understanding and appreciation of the eternal purpose of God in Christ and in the Church which is His Body.

Kevin J. Conner

CHAPTER 1

PROMISE AND PROPHECY

Scriptures: Matthew 16:15-20; 18:15-20.

When it comes to the revelation of the Church in the New Testament we discover that there is a threefold progression as to its origin and establishment; first in the Gospels, then in the Acts and then in the Epistles.

The principle of the Kingdom Seed could be applied to the revelation of the Church also. It is *"first the blade"* (The Church in the Gospels), *"then the ear"* (The Church in the Acts), and then *"the full corn in the ear"* (The Church in the Epistles) (Mark 4:28).

In our first chapter we consider The Promise and The Prophecy of Jesus who said that He would build His Church, which building is seen both in the Acts and the Epistles.

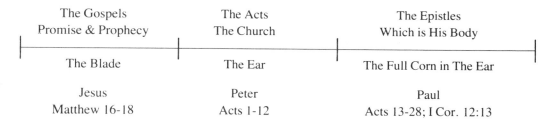

The Gospels	The Acts	The Epistles
Promise & Prophecy	The Church	Which is His Body
The Blade	The Ear	The Full Corn in The Ear
Jesus	Peter	Paul
Matthew 16-18	Acts 1-12	Acts 13-28; I Cor. 12:13

It is significant to note that in the Gospel three major words are used; these being (1) The Kingdom, (2) The Disciples, and (3) The Church. In the Acts it is also (1) The Kingdom, (2) The Disciples and (3) The Church. In the Epistles it is (1) The Church, and (2) The Kingdom, while the word ''disciple'' is not used once! The disciples of the Gospel who came into the kingdom now find their place and function in the Church!

A. **The Church in the Gospels**

There are only *two* specific references to the Church in the Gospels, and these are both found in Matthew, the Gospel of the Kingdom (Matthew 16:15-20; 18:15-20). Neither Mark, Luke nor John mention The Church.

The background of Christ's promise to build His Church is significant. The Gospel of Matthew is distinctly the Gospel of the Kingdom. Jesus Christ, the Seed of Abraham and of David, the King of the Kingdom, came to His own people, Judah, and presented to them the Kingdom of God.

Jesus preached, taught and demonstrated the power of that kingdom but Jewry generally hardened their hearts to the king and the kingdom He came to establish. It was not the type of kingdom they expected. They looked for a nationalist, carnal, earthly, political and materialistic kingdom. They looked for the kind of kingdom that would overthrow the Roman yoke of bondage. They looked for a Davidic kingdom like unto David's, of military might and power and subjugation of all Gentile enemies.

Jesus, however, presented a spiritual and heavenly kingdom that could only be entered by repentance and faith (Matthew 4:17; Mark 1:14, 15).

Hence blindness and hardness of heart and spiritual deafness settled upon Jewry as a nation.

The Sanhedrin took counsel together to crucify their Messianic King (Matthew 12:14).

The Kingdom of God was then to be taken from them and given to a nation that would bring forth the fruits thereof (Matthew 21:43).

It is with this background and setting at Caesarea Philippi that Jesus prophesied of the building of His Church (Matthew 16:15-20).

The Old Testament Church (Acts 7:38), represented in the religious leaders of the nation and in the people of Judah, had become "old wine skins". They were hard and dry and inflexible to the "new wine" of the Kingdom that Jesus came to bring. The "new wine" of New Covenant truths could not be put by Christ or His apostles into the Old Covenant wineskin Church. New Covenant truth and Old Covenant wineskins would not stay together. The one would burst the other (Luke 5:36-39).

Therefore Christ promised, and the promise becomes the prophecy, that, "Upon this Rock I will build My Church" (Matthew 16:18). It would no longer be the Church built by and upon Moses (Acts 15:21). It would be the Church that was built by and upon Christ, to whom Moses pointed. It would no longer be the Old Covenant Church of the chosen nation of Israel, but the New Covenant Church chosen out of every kindred, tongue, tribe and nation.

B. **The Church Universal** (Matthew 16:18-20).

In this passage of Scripture we have the first specific mention by Christ of the Church He was going to build. "Upon this Rock I will build MY CHURCH" (Matthew 16:18). It will be noticed that the word "Church" is in the singular, not "Churches" in the plural.

This is the first basic concept that the Head of the Church teaches concerning His Church. That is, there would be *one universal Church!*

He would build His Church — NOT Churches!

It is for this reason that, out of the many references to the Church in the Acts and the Epistles, the word is so often used in the singular. It is so used to denote the *unity* of the Church worldwide, regardless of locality.

God has given Christ to be Head over all things to *the Church* (Ephesians 1:22).

Christ is the Head of *the Church* (Ephesians 5:23).

Christ loved *the Church* and gave Himself for it that it might be a glorious *Church like unto Himself* (Ephesians 5:24-32).

The Church is the Body of Christ (Colossians 1:18). It is *the Church* of God (Acts 20:28). It is also *the Church* of Christ (Ephesians 5:32).

There is but one Church and Christ Himself is the builder and the Head of this Church. The Church "catholic" is the Church universal.

The believer needs ever to keep this fact in mind that he belongs to the ONE TRUE UNIVERSAL CHURCH.

C. **The Church Local** (Matthew 18:15-20).

The second use of the word "Church" is that found in Matthew 18:15-20.

A consideration of the concept therein reveals that here it speaks more particularly of the Church local, or the Church in a given locality.

The passage has to do with the discipline of any member who refuses to come to reconciliation with another member. The end result is that the matter is brought before the Church and if he neglects to hear the Church, then he is to be excommunicated.

It would be difficult and impossible to tell this to the Church universal but it could be done to the Church in a given locality, or the local Church.

The local Church is a small replica and yet a part of the universal Church. There is no such thing as a Country Church, or National Church, or Provincial or District Church in the Scriptures.

There is but the Church universal and the Church local.

We see that it is upon these two basic concepts as set forth in the Gospel of Matthew that all New Testament revelation in the Acts and the Epistles concerning the church, the Body of Christ, is built.

Matthew 16:15-20 speaks of the *Church Universal.*

Matthew 18:15-20 speaks of the *Church Local.*

It is for this reason that we have the *plural* use of the word "*Churches*" in a number of places in the Acts and the Epistles.

The *Churches* in Judea, Galilee and Samaria (Acts 9:31.RV.)

The *Churches* in Syria and Cilicia (Acts 15:41).

The *Churches* of Asia (I Corinthians 16:19).

The *Churches* of Macedonia (II Corinthians 8:1).

The *Churches* of Galatia (Galatians 1:2; I Corinthians 16:1).

The *Churches* of Judea (Galatians 1:22).

The *Churches* of God in Judea (I Thessalonians 2:14).

The same is true when Christ speaks to the *Churches* in Asia. Though spoken to each local *Church,* yet together they constituted the local *Churches* (Revelation 1-2-3 chapters).

What the Spirit says to the *Churches* must be heard by all, though He may address but one in a given locality. They are locally responsible to Him. He is universally responsible to all.

The *Churches* were established (Acts 16:5).

Paul was the apostle of the *Churches* of the Gentiles (Romans 16:4), which were the *Churches* of Christ (Romans 16:16). They were also the *Churches* of the saints (I Corinthians 14:33).

Read also I Corinthians 16:19; II Corinthians 8:1; Revelation 1:4, 11.

The risen Lord spoke by the Spirit to the Churches in Asia, yet each was a local Church (Revelation 2:11, 17, 23, 29; 3:6, 13, 22; 22:16).

There was a Church in each place. They were united by the Spirit of God and the life of Jesus Christ, not by organizational unity. They were one Body. Neither Jerusalem nor Rome could be the "Mother" Church to govern, organize or control any Church in any locality. Fellowship and instruction could be given but not control from any central headquarters, or central government.

IN SUMMARY the Gospel of Matthew speaks of the Church universal, "*His Church*", and yet within this one Church there would be numerous local Churches, each of which would be a replica and part of the whole. The local Churches together would comprise the universal Church.

The Church local would be in plurality, in many places (I Thessalonians 2:14).

The Church universal would be in unity in many places (I Corinthians 10:32).

The Church local would gather in the one geographical place. The Church universal would gather in every place around the world.

The Church is only separated or divided on the basis of geographical locality, but it is one in Spirit and life.

The "seed" thoughts in both of these passages in Matthew's Gospel will be developed more fully in the Acts and Epistles in our subsequent chapters. The promise and prophecy of Christ shall be fulfilled. God watches over His Word to bring it to pass (Jeremiah 1:11-12). His Word will not return unto Him void but will accomplish that which He sent it unto (Isaiah 55:10, 11).

CHAPTER 2

ACCORDING TO THE PATTERN

(The Pattern and The Glory)

Introductory:

If the Lord Jesus Christ is going to *build His Church,* it is basic that He as a ''wise master-builder'' will build it according to the Divine pattern, to God's design or blueprint.

Before any builder commences building, he draws up a plan, a design, to which He intends to build, and all other builders — subcontractors — build according to that pattern as laid out therein.

No good builder ever *gathers* a lot of material and builds it at random. The materials must be placed according to the blueprint. A heap of stones is not a house, neither is a bulk of material on a piece of land a house. All the material must be assembled in its proper and respective place and built according to the plan of the Architect.

It is a sad plight today that many, many times God's people are ''gathered together'' as a lot of material and ''spiritual stones'' but never assembled or ''built together'' as a house for the Lord, a habitation for His glory. The people are ''*multiplied*'' but not ''*edified*'' (Acts 9:31). They are ''*gathered*'' but not ''*assembled*'' into their place in God's building (I Corinthians 3:9-17).

A. God has a Pattern

The Scriptures show that the Lord God has a pattern for His Church. Jesus Christ is the Architect, the wise Master-Builder, and He will build His Church according to that pattern (Matthew 16:18-19).

God has only *one pattern* for His Church, whether local or universal. The ''scaffolding'' may vary according to the national culture in various countries, but the foundational truths and Biblical principles will be the same. In other words, God's methods may change and vary but His purpose is the same; it never changes. It cannot be over-emphasized that the Church will be built according to the Divine pattern.

We will consider some of the structures in Scripture which originated with God and were built according to the pattern shown to the builders. It will be noted that none built according to whatever design he chose, but all built according to that which was Divinely given them.

The word ''*pattern*'' is defined as follows:

1. Dictionary (Collins).

    a. A model proposed for imitation.

    b. A specimen.

    c. A shape to direct the cutting of cloth.

    d. A figure or style of ornamental execution.

2. Bible Definition (Hebrew) — Deuteronomy 4:16-18; Exodus 25:8, 9.

    a. A structure

    b. A model resemblance.

    c. A likeness (Deuteronomy 4:16-18).

    Thus all Old Testament Divinely originated structures were ''*models*'' and ''*resemblances*'' of that which finds fulfilment in the New Testament Church.

B. Old Testament Patterns

1. **The Ark of Noah** (Genesis 6:14-16).

    This is the ''*fashion*'' which thou shalt make it.

The Hebrew word "fashion" means (a) A verdict (judgment), (b) A sentence or formal decree, (c) A Divine law, (d) A Divine style.

"The make or form of anything, workmanship, the act or process of making; to mold in some manner or another" (Random House Dictionary).

"To give a specified shape to; to model according to; to model after or like something; to shape into or to something" (Oxford).

The Hebrew word "mishphat" is also translated "manner" (Leviticus 5:10; II Chronicles 30:16); "likeness" (Genesis 1:26); "similitude" (Daniel 10:16); and "order" (I Chronicles 6:32).

Thus Noah was told of the coming judgments on the earth. The Lord told him to build an ark to the saving of his household and a remnant of all creatures (Hebrews 11:7). The ark was to be built after the *fashion* that God showed him. Noah did not originate the idea or design of the saving ark. God was the Architect. Noah was the builder according to the pattern given him. The details were given to Noah. It was to be an ark of gopher wood, having rooms, pitched within and without. It was to be 300 cubits long, 50 cubits broad by 30 cubits high, having a window at the top and a door at the side. It was also to have three stories. Into it were to be brought seven of every clean beast and two of every unclean beast, by their pairs (Genesis 7:2-3). Scripture records that Noah did according to all that the Lord commanded him.

There was full obedience to the Divine pattern in the making of the ark of salvation (Genesis 6:22; 7:5, 9).

2. **The Sacrificial Altars** (Exodus 20:24-26).

In the making of sacrificial altars, God laid out His commands. These altars could be made of earth, or stone. No tool was to be used to shape the stones of the altar, but they were to be used just as they had been shaped by the hand of nature. They were shaped naturally and unhewn or polluted by the hand of man or human ingenuity.

The altars of the heathen were shaped by human hands, but the altars of the saints were according to God's pattern for worship and sacrificial approach (Genesis 8:20, 21; 12:7; 13:4, 18; 35:3; I Kings 18:30-39). All pointed to the Cross of Calvary.

3. **The Nation of Israel** (Acts 7:38).

Israel is called "The Church in the Wilderness". The whole ordering of the camp of the tribes, the priesthood, the sanctuary, the camp, the tithes and offerings, etc., surely reveals God's pattern and principle for His people (Numbers 1-8). All were positioned in the shape of the Cross and gathered to the Name of the Lord. All was according to the commandment of the Lord.

4. **The Tabernacle of Moses** (Exodus 25-40).

The details of the Tabernacle of the Lord built by Moses are found in these chapters. Nothing originated with the mind of man, not even with Moses. All the details, the measurements, the materials, the pattern originated with God Himself, the great Architect. Moses and those that helped him simply built according to the pattern shown him in the mount.

"According to *all* that I show thee, after the *pattern* of the tabernacle, and the *pattern* of all the instruments thereof, *even so shall ye make it*" (Hebrews 8:8; Exodus 25:8, 9; 26:30; Numbers 8:4).

The people obeyed Moses and the Lord and all was built according to the pattern as the Lord commanded Moses (Exodus 39:42, 43; 40:33, 34). Seventeen times in Exodus 39-40 we are told that all was done "as the Lord commanded Moses". Moses was faithful in all the intricate details of God's pattern for His House (Hebrews 3:1-5).

a.　**Pattern for the Brazen Altar**

This was the *first* piece of furniture; the place of the BLOOD of atonement; the beginning of worship. ALL other pieces were touched by this piece and the blood that was shed here. The Blood was first as far as God was concerned and man's approach to God. For man — on the altar, grate 1½ cubits high. For God — on the mercyseat, 1½ cubits high. Same level. Exalt the blood. Sin must be judged. the cross has its place. Sacrifice provided. Atonement is made. It begins worship for Israel and for the Church.

b.　**Pattern for the Brazen Laver**

The SECOND step in approach and WORSHIP was water. The brazen laver of the water of the Word. Blood, then water. The priests had the initial bath and then the daily washing of hands and feet before ministry was done. None were allowed into the Sanctuary where the other articles were without the washing of water, or with unclean hands or feet. Hands (service) and walk (feet) must be cleansed before service to the Lord. Mirror of the Word is self-judgment (Ephesians 5:26, 27; I Corinthians 11:23-32).

c.　**Pattern of the Candlestick**

Typified the Church local and universal. The light-bearer, the illuminator. Walking in the light as ministering at the Table and the Golden Altar. Cf. I Corinthians 11-12-13-14.

d.　**Pattern of Table of Shewbread**

Table of the Lord symbolized here (I Corinthians 10-11; Matthew 26:26-28; Acts 20:1-7). Discerning the Body here. Worship in the Bread of His PRESENCE. None could touch the table if unclean, only qualified priests (Leviticus 21:16-24). To *worship* Him in the bread and the wine, in faith, in His presence, every seventh day. It was not to be a form.

e.　**Pattern of Altar of Incense**

Divine movement of prayer, intercession praise and worship. Measure the altar, our prayers (Revelation 11:1-3). Present our incense-prayer to Him as our High Priest before God. His house is a house of prayer — just before the veil.

f.　**Pattern of the Ark of the Covenant.**

This article constituted the very centre of all. It was the attraction of all and all other articles received their value according to their relationship to the Ark of Glory. Here the voice of God was heard (Numbers 7:89). Here worship ascended. Here God dwelt in His glory. Here the name of the Lord was called (II Samuel 6:1-2).

Thus God laid out all the intricate details of approach and worship for the children of Israel. Nothing was arranged out of their own minds. It was His house and His furniture and all were to be in their proper place. They were to follow the Divine order in the pattern of worship.

5.　**The Sacrifices and Oblations** (Leviticus 1-7; Numbers 19).

One may read these chapters with their intricate details and wonder what the whole thing was about. But when we realize that these things in the Mosaic Covenant economy pointed to Christ and His Church, then we can find the key to understanding these details.

The commands of the Lord concerning the offerings and the offered pointed to that which would find fulfilment in Christ and His Church. The Burnt, Meal, Peace, Sin and Trespass Offerings, the sacrifice of the Red Heifer and their accompanying Oblations were to be offered before the Lord according to His sacrificial pattern. Only that which was so offered was acceptable to Him. All had to be sacrificed in His place, His way, His time and in His order.

6. **The Feasts of the Lord** (Leviticus 23; Deuteronomy 12; 16; Numbers 28, 29).

The three yearly Festival occasions of Passover, Pentecost and Tabernacles were also rich in detail, originating with God and obeyed by Israel. Presumptuous disobedience to the details of the Feasts in relation to the Sanctuary of the Lord were met by Divine judgments. All had to be according to God's pattern of approach.

7. **The Tabernacle of David** (I Chronicles 15-16; II Samuel 6; I Chronicles 6:32).

In due time when the Tabernacle of David was set up, all had to be according to Divine order. When David tried to bring the Ark of God on a new cart, he was struck in judgment because of lack of the ''due order''. The singers and the musicians waited on their office according to the order of David. Nothing was haphazard but David established God's due order of worship around the Ark of the Lord in Zion. Worship was according to the heavenly pattern. It pointed to the New Testament order of worship (Acts 15:13-18; 24:14; John 4:20-24; Ephesians 5:19; Hebrews 13:15).

8. **The Temple of Solomon** (I Chronicles 28-29; II Chronicles 1-5).

David told Solomon that he had been given ''the pattern'' of the house of the Lord, the porch, the treasuries, the upper chambers, the inner parlour and the place of the Ark of the Covenant (I Chronicles 28:11, 12). He told him that he had received ''the pattern of all that he had by the Spirit''. Nothing was left to David's imagination, or whims and fancies. All was therefore built according to the pattern given to David by the Spirit.

9. **The Temple Vision of Ezekiel** (Ezekiel 40-48).

These chapters give much detail concerning the temple of the Lord and its ordinances. The heart of the vision is given in Ezekiel 43:10-13 when the Lord told Ezekiel to show ''*the house*'' to the House of Israel, and to ''let them measure the pattern''. God wanted Israel to be ashamed for all their iniquities and failures. Ezekiel was to show them all the forms, the ordinances and the goings out and the comings in and the laws of the house. All, again, was to be according to God's pattern.

C. New Testament Patterns

1. The New Testament Church

All of these Old Testament ''patterns'' and ''structures'' pointed typically and prophetically to Christ and His Church. If God dwelt in Old Testament structures, it was only temporary, until He could dwell in His redeemed people, the Church.

The New Testament Church today is God's Ark, God's Tabernacle, God's Temple, and in the Church the sacrifices and festival occasions find spiritual fulfilment because of Christ (I Peter 2:5-9). True worship in Spirit and in truth take place here (John 4:20-24).

And just as all those things were according to God's pattern, so shall the Church be according to God's pattern. Paul said he was a ''wise master-builder'' and warned other builders to take heed how they build (I Corinthians 3:9, 10). Christ is the Divine Architect and He will build His Church to Divine design (Matthew 16:18, 19). He is the ''Wise Man'' who builds His house on the rock and His house shall stand the storms (Matthew 7:24-27; Luke 6:46-49). The Church will be built according to the pattern shown to Christ by the Father in the heavenly mount.

2. The New Jerusalem City of God (Revelation 21-22).

The final habitation of God and the redeemed is that of the City of God, the New Jerusalem, the four square City of God. About two chapters are given as to the details of this City, its measurements, materials and design. The Bible closes with a City that is built according to Divine design. It is the order of the eternities to come.

D. **The Pattern and The Glory**

As seen in each of these things, God does not have a variety of patterns. However, there is variety within this "one pattern". God does care about His pattern and how His Church is built, even though men may ridicule those who desire to build according to this pattern in the mount! It is of great significance that God's Glory only comes where all was according to His pattern. The pattern preceded the glory; the glory sealed the pattern. This very fact reveals that God was concerned about the pattern — HIS PATTERN — and that he can only really and fully put the seal of His Glory on that which is according to His pattern. The following references attest to this fact.

1. **The Tabernacle of Moses** (Exodus 39, 40).

    When Moses finished the work and all was according to God's pattern, as the Lord commanded Moses, the Glory-cloud filled the Tabernacle and none could minister by reason of that Glory (Exodus 40:33, 34). The pattern was sealed by the Glory.

2. **The Temple of Solomon** (I Kings 7, 8; II Chronicles 5:11-14).

    When Solomon had finished the work of the temple, and all was built according that the Lord God had given to him through David, the Glory-cloud filled the Temple and none could minister by reason of the Glory. The order of singers and musicians and the unity of that Tabernacle of David worship preceded that Glory. Again, the pattern was sealed by the glory!

3. **The Temple of Ezekiel** (Ezekiel 40-48).

    After the Lord had shown Ezekiel the vision of the Temple, and all had been measured according to the Divine pattern, the Glory filled the Temple of the Lord as it came by way of the east (Ezekiel 43:1-6). Once again, the pattern was sealed by the return of the glory that had departed.

4. **The Lord Jesus Christ**

    Jesus Christ is both God's Tabernacle and Temple (John 1:14-18; 2:20-21). He was perfect in all He was, all He thought, all He said and all He did. He measured up perfectly to God's pattern for man. The seal of God was upon Him and the Glory indwelt Him in fulness (John 3:33, 34; Colossians 1:19; 2:9). On the Mt of Transfiguration, the Glory of God shone through the veil of His flesh (Matthew 17:1-9; John 17). He asked the Father to clothe Him with the Glory He had before the world began.

5. **The City of God** (Revelation 21-22).

    The ultimate picture is that of the foursquare City of God. Measured according to God's pattern, the Lord God and the Lamb are the light and the Glory of this perfect City. The pattern is sealed by the Glory light of God and His Christ. It is a City whose builder and maker is God (Hebrews 11:10-16).

6. **The New Testament Church**

    Who can fail to see that the New Testament Church, God's New Covenant dwelling place, will come to measure up to the pattern under the builders thereof? Ephesians 4:1-16; 2:10-22. The Church will be built according to the Divine pattern. The end result will be that God's Glory will fill the Church. It will be the Divine seal on a finished work that is according the pattern in the Mount (Ephesians 3:17-21; Colossians 1:27; Psalms 102:13-16).

All and any minister involved in the building of God's house, the New Testament Church, should study "*the pattern*" the blueprint in God's Word, and build to it. Paul exhorts all to "take heed how he builds" (I Corinthians 3:9, 10). God can only place the seal of His Glory on that which is according to His pattern! It should be remembered that one could have "the pattern" and not have "the glory", but one cannot have "the glory" without having "the pattern". The builder should have pure motivation and desire to build according to the pattern for the glory of God and His Christ!

CHAPTER 3

WHAT THE CHURCH IS NOT

The word *"Church"* is a word which has lost most of its meaning today in comparison to what it originally meant in the Early Church times. It is a word that needs to be re-defined in our modern society. There are a number of things and groups in existence today called *"The Church"* but they certainly are not that which the Lord said He would build, nor do they measure up to that which the New Testament means when it speak of the Church!

It is these false concepts of the Church which have to be rooted out, torn down and plucked up and destroyed before the truth and reality can be built and then planted.

A. The Church is not a Material Building

The word "Church" is never used in Scripture to refer to a material building. The word "Church" is used about 140 times in the New Testament but never once used of a material building of wood or stones.

Where the word is translated "churches" in Acts 19:37 it refers to "Temple buildings" (Greek "Hierosulos", NOT "Ekklesia"). They were not "robbers of churches" nor "robbers of temple buildings".

The language used of the Church in Acts could not be applied to a material building. Note Acts 2:47; 5:11; 7:38; 8:1-3; 11:22-26; 12:1-5; 15:3, 4, 22, 41; 18:22. The Lord *added* to the Church. Herod *vexed* the Church. The Church was *persecuted.* Paul *saluted* the Church. The Churches had *rest.* Such language is hardly applicable to a material building!

It is the traditions of men that apply the word "Church" to a material building. We are "going to Church". i.e., We are going to the building where the Church meets together. The Lord did not mean that He would build "church buildings" when He said "I will build my Church". The Gates of Hades could hardly prevail against a Church building! When God rent the veil of the material temple at Jerusalem at the death of Jesus, He forever finished with material Tabernacles and Temples and material dwelling places where His glory and presence had been manifested in Old Testament times. The true temple is the Church, made up of living stones. The building is simply the place where the Church meets. The Church is a spiritual house, a spiritual temple, a spiritual building. Thus we do not "go to Church" but the Church meets together in a building, a "sheep-fold" (II Chronicles 6:18; Isaiah 66:1, 2; I Peter 2:5-9; Ephesians 2:20-22).

B. The Church is not a Denomination

The Church is not a denomination, organization or sect. The many and multiplied Churches, with their multiplied names, all claiming to be the Lord's Church are not necessarily His Church. Christ said he would build HIS CHURCH not the various churches named today. Denominationalism is contrary to the Scriptures. Denominations are the evidence of our carnality and divisions.

Thus we speak of the various denominations as Churches. For instance, The Episcopal Church, The Lutheran Church, The Methodist Church, The Presbyterian Church, The Reformed Church, The Roman Catholic Church, The Salvation Army, The Baptist Church, etc. But none of this is in the Bible. Some of the denominations claim to be "THE Church" exclusively, thus excluding all others. Yet it is absolutely necessary that we distinguish between a Denomination and "the Church". This divided condition of Christendom is indeed sinful and evidence of our carnalities (I Corinthians 3:1-6).

There are certain "divisions" that are of God (I Kings 12:24), yet on the other hand most of it is our carnality (I Corinthians 1:11-17). There are people who belong to "A Denomination" which calls itself "Church", yet they have never been born again, and thus they do not really belong THE CHURCH in the New Testament sense. They belong to "A Denomination". Thus distinguishing between belonging to a denomination and to THE Church must be recognised. One may belong to THE CHURCH and yet not to a Denomination. It is also possible to belong to a Denomination and belong or not belong to THE Church! It is also possible to belong to a "non-denominational denomination" or a "non-sectarian sect!"

Denominationalism is contrary to the Scriptures. The very fact that today there is so much "ecumenicalism" going on is self-indicting of this divided Christendom.

Denomination is defined as:

1.   The act of naming.

2.   A name or appellation.

3.   A religious sect; such as a Protestant Denomination.

4.   A Denominational System.

A Denominationalist is an advocate or believer in denominationalism; a sectarian.

Denominations are usually formed around the following:

1.   A certain form or type of Government. i.e., Apostolic, Episcopal, Presbyterian, Congregational, etc.

2.   A Doctrinal emphasis or some truth of Scripture. i.e., Holiness Church, Grace Church, Pentecostal Churches, Charismatic, etc.

3.   A Personality which God used to emphasize a truth or experience, or used by God in some awakening or revival power.

4.   An Experience. i.e., Baptist, Water Baptism; Baptism in the Holy Spirit; Holiness, Second Blessing, Covenant, etc.

Thus denominations are usually formed by a revival or restoration of some truth in which God opened the eyes to see. The people who gather to this truth and see "eye to eye" with the fresh revival are "called out" of some existing system or group to which they belonged. The result is, in due time, another Denomination is formed. Truth after truth has been restored since the time of the Reformation, with the inevitable rejection by some and acceptance by others, which resulted in further division. The ones who came out to follow the restored truth were forced to come out, start another Denomination of their own choice, in order to maintain and uphold the particular aspect of truth restored.

Hence the origin of so many Denominations and Organizations today. The tragedy is that each revival of truth finds its bitterest enemies and opponents from the previous group which had light from heaven. History repeats itself in each generation. The only thing we learn from history is that we never learn from history. Revival usually begins in the glory of God and deteriorates to the glory of the Denomination, or a Personality. It goes from the Man to the Movement to the Monument! Having begun in the Spirit, they end in the flesh. When the Spirit leaves or moves on, then man takes over, forming Doctrinal Statements or Articles of Faith, instituting Creeds, Regulations and Constitutions and By-Laws to try and maintain the Denomination. Certain of these things are necessary in "Caesar's world" but not necessary to the life of His Church!

The Lord did not mean He would build our Denominations. He does not have a variety of Churches nor will there be any such Denominational divisions in heaven. THE Church is NOT a Denomination!

C.   **The Church is Not a Nationalistic Enterprise.**

While the Church is composed of genuine believers out of "every kindred, tongue, tribe and nation", yet it is not a national thing, or even international. The Church is God's "new ethnic" in the human race. Realizing this will save people from a nationalistic spirit or national

Churches, which have rent the Church as the one Body of Christ. i.e., The CHURCH of ENGLAND! The Church of ROME! The LUTHERAN Church! The AMERICAN Society of Churches in Japan, etc. To stamp the Churches in different countries would be like saying ''The Church of JERUSALEM in China, or Japan, or America.''

National distinctions cease to exist ''in Christ'', where there is neither Jew nor Greek, bond nor free, male or female, but all one ''in Christ''. The Church is the new and holy nation, as will be seen in the following chapter.

D. The Church is not Judaism Extended

Although it is recognized that the believers of all ages are of ''one olive tree'' (Romans 9-10-11), yet it must be clearly seen that the New Testament Church is not an extension of Judaism or the Mosaic Covenant economy. There is indeed ''one fold'' (John 10:16), and ''One olive tree'' (Romans 11:16, 24), and ''The Church in the Wilderness'' (Acts 7:38). But Christianity is ''the new wine'' of the New Covenant placed in the ''new wineskin'', which is THE NEW TESTAMENT CHURCH! (Matthew 9:16). The ''old wineskin'' of the Old Covenant could not receive or contain the ''new wine'' of the New Covenant.

We may say that Christianity was born out of Judaism as ''the mother'', but it is still the new child of promise and is not as the mother. Realizing this fact will help us to realize that all Mosaic Covenant economy things are fulfilled and abolished. The sacrifices, the priesthood, the temple, the rituals and festivals all find their spiritual fulfilment in Christ and His Church. These things of the Old Covenant were abolished at the cross and cannot be brought into New Testament Christianity or the New Testament Church. It is a ''new man''.

E. The Church is not The Kingdom of God

Although it is clear that there is a relationship between the Church and the Kingdom of God (as will be seen), the Church is not the Kingdom in the fullest sense of that word. The Kingdom and the Church have much in common, but the Kingdom is larger than the Church. It includes the whole universe, the angelic hosts, as well as Old Testament saints, and the New Testament saints. In a narrower sense we may say, for the present, that the Church is confined to the believers of this present age and Dispensation of the Holy Spirit. The Kingdom is all-inclusive.

F. The Church is not a Parenthetical Plan of God

Certain Dispensationalists teach that the Church is a parenthetical revelation and plan of God. This came because of Jewish blindness and unbelief. The teaching is that the Jew rejected the King and the Kingdom, so the Kingdom was taken from them and postponed to the close of this age. During the interval period God planned the Church as a new thing. However the Church would end in failure and there would be only a remnant of faithful ones when Christ came. After this He would turn again to the Jews who would then take up the Gospel of the Kingdom. In our following chapter we will see that the Church is NOT a parenthetical plan of God but was and is the ETERNAL PURPOSE of God. Known unto God are all His works from the beginning of the world (Acts 15:18; Ephesians 3).

CHAPTER 4

WHAT THE CHURCH IS

Having seen what the Church is NOT, in this chapter we consider WHAT THE CHURCH IS from God's point of view, which has to become our point of view also.

A. **The Church is The Will of God**

The Church is the central fact of God's will. The Church is not a parenthetical revelation which came in because of Jewish blindness and unbelief in their own Messiah. Before there was a Gentile or Jew or Israelite, God had the church in mind. He desired to have a peculiar people for Himself, a Bride for His Son. The Apostle Paul speaks strongly of God's will, especially in relation to the purposes of God in the redeemed and the Church (Ephesians 1:2-11; Romans 8:26-30).

There are two aspects of the will of God that need to be recognized. One has to do with the sovereign will of God and the other the permitted will of God.

1. **The Sovereign Will of God**

   a. **Objective Will**

   Arndt and Gingrich write of the will of God. The Greek word "*thelema*" means "a determination; a choice; a decree, especially a king's decree sent somewhere by his messenger."

   ★ It is objective, what is willed, what one wishes to happen (Matthew 6:10; Matthew 26:42).

   ★ It is what one wills to bring about by his own action, since one has undertaken to do what He has willed (Ephesians 1:5, 9, 11; John 5:30; 4:34; Matthew 16:18).

   ★ It is what one wishes to bring about by the activity of others, to whom one assigns a task (Ephesians 1:1; II Peter 1:21; I John 2:17).

   Therefore it speaks of the sovereign will of God, which is over and above all creation and creatures. His will is absolute. Nothing and no one can frustrate or violate that will of God.

   Thayer says of this Greek word "that which one wishes or has determined shall be done" (i.e., objectively, thing willed) (Luke 12:47; John 5:30; Hebrews 10:10).

   The Scriptures reveal that God's will is over and above all and His will can be done in heaven and in earth (Matthew 6:10). In relation to the kingdoms of this world, He gives the kingdoms to whomsoever He wills (Daniel 4:17, 25, 32). In relation to the crucifixion of Christ, God's will was done over and above all, in spite of the part that Jew and Gentile played. God's hand and counsel had determined before what should be done (Acts 4:25-28; 2:23, 24; 3:18). All was founded on the foreknowledge of God and God's determinate counsel based on that foreknowledge.

   Jesus came to do the will of God, and He perfectly fulfilled it as the eternal Son of God (John 5:30; Luke 22:42; John 6:38; Matthew 26:42; Hebrews 10:10). He also said "Upon this Rock *I will build My Church*" (Matthew 16:18, 19).

   b. **Subjective Will**

   The Greek word "*boulema*" means "a deliberate design, that which is purposed". The thought here in subjective will is what is desired. God is not *willing* that anyone should perish. He does not *wish* this (II Peter 3:9; Matthew 18:14).

   It is not His deliberate design or purpose that people perish (John 3:16). He does deliberately design, purpose and wish that the heirs of promise believe His Word and so He attaches an oath to His promise to help their faith (Hebrews 6:17).

The Church is not merely God's wish but it is God's will. He willed it before Time began in the eternities past, before the creation and the fall of man. Nothing will frustrate God's sovereign will and design. He desires a Church. He wilis a Church. He will have this Church.

To see the perfect will of God as pertaining to the Church is to see that the Church is not a parenthetical plan of God because of Jewish unbelief. God had the Church in mind in eternity, and He willed it in eternity and manifested it in Time.

2. **The Permitted Will of God**

The Scripture reveals also that there are levels pertaining to the will of God (Romans 12:1-2). These being the following:

a. The Perfect Will of God.

b. The Permitted Will of God.

The Principle is illustrated clearly for us in Matthew 19:3-9 concerning the matter of divorce and remarriage. Divorce was never God's perfect will. God permitted it for one reason — for the *hardness* of the heart of man.

We may illustrate this fact thus:

Perfect Will

In the Beginning Genesis 1-2	Permitted Will or Accommodating Will
	After the Fall

Deuteronomy 24 — Hardness of heart

The complicating problems are seen in the fact of God's ONE WILL and Man's FREEWILL, and the bringing of them together in unity and harmony. Thus God does not compel us to go against our will but He does make us willing to go (Luke 12:41-48). The servant who knew his Lord's will and did it not shall be beaten with many stripes; the other with lesser stripes who did not know it. Following we note a number of illustrations of these two levels as pertaining to the will of God.

God created angels and man with free will, the power of choice. He did not create robots or ''zombies'' or irrational creatures or machines.

Satan manifested self-will against God's will. It was the abuse of free will. So did Adam (Isaiah 14:12-14; Genesis 3:1-6). God does not force or violate the free will He has given to man. God often permits or accommodates, in His wisdom, His will to man's failures. He makes all things work together for Himself ultimately.

A detailed study of the following accounts will reveal the two levels of God's will.

1) Abraham's two sons, Ishmael and Isaac (Genesis 16; Genesis 21; Galatians 3; Hebrews 6:12-17).

   Ishmael was not God's perfect will. God permitted his birth. He could have closed the womb. Galatians shows that these two sons are two covenants. The Law Covenant and the New Covenant. God permitted the Law Covenant. It was not His perfect will. It was of works, of the flesh, of man. Isaac was God's perfect will, even though He blessed Ishmael.

2) Israel's wanderings in the Wilderness for 40 years. Not God's perfect will. The Breach Period. God's altering His purpose (Numbers 13-14; Hebrews 3-4). Unbelief caused the promise to be postponed to another generation.

3) The Mosaic Covenant and the New Covenant (Exodus 19:1-6). The Priesthood

of the nation, then God permitted the priesthood of a tribe instead. His perfect will was the priesthood of Melchisedek.

4) Balaam and the will of God evidences this. God's perfect will was for him not to go. God permitted it the next day, then overruled the prophetic word (Numbers 22-24).

5) Melchisedek priesthood was God's perfect will. God permitted the Aaronic priesthood to illustrate the same truth (Hebrews 5-7; Exodus 19:1-6).

6) The Fall of Man into sin and the marring of the Divine image was NOT God's perfect will. But He did permit it. Otherwise we make God the originator of sin (Romans 8:26-28).

7) Jonah was in the perfect will of God to go to Nineveh. God permitted the fish to swallow him, but the fish brought him up to the level of the perfect will of God again. Thus 3 days journey permitted.

8) Paul was in the will of God going to Rome (Acts 27-28). Paul knew what would happen. God overruled in it all. The ship owner's self-will manifested, so it was not God's perfect will for Paul to be shipwrecked. Paul was caught in another man's will, but God permitted it and wrought glory for His Name on the island of Melita.

9) Divorce, as noted is never God's perfect will. He permitted it for hardness of heart (Matthew 19:3-8).

10) King Saul was not God's perfect will. God permitted Israel to have him as king. David's was God's perfect will in His way, in His time. It was God's will for Israel to have a king (Genesis 17), but not then God's time.

11) God has permitted Denominations, etc., also in Church History but these are not His perfect will. He permitted them but as His Church arises to the level of His perfect will, then many things will fade away.

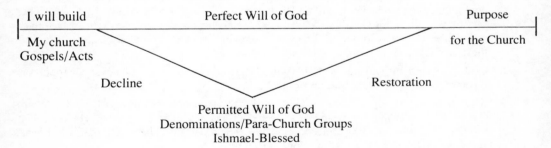

B. **The Church is The Eternal Purpose of God**

Arising out of God's will there comes purpose; the purpose of God relative to the Church.

The word "purpose" is defined as:

1. Object in view; end or aim; design; intention.

2. To design; to intend, definite object in view (Collins).

3. Greek (SC.4286), "*Prothesis*" = Plan, a setting forth; an intention; a proposal, especially referring to the Shewbread in the Temple as it was exposed before God.

   SC.4388. Greek "*Protithemai*" = To place before, to set forth, specifically to set forth with a view to be looked at, to expose to view, to exhibit, to determine.

Thus the Scriptures speak of the purpose of God. God has but ONE PURPOSE! Proverbs

20:18. Purposes are established by counsel. The Counsels in the eternal Godhead are established.

Proverbs 15:22; 24:6; 11:14. Without counsel purposes are disappointed.

Isaiah 14:27. None can disannul the purposes of God. Isaiah 55:8-11.

Isaiah 48:11. God has purposed a thing and He will also do it.

Ecclesiastes 3:1-17. There is a season and a time to every purpose under heaven.

Ecclesiastes 8:6. To every purpose . . .

Ephesians 1:9, 11. God has purposed in Himself a thing, and He works all things after the counsel of His own will.

Ephesians 3:11. It is an eternal purpose manifested in time. The Church is a manifestation in TIME of an ETERNAL Purpose.

Romans 9:11(17). God's purpose according to election will stand.

Romans 8:23; II Timothy 1:9. We are called according to that eternal purpose. We are part of the purpose of God.

Acts 11:23. Because of the above believers are to serve the Lord with purpose of heart.

Thus the purpose of God for the Church is ETERNAL. It cannot be disannulled. In the counsels of the eternal Godhead, in the Everlasting Covenant, God decreed THE CHURCH. The Everlasting Covenant is the foundation for all covenants on earth. Hebrews 13:20. Man was not the party to it, but the object of it. It was the covenant of redemption made in the counsels of the Godhead in the event of the entrance of sin into the universe.

This purpose of God was planned:

a. **Before the Foundation of the World**

John 17:5, 24; I Corinthians 2:7; Ephesians 1:4, 9, 11; 2:10; 3:11; II Timothy 1:9; Titus 1:2, 3. The hope of eternal life was promised before the world began.

b. **From the Foundation of the World**

Revelation 13:8; 17:8; I Peter 1:18-20; Titus 1:2, 3. Planned in eternity, but manifested in these last times for you.

The Church is therefore a manifestation in TIME of an ETERNAL Purpose. Because of God's foreknowledge, He could will and purpose to bring forth the Church to His glory (Romans 8:26-30) before Jew or Gentile even existed!

The believer has to totally accept the fact that Christ in His Church is the central fact of God's will and that the Church *was and is* the *eternal purpose* of God, NOT a parenthetical invention. Any other concept robs the believers both individually and corporately of proper motivation, goals and purposes as to the plan of the eternal Godhead.

A number of important things need to be noted about this purpose of God as it pertains to the Church.

1) The Purpose was determined by God Himself (Ephesians 1:9).

2) The Purpose of God for the Church is eternal (Ephesians 3:9, 10; 1:4; II Timothy 1:9; Acts 15:18; Titus 1:2).

3) The Purpose of God was hidden in the Old Testament Times (Ephesians 3:5; Matthew 13:17; I Peter 1:10-12; Romans 16:25-26).

4) The Purpose of God as a Progressive revelation (Isaiah 28:10-14; Hebrews 1:1, Amplified N.T.)

5) The Purpose of God was manifested in New Testament Times (Ephesians 3:1-6).

6) The Purpose of God will never be disannulled. God will not change His plan or

purpose. He will have a glorious Church (Ephesians 3:1-12; Colossians 1:26; Romans 16:25, 26).

7) The Purpose of God is to be realized in Christ and His Church (Ephesians 3:8-11). By the Church is to be made known the manifold wisdom of God.

C. The Church is The Mystery of God.

The *will* and *eternal purpose* of God in Christ find fulfilment in *THE GREAT MYSTERY*, which is the Church, the Body of Christ.

1. Definition of the word "Mystery"

a. Dictionary

Webster defines the word "mystery" as "something unexplained, unknown or kept secret". The Greek Priests and Philosophers often initiated their people into the mystery rites and teachings of the cultic, initiating them into the mysteries of their religion.

Collins Dictionary defines it as "a profound secret; an object of curiosity and wonder; a religious truth or doctrine, not discernible by human reason; an enigma."

b. Bible

The Greek word "*Musterion*" (SC3466), from a derivative of "*muo*" (to shut the mouth); a secret or mystery (through the idea of silence imposed by initiation into religious rites).

W. E. Vine says "among the ancient Greeks 'the mysteries' were religious rites and ceremonies practiced by secret societies into which anyone who so desired might be received. Those were thus initiated into their 'mysteries' therefore became possessors of certain knowledge which was not imparted to the uninitiated, and were called 'the perfected' " (Cf. I Corinthians 2:6-16).

A mystery, however, in the New Testament, is not an undiscovered secret, but a secret, undiscoverable by human reason, but now revealed by the Spirit of God.

Arndt and Gingrich say "Our literature uses it to mean the secret thoughts, plans and dispensations of God hidden from human reason, and therefore to be revealed to those for whom it is intended."

Young's Concordance defines the word as "That which can only be known to the initiated" (I Corinthians 2:14; Matthew 13:11-17).

The Church, therefore, is the great secret, the great mystery of God. It was hidden in God since the foundation of the world, but it was revealed to the holy men of God, the apostles and prophets by the Holy Spirit. The Holy Spirit is the one who initiates us into the mysteries of God (Ephesians 3:1-9; Deuteronomy 29:29).

Paul speaks much of "the mystery" in Ephesians, the Epistle of the Church.

★ Ephesians 1:9. The *mystery* of His will.

★ Ephesians 3:3. By revelation He made known unto me the *mystery*.

★ Ephesians 3:4. Understand my knowledge in the *mystery* of Christ.

★ Ephesians 3:9. To make all men see what is the fellowship of the *mystery*.

★ Ephesians 5:32. This is a *great mystery* but I speak of Christ and His Church.

★ Ephesians 6:19. The *mystery* of the Gospel.

2. Stewards of the Mysteries of God (I Corinthians 4:1, 2).

Paul counted himself a steward of the mysteries of God. The word "stewardship" means "dispensation". It speaks of a householder, one who manages anothers affairs. It involves

(a) Responsibility, and (b) Faithfulness, and (c) Accountability (Matthew 25:14-30; Luke 12:41-48; I Peter 4:10).

Paul was given "a dispensation of the Gospel" (I Corinthians 9:16, 17). He speaks of the dispensation of the grace of God, and the distinctive Gospel entrusted to him (Galatians 2:7, 18; 1:6-12; I Timothy 1:1; Ephesians 3:1-2; Colossians 1:25; Romans 2:16; 16:25).

The Holy Spirit initiated Jesus, Paul, John and the New Testament writers into the mysteries of God and they were good stewards of those mysteries (Proverbs 25:2; I Corinthians 2:9, 10). The heathen temples and priesthood were but the counterfeit of the Divine.

3. **Mysteries in the New Testament**

There are about 19 particular mysteries spoken of in the New Testament, by Jesus, Paul and John the Beloved Apostle.

a. **By Jesus**

The Mysteries of the Kingdom of Heaven in parabolic form (Matthew 13:11; Mark 4:11; Luke 8:10).

b. **By Paul**

1. The Mystery of God's will in the fulness of times (Ephesians 1:9-11).
2. The Mystery of the Father and of Christ (Colossians 2:2, 3).
3. The Mystery of Christ (Colossians 4:3).
4. The Mystery of the Gospel (Ephesians 6:19).
5. The Mystery of Godliness (I Timothy 3:16; John 1:1-18; 14:6).
6. The Mystery of Iniquity (II Thessalonians 2:1-12).
7. The Mystery of the Faith (I Timothy 3:9).
8. The Mystery of the Wisdom of God (I Corinthians 2:7-10).
9. The Mystery of the Body of Christ (Ephesians 3:1-11; Romans 16:24, 25).
10. The Mystery of Christ in you (Colossians 1:26-28; Galatians 2:20).
11. The Mystery of Israel's blindness (Romans 11:25).
12. The Mystery spoken in unknown tongues (I Corinthians 14:2).
13. The Great Mystery of the marriage of Christ and His Church (Ephesians 5:23-33).
14. The Mystery of the resurrected and immortalized saints (I Corinthians 15:51-55; I Thessalonians 4:15-18).

c. **By John**

1. The Mystery of the Seven Stars and Lampstands (Revelation 1:20).
2. The Mystery of God (Revelation 10:7).
3. The Mystery of Great Babylon (Revelation 17:5-7). The Mother of Harlots.

However, Paul gives us an admonition in I Corinthians 13:2. Though I understand all mysteries and have not love, I am nothing.

All of these mysteries basically fall into two Mysteries; the Mystery of Godliness and the Mystery of Iniquity. Or, Satan and his hosts against God and His hosts. Both streams of mysteries run parallel from the beginning of human history to the end of this age.

THE CHURCH is indeed "*the great mystery*", once secret, and hidden in the mind of God but now revealed to be His eternal purpose and will.

D. **The Church is The New Ethnic — The Holy Nation**

According to I Corinthians 10:32 there are basically three ethnic divisions in the human race. These are the Jews (Israel), the Gentiles and the Church of God. God is at work in the nations, forming the third ethnic division — The Church. This relates to the Jew and the Gentile being baptized into One Body. It is not a nationalistic, or international thing, but ONE NEW MAN (Ephesians 2:11-22; I Corinthians 12:13).

Peter's ministry is primarily to the Jews in Acts 1-12.

Paul's ministry is primarily to the Gentiles in Acts 13-28. However, Paul is the apostle who sees both baptized in ONE BODY, the NEW MAN, the new creation Body of Christ.

It is very important to see this truth as it will help us to understand why and how we may use Old Testament things in application to the New Testament Church. (The following is taken from *"Interpreting the Scriptures"* by Conner/Malmin on the Ethnic Division Principle of interpreting Scripture).

1. **Definition of the Word**

   The word "ethnic" has to do with the basic divisions of mankind distinguished by culture. The following are the main words used in Scripture relative to the ethnic divisions of mankind:

   A. **Old Testament Hebrew:**

Ummah	= "a collection; i.e., community of persons"	
	Translated:	
	Nations —	Ezra 4:10; Daniel 3:4, 7, 29.
	People —	Numbers 25:15; Psalms 117:1.
Goy	= "a massing; a foreign nation; hence a Gentile"	
	Translated:	
	Gentiles —	Genesis 10:5; Isaiah 11:10; 42:1, 6; 49:22; 54:3; 60:3, 5, 11, 16.
	Heathen —	Psalms 2:1, 8; 102:15; Jeremiah 10:2; Ezekiel 11:12, 16; 39:21; Malachi 1:11.
	Nation(s) —	Genesis 10:31, 32; Deuteronomy 9:1, 4, 5; I Chronicles 16:20; Psalms 22:27, 28; Isaiah 2:2, 4; 52:15; Malachi 3:12.
	People —	Joshua 10:13; II Kings 6:18; Daniel 11:23.
Leom	= "to gather; a community"	
	Translated:	
	Nation —	Genesis 27:29; Psalms 47:3; 57:9.
	People —	Genesis 25:23; Psalms 148:11; Isaiah 55:4
	Folk —	Jeremiah 51:58.
Am	= "a people (as a congregated unity); especially, a tribe"	
	Translated:	
	Folk —	Genesis 33:15; Proverbs 30:26.
	Nation(s) —	Exodus 21:8; Deuteronomy 30:3; I Chronicles 16:24; Psalms 108:3.
	People —	Psalms 29:11; 102:18, 22; Habakkuk 3:13; Zechariah 8:6; Malachi 1:4.

   B. **New Testament Greek:**

Ethnos	= "a race (as of the same habit); i.e., a tribe; specially a foreign (non-Jewish) one"	
	Translated:	
	Gentile —	Matthew 10:5, 18; Mark 10:42; Acts 4:27; Romans 9:24, 30.

Heathen —	II Corinthians 11:26; Galatians 1:16; 3:8.
Nation(s) —	Mark 11:17; John 11:50-52; Acts 14:16; Romans 4:17, 18.
People —	Romans 10:19.

Genos = "offspring, family, nation, the aggregate of many individuals of the same nature, kind, sort, species"

Translated:

Born —	Acts 18:2, 24
Country(man) —	Acts 4:36; II Corinthians 11:26.
Diversity —	I Corinthians 12:28
Generation —	I Peter 2:9
Kind (red) —	Matthew 13:47; Acts 7:13, 19
Nation —	Mark 7:26
Offspring —	Acts 17:28, 29; Revelation 22:16
Stock —	Acts 13:26; Philippians 3:5.

The above words indicate that an ethnic group is to be viewed as a community of persons sharing the same ancestry and participating in the culture. These words are applied to Israel/Judah, Gentile nations, and the Church.

2. **Classification**

The apostle Paul recognized that while God is no respecter of persons, He has instituted certain ethnic divisions and distinctions. Paul noted the three basic divisions in the human race in I Corinthians 10:32. "Give none offence,

neither to the Jews,
nor to the Gentiles,
nor to the Church of God."

Thus, in God's mind, the three main divisions of the human race are the Jews, the Gentiles and the Church of God. The Word of God must be rightly divided in relation to these three classes of people.

3. **Origination**

From the creation of Adam to the Tower of Babel (Genesis 1:1; 11:9), mankind was one race, speaking one language. The event recorded in Genesis 11 gives us the background of the reason for the division of mankind into diverse nations. The origin of the nations is described in this chapter. Out of these nations God chose a nation for Himself and for His own redemptive purposes. In the Old Testament there are two major ethnic divisions: the chosen nation Israel, and the Gentile nations. The New Testament introduces the third major ethnic division, which is the Church, composed of both Jew and Gentile.

a. **The Chosen Nation**

1) **The Choice** — Scripture reveals that Israel was the nation which God chose to fulfill His own purposes. God took Israel as a nation from the midst of the nations and made a great nation out of them by His statutes, laws and judgments (Deuteronomy 4:6-8, 34). In the covenant with Abraham God said He would make him a great nation (Genesis 12:2, 3). God also promised Abraham that He would make him the father of many nations (Genesis 17:1-7).

2) **The Reason** — God chose Israel to be a special people to Himself above all the people on the earth because of His love and the covenant He made with Israel's fathers, Abraham, Isaac and Jacob (Deuteronomy 7:7-9; 9:1-6). There were a number of things involved in the purpose for this Divine choice:

a) Chosen to *bless* all nations (Genesis 9:27; 12:2, 3; 17:4-7; 18:18; 22:16-18).

b) Chosen to receive the *oracles* of God (Romans 3:2).

c) Chosen to receive the *blessings* of God (Romans 9:4, 5).

★ The Adoption — Adopted as God's son from among the nations (Exodus 4:22, 23).

★ The Shekinah Glory of God — The visible manifestation of the presence of God in the Glory–Cloud.

★ The Covenants — The Abrahamic, the Mosaic, the Palestinian, the Davidic and the New Covenant.

★ The Giving of the Law — The moral, civil and ceremonial laws.

★ The Service of God — The Tabernacle of Moses, the Tabernacle of David, the Temple of Solomon, with their respective orders of worship.

★ The Promises — Particularly as they relate to the Seed (as the sand and as the stars) and the Land.

★ The Fathers — Abraham, Isaac and Jacob being particularly the three fathers of Israel (Exodus 3:6; Genesis 48:15, 16).

★ The Messiah — As pertaining to His human nature (Romans 1:3)

The summation of these shows the choice of Israel as a nation to receive and be the guardians of the written Word; and to be the progenitors of the Living Word through which all nations would be blessed.

3) **The Division**

Israel was a united nation from the time of the Exodus under Moses through the reigns of Saul, David and Solomon — under whom the nation reached its highest glory. After the death of Solomon the nation was divided into two houses, two kingdoms, two nations, known as Israel and Judah (I Kings 11, 12). God permitted this division in order to fulfill His distinctive purpose for each house or nation. It must be recognized that from that time on there were two dynasties, two kingdoms and two destinies. These two nations went into two different captivities, to two different places, at two different times, under two different world kingdoms. Israel went into captivity to Assyria and Judah to Babylon. This the prophets of each nation clearly foretold beforehand.

Therefore, in interpreting the prophets, the distinction between the kingdoms to which they were prophesying must constantly be kept in mind. Some prophecies were distinctly given to Israel and others to Judah; these should not be confused. The Lord foretold through the prophet Jeremiah that He would make a New Covenant with the House of Israel and with the House of Judah (Jeremiah 31:31-34; Hebrews 8:8-13). The prophet Ezekiel foretold that God would make Israel and Judah (two sticks) one in the hand of the Son of Man (Ezekiel 37:15-19). "And I will make them one nation in the land upon the mountains of Israel; and one king shall be king to them all: and they shall be no more two nations, neither shall they be divided into two kingdoms any more at all" (Ezekiel 37:22). This union can come about only through the New Covenant in the Lord Jesus Christ.

b. **The Gentile Nations**

1) **Their Condition** — In Scripture the term "Gentiles" is used to refer to all nations besides Israel/Judah. It denotes all peoples not in Covenant relationship with God, as Israel was. Paul aptly describes the condition of the Gentiles in Ephesians 2:11, 12.

★ Gentiles in the flesh — as to natural and national birth.

★ Uncircumcision in the flesh — not in Abrahamic Covenant relationship with God.

★ Without Christ — having no Saviour; no Anointed One.

★ Aliens from the Commonwealth of Israel — estranged and outlawed from the rights of Israel as a nation (unless they became proselytes).

★ Strangers from the Covenants of Promise — the Abrahamic, Mosaic, Palestinian and Davidic Covenants, and the promises, privileges and blessings therein.

★ Having no hope — no Messianic expectation.

★ Without God in the world — having general, but no special revelation of God.

★ Afar off — no nearness of relationship to God.

Paul, later on in the same Epistle, summarized the spiritual condition of the Gentiles as "having the understanding darkened, being alienated from the life of God through the ignorance that is in them, because of the blindness that is in their heart" (Ephesians 4:18; read also Romans 1:18-32).

2) **Their Salvation**

The writers of the Old Testament Scriptures were concerned primarily with the chosen nation and only dealt with the Gentile nations as they related to it (Deuteronomy 32:8; Acts 17:26). However, the Scriptures also plainly declare that God is no respecter of persons (Acts 10:34, 35). As already noted, Israel was chosen as a nation to eventually bless all other nations. The following Scriptures attest to this fact:

★ All nations to be blessed through the seed of Abraham (Genesis 22:18).

★ All families of the earth be blessed (Genesis 26:4).

★ All kindreds of the nations to worship God (Psalms 22:27, 28).

★ All nations to flow to the house of the Lord (Isaiah 2:2, 3).

★ Gentiles to seek the Root of Jesse (Isaiah 11:10).

★ Messiah to sprinkle many nations with His blood (Isaiah 52:15).

★ Many nations shall be joined to the Lord in that day (Zechariah 2:11).

★ The name of the Lord to be great among the Gentiles (Malachi 1:11).

★ The Gentiles shall trust in His name (Matthew 12:21).

The great commission involves the taking of the Gospel of Christ to every creature, making disciples of all nations (Matthew 28:19; Mark 16:15; Luke 24:47; Acts 1:8). The Book of Acts shows God's turning from the chosen nation to the Gentile nations in order to take out of them a people for His Name (Acts 9:15; 13:44-49; 14:1, 2; 15:14-18; 28:23-31). The Scriptures clearly show that the Gentile nations would be blessed through the chosen nation by "the Seed" — Messiah. "And the Scripture, foreseeing that God would justify the heathen through faith, preached before the Gospel unto Abraham, saying in thee shall all nations be blessed" (Galatians 3:8).

c. **The Church**

1) **Definition of the Church** — The third group mentioned by Paul in I Corinthians 10:32 is "the Church of God." The word Church is a translation of the Greek word EKKLESIA, which is made up of two other words: EK, which means "out of" and KALEO, which means "to call." Thus the word EKKLESIA means literally "the called out ones." It is used in Scripture to refer to the nation of Israel and to the Christian community of believers, whether in heaven or on earth.

a) Israel — The Church in the Wilderness (Acts 7:38).

    b)   Saints in Heaven (Hebrews 12:23).

    c)   Saints on Earth (Revelation 1:11).

In these three the word "Church" is used in its two basic senses: universal and local. We understand the universal Church to include the redeemed of all ages both in heaven and earth, and the local Church to be a visible expression of it.

2)   **Composition of the Church** — The Church, as it is revealed in the New Testament is composed of both Jew and Gentile. As God called Israel as a nation from the midst of the nations and constituted them as His Church in the Old Testament, so God now calls people unto Himself out of every nation, whether Jew or Gentile, and constitutes them as His Church in the New Testament. The New Testament Church is revealed as the Body of Christ composed of Jew and Gentile:

★   Christ is the builder of His Church (Matthew 16:18).

★   The Lord adds to His Church (Acts 2:47).

★   Christ is the Head of the Body, the Church (Colossians 2:19).

★   The Church is Christ's Body (Ephesians 1:22, 23).

★   Jew and Gentile are all baptized into one Body (I Corinthians 12:13).

★   Jew and Gentile are one new man in Christ (Ephesians 2:15, 16).

★   Jew and Gentile are fellow-heirs in the same Body (Ephesians 3:6).

Thus the Church, being the third major ethnic division, is a called out company, consisting of Jew and Gentile, circumcision and uncircumcision, chosen nation and Gentile nations in the one Body of Christ. National divisions are determined by natural birth, but by spiritual birth all national distinctions cease to exist, for "there is neither Jew nor Greek, there is neither bond nor free, there is neither male nor female: for you are all one in Christ Jesus" (Galatians 3:28). "For in Christ Jesus neither circumcision avails anything, nor uncircumcision, but a new creature" (Galatians 6:15).

3)   **Significance of the Church** — This Church taken out of every kindred, tongue, people and nation (Revelation 5:9) now constitutes God's nation. It is the true Israel of God entitled to the spiritual promises in the Abrahamic Covenant:

★   Those in Christ are "an holy nation" (I Peter 2:9).

★   The Kingdom of God was taken from Judah and given to a nation that would bring forth the fruits thereof (Matthew 21:43).

★   The prophets foretold of a righteous nation that would keep the truths (Isaiah 26:2).

★   Salvation was offered to a nation not yet called by His Name (Isaiah 65:1 with Romans 10:20, 21).

★   All those who are new creatures in Christ constitute the Israel of God (Galatians 6:15, 16).

★   The Gentile by faith in Christ is brought into the commonwealth of Israel (Ephesians 2:12).

★   The believing Gentile is grafted into the olive tree of Israel (Romans 11).

★   The Israel after the flesh are necessarily the Israel after the Spirit (Romans 9:6-8).

★   The true Jew and true circumcision are of the heart and in the spirit, and not of the flesh or the letter (Romans 2:28, 29).

★   The believers in Christ are Abraham's seed and heirs according to the promise (Galatians 3:16, 29).

These Scriptures attest to the fact that the Church, composed of Jew and Gentile, is God's holy nation, the true Israel of God, the seed of Abraham, and the called out company. This is the ''mystery'' revealed to Paul: that Jew and Gentile would become one Body in Christ (Ephesians 3:1-9).

The Church is God's spiritual and eternal Israel. The interpreter must realize that the name ''Israel'' is used in Scripture to refer to:

a) The Patriarch Jacob (Genesis 49:1, 2).

b) The twelve tribes of ''Israel'' (Exodus 19:3).

c) The 10-tribed House of Israel, the northern kingdom (I Kings 12:21).

d) The 2-tribed House of Judah, the southern kingdom (Ezra 6:21) — spoken of here as the children of Israel.

e) The Church, the spiritual Israel of God (Galatians 6:16; Romans 9:6).

In conclusion, it can be seen that the three main ethnic divisions mentioned by Paul in I Corinthians 10:32 are supported by the testimony of Scripture. These three distinctions can be traced through the Book of Acts in the development of the New Testament Church. Therefore, this Church of which Christ speaks is to be composed of the redeemed of every nation, but these national distinctions were to cease in the Church, the Body of Christ, the one new man (Ephesians 2:14-16).

E. **The Ekklesia** — Matthew 16:18, 19; 18:15-20.

W. Barclay, in *New Testament Words* (pp. 68-72) gives some excellent information concerning the true meaning of the word ''Church'', which is adapted here. The New Testament word for ''Church'' is a most important word in New Testament words. It has a double background. It comes from two Greek words: EK, meaning ''out of'', and KALEO meaning ''to call.''

1. **The Hebrew Background**

The Septuagint Version translates the word ''Qahal'' (or Kahal), coming from the root word ''to summon'', as ''assembly'' or ''congregation'' of the people of Israel. Note — Deuteronomy 18:16; Judges 20:2, Assembly. I Kings 8:14; Leviticus 10:17; Numbers 1:16, Congregation.

This Hebrew word occurs over 70 times in the Septuagint. In Hebrew sense it means ''God's people called together, in order to listen to or to act for God.''

KAHAL Jehovah = ''the called and assembled people of God.'' Or, the Congregation or the Assembly.

Numbers 10:7; 20:10; I Kings 8:14; I Chronicles 29:20; Psalms 40:9; 107:32; 149:1. Kahal = Septuagint Version for ''Ekklesia''. They assembled before the Door of the Tabernacle to hear God speak.

Thus a congregation is a company of people who have been ''called out'' of their tents or dwelling places, and have ''come together.'' This is the Hebrew ''Qahal''.

2. **The Greek Background**

Greek background of the word ''Church'' in Paul's day is seen in the following. In the great classical days of Athens, the EKKLESIA was the convened assembly of people. It consisted of all the citizens who had not lost their civic rights. Apart from the fact that its decisions had to conform to the Laws of the State, its powers were to all intents and purposes unlimited.

It:

a. Elected and dismissed Magistrates.

b. Directed the policy of the City.

c.   Declared war, made peace, contracted treaties and arranged alliances.

d.   Elected generals and other military officers.

e.   Assigned troops to different campaigns and dispatched them from the city.

f.   Ultimately was responsible for the conduct of military operations.

g.   Raised and allocated funds.

These meetings began with prayer and sacrifice. It was a true democracy. Two great watchwords were ''equality'' and ''freedom''. All had equal rights, and equal duty to take part. In cases of ostracism or banishment, at least 6000 citizens had to be present.

Thus for the secular Greek society, the word EKKLESIA came to mean ''assembly of free citizens who were called out of their homes and/or places of business to assemble together and give consideration to matters of public interest.''

Cf. Ephesians ''assembly'' (Ekklesia — to illustrate this).
Acts 19:32, 39, 41. Acts 7:38. Israel was the Church in the Wilderness, God's Ekklesia.
Exodus 12:3, 6. The children of Israel were the whole assembly, called together by Moses and told what to do in their homes for their deliverance. They had the Lamb for a house, as the congregation of the Lord and were summoned together to hear the word of the Lord through Moses.

''Congregation'' (SC.6951) also means ''convocation, assemblage. The congregation was gathered by the Trumpet; a summons (Numbers 10:7).
Psalms 22:22. In the midst of the *congregation*.
Psalms 35:18. Give thanks in the great *congregation*.
Psalms 149:1. Praise Him in the *congregation* of the saints.
When Israel was called together out of their tents or homes to the Door of the Tabernacle of the Congregation, that was THE CHURCH, THE ASSEMBLY, THE CONGRE-GATION! NOT just ''called out ones'' but ''called out TO ASSEMBLE TOGETHER!''

Greek = Ekklesia. Latin = Ecclesia. The Church is God's assembly, God's muster, and the Convenor is God Himself. It is the free citizens of the heavenly community summoned by the Gospel trumpet to assemble together to hear from God. In the New Testament the word ''Ekklesia'' is used 114 times, and 110 of these of the Church!

The Church therefore is not just used in the exclusive sense of being ''picked out'' from the world. In the Hebrew and Greek sense, it was not exclusive but *inclusive*. The summons was not to any selected few. It was a summons from the State to every man to come and shoulder his responsibilities. Today it is a summons from God to every man to come, listen, acknowledge the Word of God.

In essence therefore, the Church (The Ekklesia) is a body of people, not so much assembling because they have chosen to come together, but because they have been chosen to come together to assemble, because God has called them to Himself; not so much to share their own thoughts and opinions, but assembling to listen to the voice of God.

It is the ''called out company'', and ''assembled together'' people (Revelation 5:9). It consists of living people, an organism and not a mere organization.

IN CONCLUSION:

A.   Abraham was ''called out'' of Ur of the Chaldees, out of Babylon (Genesis 12:1; Hebrews 11:8).

B.   Israel was ''called out'' of Egypt's world, religion, life and world. They were called to be a peculiar treasure to God, a chosen and holy nation unto the Lord, the Church in the Wilderness (Acts 7:38). A marvellous and prophetic picture of the Church.

C. The House of Judah was "called out" of Babylon unto restoration of the Temple at Jerusalem. These things are types and ensamples (I Corinthians 10:6, 11).

D. The New Testament Church is also "called out" of every kindred, tongue, tribe and nation to be His Church (Revelation 18:1-4; II Corinthians 6:14-18; Hosea 11:1. Revelation 5:9).

E. This calling is:

1) Being called out of darkness into light (I Peter 2:9).
2) Being called to a vocation (Ephesians 4:1).
3) Being called to a calling of hope (Ephesians 4:4).
4) Being called with a holy calling (II Timothy 1:9).
5) Being called to a high calling (Philippians 3:14).
6) Being called to a heavenly calling (Hebrew 3:1).
7) Being called unto eternal glory by Christ Jesus (I Peter 5:10).
8) Being called to His kingdom and glory (I Thessalonians 2:12).

    Read also I Peter 1:14-16; 2:1-12; I John 2:14-17; James 1:27; Romans 8:30; II Corinthians 7:1; Matthew 2:15; Exodus 4:22, 23.

The Church consists of those who obey the call, world-wide, regardless of nation or culture. Called out from the world, the flesh, and the Devil, they come to hear from God. It is the Church of the Firstborn ones (Hebrews 12:22-24. Hebrews 2:12 with Psalms 22:22 where "Congregation" is translated "Church").

THE CHURCH is the burden of Ephesians 1:22; 3:10, 21; 5:23, 24, 25, 27, 29, 32. The Church is not national, international, denominational, undenominational, sectarian or non-sectarian — it is ONE NEW MAN, a NEW THING that God has created in the earth.

CHAPTER 5

WHAT THE CHURCH IS TO BE

We ask ''What kind of a Church is the Lord building?'' What type of Church is it to be? There are three major things that the New Testament reveals concerning what His Church is to be.

A. **The Church Militant and Victorious** — Matthew 16:15-20.

The Church in this passage is to be a Church militant and victorious. This is what the Church is to be in earth, as to its outward expressions, as far as the world is concerned and the kingdom of darkness.

Fuller details of these things will be taken up in due time but for the present we note this in outline form.

1. A Church built on the Rock foundation — Christ.

2. A Church built by Christ Himself, who is the Architect and Head.

3. A Church composed of called out and assembled ones.

4. A Church militant against the Gates of Hades. A Church not ''holding the fort'' but ''storming the forts'' of darkness (Ephesians 3:9, 10).

Genesis 22:17. The conflict with the Gates of the enemies. Genesis 24:60. The Church to be victorious in battle, conquering and to conquer. Ephesians 6:10-20. The armour of God needed for battle. II Corinthians 10:1-5. The weapons of our warfare are not carnal but mighty through God. Not militant spirit as seen in the Dark Ages and the Christian Crusades; religious and ''holy wars''. Our Kingdom is not of this world system, hence we do not fight physically. The warfare is spiritual, with principalities and the powers, rulers of the darkness of this world, and wicked spirits (John 18:36, 37; Revelation 12:10, 11; Acts 12:10; Psalms 9:13; Isaiah 38:10; Matthew 7:13; Genesis 28:17; Isaiah 26:2).

The Gates are always symbolical of where the ancients held their meetings for counsel, business, amusement, etc., at their cities. They were to them what Law-Courts, Town-Halls are for us today.

The Gates of Hades — Conflict with the Kingdom of Darkness (Genesis 3:15). The Church, like ''the woman'' is at warfare and enmity with the serpent, the Devil. Satan shall not prevail. The Church shall prevail.

5. **A Church having the Keys of the Kingdom.**

''I will give thee the keys of the kingdom of heaven'' (Matthew 16:19). Note the following keys in Scripture.

a. The key of knowledge — Luke 11:52.

b. The key of David — Revelation 3:7; Isaiah 22:21, 22.

c. The keys of Death and Hades — Revelation 1:18.

d. The key of the Bottomless Pit — Abyss — Revelation 9:1; 20:1.

e. The keys of the Kingdom of Heaven — Matthew 16:19. Used in the Book of Acts.

The key is always significant of power and authority; to open and shut doors, to let people in or lock them out; to lock or unlock that which is closed. As will be seen, Peter opened the door of faith to Jewry at Pentecost, and then to the Gentiles in Acts 10-11. The one holds the keys holds authority of the Kingdom. These are not the keys of the Church, but the keys of the kingdom.

6. **A Church having a Binding Ministry.**

This relates to (a) The Gates of Hades in conflict against the Church. The Church is to have power to *bind* those who oppose. Principalities, powers and wicked spirits have to be bound. FIRST bind the strong man, then spoil his house (Matthew 12:29; 13:30). The tares are bound into bundles first.

Matthew 18:15-18. In the matter of Church discipline the person is bound.

Mark 5:3; Revelation 20:2; Psalms 105:22-26; 149:8. Satan is to be finally bound for 1000 years.

The Word of God cannot be bound (II Timothy 2:9).

7. **The Church is to have a Loosing Ministry.**

This relates to (b) The Keys of the Kingdom. The Church is to have a *loosing* ministry. Luke 13:16. "Ought not this woman, a daughter of Abraham, whom Satan hath bound, be *loosed?*"

John 11:44. Lazarus had to be loosed from the graveclothes of death.

Psalms 102:20; Mark 7:35. Satan binds his captives. The Church is called to loose them, and bind the powers that bound.

Whatsoever ye bind shall be bound . . . whatsoever ye loose shall be loosed.

8. **The Church in Earth is connected with heaven.**

Whatsoever is already bound in heaven shall be bound in earth, and whatsoever is loosed already in heaven shall be loosed on earth. Hence the Church needs the mind of Christ, her Head. The Church on earth is to be one with the Lord in heaven (Matthew 28:19). All power is His in heaven and earth.

Mark 16:15-20. They went forth, preaching, the Lord in heaven working with them confirming the Word with signs following. Matthew 6:9. Thy Kingdom come, thy will be done in earth as in heaven. The will of God is to be done through the Church, the Body of Christ.

Genesis 14. Melchisedek, blessed Abraham of the Most High God, Possessor of heaven and earth. Earth is utterly dependant on heaven, to be one with heaven. Deuteronomy 11:1-10, 21. Unless heaven works with earth, then all earth will fail in powerless, meaningless form and ceremony. There must be total dependence on the Lord in heaven.

B. **The Church is To Be a United Church** — John 17

The prayer of Christ is practical and prophetic. The Lord undoubtedly saw the divisions that would come in Christendom and thus prayed that the world might see a united Church, a Church at unity in and with itself. Unity is one of the most powerful forces in earth, whether for good or evil. The Tower of Babel proved this until God confused the wicked unity of one speech and one language (Genesis 10-11).

1. **Church**

The use of the word "Church" in many places speaks of the ONE Universal Church. When the word "Churches" is used it speaks of this ONE CHURCH in various localities. The only reason for distinction in the Church is a geographical setting — nothing else!

We note the use of the word "Church" in some of the important passages:

a. I will build My Church (not Churches) — Matthew 16:18, 19.

b. The Lord added to the Church — Acts 2:47.

c. Great fear fell on the Church — Acts 5:11.

d. There was persecution against the Church — Acts 8:3.

e. Saul made havoc of the Church — Acts 8:1-3.

f. THE CHURCH throughout the whole of Judea, Galilee, Samaria had rest. Not Churches as in (Acts 9:31) KJV. See Weymouth, Numerical, Goodspeed, Moffatt, Amplified, RSV.

g.   The Church in the Wilderness, one Church, though 12 Tribes — Acts 7:38.

h.   Elders of the Church — Acts 20:17.

i.   A glorious Church — Ephesians 5:25-27.

j.   Head over the Church — Ephesians 1:22.

Thus the word "Church" is used of the One Universal Church about 80 times. Then the word is used of local and scattered groups in various geographical locations about 40 times. "Church of God" is used about 8 times, and "Churches of Christ" is used once (Romans 16:16).

Names of the Church are taken up further in Chapter 8.

2.   **One Accord, One Heart, One Mind**

The Early Church was of one accord, one heart and one mind (Acts 1:14; 2:1; 2:46; 4:32; 5:12; 8:6; 15:25; Philippians 1:27; 2:2). There the Lord commanded the blessing (Psalms 133).
The Lord will give them one heart (Ezekiel 11:19).
The trumpeters and singers made one sound (II Chronicles 5:13-14).

3.   **Symbols of Unity and Oneness**

a.   There is one body but many members — I Corinthians 12:12, 18.

b.   There is a sevenfold oneness here — Ephesians 4:4-6.

c.   One Tabernacle — Exodus 25-40.

d.   There was only one Temple — II Chronicles 1-5.

e.   Christ and His Bride are to be one in marriage — Ephesians 5:23-32.

f.   Must discern the oneness of the Body — I Corinthians 10:16, 17; 11:27-30.

g.   The Lord is making Jew and Gentile one new man — Ephesians 2:11-16.

h.   Christ died to gather all scattered together in one — John 11:50-52.

i.   There is one body but various offices and functions — Romans 12:1-5.

j.   There is one head of this one body — Colossians 1:18.

k.   The two sticks are to be one in the hand of the Son of Man — Ezekiel 37:17.

l.   There shall be one fold and one shepherd — John 10:16.

m.   Brethren in unity receive the anointing of the High Priest — Psalms 133.

n.   He will gather together in one all things in Christ — Ephesians 1:10.

o.   Noah's ark was three-storied yet one ark — Genesis 6-8.

p.   The Lampstand was 7 branches yet one Candlestick — Revelation 1:20. So the 7 local Churches, yet one Church. Revelation 1-2-3.

q.   Unity in time of restoration from Babylon — Ezra 3:1; Nehemiah 8:1. Isaiah 52:8; Ephesians 4:13-16. The fivefold ministries to bring unity in the Body.

r.   We being many are one body and one bread — I Corinthians 10:16-17.

s.   To have the same mind, speak the same thing, have the same judgment — I Corinthians 1:10.

t.   The vine and the branches are one by union life — John 15.

u.   One husband, Christ — II Corinthians 11:2.

Thus the Body is to be one. There is to be no schism in the Church (Romans 12:4, 5; Ephesians 5:30; Ezekiel 34:23; 37:24).
The unity in the Godhead is to be manifested in the Church (I John 5:5-8).
The Church is to come to a perfect man (Ephesians 4:12-16).

4.   **That they all might be one** — John 17.

This is the prayer of Christ. Christ foresaw the schisms, divisions and the heresies which would rend the Church. His prayer must be answered before He returns "that the world may know" that the Father sent the Son. He prays for the Church, not for the world. The same unity which exists in the Godhead, as Father, Son and Holy Spirit, is to be in the Church. The Godhead is equal as three persons, yet unity manifested in the three persons, in distinctive operation, ministry and manifestation.

This is to be in the many-membered Body of Christ. It is not a man-made or man-coerced unity, or unity of the flesh, but of the Spirit of God; "Even as we are one."

Note the four things that Christ gave to the Church that they might be one. At least five times Jesus prayed that they all might be one — vs 11, 21, 22, 23. He counts those things that are not as though they were — Jeremiah 1:10; Isaiah 55:9-10; Romans 4:17; Ephesians 3:21.

a. **Unity in the Name of God** — vs 6, 11, 12, 26.

Denominational names and sectarian names divide the Church. There can only be unity in the Name of the Lord Jesus Christ (Ephesians 3:14, 15). It is the "family name" — the uniting name of God's people, His Name in the Church.

b. **Unity in the Word of God** — vs 6, 8, 14, 17, 19, 20.

One in truth. The unity of the faith (Ephesians 4:9-16) by the Word and the revelation of God. The Spirit of God is to bring unity in the Word of God. Doctrinal divisions do not exist in the Godhead.

c. **Unity in the Glory of God** — vs 2, 4, 5, 10, 22, 24.

One in His glory. The glory of God and Christ. Not the glory of men, or of the movement, but His glory (Ephesians 3:21). Unto Him be glory in the Church.

d. **Unity in the Love of God** — vs 23, 24, 26.

God is love. The very nature of the Godhead manifest. I John — The Epistle of Love, Light and Life (John 3:16).

Here we have the very secret and power of unity, the glory of unity, the perfection of unity, (vs 21, 22, 23). The Lord has purposed this kind of Church and nothing in heaven or hell or earth will frustrate this purpose. There will be a Church that will be "one as we are one". His prayer will be answered.

C. The Church to be a Glorious Church

Ephesians 5:23-32. The revelation given to Paul concerning the Church as the great mystery, the Bride of Christ, shows the ultimate intention of the Lord for His Church. This is Godward in its truth even as the earlier revelations were outward and inward in their truths.

The Church is to be:

1. A sanctified Church that is holy, separated unto the Lord.
2. A cleansed Church, by the washing of water by the Word.
3. A glorious Church, clothed with glory and bringing glory to Christ.
4. A Church without spot or wrinkle, even as the Old Testament sacrifices were to be without spot, wrinkle, blemish or any such thing.
5. A holy Church, separated from sin.
6. A Church like unto Christ so that He can be united to her and not have a unequal yoke in this marriage.

The word has gone forth out of the mouth of the Lord and the zeal of the Lord of Hosts will perform it (Isaiah 55:9-11). This is the kind of Church He will have.

D. **The Sin of Sectarianism in the Church**

One of the greatest inditements against the Church is its numerous divisions. These divisions are the evidence of carnality in all its subtle forms (I Corinthians 3). Sects are the works of the flesh, and many times have the influence of an evil spirit behind them.

Paul spoke of these evil divisions (Romans 16:17, 18; I Corinthians 1:10). In Galatians 5:14-24 he lists *strife, seditions and heresies* as works of the flesh. These all speak of sectarian divisions among Christians.

1. *Variance* (Greek "eris") — Romans 1:29; 13:13; I Corinthians 1:11; 3:3. Translated as debate, strife, contentions, strife, in these verses. Also II Corinthians 12:20; Philippians 1:15; I Timothy 6:4; Titus 3:9.

2. *Strife* (Greek "eretheia"). Translated contention, strifes, contention, strife in Romans 2:8; II Corinthians 12:20; Philippians 1:15; 2:3.

3. *Seditions* (Greek "dichostasia"). Translated divisions in Romans 16:17; I Corinthians 3:3.

4. *Heresies* (Greek "hairesis"). Translated sect and heresies in these verses: Acts 5:17; 15:5; 24:5; 24:14; 26:5; 28:22; I Corinthians 11:19; II Peter 2:1; and heretic in Titus 3:10.

Thus to have a party-spirit or one's own opinion contrary to the Word of God is to be sectarian. The Pharisees were a sect and condemned all other peoples. When any group sets itself up as being right and all others wrong, and refuses to fellowship or co-operate with any others, that is sectarianism.

It is possible to be more sectarian in a "non-sectarian sect" and more denominational in a "non-denominational" group that those in a denomination. Sectarianism many times has an evil spirit behind it, and an evil attitude. This is evidenced in Church history by the persecutions, the bitterness, hatred, envy, jealousy, anger and slander that has manifested itself in believers in these times. God hates all forms of sectarianism for it divides the One Body of Christ.

CHAPTER 6

THE CHURCH AND THE KINGDOM

One of the greatest areas of controversy and confusion is that which pertains to the distinction and relationship of the Church and the Kingdom.

Dispensationalists speak of the Kingdom as being a Jewish thing and the Church as being a parenthetical plan of God after the Jews rejected the King, Jesus Christ. They teach that the Kingdom was postponed during this Dispensation of the Holy Spirit, and that the Church is God's temporary purpose in this period of time of Jewish unbelief.

However, this is very far from the truth of Scripture as it pertains to both the Church and the Kingdom.

Questions are asked: Are the Church and the Kingdom synonymous? Is the Church in the Kingdom or is the Kingdom in the Church? Is the Church Gentilish and the Kingdom Jewish? Is the Kingdom past, present or future? Materialistic? Spiritual?

A. **The Kingdom Defined**

The word ''Kingdom'' is made up of two words: ''King's Domain'' = King-Dom. It is the territory or area over which a King rules and reigns; the King's Domain. God's Kingdom is the reign or the rule of God, whether in heaven or earth. It is the purpose of God — the extension of God's rule.

Greek = ''*Basileia*''. It speaks of the sway, rule, administration of a king. The royal reign of the kingdom of God. One cannot separate the King and the Kingdom as far as God is concerned.

The word ''Kingdom'' is used about 160 times in the New Testament.

1. **How long has the Kingdom of God been in existence?**

   a. The Kingdom of God is an *everlasting* Kingdom (Psalms 145:10, 13; 103:19; Daniel 4:3). There has never been a time when the Kingdom of God has not been in existence. It has neither beginning nor end.

   b. The Kingdom of God is sovereign, ruling over kingdoms (Psalms 103:19; Revelation 11:5).

   c. The Kingdom of God is all-inclusive, including within itself, its domain, the total universe, the elect angels, heaven, the fallen angels and all creatures and mankind on this earth. All are under His control and dominion. None could exist or act without His sustaining power (Psalms 103:19; Exodus 15:18, Psalms 145:10-13).

2. **What is the difference between the Kingdom of God and the Kingdom of Heaven?**

   There is no difference between these terms; they are synonymous. A comparison of the following Scriptures shows that what is said of the Kingdom of God is also said of the Kingdom of Heaven (Matthew 23:22).

Kingdom of Heaven	Kingdom of God
Matthew 4:17	Mark 1:14
Matthew 5:3	Luke 6:20
Matthew 10:7	Luke 9:2
Matthew 11:11	Luke 7:28
Matthew 13:11	Luke 8:10
Matthew 13:31	Luke 13:18, 19
Matthew 19:14	Mark 4:30, 31
Matthew 19:23, 24	Luke 18:24

Matthew (writing particularly for Jewish converts) almost invariably uses the expression "Kingdom of Heaven", while Mark, Luke and John substitute "Kingdom of God."

It was customary among the Jews to use the word "Heaven" for God, and in Matthew 23:22 the Lord Himself states that to swear by heaven is to swear by "the throne of God and by Him that sitteth thereon."

B. **The Progressive Revelation of the Kingdom**

In each age there has been a further or progressive revelation of the Kingdom of God. This is the purpose of God for His kingdom to be manifested.

1. **The Kingdom of God in Heaven — Time Past**

    Matthew 6:6-9; Psalms 102:19; 145:10-13. The angels and the archangels were created as subjects of the heavenly kingdom in the eternity past. Sin brought confusion and originated a rebel kingdom of Satan and fallen angels here (Revelation 16:10; John 8:44; II Peter 2:4; Jude 6).

2. **The Kingdom of God in Eden**

    Genesis 1-2. God created Adam and Eve giving them dominion and rulership over the earth. In and through them God desired to rule and reign. His Kingdom was to be established in the earth, in Adam's race. However, as instruments for the expression of God's Kingdom, they failed because of sin and sold all their unborn generations over to Satan and the Kingdom of Darkness.

3. **The Kingdom of God in Patriarchal Times**

    Noah, Abraham, Isaac and Jacob were faithful patriarchs and covenant men. In them was illustrated and demonstrated the Kingdom of God in the earth. The promises of King Messiah were preserved in these men who were the instruments for the expression of God's Kingdom. These men, though imperfect, knew the rule and reign of God in their hearts and lives in the midst of corrupt and apostate nations about them. (Genesis 8-50 Chapters).

4. **The Kingdom of God in Israel**

    Exodus 19:1-6. In due time God brought forth the nation of Israel, and chose it out of the midst of other nations (Deuteronomy 4-5). In this nation He established more fully His Kingdom, His laws. Israel was a theocracy. God was their King (Numbers 24:5-7; Deuteronomy 7:6-8).

    God intended Israel to be the instrument in earth to demonstrate His rule and reign to other nations; to give all nations the revelation of the true God.

    Saul (I Samuel 9-10), David (I Samuel 16; I Chronicles 10:14), Solomon (I Kings 1:46) were the first kings to reign over a united nation. In due time the Kingdom of Israel was divided into two houses, the House of Israel and the House of Judah (I Kings 11-12; Ezekiel 16; Ezekiel 23). Both houses had prophets of God sent to them to remind them of the Laws of God. The tragedy is that Israel failed to be all that God intended them to be. For this reason God allowed the captivity of both houses; the House of Israel going into Assyrian Captivity and the House of Judah into Babylonian Captivity.

5. **The Kingdom of God in the Gentile World**

    During the Captivity of Israel and more especially that of Judah, God used the Gentile nations to be the instrument of His rule and reign in the earth. The Book of Daniel especially shows the sovereignty of God's Kingdom. He rules in the heavens and the earth and He gives the Kingdom to whomsoever He will (Daniel 2; Daniel 4; Psalms 9:16; Ezra 1:1-4; Daniel 7:9-14, 26, 27; Psalms 22:28, 29; I Kings 2:15; II Samuel 16:8; II Chronicles 36:22, 23; Daniel 4:17, 25; 32-35).

Thus Assyrian, Babylonian, Medo-Persian, Grecian and Roman Kingdoms were given the reign, under God, over the people of God because of their failure.

6. **The Kingdom of God in Christ**

God held the House of Judah in the land of Palestine until the advent of the King, Jesus Christ. The Gospel of Matthew is the Gospel of the King and the Kingdom. Jesus preached, taught and demonstrated the Kingdom of God. He gave the laws of the Kingdom in Matthew 5-6-7. He presented the rule and reign of God to the House of Judah (Matthew 4:17, 23-25). The King was actually the personification of the Kingdom of God in the earth.

★   Jesus preached the Gospel of the Kingdom — Matthew 4:23; Mark 1:14; Acts 1:3.

★   Jesus taught the Kingdom of God was at hand — Matthew 4:17; Mark 1:15.

★   Jesus showed that His ministry ushered in the next stage of the Kingdom — Matthew 12:24-28; Luke 11:20; 16:16.

★   Jesus told His disciples to preach the Kingdom of God — Matthew 10:7; Luke 9:2, 60; 10:9-11.

★   Jesus taught His disciples to pray "Thy Kingdom come" — Matthew 6:6-9; Luke 11:2.

★   Jesus told some of the disciples they would not die until they had seen the Kingdom of God come with power — Matthew 16:28; Mark 9:1; Luke 9:27.

★   Jesus said He would not eat and drink of the fruit of the vine until He did it anew in the Kingdom — Matthew 26:29; Mark 14:28; Luke 22:16-18.

This was demonstrated in the communion times He had with them after His resurrection — Acts 1:4; 10:41; John 21:13; I Corinthians 11:23-34.

However, because the Jews had such a nationalistic and materialistic concept of the Kingdom of God, they rejected their King and crucified Him (Matthew 26-27). But, contrary to the Dispensationalists, the Kingdom was not postponed until the end of the age and the lifting of Jewish blindness and unbelief, nor was the Church brought in as a parenthetical plan. The Kingdom was transferred over to the Church. The Kingdom was taken from Jewry and given to a nation, which was the New Testament Church (Matthew 21:41-46; I Peter 2:5-9).

7. **The Kingdom of God in the Church**

That there is a relationship between the Church and the Kingdom is evident from Matthew 16:18,19. Jesus said "Upon this Rock I will build My CHURCH and I will give unto thee the keys of the KINGDOM of heaven."

As will be seen, the Church now becomes the instrument for the demonstration of the Kingdom of God in the earth. It is also the final instrument for that ministry. The Church is entrusted with the administration and authority of the Kingdom in earth; symbolized by the "Keys of the Kingdom" given to it. This will be seen more fully at the close of this chapter.

8. **The Millenial Kingdom**

There is a further aspect of the Kingdom of God as to its manifestation in earth and that is the 1000 years reign of Christ on earth with the saints (Daniel 2; Daniel 7; Revelation 20:1-10).

However, there is much controversy and confusion over the fact and nature of this aspect of the Kingdom. It is not the purpose of this text to deal with this matter, but simply to note that this is just the final aspect of the Kingdom revelation in earth after Christ's second advent.

9. **The Kingdom in Eternity**

    The final aspect of the progressive revelation of the Everlasting Kingdom of God is that which takes place at the close of the 1000 year period. Paul says "Then cometh the end when he (Christ) shall have delivered up the Kingdom to the Father" (I Corinthians 15:24-28).

    Here we complete the cycle. The Everlasting Kingdom has been expressed in its sevenfoldness in earth, reaching from eternity to eternity in its completeness.

IN SUMMARY then, the Kingdom of God is the rule and reign of God over the universe and all creatures therein, angelic and human. There has been and is but ONE KINGDOM of God, but the instruments through which this one Kingdom has been expressed have varied. The final instrument for the expression and manifestation and demonstration of the Kingdom of God is THE CHURCH! The instrument of God has changed over the centuries but the purpose of God has never changed!

C. **The Church and The Kingdom**

Having defined and followed the cycle and progressive revelation of the Kingdom of God from eternity to eternity, through time, we consider more fully the Kingdom in relation to the Church.

1. **Distinction and Relationship**

    The Church and the Kingdom are distinct, yet related. The Kingdom is the universal reign of God over all creation and creatures and the universe of worlds, including in itself angels and men.

    The Church is composed of redeemed believers, out of every kindred, tongue, tribe and nation. The Church does not include the angelic hosts. So we may say that the angelic hosts are in the Kingdom, but only the redeemed are in the Church and also in the Kingdom.

    The Kingdom is eternal and unlimited. It is all encompassing. The Church is God's eternal purpose, manifested in time. It is limited to those of mankind who are redeemed by Christ.

    The Church becomes the instrument for the full demonstration of the Kingdom. God's Kingdom — His rule and reign — is to be established in the Church. The Church is in the Kingdom and the Kingdom is in the Church. But the Church is not the totality, but only a part of the Kingdom of God. The Kingdom is far more inclusive than the Church.

    This distinction, yet relationship between the Church and the Kingdom needs to be recognized and understood to avoid confusing the real issues involved in both. We do not pray "Thy *Church* come" but the Church prays "Thy *Kingdom* come" (Matthew 6:6-10). Nor do we preach "The Gospel of the *Church*", but the Church preaches the Gospel of the Kingdom (Matthew 24:14).

2. **The Church and The Kingdom**

    The word "Church" is used about 115 times, and the word "Kingdom" about 160 times in the New Testament.

    A study in the Book of Acts, along with other major Scriptures from the Gospels shows that the early Church was indeed the channel, the instrument, the vehicle and vessel for the expression of the Kingdom of God. It was through the Church that the Kingdom of God was extended in the earth in the hearts of men. We note some of the major truths concerning the Kingdom in these verses:

    ★   Christ would build His *Church* and give her the keys of the *Kingdom* — Matthew 16:18, 19.

    ★   Repentance and faith are the doorway into the Kingdom (Matthew 3:2; 4:17, 23).

★ The Kingdom is at hand (Mark 1:14, 15; Hebrews 6:1; Acts 2:34-42).

★ One must be born again from above by spiritual and heavenly birth to enter the Kingdom (John 3:1-5). If the Kingdom was postponed, then it means that none could be born again until then!

★ Regeneration is a translation out of the Kingdom of Darkness into the Kingdom of Light and love (Colossians 1:13, 14).

★ The Kingdom of God is righteousness, peace and joy in the Spirit (Romans 14:17; Matthew 6:33).

★ The Kingdom of God is not of this world system (John 18:36; Matthew 6:9, 10; Luke 17:20, 21).

★ The Gospel of the Kingdom is to be preached in all the world for a witness all nations before the end comes (Matthew 24:14; Mark 16:15-20).

★ The Law and the Prophets were until John; since that time the Kingdom is preached (Luke 16:16; Matthew 5:17, 18; 11:13; 12:28).

★ The Kingdom was taken from Jewry and given to the holy nation, which is the Church (Matthew 21:42-46; I Peter 2:5-9).

★ Believers are the good seed of the Kingdom in the Kingdom in its mystery form (Matthew 13:37, 38; Mark 4:11; Matthew 8:11; Luke 13:28, 29).

★ We are to seek first the Kingdom of God (Matthew 6:33; Luke 21:31).

★ The Kingdom of God is within the heart (Luke 17:20).

★ The Church taught and preached and demonstrated the power of the Kingdom of God in the Book of Acts.

a) Jesus spoke to the disciples of the Kingdom of God (Acts 1:3-6).

b) Philip, from the Church at Jerusalem, preached the Kingdom of God, as and Evangelist (Acts 8:1, 12).

c) Paul preached the Kingdom of God (Acts 14:22; 19:8; 20:25), as an apostle from the Church.

d) John and Paul, apostles of the New Testament Church, believed they were then in the Kingdom (Revelation 1:9; Colossians 4:11; Acts 28:23, 31).

e) Jesus Christ is the King-Priest after the order of Melchisedek (Hebrews 7:1, 2; Revelation 15:3; I Timothy 1:17; 6:15; Revelation 19:16), and the Church is also a Royal Priesthood after the same order (Revelation 1:6; 5:9, 10; I Peter 2:5-9; Romans 5:17, 21).

f) Believers were born into the Kingdom as subjects of the Kingdom (John 3:1-5), and they were added as members to the Church (Acts 11:24; 2:41-47).

g) The Church preached the Gospel of the Kingdom, for there is only *one Gospel for Jew and Gentile*. It is spoken of as:

1) The Gospel of the Kingdom (Mark 1:14, 15; Matthew 24:14).

2) The Gospel of Jesus Christ (Mark 1:1).

3) The Gospel of God (Romans 1:1).

4) The Gospel of His Son (Romans 1:9).

5) The Gospel of the Grace of God (Acts 20:24).

6) The Glorious Gospel (I Timothy 1:11).

7) The Everlasting Gospel (Revelation 14:6).

8) The Gospel of the Circumcision (Galatians 2:7).

9) The Gospel of the Uncircumcision (Galatians 2:7).

10) The Gospel (Mark 16:15-20).

11) The Gospel of Paul (Galatians 1:6-9; Romans 2:16; 16:25).

THE CHURCH today is the agent for the demonstration of THE KINGDOM of God in the earth. Though the Church and the Kingdom are distinguishable, they are indivisible in God's eternal purpose!

CHAPTER 7

THE CHURCH IN THE OLD TESTAMENT

One of the greatest truths to be discovered is the revelation of the Church in the Old Testament. Many Dispensationalists teach that the Church is nowhere to be found in the Old Testament, that the Church is only a New Testament revelation. They say that the Old Testament prophets did not see the Church as it was not revealed to them. They also teach that because the Church was a parenthetical plan of God, during Jewish unbelief and blindness, the Church could not be seen by the Old Testament saints. Hence it was given especially to Paul. In this chapter we consider the fallacy of such teaching, for, the New Testament Church was both prophesied and typified in Old Testament times.

A. **The Church Prophesied**

As has been seen in Chapter 4 *"What the Church Is"*, Section D, The Church is God's New Ethnic.

The Old Testament clearly foretold the coming in of the Gentiles into blessing in the Kingdom of God. The New Testament shows the beginning of the fulfilment of these prophecies when the Holy Spirit was poured out on the Gentiles, and then the Gospel going to the whole Gentile world. Many Dispensationalists place these Scriptures of the Gentiles coming into blessing into the Millennial Kingdom for a Jewish ministry instead of realizing these Scriptures are for this present dispensation — not a future one!

Paul is especially the apostle to the Gentiles, and it is Paul who is the great exponent of the Church as the Body of Christ, made up of Jew and Gentile (Ephesians 3:1-6).

We note again, with additional Scriptures, the Old Testament prophecies of the Gentiles coming into Christ by the Gospel — not in an age to come but in this present age.

★   All nations were to be blessed by the seed of Abraham (Genesis 22:18).

★   All the families of the earth were to be blessed by Abraham's seed (Genesis 26:4).

★   All kindreds of the nations would worship the Lord (Psalms 22:27, 28).

★   In the last days all nations would flow to the house of God (Isaiah 2:2, 3).

★   The Gentiles would seek the Root of Jesse (Isaiah 11:10).

★   Many nations would be sprinkled with the blood of Messiah (Isaiah 52:15).

★   Many nations would be joined to the Lord in that day (Zechariah 2:11).

★   The Name of the Lord would be great among the Gentiles (Malachi 1:11).

★   In His Name the Gentiles would trust (Matthew 12:21).

The Old Testament prophets especially foretold the days when the Gentile nations would flow to Israel and the Kingdom of God. Many times these prophecies are placed for fulfilment in the future age. However, the New Testament writers and especially Paul, the apostle to the Gentiles, show how the writings of the prophets were in the process of fulfilment right then, as the Holy Spirit was poured out on the Gentiles unto salvation.

Isaiah is the great "evangelist-prophet" of the coming of Messianic Times and there are more prophecies of the Gentiles coming into blessing in Isaiah than all the other Major and/or Minor Prophets put together.

A careful reading of Isaiah 11:10; 42:1,6; 49:6, 22; 54:3; 60:3, 5, 11, 16; 61:6, 9; 62:2; 66:12, 19; shows the prophesied blessing upon the Gentiles. In Romans 9-10-11 Chapters, Paul shows how the natural branches of the Israel Olive Tree were broken off because of unbelief and the believing Gentiles of the wild olive tree are now grafted in by faith. Here the Gentiles become one with the Israel Olive Tree, partaking of its root and fatness through Christ. Note the quotations of Paul from the Old Testament concerning Gentile blessing, especially in Romans 15.

Romans 15:9   with Psalms 18:49; II Samuel 22:50. The heathen are Gentiles.
Romans 15:10   with Deuteronomy 32:43. The nations are Gentiles.
Romans 15:11   with Psalms 117:1. Gentile nations rejoice with Israel.
Romans 15:12   with Isaiah 11:10; 42:1; Matthew 12:18-21.
Romans 15:21   with Isaiah 52:13-15. Gentiles would see and hear and understand while Jewry would fail to understand.

Paul, as the apostle to the Gentiles, quotes these great Gentile prophecies from Moses, David and Isaiah (Romans 15:16-20).

In Acts 10-11 Peter is the agent who, by the Gospel, opens the door of faith to let the Gentiles into the Kingdom of God. The Holy Spirit seals this fact. In Acts 15 the great controversy is settled by James quoting from Amos about the Gentiles coming into blessing in the Tabernacle of David (Amos 9:11-15). Christ told his disciples to make disciples of ALL nations (Matthew 28:18-20; Mark 16:15-20; Luke 24:47; Acts 1:8). Through Christ all may become the seed of Abraham (Galatians 3:16, 29).

The summation of all this is given to Paul when he says that Jews and Gentile are baptized by one Spirit into *one Body,* the Church of Jesus Christ (I Corinthians 12:13; Ephesians 3:1-10).

When we see that the Gentiles come into THE CHURCH through Christ, then we can understand Old Testament prophecy of blessing on the Gentiles. Although the word *"Church"* is not used in the Old Testament specifically (though "Qahal" = Congregation and Assembly is), yet the word *"Gentiles"* is used. Whenever these references speak of Gentiles coming into blessing with the true Israel of God, that is the Old Testament way of speaking of the New Testament Church.

It is in this way THE CHURCH was prophesied of in the Old Testament by the prophets.

B. The Church Typified

The Old Testament clearly prophesied of the coming of the Gentiles into the Kingdom of Messiah. The thing that was hidden from them, not understood by them, was the revelation that The Church would be THE BODY of Christ made up of both Jew and Gentile (Ephesians 3:1-6).

However, though this aspect of the Church may have been a mystery to them, and hidden from them, the Church was foreshadowed and typified also in the Old Testament. The Church was both prophesied and typified. When the New Testament apostles received the full revelation of the Church, they continually appealed to the Old Testament Scriptures, both prophetically and typically (Romans 16:25, 26; I Corinthians 10:6, 11). They saw that many things were Old Testament types and symbols of the Church. These were foreshadowings of the New Testament Church.

It was not that these things were types to them in the Old Testament but they become types unto us upon whom the ends of the age are come.

Peter says the prophets did not understand some of their own prophecies, but he says that it was revealed to them that they were not only speaking to their own generation but also to our generation which is experiencing the outpouring of the Holy Spirit (II Peter 1:16-21; I Peter 1:10-12). They spoke for our age timeless truths. Jesus said the prophets would love to have seen and heard the things happening in our age (Matthew 13:10-17).

★   Moses would like to have seen the New Testament Church and Priesthood (I Peter 2:5-9).

★   Isaiah would love to have seen Pentecost (Isaiah 28:10-12).

★   Joel would like to have been in the Upper Room (Acts 1-2).

★   Enoch would like to see the translation of saints (Jude 14, 15).

★   Israel would like to see the true Passover (Exodus 12).

★   Elijah and Elisha would like to see Christ's ministry, lepers cleansed, dead raised.

★ Jonah would like to see Christ's 3 days experience (Matthew 12:39-40).

★ Abraham saw Christ's day (John 8:56-58).

So the prophets ministered to their own generation and also unto ours. Hebrew 1:1, 2.

Many believers see that the prophets foretold THE CHRIST, but fail to see also that they foretold THE CHURCH just as clearly. National blindness concerning Jewry has robbed the Church of these truths.

These things became ''types'' to us (Greek *''Tupos''* = ''to strike, make an impression, a blow, a mark left by a blow''). (John 20:25; Acts 7:43; Romans 5:14; 6:17; Acts 7:44; I Corinthians 10:6, 11).

Because the following chapter lists a number of various types, symbols and names of the Church in both Old and New Testament, we note in brief just several of the major Old Testament types of the Church which are substantiated by the New Testament writers.

1. **Adam and Eve** (Genesis 1-2 with Ephesians 5:23-33; Romans 5:14).

    There is no mistaking Paul's use of the marriage relationship as a type of the marriage of Christ and His Church. Paul goes back to the first sinless marriage of Adam and Eve as being prophetic and typically of Christ and His Bride. It is a type rich in details.

2. **Israel Nation** (Exodus 1-19; Acts 7:38).

    Israel is spoken of as ''The Church in the Wilderness.'' Without doubt there are numerous things in Israel's experience which become typical of the New Testament Church. This is seen by the many references of the New Testament writers (I Corinthians 5; 10:1-11).

3. **The Tabernacle and Temple** (Exodus 25-40; II Chronicles 1-5; Ephesians 2:20-22; I Corinthians 3:16; 6:19).

    The Tabernacle and Temple were God's dwelling place, the habitation of His Name, Presence and Glory. The New Testament uses such things as being symbolical and typical of Christ and also His Church (John 1:14-18; 2:18-22; Hebrews 3:1-5; I Peter 2:5-9; 4:17).

    Both Tabernacle and Temple are rich in symbolic and typical truths of both Christ and His Church.

Thus the New Testament continually uses Old Testament pictures, types and symbols to illustrate the revelation of the Church. The Church was indeed both prophesied and typified under the former dispensation, even though the Old Testament writers did not have full insight into their own utterances and ordinances. I Peter 1:9-12; II Peter 1:19-21.

In a subsequent chapter we will consider ''The Mystery Body of Christ'', made up of Jew and Gentile, which was revealed to Paul but NOT to the Old Testament saints.

CHAPTER 8

SYMBOLS, TYPES AND NAMES OF THE CHURCH

Having seen that the Church was both prophesied and typified in the Old Testament, we note a number of types and symbols as well as names and titles of the Church in both Old and New Testaments. The very fact that the New Testament writers repeat the same things show that these may be viewed as types and symbols and that the Hermeneutical Principles of Type and Symbols may be safely applied.

A. **Symbols and Types of the Church**

1. **In the Old Testament**

    a.   The Garden of Eden — Genesis 1-2; Song 1-8.

    b.   The Tabernacle in Eden; the glory, worship and sacrifice — Genesis 3.

    c.   Adam and Eve — Genesis 2-3. Christ and His Bride — Ephesians 5:23-32. Romans 5:14.

    d.   Altars of sacrifice — Genesis 3:8. Lamb slain. Revelation 13:8.

    e.   The Ark of Noah — Triune salvation of God. Genesis 6-8. Christ and His Church.

    f.   The Tabernacle in the Wilderness — God's Dwelling. Exodus 25-40; Ephesians 2.

    g.   Israel — The Church in the Wilderness. Acts 7:38.

    h.   Israel, as the Holy Nation — Exodus 19:1-6; I Peter 2:5-10.

    i.   Enoch, the Translated Saint — Genesis 5; Hebrews 11:5, 6.

    j.   Noah — Rest after Judgment — Genesis 6-8.

    k.   Jacob — The Anointer of Bethel, The House of God — Genesis 28.

    l.   Jacob's Ladder — Genesis 28; John 1:51.

    m.   Joseph, the beloved son — Genesis 37-50.

    n.   Priestly ministry of Aaron and Levites — Exodus 28-29; Leviticus 8-9.

    o.   The Golden Candlestick — Exodus 25:31-40; Revelation 1-2-3.

    p.   The Vineyard of the Lord — Isaiah 5; Matthew 21; John 15; Psalms 80.

    q.   The House of the Lord — Isaiah 2:1-5. Temple of Solomon. Joshua 22:19; Isaiah 57:15; Ephesians 2:21-22; Isaiah 56:7.

    r.   The Flock of God — Jeremiah 23; Ezekiel 34; John 10.

    s.   The Bride of Jehovah — Isaiah 54; Revelation 21:9.

    t.   The Life of Samson — Weak, strong, falling, restored Man — Judges 13-16.

    u.   Ezekiel's Valley of Dry Bones — Ezekiel 37.

    v.   The Firstborn — Numbers 1-2-3; Hebrews 12:22-24.

    w.   The Army of the Lord — Exodus 13-14; Numbers 1-2-3.

    x.   The Heritage of the Lord — Joel 3:2.

    y.   The Branch of the Lord — Isaiah 4:1-4.

    z.   The Congregation of the saints — Psalms 149:1; 89:7.

    It will be seen that many of these things are repeated also in the New Testament.

2. **In The New Testament**

    a.   The House of the Lord — Hebrews 3:6; I Peter 2:5; I Timothy 3:15; I Corinthians 3:16.

b.   The True Israel of God — Galatians 6:16; 3:16, 29; Romans 9-10-11.

c.   The Olive Tree — Romans 9-10-11.

d.   The Mystery Kingdom — John 3:1-5; Romans 14:17; Matthew 13.

e.   The Sons of God — Romans 8:1-19; Exodus 4:22-24; John 1:12-14; I John 3:1-2.

f.   The New Jerusalem Bride City — Revelation 21-22; Matthew 5:14; Hebrews 11:10-16.

g.   The Royal Priesthood — Revelation 1:6; 5:9, 10; Hebrews 7; I Peter 2:5-9; Psalms 133.

h.   The Flock of God — John 10; Psalms 80:1-2; Acts 20:20-28.

i.   The Army of the Lord — Ephesians 6:10-18.

j.   The Church or the Assembly — Ephesians 3:1-12. Hebrews 12:22-24.

k.   The Body of Christ — I Corinthians 12:27; Ephesians 1:22, 23; Colossians 1:18.

l.   The Camp of the Saints — Revelation 21-22; Numbers 1-2-3.

m.   The Royal Seed of Abraham — Galatians 3:16, 29; Genesis 22.

n.   The Overcomers — Revelation 1-2-3.

o.   The Church of the Firstborn — Colossians 1:17, 18; Hebrews 12:22-24.

p.   The Holy Nation — I Peter 2:5-9; Exodus 19:1-6.

q.   The Golden Candlestick — Revelation 1-2-3.

r.   God's Husbandry — I Corinthians 3:9.

s.   God's Heritage — I Peter 5:3.

t.   Mt Zion — Hebrews 12:22; Revelation 14:1-2.

u.   The Pillar and ground of truth — I Timothy 3:15.

v.   The Vine and Branches — John 15.

w.   The Bride of Christ — Ephesians 5:23-32.

x.   The Light of the World — Matthew 5:14; John 8:12; Isaiah 60:1-3.

y.   Peculiar Treasure/People — I Peter 2:5-9; Matthew 13:44; Exodus 19:3-6.

z.   God's chosen people — I Peter 2:9; Deuteronomy 10:15; II Corinthians 6:16; Psalms 100:3.

The Church is God's Witness in the earth (Acts 1:8; Isaiah 43:10).

The Church is God's New Covenant people (Isaiah 43:21; Exodus 6:7). Natural Israel were cut off because of unbelief, except for a remnant (Romans 11:5, 20). Gentiles are grafted in by faith and grace.

These promises are New Covenant promises (Galatians 3:29; Hebrews 8:6-13; Jeremiah 31:31-34). God is visiting the Gentiles to take out of them a people for His Name (Acts 15:14; I Peter 2:10). This people is God's holy nation, composed of Jew and Gentile.

So God has given many pictures of Israel, His people in the Old Testament, which the New Testament now applies to the New Testament Israel of God. The same language is used of both Old Covenant and New Covenant people. Each picture gives a new and different facet of truth of His people. They are pictures of relationship between Christ and His Church. One cannot see Christ without seeing His Church and vice versa.

In order to gain insights into each of the above symbols and types of the Church, used in the Old Testament and then confirmed by the New Testament, the Hermeneutical Principles of Interpretation that should be used are:

★   The Symbolic Principle

★   The Typical Principle

The Old Testament was preparatory to the New Testament, as the bud to the flower.

B.   **Names and Titles of the Church**

The Church or the Ekklesia is known under various names or titles also in the Scripture. The most frequent is ''The Church'', used about 114 times, 96 speaking of the ''local Church'' and 18 speaking of the ''universal Church''. The one speaks of saints in a given locality, the other is all-inclusive of saints in heaven and earth. The multiplied names of denominations and organizations and sects are but the making of men. They speak of the names of Babylon and generally are a terrible testimony to our divisions. There is but ONE NAME God has given to the Church and the believers collectively and that is simply ''The Church''. The Name that the Church is to bear is THE NAME of the LORD JESUS CHRIST! (Ephesians 3:14, 15). It is the family name, the uniting Name. None dare place upon the Tabernacle, or the Temple, where God's Name was recorded, their own tribal name. Israel, consisting of twelve tribes with their own names, was collectively known as ''THE CHURCH in the Wilderness'' (Acts 7:38).

Following are the various designations in the New Testament of the Church of our Lord Jesus Christ.

1. The Church in the Wilderness. Used once of Old Testament Israel (Acts 7:38).

2. The Churches of Christ. Used once only (Romans 16:16).

3. The Church of God. Used 6 times (I Corinthians 1:2).

4. The Churches. About 37 times (Acts 9:31).

5. The Church. Approximately 76 times (Acts 18:22).

6. The Church of the Firstborn (Hebrews 12:23). Once only.

7. The Church of the living God. Once only (I Timothy 3:15).

8. The Churches of God. Once only (I Thessalonians 2:14).

9. The Church of the Thessalonians in the Father and in Christ (II Thessalonians 1:1). Once only.

10. The Church which is His Body (Ephesians 1:22-23). Several times.

11. The Body of Christ (The Body of the Anointed One). Above 20 times (I Corinthians 12:27).

12. The Christ (I Corinthians 12:12). Head and Body together constitute ''the Christ''.

(Note — Acts 19:37. ''Robbers of Churches'' = Greek ''*Hierosulos*'', Robbers of the Temple buildings, NOT ''Churches'' as congregation of the Lord.)

THE CHURCH therefore is the corporate title of the people of God, regardless of their geographical locality.

CHAPTER 9

THE CHURCH, GOD'S BUILDING

As already dealt with there are numerous types and shadows of the Church. In this chapter we take one of these types and develop it more fully; that is, the picture of the Church as God's building, God's habitation.

In contemplating the Church we see that Christ is the Builder, the Church is His Building and He has chosen to have others build with Him, according to His pattern. Paul said that he was called to be a wise master-builder and he warned others to take heed to the material they put into God's building and how they build.

A.   The Builder and The Builders

1.   Christ is The Builder

He Himself said "Upon this Rock I WILL BUILD My Church" (Matthew 16:18). If the Lord is not building the house, then all labour is in vain by those who build it (Psalms 127:1). Men will build organizations, denominations, a sect or his own kingdom but it is not necessarily HIS CHURCH.

Christ is "the wise man" who builds His house upon the rock (Matthew 7:24-27) and it will stand the storms that beat against it. The Church is His house over which He rules as the Son of God (Hebrews 3:1-6; I Timothy 3:15; I Corinthians 3:9; Ephesians 2:21-22).

★   The Church is typified in the Tabernacle of Moses.

★   The Church is typified in the building of the Tabernacle of David (I Chronicles 17:5). Read also Acts 15:15-18; Amos 9:11-13.

★   The Church is typified in the temple of Solomon (I Kings 8:8-13).

★   Jesus Christ is both Tabernacle and Temple, and the Church is His Body (John 1:14-18; 2:18-21).

★   The Church is the city whose builder and maker is God (Revelation 21-22; Hebrews 11:10-16).

The prophet Zechariah foretold the fact that Christ would be a King-Priest on the throne and he would build His house and bear the glory (Zechariah 4:9; 6:12, 13).

The first and most important question to be answered is this. "Is CHRIST building His house?" If not, all our labour is in vain.

2.   Building by the Spirit

The Church is not a material but a spiritual house built of lively stones (I Peter 2:5-9).

The Church is to be built up as the habitation of God by the Spirit (Ephesians 2:20-22).

Just as the Tabernacle of Moses, the Temple of Solomon was built by the revelation of the Spirit upon people; so Christ is building His Church by the power of the Spirit. The Book of Acts is the Acts of the Holy Spirit as Christ began to build His Church. It is not by might nor by power but by My Spirit, saith the Lord (Exodus 36:1-6; I Chronicles 28:11-19; Zechariah 4:6; I Corinthians 12:13; Acts 2:1-4).

3.   Building According to the Pattern

The Greek noun for "building" is "*Oikodome*" ("Oikos = a home, and dome") = to build. The verb "*Oikodomeo*" is translated "build" (ed, ers, edified, eth, ing), edification, built and built up.

The Church is God's building, God's edifice.

As the Tabernacle of Moses and Temple of Solomon were built according to the Divine pattern, so Christ will build His Church according to the Father's pattern given to Him.

B. **The Builders — The Ministries and Believers**

A study of the following Scriptures reveal that, not only is Christ THE Builder by the Spirit, but He also builds through other people, as sub-contractors. This has been typified in the Old Testament buildings and habitations of God.

1. **Moses and Builders**

    Moses was the builder, the wise master-builder, of the Tabernacle of the Lord in the wilderness. However, with him were other builders who built according to the pattern given to him from the Lord God. All was built by the wisdom and Spirit of God (Exodus 25-40; 36:1-7).

2. **Solomon and Builders**

    Solomon was the builder of the temple of the Lord. All was again built to the pattern by the wisdom and Spirit of God (I Chronicles 28-29; II Chronicles 1-7). He had other builders with him also.

3. **Christ and Builders**

    Jesus Christ is the Builder of the New Testament Church. It is also being built by the wisdom and Spirit of God according to the Divine pattern. However, He has seen fit to call other builders (sub-contractors) to build with Him, under His direction and supervision.

    The five-fold ascension gift ministries of Apostles, Prophets, Evangelists, Pastors and Teachers are called to build the Church, to edify it (Ephesians 4:9-16). Paul, the apostle, said he was a wise, skilful architect, master-builder of God's house, and called on other builders to be careful how they built and what materials they used (I Corinthians 3:9-16).

    Sub-contractors are God's workmen, co-workers with Christ, in a spiritual building. No one can do it all, but all are inter-dependent on others ministries and abilities and talents.

    The Church, God's house, is built on the foundation laid by the apostles and prophets (Ephesians 2:20-22). In the foundations of the City of God, whose Builder and Maker is God, are the names of the 12 apostles of the Lamb (Revelation 21-22; Hebrews 11:10, 16).

    No one ministry can do the whole work. As in the building of a material house, by sub-contractors, so in the spiritual house of the Lord. Electricians, plumbers, carpenters, roofers, etc., all specialize in their own areas of building, yet all are inter-dependent on the other. So it is in the fivefold ascension-gift ministries who specialize in their God-given grace (Ephesians 2:20-22; 4:9-16; I Corinthians 12).

    All believers are also involved in building according to the measure of the grace-gifts given to them by Christ and the power of the Holy Spirit (I Corinthians 3:9; Romans 12:1-8).

    I Corinthians 12; Romans 12:1-8; I Peter 4:10, 11 list some of the grace-gifts that are given to the members to build the house of God.

C. **The Building — The Church**

The building in which Christ, His ministries and believers are involved is made up of PEOPLE — not a material building. It is a *living building,* made up of *lively stones,* the people of God (I Peter 2:5-9; Ephesians 2:20-22).

Many times people become caught up and wrapped in building a material building and forget the building up of the Church, composed of the people of God. God's purpose is to build up A HOUSE for His habitation by the Spirit. There are two facets to building people:

1. **Multiplication** — Evangelism

    In building a natural house, the first thing to do would be to gather all the material together. So in the spiritual. Evangelism, personal and public, is the gathering together of the "lively stones." However, a heap of stones is not a building. Gathered stones, from the quarry, are but the materials. They have to be cut and shaped, hewn and measured, and then fitted together. This is beautifully illustrated in the building of Solomon's temple and his own house (I Kings 5:17, 18; 6:7; I Peter 2:5-9).

The stones have to be prepared to fit into their place (Isaiah 51:1-2; Ephesians 2:19-22).

The Church in the Book of Acts, by evangelism, "*multiplied*" (Acts 6:1, 7; 9:31; 12:24 with Genesis 1;22, 28; 22:17; Hebrews 6:14). The disciples were multiplied (Acts 7:17). Evangelism is simply gathering stones, rough, unhewn and unplaced stones. The "stone-masons" work on them. i.e., The fivefold ministries (Ephesians 4:9-16).

2. **Edification** — Assembling

Multiplication is not necessarily edification! We can have a heap of stones and say "crawl in", but that is NOT a house! Multiplication should lead to edification. BOTH are needed. One without the other is useless, but the one precedes the other. There must be assembling together, ASSEMBLING people into a spiritual building. I will BUILD My Church (Greek "*oikodomeo*", which means "to build") as you would a building. The individual stones need to be cut, to fit together corporately. The Churches were multiplied . . . edified (Acts 9:31). Thus "to be built up, to be placed, to be put in order, or to be arranged." This is structure. Fit stones, stones finding their place (Hebrews 10:25; I Corinthians 11:17, 18, 20, 33, 34), assembling together.

D. **The Materials in the Building**

Paul in I Corinthians 3:9-15 (Amplified New Testament) tells us all to "take heed how we build." This has to do with our works. In Moses' Tabernacle and Solomon's Temple there were various materials, all of Divine order.

1. Gold —	)	All imperishable, can stand the pressure,
2. Silver —	)	fire, purification test.
3. Precious stones —	)	Purify the spoils of war (Numbers 31:21-24).

1. Wood —	)	
2. Hay —	)	Perishable, fire reduces all to nothing but ashes.
3. Stubble —	)	

The fire tests and appraises the character and worth of each person's works (Job 23:10).

Gold — speaks of that which is Divine, of God.
Silver — speaks of that which is of redemption.
Precious stones — speaks of that which is formed as a gem, gifts of the Spirit (Proverbs 17:8).
Works have to be tested as to our motivation.
Works according to the WORD = Gold.
Works inspired and energized by the SPIRIT = Silver.
Works motivated by the LOVE of God = Precious stones.

Only works that are according to the WORD of God, inspired by the SPIRIT of God and motivated by the LOVE of God will stand the fire tests "in that day" (II John 8). We have to look to ourselves that we receive a full reward. Other works are reduced to ashes, and thus we are saved, so as by fire. "Remember Lot's wife," (Luke 17:32).

E. **Things that Build or Edify**

There are a number of things that edify both individually and corporately. The test is always, Does what I am saying, doing and being edify? (I Thessalonians 5:11; I Corinthians 14:26; 10:23.) Seek to excel to the edifying of the Church.

1. The Word of God, the Word of grace, builds up, as well as obedience to that Word (Acts 20:32; Matthew 7:24-27). Hearing and doing builds the house.

2. Praying in the Spirit in the most holy faith builds up (Jude 20). Unbelief, doubt and fear tear down and destroy.

3. The love of God builds up (I Corinthians 8:1).

4. The right kind of communication builds up (Colossians 4:6; Ephesians 4:29).

5. The peace and harmony of the Lord builds up (Romans 14:19; Matthew 5:3-12).

6. The endeavour to please our neighbour in love builds up (Romans 15:2).

7. The being rooted and established in the faith builds up (Colossians 2:7).

8. The five-fold ministry ascension gifts build up (Ephesians 2:20-22; 4:11, 12).

9. The members of the Body ministering to one another builds up (I Corinthians 14:26; Note ''edify'' in this chapter; Ephesians 4:12-16).

10. The speaking in tongues edifies oneself (I Corinthians 14:3-5).

11. The gifts of tongues and interpretation edify the Church also.

12. The gift of prophecy edifies the Church (I Corinthians 14:3-5, 12).

13. Spiritual sacrifices edify also (I Peter 2:5; Hebrews 13:15, 16).

We cannot edify others unless we ourselves are edified (I Corinthians 14:3, 5, 12, 17, 26).

Paul could use his power to edify or destroy (II Corinthians 10:8; 12:19; 13:10).

The Lord desires to build His house, to make it a glorious living edifice.

CHAPTER 10

THE FOUNDATION ROCK-STONE

In the building of a building, the first and most important thing is to lay a proper foundation, for upon this the whole structure stands or fall. The foundation is the beginning of the structure.

If the foundations be destroyed, what can the righteous do? (Psalms 11:3). In the purchase of a house people generally look at the foundations first.

A. Importance of the Foundation

All depends on the foundation as to whether a building will stand the storms. Matthew 7:24-27. The two builders illustrate this. The wise builder laid the foundation upon a rock. The foolish built without a foundation. Luke 6:46-49; 14:29. The wise man laid the foundation upon a rock foundation. He counted the cost of building the house lest he be not able to finish it and people mock him. Matthew 16:18, 19. Upon THIS ROCK I will build My Church, Jesus said.

B. Symbolic Foundations

In the Old Testament structures, originating with God, we see that each had a proper foundation Divinely laid.

Psalms 87:1. His foundation is in the holy mountains.

1. The Tabernacle of Moses was built, not on the sand, but upon the foundations of the silver sockets of redemption (Exodus 26:19, 21, 25).

2. The Bethel House of God was founded upon the Rock/Pillar anointed with oil (Genesis 28:12-28).

3. The Tabernacle of David was pitched in the rocky fortress of Mt Zion (I Chronicles 17).

4. The Temple of Solomon was built upon the foundation in Mt Moriah, upon the typical sacrifice of an only begotten son, a threshing floor, and 3 days of judgement and the price of silver (II Samuel 24:18-25; Genesis 22; I Chronicles 1-7; II Chronicles 3:1, 2).

5. The City of God, whose Builder and Maker is God, is a city with twelve foundations.

6. The New Testament also has proper foundations. Paul said "I laid the foundation" (I Corinthians 3:9-15). Paul did not try to build his Churches on another man's foundation" (Romans 15:20).

7. The Great Pyramid has its solid foundation stones. If we take the Church as a pyramid, then we may apply (a) The Chief Cornerstone, and then (b) The Capstone to Christ Jesus (Isaiah 28:16; Ephesians 2:20, 22). Christ is the cornerstone, from which the whole building takes its alignment; it is the alignment of two walls. The stone of the corner is the foundation stone.

   Then the head of the corner is the capstone, the final stone, the Headstone, the keystone, that locks all the structure together as one (I Peter 2:6).

   Thus Christ is the First and the Last, the Beginning and the Ending, the Alpha and Omega, the Author and Finisher, the Cornerstone and the Capstone (Revelation 1:10; Hebrews 12:2; Romans 9:33).

C. **Who or What is the Foundation?**

I Corinthians 3:9-15. Paul clearly says "I laid the foundation . . . other foundation can no man lay than that is laid which is CHRIST . . ." All involved in His person is in this fact; all He is, all He said, all He did. The Church is NOT built on the personalities of the apostles or prophets, but on Christ Jesus, WHO He is, WHAT He has done, and ALL He said!

The theme of "The Rock/Stone" may be followed throughout Scripture. Sufficient for this chapter are some of the major references to this progressive revelation.

1. The Bethel Anointed Stone (Genesis 28:12-22). The builders rejected it, but it became the Anointed Pillar and Rock.

2. The Deity of the Rock (Psalms 18:31, 46; 28:1; 62:7; 89:26).

3. The Rock that begets other rocks (Deuteronomy 32:4, 15, 18, 30, 31, 37).

4. The Anointing of the Rock (Genesis 28:12-22; I Corinthians 10:1-4; John 1:41, 42).

5. The Shepherd ministry of the Rock (Genesis 49:24).

6. The Crucifixion and Smiting of the Rock (Exodus 17; Psalms 118:22; Matthew 21:42-44; I Corinthians 10:1-4; Acts 4:11; I Peter 2:5-9). The Rock was rejected, despised, refused and smitten.

7. The Rock as a Stumblingstone (Romans 9:30-33; I Peter 2:1-9).
    Jewry stumbled through unbelief and rejection of faith-righteousness.

8. The Rock that becomes the Foundation Stone in Zion (Isaiah 28:16; Matthew 16:18, 19); or the Cornerstone, if a Pyramid (Ephesians 2:20-22; II Timothy 2:19).

9. The Rock of Offence to those who reject Him (Psalms 118:22; Acts 4:11; Luke 7:23; John 16:1; Galatians 5:11; I Peter 2:5-9).

10. The Rock that becomes the Smiting Stone (Daniel 2; Matthew 21:44-46). There is absolutely no mistaking the fact that THE ROCK, THE STONE, is Christ Jesus Himself! It is not Peter but the ONE WHOM PETER CONFESSED!

D. **Who Lays the Foundation?**

The foundation — Christ — is laid by the apostles and prophets (Ephesians 2:20-22). The twelve apostles of the Lamb are in the foundation of the City of God. This speaks for the same fact (Revelation 21:14-19).

So Moses laid the foundation of the silver sockets for the Tabernacle, as the apostle of the Church in the Wilderness, with Aaron the prophet.

So David laid the foundation of the Tabernacle of David in rocky Mt Zion. So Solomon built upon the foundation laid by David in the Temple building in Mt Moriah.

The *foundation doctrines* of the apostles has already been laid (Acts 2:42), and all other ministries, apostles and prophets, will simply 'lay' that foundation!

E. **The Foundation Principles** (Hebrews 6:1, 2).

The wise man, according to Luke, laid the foundation on a Rock (Luke 6:48, 49). There is a two-fold thought here; (a) The ROCK is the foundation, and (b) The foundation is also laid on that rock foundation.

So we may say that CHRIST is THE Foundation Rock, and THE FIRST PRINCIPLES of the Doctrine of Christ are "the foundation" laid on THE Foundation Christ. "Upon *this rock* I will build My Church". Note how Christ spoke of "this bread", and "this Gospel", and "this temple" to the people. People looked at the wrong thing so much, when He was speaking of Himself (John 2:18-22; 6:34, 51-57; Matthew 24:14; Matthew 16:18).

after the Babylonian Captivity had ended. All point to Christ and His Church).

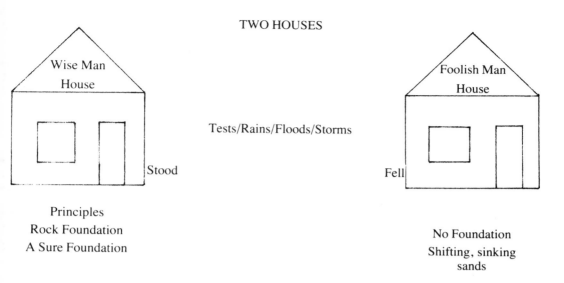

TWO HOUSES

Wise Man House

Foolish Man House

Tests/Rains/Floods/Storms

Stood

Fell

Principles
Rock Foundation
A Sure Foundation

No Foundation
Shifting, sinking
sands

Christ is THE FOUNDATION Rock and Stone. The Church that is built upon His person and all involved in that will stand the tests of the coming storms. The false Church will have a great fall.

CHAPTER 11

THE CHURCH IN THE BOOK OF ACTS

Having seen the Church as to its Divine origin as set forth in promise and prophecy in the Gospel of Matthew, we turn to the Book of Acts to see the progression of this prophetic word.

The thoughts there are in "seed form" and now watered by the Holy Spirit in the Acts of the Apostles. The revelation of the Church in the Acts and the Epistles especially grew out of that Gospel "seed".

There are basically two aspects of the Church as seen in the Gospel of Matthew; the Church Universal and the Church Local (Matthew 16:18, 19; 18:15-20).

A. The Church Universal

Matthew 16:18, 19 especially refers to the Church Universal. "My Church" — NOT Churches! ONE Church, even as there was but ONE Tabernacle, and ONE Temple. We saw this in Chapter One. The Book of Acts shows clearly how the early believers accepted this concept and outworking. The early believers counted themselves as part of the one universal Church, wherever they were, in whatever locality they lived.

As noted in Chapter Four, E, on the "Ekklesia", as the citizens of Athens, wherever they were, and wherever they assembled together, counted themselves a part of the city of Athens, so the believers, whenever and wherever they gathered together, counted themselves as part of the heavenly city of Jerusalem. They would gather together to the Heavenly Zion, Heavenly Jerusalem, to the General Assembly and Church of the Firstborn ones (Hebrews 12:22-24).

The earthly Jerusalem, where the Church began under the Pentecostal outpouring of the Spirit symbolized this truth.

The disciples were part of the one universal Church, the Church that Christ said He would build (Matthew 16:18).

They were "added to the Church" (Acts 2:47).

Christ was the Head of the Church (Ephesians 1:22).

The wisdom of God was known by the Church (Ephesians 3:10, 21).

The Church is the Body of Christ (Ephesians 5:23-32; Colossians 1:18, 24).

The Church is His House (I Timothy 3:5, 15).

Christ was in the midst of the Church, His worshipping congregation (Hebrews 2:12).

The Church universal spoke of the mystical union in a spiritual Body of the habitation of the Spirit, having Jesus as its Head, of all believers everywhere at all times. It is not spoken of in a visible sense but it is an invisible union of all true believers in Jesus Christ (Ephesians 3:21; 2:19-22; Hebrews 12:22, 24).

B. The Church Local

However, within this one universal Church, there were many Churches in many and various localities, all replicas and part of the whole. The concept was from the whole to the part, and part to the whole. This concept maintained the unity of the Church universal and the Churches local.

The second use of the word "Church" in Matthew's Gospel seeds the best concept of a Local Church.

Matthew 18:15-20. This passage is applicable to the Church local, for it is evident that if it is a brother that comes under the need of discipline and it must be told to the whole Church, then it would have to be sent worldwide if it meant the Church universally.

★ **Where** — anywhere, regardless of place (Deuteronomy 12:15-18; 16:2, 22). In the Old Testament the only place that was allowed by the Lord for Israel to meet was either the Tabernacle or the Temple where God chose to place His Name.

Jerusalem was the PLACE where His NAME was recorded, and all gathered together there for worship and festival times.

In the New Testament, we gather to the place where HIS NAME is, and this is in the Church. Where two or three gathered together IN My name (I Corinthians 1:1-2).

Jesus Christ is now THE TEMPLE, or THE TABERNACLE (John 1:14-18; 2:18-21).

★ **Two or Three** — the persons, the believers, the smallest possible grouping of believers, as a cell. However, not just one person, but minimum of two or three.

★ **Gather Together** — constitutes the assembly, harmonize together, make a symphony and it is the coming together that makes the Church.

★ **Into My Name** — the only true place and person of worship; not into denominational names. Tabernacle and Temple were built for His Name to dwell. Now it is the Church.

★ **There I AM in the midst of them** — Gathering in or into his Name is the guarantee of His Presence in the midst. The risen Lord present in the midst as Head of the Church. Exodus 3:14, 15; Deuteronomy 16:5, 6; I Kings 8:15-21.

★ **Binding and Loosing Ministry** — As in Matthew 16:18, 19 in relation to the Gates of Hades, so here the same ministry in regards to Church discipline.

It is this that constitutes a Local Church. Where believers gather together in true and spiritual harmony, of one accord, in one place, unto His Name then the Lord is in the midst of them. Whether in a home, or building or any geographical place, then if it is UNTO HIM in gathering, He is there.

As the Church in Jerusalem began to fulfill the great commission, then the Church spread into many different localities. We see the development and establishment of numerous local Churches, yet each counting themselves a part of the whole. Any member of the Church was a member of the Church both locally and universally. As in the Roman concept, any Roman citizen, wherever meetings were held, was a part of the great concept of Rome. There was no meaning apart from Rome. They were part of a great unity. Any citizen coming into town was automatically and without introduction a member of the group. Though separated from Rome geographically, he was part of it in spirit. So with the Church. The believers were connected in spirit, not with earthly cities, but with THE HEAVENLY CITY, Jerusalem, of which the earthly Jerusalem was the symbol.

We note now the development of the Local Churches in Acts and the Epistles.

1. **The Church in The City**

   The following shows the concept of the Church in a city. ONE Church in ONE City, yet within this city were many congregations, part of the whole. There were no buildings large enough to house the many believers, generally speaking, so they met in homes, etc., yet were the Church in that city.

   a. **The Church at Jerusalem** (Acts 8:1; 11:22).

      Acts 1. The Lord, Head of the Church, here gives the final teachings concerning the Kingdom, after 3½ years ministry with the Twelve Apostles.

      Acts 2. Birthday of the Jerusalem Church by the outpouring of the Spirit. About 3000 souls added to the Church, added to the 120 initial company. The Lord added daily to the Church at Jerusalem.

      Acts 3-4. The healing of the lame man. Unity. Signs and wonders done. Grace.

      Acts 5. Apostolic discipline for sin against the Holy Spirit. Fear fell.

Acts 6. The choosing of the first Deacons at Jerusalem.

Acts 7. Stephen, the first Deacon-martyr in Jerusalem.

Acts 8. Philip, the first Deacon-Evangelist ministers at Samaria, from Jerusalem because of persecution.

Acts 10-11. The Lord sends Peter from Jerusalem to the Gentiles, who experience the same outpouring as did the Jews at Pentecost. Caesarea.

Acts 12. James, the first Apostle-martyr. Peter is delivered by a miracle.

Acts 15. The great Jerusalem Council over the matter of the Gentile and the Law Covenant and New Covenant. Legalism battle.

Acts 21:15-40; Acts 22-23. Paul taken prisoner at Jerusalem here, testifying very strongly and before the religious leaders of the nation. From here he is taken to Rome.

The history of the Jerusalem Church shows its decline from that early glory into legalism, sectarianism and bigotry because of the legalistic Judaizers mixing Law and Grace. These were Paul's greatest problems. Centralization dangers are seen also.

However, the Jerusalem Church laid the foundation. There were the fivefold ministries, elders and deacons, local government, healing, supernatural manifestations of the Spirit, the apostles doctrine, repentance, faith, water baptism, Holy Spirit baptism, fasting and prayer, laying on of hands, visions, trances, miracle transportation, angelic visitation, spiritual gifts, Divine discipline, the redemptive truths of Messiah Jesus. etc.

Any other Church born out of Jerusalem must need to continue stedfastly in the apostles doctrine, the faith that was once delivered to the saints (Jude 3).

b.   **The Churches of Judea, Galilee and Samaria** (Acts 9:31)

As the Gospel spread, so Local Churches arose in these cities also.

Acts 1:8; 2:9, 14; 5:16; 8:1; Galatians 1:22. Many converts were gathered in the cities of Judah, where Christ and His apostles had ministered previously.

Acts 8:40. Azotus of Judea.

Acts 9:31. Churches in Judea and Galilee.

Acts 9:32-34. Lydda, Saron, Joppa cities had believers also.

Acts 10:36, 37. Churches in Judea and Galilee.

Acts 11:1, 29. Brethren from Judean Churches trouble the Gentiles.

Acts 15:1; 21:10. Agabus was a prophet from Judea.

Thus under Peter's ministry Churches are established in Judea, with signs and wonders and apostolic doctrine. Jerusalem reproducing herself.

c.   **The Church in Samaria**

Acts 1:8; 8:1-25; 9:31; 15:3. Philip the Evangelist, from the Church at Jerusalem preached Christ in the city of Samaria. Signs, wonders, exorcism, salvation, water baptism took place under his ministry. This was the harvest time spoken of in John 4:35-38. The city was stirred. Then Peter and John, apostles from Jerusalem, minister the Holy Spirit to the Samaritans.

d.   **The Church at Caesarea**

Acts 10-11; 21:7-16. Planted by Peter an apostle, under a sovereign outpouring of the Holy Spirit on the Gentiles.

Acts 23:33-35; 24; 25; 26; Acts 18:22. Paul testified and ministered here also.

e.   **The Church at Antioch**

Acts 11:19-21. The word was planted here by unknown and unnamed disciples under the persecution of the Church at Jerusalem. The believers were scattered and so was the Seed of the Word. Acts 8:1; 11:19.

Acts 6:5. One of the deacons was a proselyte of Antioch.

Acts 11:22-26. Barnabas sent forth from the Church at Jerusalem to Antioch. Seeks for Saul and brings him to minister at Antioch. The Disciples were first called Christians at Antioch.

Acts 11:27-30. Prophets from the Church at Jerusalem foretell at Antioch the coming famine, and prepared for it.

Acts 13:1-3. There were prophets and teachers at Antioch. This Church became the great missionary Church to the Gentiles. Many Churches established out of here by Paul's ministry, as the missionary to the Gentiles.

Acts 15:1-4, 22-35. The Church at Antioch was troubled by Jerusalem Judaizers and the law-grace teaching and legalism. The Conference settled this problem by the Word of God. Acts 15:35.

Acts 16-20 shows a number of Churches established by Paul.

Acts 14:23. Elders were appointed in every local Church.

Galatians 2:11; II Timothy 3:11. Paul contended with Peter at Antioch over his compromise with the legalizers.

Antioch not founded by apostles, but an unnamed group, but then established under apostolic ministry. Gentile Churches needed teaching as they did not always have the Scriptures as did the Jews. Jewish believers needed interpretation and spiritual application of Scripture truths they already knew. To the Gentiles all was new material and lifestyle. Thus from Antioch we have three great missionary journeys of Paul in establishing Gentile Churches.

From Jerusalem to Antioch, Peter to Paul, Jews to Gentiles is the order in Acts. Acts 1-12 is Peter's ministry while Acts 13-28 is Paul's ministry. Both are responsible for the founding of local Churches; Peter from Jerusalem, Paul from Antioch.

f.   **The Churches of the Gentiles** (Romans 16:4).

There were many cities where Paul founded local Churches amongst the Gentiles.

We list a number of the cities here. The Church in a City is the order.

★   The Church at Babylon (I Peter 5:13).

★   The Churches in the cities of Asia (Revelation 1-2-3).
       Christ wrote, through John, to each of 7 of the local Churches in 7 cities.
       Church of Ephesus (Revelation 1:11; 2:1-7).
       Church of Smyrna (Revelation 2:8-11).
       Church of Pergamos (Revelation 2:12-17).
       Church of Thyatira (Revelation 2:18-29).
       Church of Sardis (Revelation 3:1-6).
       Church of Philadelphia (Revelation 3:7-13).
       Church of Laodicea (Revelation 3:14-22).
       Thus each letter sent to each local Church — NOT 'headquarters' anywhere!

★   The Church at Cenchrea (Romans 16:1).

★   The Church at Corinth (I Corinthians 1:2; II Corinthians 2:1).

★   The Church of Thessalonica (I Thessalonians 1:1; II Thessalonians 1:1).

★   We list other cities where believers were gathered together. Any believers who met together constituted a local Church. They were the called out and assembled ones in that city. They were THE CHURCH in THE CITY!

Many other cities are mentioned and even though the word "Church" is not specifically mentioned, yet our definition of the Church shows they were such.

★   Damascus (Acts 9:10, 19). Saul converted here and under Ananias, receives healing, water baptism and Holy Spirit, and a prophetic word. Saul began ministry here also (Acts 22:1-11; 26:12-20; Galatians 1:17; II Corinthians 11:32, 33).

It was a memorable place of testimony for Saul.

★   Cyprus — Salamis and Paphos (Acts 13:1-6).

★   Perga in Pamphilia (Acts 13:13; 14:25).

★   Antioch in Pisidia (Acts 13:14, 15, 24).

★   Iconium (Acts 13:51; 14:1-5; 16:2).

★   Lystra (Acts 14:6-8).

★   Derbe (Acts 14:6, 20, 21; 15:36; 16:1-7).

★   Troas (Acts 16:6-10; 20:5-12).

★   Philippi of Macedonia (Acts 16:9-40; Philippians 1:1).

★   Thessalonica (Acts 17:1; I Thessalonians 1:1; II Thessalonians 1:1).

★   Berea (Acts 18:10-14).

★   Athens (Acts 18:16-34).

★   Corinth (Acts 18:1-18; I Corinthians 1:1, 2; II Corinthians 1:1, 18, 19).

★   Ephesus (Acts 19-20; Ephesians 1:1; Acts 20:17; Revelation 2:1).

★   Miletus (Acts 20:15-36).

★   Tyre (Acts 21:1-6).

★   Sidon (Acts 27:1-6).

★   Melita (Acts 28:1-10).

★   Syracuse (Acts 28:11, 12).

★   Rhegium (Acts 28:13).

★   Rome (Acts 28:14, 28-31; Romans 1:7).

Acts 2:10; 18:2; 23:1; Romans 1:7, 15. Strangers from Rome at Day of Pentecost, undoubtedly founded the Church there. Paul's Epistle to them shows his desire to see them and impart to them.

★   Church at Colossae (Colossians 1:2).

Thus we have about 38 places and names and in these cities were groups of believers, large or small, and these constituted the Church in the city.

2. **The Churches in the Provinces**

We consider now references to the Churches in the Provinces. These were local Churches in the cities in Provinces.

★   The Churches throughout Judea, Galilee and Samaria (Acts 9:31).

★   The Churches in Syria and Cilicia (Acts 15:41).

★   The Churches of Asia (I Corinthians 16:19; Revelation 1-2-3).

★   The Churches of Galatia (Galatians 1:2, 11; I Corinthians 16:1).

★ The Churches of Judea (I Thessalonians 2:14).

★ The Churches of the Gentiles (Romans 16:4).

★ The Churches of Macedonia (II Corinthians 8:1).

The word "Church" or "Churches" as above refer to local gatherings of believers in local cities, different localities.

It is not "The Church" in Asia, or Macedonia, or Syria, etc., but "Churches".

3. **The Church in the House**

The Church in the house is mentioned several times. Not having buildings in those days, many Churches would gather in homes and that constituted "The Church in the home", or the house-church.

★ Romans 16:5. At Rome.

★ I Corinthians 16:19. To Corinth. Church, in order under Christ (Matthew 18:20).

★ Colossians 4:15. At Colossae.

★ Philemon 2. At Colossae.

Every Home should be a miniature Church, in order under Christ.

Thus we have two definable areas of a local Church, which are (1) A CITY, and (2) A HOUSE.

Church in a city — about 38 times.

Church in a House — 4 times.

Church in a Province — about 36 times in all.

Church universal — about 20 times.

Church local, not exactly defined — about 16 times.

Church in a city — not once.

Church in a province — not once.

Church in the Wilderness — once.

Assembly (of the city of Ephesus) — 3 times.

The local Church meets as members, joints and bands, working together in harmony. Ephesians 4:3; Colossians 3:14; I Corinthians 1:9; I John 1:3, 4; Acts 2:1; 13:1-6.

The separation of Churches was only on the basis of geographical location, and nothing else. They were one spiritually though separated geographically. I Corinthians 7:17. "All the Churches".

C. The Church and The Churches

It is important to note what the Apostles, the founders of the Church, did NOT do with these Churches.

1. They did NOT create a Denominational Church of all local Churches.

2. They did NOT use Jerusalem or Rome as "the Mother Church".
Though Jerusalem reproduced itself, there was no centralization nor was Jerusalem the "headquarters" for all the Churches. CHRIST was Headquarters!

3. They did NOT have Country Churches. i.e., The Church of ENGLAND in Japan, etc.

4. They did NOT have Provincial Churches. There were Churches in the Provinces but never the CHURCH in Galatia, Macedonia, etc.

5. They did NOT have a National Church. The JEWISH Church in Corinth, etc.

6. They did NOT have a District Church and bring all Churches under a District.

ALL CHURCHES were locally governed. They were autonomous, and reproduced themselves accordingly. They were not welded into a great organization, nor was the unity an organizational unity, but unity of the spirit, by the Spirit.

However, there was not extreme independence in these local Churches either.

1. They DID have a spiritual unity in Christ.
2. They DID recognize each other's sovereignty under Christ's headship.
3. They DID share with each other, and minister to each other as possible.
4. They DID receive ministries from each other.
5. They DID recognize that the revelation of Christ to one could be profitable for all Churches (Revelation 1-2-3). What He saith to the Churches, although spoken to one local Church in particular.
    I Thessalonians 2:14; I Corinthians 4:17; 7:17; 16:1.

Thomas M. Lindsay, in *"The Church and the ministry in the EARLY Centuries"* (p.4,5), summarizes his thoughts on the Church:

"Thus TO THE JEW the Ecclesia had been the Assembly of the Congregation of Israel summoned to meet at the Door of the Tabernacle of Jehovah by the blowing of the silver trumpets.

TO THE GREEK the Ecclesia was the sovereign assembly of the Greek free City-State, as summoned by the Herald blowing his horn through the city street.

TO THE CHRISTIANS the Church was to be the congregation of the redeemed, and therefore the free, summoned by the Heralds of Christ to continually appear in the presence of the Lord, who is always in the midst of them.

The Old Testament Ecclesia had been the Congregation of Jehovah (Psalms 74:2). It was in the future to become the Congregation of Jesus the Christ (Galatians 6:16). It had been the self-governing Greek republic ruled by elected office-bearers, but hereafter communities of Christians were to be the Ecclesia, self-governing societies where the individual rights and responsibilities of the members would blend harmoniously with the common good of all."

The term ECCLESIA has its home in Pauline literature and used about 115 times in the New Testament, 86 of these times by Paul in his Epistles and in the Acts of the Apostles.

In the majority of cases the word "Church" denotes a local Christian community, varying in extent from all the Christian Congregation within a Province of the Empire to a small assembly of Christians meetings together in a house of one of the believers.

The following classification of this word "Church" is based on that of Dr. Hort:

a. **The word 'Ecclesia' in the singular and with the article is used to denote:**
    1) the original Church of Jerusalem and Judea when there was no other (Acts 5:11; 8:1-3; Galatians 1:13; I Corinthians 15:9; Philippians 3:6).
    2) The sum total of the Churches in Judea, Galilee and Samaria (Acts 9:31). Note — Word here in many translations is in the singular.
    3) The Local Church in a particular named city. (Refer to list of Churches in cities).
    4) The ASSEMBLY of a Local Church (Acts 15:22; I Corinthians 14:23).
    5) The House Church (I Corinthians 16:5, 19; Colossians 4:15; Philemon 2).

b. **The word 'Ecclesia' in the singular and without the article is used to denote:**
    1) Every Local Church within a definite district (Acts 14:23).
    2) Any or every Local Church (I Corinthians 14:4; 4:17; Philippians 4:15; and probably I Timothy 3:5, 15).
    3) The ASSEMBLY of the Local Church (I Corinthians 14:19, 35; 11:18; 3 John 6).

c. **The word 'Ecclesia' is used to denote:**

1) the sum total of Local Churches in definite districts, the name being given according to locality. Refer to Churches in the Provinces (I Thessalonians 2:14; Galatians 1:22; I Corinthians 16:1; Acts 15:41; 16:6; II Corinthians 8:1, 19; I Corinthians 16:19; Revelation 1:4, 11, 20; 2:7, 11, 17, 29; 3:13, 22; 22:16).

2) An indefinite number of Local Churches (II Corinthians 11:8, 28; 8:23, 24; Romans 16:4, 16).

3) The sum total of all the Local Churches (II Thessalonians 1:4; I Corinthians 7:17; 11:16; 14:33; II Corinthians 12:13).

4) The ASSEMBLIES of all the Local Churches (I Corinthians 14:34).

d. **The word 'Ecclesia' is used in the singular to denote:**

1) The one Universal Church as represented in the individual Local Church (I Corinthians 10:31; 11:22 [and probably 12:28]; Acts 20:28 and [perhaps] I Timothy 3:5,15).

2) The one Universal Church absolutely (Colossians 1:18, 24; Ephesians 1:22; 3:10, 21; 5:23, 25, 27, 29, 32).

This shows us how the word "Church" can be used to denote communities of various sizes, from the sum total of all Christian communities everywhere down to the very small gathering which met in the house of Philemon.

The Church can be present in many places at the same time and in such a way that, as Ignatius says, "Where Jesus Christ is, there is the WHOLE Church." Paul counted the congregation at Corinth as the Body of Christ, not A BODY, but THE Body of Christ. Christ is not divided. The Body is one, locally, universally. The Local Church may do what the universal Church may do in miniature form, as to its worship, communion and ministry of the Word, according to the measure of the gifts of Christ in its midst in the members.

THE CHURCH UNIVERSAL meeting in every place is a unity (I Corinthians 10:32).

THE CHURCH LOCAL meeting in many places is a plurality (I Thessalonians 2:14).

IN SUMMARY:

The Church Local as a replica and representative of the Church Universal may be defined as:

★ A group of believers in a given locality (Matthew 18:20).

★ Gathered to the person of Jesus Christ for worship (John 4:24).

★ Marked out by a confession of faith (Romans 10:9, 10).

★ Living a disciplined life (Matthew 18:15-20).

★ Under the oversight ministries Christ has set in the Church (Ephesians 4:9-16; I Timothy 3; Titus 1).

★ Obeying the teaching of Christ according to the Great Commission (Matthew 28:19, 20).

★ Established in the first principles of the doctrine of Christ (Hebrews 6:1, 2), which is the apostles doctrine (Acts 2:42).

★ Keeping the memorial of Christ's death and resurrection (I Corinthians 11:23-34).

★ Locally governed under Christ's headship, yet recognizing their unity in spirit with all other believers in their locality as well as world-wide (Revelation 1:11; Philippians 1:1; Matthew 16:18, 19).

★ Excercising the authority of Christ by use of the keys of the kingdom which are given to the Church (Matthew 16:18, 19).

★   Not forsaking the gathering of themselves together to worship the Father, to glorify Christ, to edify one another, to extend the kingdom of God in the earth (Matthew 24:14; John 4:20-24; I Corinthians 11-12-13-14).

CHAPTER 12

MINISTRIES OF PETER AND PAUL

In relation to the Church in the Book of Acts it is also important to recognize the distinctive place and part that the apostle Peter and the apostle Paul played. It should be seen that these major apostles, along with other apostles and believers were in a great transitional period of time.

They were coming out from the Old Covenant economy under Moses into the New Covenant economy under Jesus.

Much revelation was coming to them and in the transitional period there were a lot of adjustments to be made. This especially involved the Jew and the Gentile coming together in one Body, the New Covenant Church. This will be developed more fully in Chapter 14.

Sufficient for this Chapter is to see the distinctive roles of Peter and Paul in the progressive revelation and development of the Church.

A. The Apostle Peter

After Peter's revelation and confession of Christ as the Son of the living God, Jesus foretold the fact that He would build His Church. Along with this prophecy Christ specifically said to Peter: ''I will give to thee the keys of the kingdom of heaven'' (Matthew 16:19).

What were these ''keys''? Did Peter use these keys? When? Where?

The Book of Acts reveals the fulfilment of this word of Christ to Peter. In the Acts we see Peter distinctly using these keys in relation to two ethnic divisions of the human race.

1. To the Jew

On the Day of Pentecost, with the initial outpouring of the Spirit on the 120 in the upper room, it is Peter, standing with the eleven, who gave the initial call to the Jews, gathered out of many nations, to enter the Kingdom of God (Acts 2:1-36). The response was tremendous as 3000 Jews accepted Jesus as the Messiah, repented, believed and were baptized.

The Scripture says they continued stedfastly in the apostles doctrine, fellowship, breaking of bread and prayers (Acts 2:37-47). The Lord added to the Church daily those that were being saved.

Shortly, another 5000 believed, and then multitudes were added to the Lord (Acts 4:4; 5:12-17; 6:7).

Acts 1-7 gives the account of the work of the Holy Spirit in the formation of the early Church, Peter being the major channel being used at this time.

2. To the Gentile

In due time, the Lord moved upon Peter to take the Gospel to the Gentiles. It is the apostle Peter again, who uses the keys of the Kingdom to let the Gentiles in (Acts 10-11). While Peter ministered the Word, there is the next sovereign outpouring of the Holy Spirit on the Gentiles, as on the Jews at the beginning. It was Peter originally who ''opened the door of faith'' unto the Gentiles as well as to the Jews (Acts 14:27).

Thus Peter used the keys Christ had given him to open the door to both ethnic divisions. Relative to Peter's apostolic ministry, Jew and Gentile experience the sovereign outpourings of the Holy Spirit.

Acts 1-12 especially set Peter out of the dominant apostle, the apostle of the circumcision.

B. **The Apostle Paul**

It is in Acts 9 that we have the account of the miraculous conversion of Saul, who was to become the apostle Paul.

From Acts 13-28 the scene shifts from Jerusalem to Antioch, from the emphasis on the work of the Holy Spirit among the Jews to the emphasis on the work of the Holy Spirit among the Gentiles. It also shifts from the ministry of Peter the apostle to Paul the apostle.

The roles of these two men become more distinctive. They come into sharper focus. Peter is the apostle that Christ, the risen and ascended Head of the Church, uses to open the door of faith initially to both Jew and Gentile. But it is the converted Jew — Paul the apostle that the same Christ uses to step into that door opened to the Gentiles (Acts 14:27).

Even though Paul always took the Gospel "to the Jew first" (Romans 1:16) in the cities that had Synagogues, yet he is expressly sent as the apostle to the Gentiles (Acts 9:15, 16).

Jewish unbelief and hardness of heart was settling on the nation as a whole, but the Gentiles responded to the saving Gospel. The prophetic word of the prophets that Christ would also be "a light unto the Gentiles" was being fulfilled (Acts 13:46-49; 14:2, 3, 26, 27; 22:21; 26:13-20; 28:23-28).

The great conflict is that found in Acts 15 where the council of apostles and elders meet together to discuss the matter of Jewish and Gentile salvation. The Judaizing teachers tried to make the believing Gentiles as Jews, having Jesus and Moses in each hand. They were confusing the Old and the New Covenant economies of Law and Grace.

After much dissension and disputation, Peter rose and told how God had poured out His Spirit on both Jew and Gentile apart from works and ceremonies of the Law (Acts 15:6-11).

Barnabas and Paul told of God's grace and power among the Gentiles apart from the Law economy (Acts 15:12).

Finally, James concluded with a word of wisdom from the prophet Amos 9:11. The Lord had foretold the fact of the Gentiles coming in, apart from the Law, to the Tabernacle of David — NOT the Tabernacle of Moses (Acts 15:13-18).

The end result was a recognition and acceptance of the distinctive and unique ministries of Peter and Paul. Peter was the apostle to the Jews, the Circumcision, and Paul was the apostle to the Gentiles, the Uncircumcision. Both were received with the right hands of fellowship, as all recognized the distinctive grace given to each in their area of ministry (Galatians 1-2). The Jews did not have to live as the Gentiles, nor the Gentiles as Jews as far as the ceremonial laws was concerned. All were "in Christ" and baptized by the same Spirit into the same body (I Corinthians 12:13). Believing Jews and Gentiles were all in the same good olive tree (Romans 9-10-11). But this matter is taken up in Chapter 14 — The Church in the Epistles.

CHAPTER 13

CHURCH MEMBERSHIP IN THE NEW TESTAMENT

There were two sides to Church membership; the Divine side emphasized in Matthew and the human side as set out in the Book of Acts. However, neither should be separated, for each complement the other, and one side should not be used against the other side.

Many times Church membership is looked upon negatively because of misunderstanding or various other reasons which will be considered in due time. We consider what the Scriptures have to say on this area.

A. The Divine Side — Sovereignty

What happened in the experience of Peter relative to Christ's prophecy certainly can be received in embryonic form of that which must happen in every member of the true Church.

1. **In the Gospels**

    In Matthew 16:13-19 we may see the following outline.

    a. **Two Persons**

        Christ Jesus, the Son of the Living God.

        Peter — typical of every believer who becomes a member of the true Church. "Simon" means "Hearing", and "Son of Jona" means "Son of a Dove". It points to the matter of spiritual hearing that comes through hearing the Holy Spirit who is likened to a Dove.

        "Peter" means "A Stone". He is a sample of the lively stones of I Peter 2:5.

        Greek Petros = Movable Rock, that is, Peter.

        Greek Petra = Massive bed-rock. That is Christ Himself. City of Petra was a Rock City. Christians, like Peter, are lively stones and all are to be built together on THE ROCK Christ Himself, as His house.

        Christ is THE ROCK/STONE. Peter is a Stone. Believers are lively stones. John 1:41, 42. Cephas = A Stone. I Peter 2:5-9.

    b. **Two Questions**

        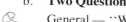

        General — "Whom do men say that I the Son of Man am?"

        Personal — "Whom do ye say that I am?"

    c. **Two Answers**

        General — "Some say John the Baptist, Elijah, Jeremiah, or one of the Prophets."

        Personal — "Thou art the Christ, the Son of the living God."

    d. **Two Sources of Revelation**

        Flesh and blood. Carnal, human reason. Sense knowledge (Galatians 1:16; Ephesians 6:12; I Corinthians 15:50).

        The Father God. Divine revelation. Revelation knowledge (Matthew 16:17; Galatians 1:15, 16).

    e. **Two-fold Revelation**

        The Father God revealed the Son of God to Peter by inner revelation. Flesh and blood cannot reveal who the Christ of God is. Peter becomes typical of the multitude who would form His Church after receiving the same inner revelation. Each member of Christ's Church must have this inner personal revelation. No man, flesh and blood, can impart it (Galatians 1:15, 16; Matthew 11:25-27; 16:17).

The Son reveals the Church (Matthew 16:18), that he would build His Ekklesia. So the Lord adds to the Church those that receive the revelation of who He is from the Father God.

1) **Thou art the Christ**

That is, the Anointed, the Messiah. Foretold by the Prophets (Daniel 9:24-27; John 1:41; 4:25-29; 7:41-42; 9:22; 7:27). Many Jews accepted Jesus as the Messiah, the Christ, but were excommunicated if they voiced or confessed Him as such (John 10:24). The Jews generally believed that Messiah would be sent of God, a Prophet like unto Moses or Elijah, and that He would be David's Son, The Son of Man. Jesus used the Scriptures pertaining to the Messiah and applied them to Himself as the fulfilment of these Scriptures. Many Jews believed He was the Messiah by His words, deeds and miracles. But it is over the next part of the revelation that the greatest division came.

2) **The Son of the Living God**

The Son of God spoke of Deity. Many Jews accepted Him as the Christ, but not the Son of God. Through misinterpreting the Messianic Scriptures, Jewry could not see that Messiah would also be the Son of God. The union of both Divine and Human in one Messiah was confused. The great tenet of faith for centuries was that "The Lord our God is ONE Lord" (Deuteronomy 6:4, 5).

Jewry rejected the triunity of God. They refused to accept that God had a Son. It was this confession of Sonship that caused Jesus to be crucified. Not for his claim as Messiah but for His claim as the Son of God, making Himself equal with God (John 19:7; 10:22-39; 5:18; Matthew 26:63-68; 27:40-43).

Their own Old Testament Scriptures taught the Sonship of the Messiah, and that this Son would be born of a virgin, and would be God incarnate as well the Messiah, David's greater Son (Proverbs 30:1-4; Psalms 2; Isaiah 9:6-9; 7:14; Genesis 3:15). All these references show that Messiah would be the God-Man. Hence it was direct revelation that Peter and others confessed Jesus as THE SON OF GOD! Read John 1:41, 49; 1:24-39; 9:22-28; Matthew 16:16, 17). This was revealed to the heart of Peter by the Father God.

To worship Jesus as God incarnate meant idolatry and blasphemy and was punishable by death, if this fact were not so. To reject Jesus, as God's Son, was to reject God Himself.

As it came to Peter by revelation, so must it come to all who constitute the members of His Church (Matthew 11:25-27). This confession involved, by implication, His virgin birth as well as His Deity — God manifest in the flesh. Jesus is the God-Man. Deity and Humanity. Son of God and Son of Man (Luke 1:32-35; 3:22; Matthew 17:5). He is God's Son, not the son of Joseph.

f. **Two-fold Confession**

There was also a two-fold confession; by Peter "Thou art the Christ"; by Jesus to Peter — "Thou art Peter". Peter confessed Christ. Jesus confessed Peter (II Timothy 1:19; Matthew 10:32; John 6:44, 45; Matthew 11:25-27; John 10:3; Luke 10:18; John 1:41, 42). If we confess Him before men, He will confess us before His Father. Peter — a rock fragment.

However, note that, while Jesus blessed Peter in verses 16, 17 for his revelation and confession he received of God, He rebuked him in verses 21-23 for his thought received and expressed from Satan.

The Church is not built upon Peter who confessed but upon the ONE Peter confessed. Peter is a fallible man. Christ is the infallible Son of God. Truth is always greater that the one who utters it (Ephesians 2:20-22; I Corinthians 3:9-15).

2. **In the Acts**

The Book of Acts confirms that which was in the Gospel as well as adds other thoughts as far as the Divine side of Church membership is concerned. They that believed Christ was the Son of the Living God were "added to the Church" and "*added to the Lord*" (Acts 5:14; 8:37; 11:24; 15:9-11).

One cannot join Christ's Church, like joining a club. One must be joined to the Lord by the Spirit before being added to the Church (Acts 5:13, 14). This is of first and primary importance. None can be added to the Church unless first added to the Lord. Christ is the Head of the Body and one must be added to Him as a member of that Body in order to be a member of the Church universal. Membership is a spiritual first of all. There must be that spiritual revelation and relationship and union with Christ as the sure foundation of Church membership.

B. **The Human Side-Responsibility**

In the above we have seen the sovereign side of Church membership, the Divine and inner revelation to the heart of who Christ is and the confession thereof unto salvation (Matthew 16:13-16; Romans 10:9-17).

In the Book of Acts we see further factors from both Divine and human sides concerning membership in His Church. Believers were first "*added to the Lord*" and then "*added to the Church*" (Acts 2:41-47).

On the Day of Pentecost Peter declared the Word concerning Christ crucified, buried, resurrected, ascended and glorified at the Father's right hand. He declared the name of the Godhead bodily for baptism and laid the foundation message for Church membership. It is the same apostle who received that revelation in Matthew. We note the response to the Gospel before they were "added to the Church".

1. **Repentance from Sin**

True repentance actually involves two factors. On the negative side it is repentance from sin, and on the positive side, faith towards God.

It is of absolute and foundational importance before one can be in His Church.

a. Repentance was the message of the Prophets. Turn to the Lord, they cried continually to Israel (Ezekiel 3, 18, 33).

b. Repentance is the first word of the Gospel of Christ.
   - ★ John the Baptist's first word (Matthew 3:2).
   - ★ Christ's first word (Matthew 4:17).
   - ★ The disciples taught repentance (Mark 6:12).
   - ★ Repentance to be preached to all (Luke 24:47).
   - ★ Peter declared this at Pentecost (Acts 2:38).
   - ★ Paul preached the foundation of repentance (Acts 26:20).

c. God commands all men everywhere to repent (Acts 17:30).

d. It is God's desire for all to repent (II Peter 3:9).

e. Christ came to call men to repentance (Luke 5:32).

f. Repentance is necessary for salvation from damnation (Luke 13:3, 5).

g. The Churches are called to repent and maintain this state before the Lord (Revelation 1-2-3).

   It is important to understand what repentance is not, for there are many false concepts of repentance today.

   1) It is not conviction of sin (Acts 24:24, 25; Genesis 6:3). Conviction precedes

repentance, but not all who are convicted repent.

2) It is not worldly sorrow (II Corinthians 7:10). Worldly sorrow is simply being sorry for getting caught but not for the crime committed.

3) It is not reformation. Reformation is 'turning over a new leaf' but not genuine repentance.

4) It is not being religious. The Pharisees in Christ's time were extremely religious but they were hypocrites. They did not know Christ (Matthew 5:20; 3:7, 8).

5) It is not 'only believe-ism' or mental faith. Mental faith is merely a mental acceptance and assent to a set of creeds or doctrines without any change in the life. It is a dead faith (James 2:19-20).

In the Old Testament times the word "repent" meant "to pant, to sigh, to groan, to lament, to grieve about one's doings". It is linked many times with the call "to turn" or "return". It involved a right about face, from running away from God to coming towards God.

In the New Testament the Greek word means "to change one's mind or purpose". There must be both the *internal* as well as the *external* change. If there is the former there will be the latter, although one can have the latter without the former. It also signifies a "change of heart".

Repentance is brought about the Holy Spirit (II Timothy 2:25; Acts 3:26; John 16:9-16; Acts 5:30, 31).

Repentance is also man's response to the conviction of the Spirit (Luke 15:18-20; Romans 2:4; Revelation 3:19).

The *mind, emotions and will* are all involved in repentance also. There must be a change of mind, genuine sorrow for sin, and an act of the will to turn from sin unto God.

True repentance also has its *fruits* (Luke 3:8). These manifest are:

★ Godly sorrow for sin (II Corinthians 7:9-11).

★ Abhorrence of self and humiliation of soul (Job 42:5, 6; Luke 10:13; 18:13).

★ Confession of sins and cry for mercy (I John 1:9; Psalms 32:1-5; 51:1-4; Luke 15:21; 18:13, 14; Hosea 14:1, 2).

★ Turning from and forsaking of sin (Matthew 12:41; Ezekiel 14:6; 18:30; Isaiah 55:7; Jonah 3:5-8).

★ Godly hatred of sin (Ezekiel 36:31-33).

★ Turning to the Lord in faith (Acts 26:20; I Thessalonians 1:9).

★ Restitution where possible (Leviticus 6:1-7; Luke 19:8).

There is joy in heaven over those who repent (Luke 15:7, 10). On the Day of Pentecost the call was to REPENT before any one was added to the Church.

2. Faith Towards God

Genuine repentance and faith are inseparable; they are inter-dependent on each other. It is impossible to have genuine faith without genuine repentance however. To turn *from* something is to turn *to* something. To turn from sin is to turn towards God. Note — I Thessalonians 1:9; Acts 26:18-20; Acts 20:21.

Faith is the second word of the Gospel (Mark 1:15).

The word "faith" means "trust, firm persuasion, assurance, firm conviction, confidence in another or another's word."

"Faith toward God is simply to trust God, to have confidence in Him and His Word. To believe what God has said, that his Word is true and what He has promised, He will perform.''

Faith is necessary for salvation (Mark 16:16; Ephesians 2:8).

Without faith we cannot please God (Hebrews 11:6).

Whatsoever is not of faith is sin (Romans 14:23).

Faith comes by hearing the Word of God (Romans 10:17).

Christ is the author and finisher of our faith (Hebrews 12:2).

Faith is implanted in the heart upon true repentance as a SEED which has all the potential of growing into full and perfect faith (Romans 12:3). To do so it must be nurtured by the Word of God and quickened by the Holy Spirit (Luke 17:5, 6).

Implicit in Peter's call to repentance is faith. True faith is obedience (James 2:14-26). Faith without obedience is dead.

3. **Water Baptism**

Matthew 28:18-20; Mark 16:15-20; Romans 6:1-3; Acts 2:37-41.

Water baptism was involved in the initial steps of being ''added to the Church'' in the Book of Acts (Acts 2:47). 41

The Jews were familiar with ''the doctrine of baptisms'' or ''divers washings'' (Hebrews 6:1, 2).

a. Aaron and his sons were wholly bathed in water when consecrated to the Priesthood ministry (Exodus 29:4; Leviticus 8:6).

They washed at the laver before ministry in the Sanctuary (Exodus 30:17-21).

b. The leper cleansing involved bathing in water to be admitted back into the camp of the saints (Leviticus 14:8, 9).

c. Israel experienced the waters of purification from the ashes of the red heifer (Numbers 19).

d. Israel as a nation had experienced baptism in the Red Sea unto Moses the Mediator of the Old Covenant (I Corinthians 10:1-3).

e. Gentile proselytes were baptized as converts into the Jewish faith.

The word ''baptism'' means ''to dip, to overwhelm, to plunge, to submerge''. It is to dip something beneath the surface of water or some other fluid.

John the Baptist came preaching repentance and water baptism (Mark 1:4; Luke 3:3; Matthew 3:1-2). Christ's disciples also baptized others (John 4:1-2).

John's baptism was an acknowledgement of their sins and desire to be cleansed before God and a preparation in faith of the heart to receive the coming Messiah.

After Christ's death, burial and resurrection He ordained Christian baptism. Matthew 28:19, 20; Mark 16:16. Christ told His disciples to baptize disciples. In baptism believers are identified with the death, burial and resurrection of the Lord Jesus Christ (Romans 6:1-4).

In baptism circumcision of the heart takes place by an operation of the Spirit (Genesis 17; Colossians 2:12-14).

In baptism the believer has the triune Name of the triune God invoked upon him (Matthew 28:19-20; Acts 2:38; 8:16; 10:48; 19:5). The Name of the Lord Jesus Christ is the Name of the Fulness of the Godhead bodily. It is the family Name (Ephesians 3:13, 14).

Water baptism is an act of faith and obedience to the commands of Christ.

Peter's message therefore involved Repentance and Faith and Water Baptism.

4. **Baptism in the Holy Spirit**

    Acts 2:1-4; 2:37-40; I Corinthians 12:13; Acts 1:5, 8; John 3:31-33.

    Peter also said that they would receive the promise of the Holy Spirit coming upon them.

    In the Old Testament the Spirit was only available for the select few (Exodus 31:3; Judges 11:29; Numbers 24:2; 11:25; Isaiah 11:2; I Samuel 10:1-10; 16:14).

    However, the Prophets also spoke of the coming outpouring of the Holy Spirit on all flesh (Isaiah 44:3; 28:11-12; Joel 2:28-29).

    Jesus also spoke much of the coming Holy Spirit and His ministry (John 1:33; 7:38-39; 16:1-16; Acts 1:4, 5; 2:33; 19:2).

    In the Book of Acts the evidence of the reception of the Holy Spirit was speaking with other tongues (Acts 2:1-4; 8:14-17; 10:44-48; 19:1-6; 9:17, 18).

    The Godhead is thus involved in Church membership.

    ★   The Father reveals the Son (Matthew 11:25-27; 16:13-17).

    ★   The Son is confessed as the Christ, the Son of the Living God (Acts 8:37).

    ★   The Son imparts the Holy Spirit who sets in the Church, the Body of Christ (I Corinthians 12:3; Acts 2:41, 47).

        They did not just "join up" in the early Church. They were added to the Church, AFTER they responded to these steps laid out by Peter in the intial Pentecostal message.

        God's way has not changed! Man has changed God's ways and needs to return to the foundation laid at Pentecost by the apostle Peter.

C. The Church at Jerusalem

Both the Gospels and the Acts imply that there was some definite evidence of belonging to the Church. Believers were numbered and accounted for. Otherwise, how did they know who were "added" to them or not? In other words, there was a visible and practical expression of Church membership and identification. It was not enough to belong to "the Church invisible and mystical" but it was practically expressed by belonging to "the Church local and visible".

On the Day of Pentecost the first 3000 converts were "added to them" (i.e., The 120 disciples, Acts 2:41), and "added to the Church" (Acts 2:47). They became identified with the Church at Jerusalem, the Church in that city and locality.

Was there some record of membership in the early Church? The following Scriptures show that they knew who belonged or identified with them.

1. Jesus chose 12 apostles, named and numbered (Luke 9:1, 2).

2. Jesus later chose 70 others as His own (Luke 10:12).

3. Over 500 brethren saw Jesus in His ascension (I Corinthians 15:1-3).

4. Before Pentecost 120 disciples gathered in the Upper Room (Acts 1:15). The number of the names were about 120.

5. At and after Pentecost multitudes were brought to Christ and into the Church which He said He would build.

6. There were added to the Church 3000 souls (Acts 2:41, 47).

7. About 5000 believed also (Acts 4:4).

8. The number of the disciples multiplied greatly in Jerusalem (Acts 6:7).

9. At least 10,000 believers were numbered in these Scriptures. In AD70 history says over one million Christians fled from Jerusalem before its destruction and not one Christian was known to have lost his life.

One can have Church membership in any local Church or Denomination, but one must be added to the Lord FIRST, otherwise Church membership is not recognized by Him. However, a practical expression of membership is evidenced in being *added* to some New Testament local Church.

Acts 2:37, 38 lays down the standard and evidences for New Testament Church membership. These have never changed — in God's mind! These evidences were tangible and visible!

D. Old and New Testament Records

It may be asked: "Is it Scriptural to have some kind of Church Roll or Records? Yes! The Old and New Testament refer to books where the names of God's people were kept for records. It would be impossible to fully take care of God's sheep if no one knew where they went, or if they really belonged to some Local Church. Just belonging to the Church universal is abstract and vague.

1. **Old Testament**

    a. The Israelites had their names in the Books of the Genealogy of the Nation. They were numbered before the Lord (Numbers 1-2).

    b. The Levites were also numbered before the Lord before they could minister in the priestly offices (Numbers 3).

    c. Everyone numbered in Israel had to be redeemed with silver (Exodus 30:11-16; I Chronicles 21; II Samuel 24).

    d. The remnant from Babylon had to be registered in the book in order to be in the priesthood (Ezra 2:62, 63; Nehemiah 7).

2. **New Testament**

    a. The Church of the Firstborn have their names written in heaven (Hebrews 12:22-24). None can add these names or take them away but the Lord.

    b. The great shepherd calls His own sheep by name (John 10:3, 14).

    c. The redeemed of all ages have their names also written in the Book of Life (Philippians 4:3; Revelation 13:8, 17:8; 20:12-15; 21:27). "When the roll is called up yonder" all believers will be there.

    Thus God Himself keeps records! God keeps the names and numbers of the saints in His roll. If God Himself does this, then there should be no problem if human beings who are finite do likewise. God knows who is in His book or not (Revelation 3:5). He will not blot names out of His book who overcome. In God's book every member of our natural body was written (Psalms 139:13-17). How much more the members of the Body of Christ?

    NOTE: — Legal requirements stipulate that proper records of membership be kept in relation to Church funds, holding of property, taxes, etc. This cannot be just an unreal, unseen and invisible, mystical method of record keeping! We must render to Caesar what belongs to Caesar in these matters.

E. Membership Confirmation

Most historic Churches have some form of confirmation in which a person is admitted into full Church membership privileges and responsibilities. This varies from group to group. It should be recognized that certain ceremonies for confirmation are not to be found in the Bible. However, the Scriptures do show that there is a truth in confirmation.

1. **What Does the word "Confirm" mean?**

    a. Webster defines the word to mean "to make firm, or firmer, to strengthen; to establish; to encourage".

Also, "to make certain; to give new assurance of truth; to verify; to ratify; as to confirm an agreement, promise, covenant or title" (i.e. In the USA the Senate confirms or rejects the appointments brought before it by the President of the United States).

New Century Dictionary adds, "To make valid or binding by some formal or legal act".

The Bible definition gives the word a wide variety of meanings, as follows:

"To fill, accomplish or to strengthen, establish, fix, prepare, prevail, encourage; to ratify, make authoritative, to interpose (as arbiter), to ratify (as surety); to make firm, make secure, fast, stable".

b. **What Examples of Things Being Confirmed do we have in the Scriptures?**

1) **Covenants** were confirmed (Daniel 9:27; Galatians 3:15-17).

2) **Promises** were confirmed (Romans 15:8).

3) **Letters** were confirmed (Esther 9:29-32).

4) **Words** were confirmed (I Kings 1:14; Ezekiel 13:6; Daniel 9:12).

5) **Inheritances** were confirmed (Psalms 68:9).

6) **The Gospel** of Jesus Christ was confirmed with signs following (Hebrews 2:3; Isaiah 44:26; Philippians 1:17; Mark 16:20).

   We speak of people who are "confirmed alcoholics" or "confirmed atheists".

c. **Do we have Examples of People being Confirmed?**

Yes! The Scriptures show that God's people were confirmed, strengthened, established, encouraged and given assurance of the truth of the Gospel in the New Covenant.

1) Kings were confirmed in their office as King (I Chronicles 14:2).

2) Paul and Barnabas confirmed the souls of the disciples in the Churches they established (Acts 14:21-23).

3) Judas and Silas, as prophets of God, exhorted and confirmed the people of God (Acts 15:32).

4) The Corinthian Church was called on to confirm their love to the repentant excommunicated (II Corinthians 2:8).

5) The believer is to be confirmed unto the end (I Corinthians 1:6-8).

6) Feeble believers are to be confirmed (strengthened) (Isaiah 35:3 with Hebrews 12:12, 13).

7) The disciples in Galatia and Phrygia were strengthened (confirmed) by Paul's ministry (Acts 18:23).

d. **How may Local Church Membership be Confirmed?**

1) By the laying on of the hands of the oversight and prayer.

2) By extending the right hand of fellowship (Galatians 2:8, 9).

3) By a verbal commitment, or public affirmation, whereby the believer enters into covenant relationship and is willing to receive the privileges, and assume the responsibilities and accept the discipline of the Local Church of which he is a member.

   "An oath for confirmation . . ." (Hebrews 6:16, 17).

   "When thou vowest a vow, defer not to pay it . . ." (Ecclesiastes 5:4, 5).

   To commit onself is "to pledge; to entrust; to put in custody or charge; to bring together".

This confirms to the whole congregation that this person is recognized and responsible as a member and to be received as such. It confirms that both leadership and membership are committed to each other.

NOTE: — Confirmation may be experienced several times in a believer's life.

★ Confirmation after confession of faith at water baptism (I Corinthians 1:6-10).

★ Confirmation by being received into Church membership.

★ Confirmation by the laying on of hands and presbytery (I Timothy 1:18; 4:14; 5:22; II Timothy 1:6).

★ Confirmation at time of ordination (Acts 6:6; 13:1-4).

★ At other times as the Holy Spirit directs.

Confirmation, then, is a means of grace whereby members of the Local Church are strengthened and established in the faith of Jesus Christ and committed to the will of God (Read also II Corinthians 1:21; Colossians 2:7; Nehemiah 12:9). "The God of all grace . . . make you perfect, establish, strengthen, settle you." I Peter 5:10.

F. Why Do Many People reject Practical Church Membership?

Many believers reject any form of Church membership. Various reasons may be mentioned, some of which are as follows:

1. Fear of being hurt, having been hurt by other shepherds (Ezekiel 34; Jeremiah 23; John 10.)

2. Fear of legalism, and threats.

3. Do not believe it is Scriptural, as belong to the Church mystical, invisible, universal.

4. Do not have a submissive spirit.

5. Desire to be self-governing, self-directing, lawless, go it alone, independent, "Jesus and me, I need nobody else", attitude.

6. Do not want to support a Church financially with tithes or offerings.

7. Do not desire to come under correction, discipline or protection (Cf. I Corinthians 5).

8. Do not want to be committed to anything local or visible.

9. Do not want to be responsible and accountable to anyone.

G. What are some of the Blessings of Practical Church Membership?

1. Security in the family of God. Everyone needs a sense of security.

2. Fellowship — a sense of belonging, company of God's people.

3. Protection from wolves (Hebrews 13:7, 17; Acts 20:28-32).

4. Spiritual food and nourishment from the word of God.

5. Discipline and correction and adjustment where necessary (I Corinthians 5:13).

6. Ministry of life, healing and health by the members of the Body (James 5:14).

7. The Communion Table — Life of the risen Lord.

8. Love, care and concern in a practical way by the Oversight ministries (Ephesians 4:9-16).

9. Support of the ministries and the Church by tithes and offerings and the blessings of an open heavens (Malachi 3:8-11).

One cannot expect to receive all the *blessings* and *benefits* of the Lord's Church when one is not willing to be committed to the *responsibilities* of membership! Membership may be transferred to other Local Churches if a person moves geographically.

H. **Maintaining Healthy Church Membership**

There are four major and very embracing things by which a good, healthy, Church membership can be maintained. These are found in Acts 2:42.

1. **The Apostles Doctrine**

The Apostles Doctrine may be defined in the First Principles of the Doctrine of Christ in all its ramifications (Hebrews 6:1-2).

These Scriptures should be read as they all show the importance of believers being established in sound doctrine (Matthew 16:12; Colossians 2:22; Ephesians 4:4; Revelation 2:14, 15, 24; Hebrews 13:9; Mark 7:7; John 7:17; Deuteronomy 32:2; I Timothy 4:1; 4:6, 13, 16; Titus 1:9; 2:1, 7, 10).

2. **Fellowship**

Fellowship through continuance in the Apostolic Doctrine (Psalms 94:20; I John 1:3-7; Ephesians 3:9; I Corinthians 1:9; I Corinthians 1:9; Galatians 2:9; Philippians 1:5; 2:1; 3:10; II Corinthians 6:14; Ephesians 5:11; I Corinthians 10:20).

There is fellowship with the Father, the Son and the believers. There can be no true fellowship with doctrines of devils.

3. **Breaking of Bread**

The Lord's Supper, which is spiritual meat and drink, the communion of the body and blood of Jesus (I Corinthians 11:23-34; I Corinthians 12; 10:1-21; 5:1-10; John 6; Matthew 14:19; 15:36; 26:26-28; Acts 20:7; Luke 24:35).

Jesus can be known in the breaking of bread. The Table of Shewbread fulfilled.

4. **Prayers**

The fulfilment of the altar of incense in the Church. Prayers, intercessions is contact with the risen Head in heaven. He ever lives to make intercession for us. A prayerless believer is a powerless believer.

Revelation 5:8-10; Acts 1:14; 4:31; 13:3; Jude 20; Hebrews 7:27; Revelation 8:1-4.

CHAPTER 14

THE CHURCH IN THE EPISTLES

Having pursued the concept, birth and development of the Church in the Gospel, and the Acts, we come now to consider the revelation of the Church as in the Epistles, especially the Pauline Epistles.

As already noted, we have "first the blade" (The Church in the Gospel), "then the ear" (The Church in Acts), and then "the full corn in the ear" (The Church in the Epistles (Mark 4:28).

It is especially to Paul that the revelation of the Church as the "great mystery" is given, the mystery Body of Christ.

A. The Mystery Body of Christ

There are many mysteries in the Word of God, as previously listed, but the distinctive mystery, relative to the Church is "The Mystery Body of Christ". The word "Church"has been used but twice in the Gospels. The word "Church" or "Churches" is used many times in the Acts, where the Church is coming into manifestation and operation. However, when it comes to the Epistles, especially Paul's writings, we see the revelation of THE MYSTERY, even THE CHURCH as the BODY OF CHRIST!

The expression "The Body" is not used in the Gospel nor the Acts as it pertains to the Church. But it is a most frequent expression in the Pauline Epistles. The word "Mystery" has been defined as "That which can only be known to the initiated". Its distinct and unique revelation is given to Paul concerning Christ and His Church. We note this again in Ephesians 3:1-9.

1. Paul states that it was by revelation God made known to him "the mystery". Verse 3 (Ephesians 1:9; I Corinthians 2:8-10).

2. He speaks of the Mystery of Christ. Verse 4.

3. This Mystery was not made known to the sons of men in other, or Old Testament, times as it is now revealed to His holy apostles and prophets by the Spirit. Verse 5.

4. The Mystery is defined as the Jews and Gentiles being brought into "one body". Verse 6.

5. Paul desired that all men might see what is the fellowship of "The Mystery" which from the beginning of the world was hid in God and hid from generations and ages. Colossians 1:25-27; Ephesians 3:9.

6. The purpose of the Mystery is declared in Ephesians 3:9, 10, 21. To the intent that now unto the principalities and powers in heavenly places might be known by the Church the many sided wisdom of God.

Thus the Scriptures reveal that the Church was a Mystery hidden from previous generations. It was revealed to the apostles and prophets by the Spirit, after the death, burial, resurrection and ascension of the Lord Jesus Christ and the outpouring of the Holy Spirit.

The Old Testament saints did not see the Church, and many times did not understand their own utterances until it was revealed to them that their prophecies were partially for their own generation but were also for another generation. II Peter 1:19-21; I Peter 1:9-12; Matthew 13:10-17.

For this reason the prophets would love to have heard and witnessed that which took place under the ministry of Christ and the apostles, as well as that which takes place in the New Testament Church Age.

The Church is God's eternal purpose in Christ even before the world began (II Timothy 1:9, 10; Ephesians 1:9-11; 3:11; I Corinthians 2:7). The Godhead planned the whole thing in the counsels of eternity (Romans 8:29-30). The Church age is the age to which all others pointed and upon which the future ages proceed (Ephesians 3:5, 9). Creation itself made way for redemption. We are in the end of the ages (Colossians 1:26; I Corinthians 10:11; Hebrews 9:26).

Thus Paul is clear on the fact that this mystery was kept secret since the world began. "According to the revelation (Greek *'Apokalupsis'*, as Revelation 1:1), which was kept secret (silent) since the world began, but now is made manifest (disclosed) and by the Scriptures of the prophets made known, according to the commandment of the everlasting God, made known to all nations for the obedience of faith." This revelation which can only be known to the initiated was kept secret, but the time came when it was manifested, revealed, disclosed, uncovered and unveiled to the New Testament apostles and prophets, especially to the apostle Paul.

And when it was uncovered, it was seen to have been in the Scriptures of the prophets and shadowed until the appointed time. This is why Paul and other New Testament writers continually appeal to and quote the Old Testament prophets and apply their writings to the Church.

The "time element" as to why this mystery could not be revealed was that this mystery centred in the Son of God, our Lord Jesus Christ, and thus the mystery could not be seen nor could anyone be initiated into it, until after the finished work of Calvary and the glorification of the Son of God. In other words, it could not be revealed until after His death, burial, resurrection, ascension and glorification followed by the outpouring of the Holy Spirit (Luke 24:27, 44-46; Acts 3:19-21).

It was distinctly the work and ministry of the Holy Spirit to initiate one into the mystery of the Church, the Body of Christ. The Spirit revealed to the prophets that they spoke to another age, the Church age.

B. What Actually is "The Mystery"?

The actual mystery is a twofold truth as seen here. That is, the Gentiles coming into blessing in Christ, and the Jew and Gentile coming together in one Body. Ephesians 3:6; Colossians 1:24-27. The Body is THE CHURCH that He said He would build. We consider this in more detail here. The former has been dealt with under "The New Ethnic".

1. The Gentiles coming into blessing in Christ

The Gentiles were called to be fellow-heirs, of the same body, and partakers in Christ by the Gospel (Ephesians 3:1-6).

Many Old Testament Scriptures speak of the Gentiles coming into blessing. The prophet Isaiah is especially the Evangelist-Prophet who speaks of Gentile blessing through Christ. Paul was chosen to be the apostle to the Gentiles (Romans 11:13; Isaiah 42:1-16; 49:6-12, 22; 54:3; 60:1-5, 11, 16; 66:19; Malachi 1:11). Read also Jeremiah 16:19; Luke 2:32; 1:32-33; Galatians 3:8, 14-16; Isaiah 11:10; Colossians 1:24-27.

This blessing would only come through Christ, the Saviour of the world (Matthew 12:18-21; John 12:20-24; Galatians 3:14; Romans 9, 11:11; Romans 15). God chose Israel as a nation to bring forth the Saviour who would bless all the nations.

In the Acts we see the Gentiles coming into blessing in Christ. The Great Commission was that the Gospel go to every creature, everywhere, in all nations, both Jew and Gentile (Matthew 28:19; Mark 16:15-20; Acts 1:8).

In the Gospel odd Gentiles received blessing, but it remained for the fulness of blessing to come on the Gentiles after Christ's death, resurrection and ascension and the outpouring of the Holy Spirit (Matthew 15:21-28; Luke 7:1-10; John 4; Luke 4:24-28; 17:16). These Gentiles reached over by faith into the new dispensation and were blessed.

Under the Old Testament, Gentiles could come into Israel by circumcision (Genesis 17). But it was not until THE SEED of Abraham, Christ, came that the Gentiles could come into the fulness of the New Covenant blessing. At the cross the "middle wall of partition" was broken down (Ephesians 2:12-22; Acts 9:15; 13:42-48; 14:2-5, 27; 18:6; 21:11-25; 22:21; 26:17-23; 28:28).

Under the Old Covenant God chose one nation. Under the New Covenant, God chooses out of every nation those who constitute His Church (I Kings 8:38-43; Psalms 138; Psalms 102:13-22; 22:17; 98:1-14; 66:1-4; 67:1-7; 86:9; 72:17; Isaiah 19:25; Zechariah 2:8-12; Psalms 2:8; 65:1-2; Isaiah 40:5; 55:4-5; Acts 15:3-21; Psalms 117:1-2; Isaiah 11:10-11; Psalms 105:6, 43).

These Scriptures should be read and considered for they speak of the Gentiles coming into blessing IN THIS AGE, not in another future age. The prophets saw the Gentiles coming into blessing. Many believers place these Scriptures in A COMING AGE instead of realizing that it began in Acts and is still in fulfilment in our day.

2. **Jews and Gentile in the same Body**

It is around this chief truth that the problems arise in the Book of Acts, as well as in the world today. Not only were the Gentiles to come into blessing in Christ, but JEW AND GENTILE were to be made members of the SAME BODY, The mystery Body of Christ!

The Acts surround two major apostles, Peter and Paul. Also these two apostles involved the two ethnic divisions, Jew and Gentile, or Circumcision and Uncircumcision.

There is progression in the going forth of the Gospel in Acts.
Acts 1-7 chapters. Jerusalem and Judea. Ministry to the Jews.
Acts 8. Ministry to the Samaritan, then to the Ethiopian.
Acts 10-11. Ministry to the Gentiles under Peter.

Thus Shem, Ham and Japheth come into blessing in the tents of Shem (Genesis 9:24-27).

Acts 1-12 involves Peter's ministry; Acts 13-28 involves Paul's ministry.

In Acts 10-11 the Lord sends Peter to the Gentiles to open the door of faith to the Gentiles. In Acts 11 the Jewish brethren contend with Peter for going down to the Gentiles, but when Peter relates what God had done then the contention is settled.

In Acts 15 we have the problem of the Gentiles and the Judaizing teachers. The legalizers desire to bring the Gentiles under the Law of Moses while the Jews did not want to be as Gentiles. They all see that God is visiting the Gentiles to take out of them a people for His Name. However, there was great danger of having two distinct Churches; the Jewish Church, composed of Jewish believers in Christ, holding the Mosaic Law — The Church of the Circumcision; and the Gentile Church, composed of the Gentile believers in Christ — The Church of the Uncircumcision. What was God's answer to the problem?

This answer is given by revelation to Paul, the apostle to the Gentiles. He was chosen in Acts 9, preparatory to the visit of Peter in Acts 10-11 to the Gentiles. The Mystery is revealed to Paul that the Gentiles with the Jews were to be ONE BODY — not two difference ethnic bodies (Ephesians 3:1-9).

At the cross the middle wall of partition between Jew and Gentile was broken down (Ephesians 2:11-21). To erect this wall would be to nullify the work of the cross. God was making of Jew and Gentile ONE NEW MAN (Ephesians 2:15; Colossians 3:9-11). The NEW MAN is neither Jew nor Gentile. The "Old Man" is nationalistic, either Jew or Gentile. But the old man was nailed to the cross in death and judgment. The new man is Christ Jesus, the Last Adam, in His redeemed.

In Christ there is neither Jew nor Gentile (Galatians 3:28).

It is the New Creature alone that God accepts (II Corinthians 5:16, 17).

This constitutes the new Israel of God (Galatians 6:16). The new man is neither a Jewish man nor a Gentile man. It is the BODY OF CHRIST. The union, by spiritual birth, of all believers, out of all nations, who are in Christ. This is THE CHURCH. The Body of Christ, therefore, is not national, international, denominational nor undenominational —

it is a spiritual body, a new ethnic division, as already seen. The "key" verse to this is found in I Corinthians 12:13. "By *one Spirit are we all baptized into ONE BODY whether we be Jews or Gentiles, bond or free . . .*"

It is the Holy Spirit who settles the issue in the Book of Acts concerning the Body of Christ. There cannot be two separate or distinct Churches. There cannot be a Gentile and a Jewish. There is ONE CHURCH, the ONE BODY of Christ. How this revelation would, could and should settle the "nationalistic" spirit on the "mission field" in so many places if it was received.

In Acts 2, the Holy Spirit baptized the Jews into the mystery Body of Christ. In Acts 10 the same Holy Spirit baptized the Gentiles into the same mystery Body. Thus, washed in the same blood (Acts 20:28, the blood of God NOT Jewish blood!), baptized into the same Name, and baptized in the same Holy Spirit, Jew and Gentile are in the same Body, the mystery Body of Christ.

Note Paul's emphasis on the Body of Christ in these passages of Scripture:

★   The Church is the Body of Christ, the mystery unveiled (Ephesians 3:1-12).

★   Christ is the Head of the Body, which is the Church (Colossians 1:18, 24).

★   The Church is His Body, the fulness of Him who filleth all in all (Ephesians 1:22, 23; Colossians 3:15).

★   There is one body (Ephesians 4:4).

★   There is one bread, one body (I Corinthians 10:17).

★   There is one body but many members. The natural body typifies the spiritual body, the Church (I Corinthians 12:13-27).

★   Christ is the Saviour of the body, His Church (Ephesians 5:23-32).

★   There are many members but one body (Romans 12:1-6).

★   There is the communion of the body of Christ (I Corinthians 10:16, 17; 11:24-29).

★   Jew and Gentile are dead to the Law by the Body of Christ (Romans 7:4).

★   Jesus spake of the new Temple as the temple of His body (John 2:12-22).

C.   The Spirit and The Word

It is important to understand the related ministries of the Spirit and the Word relative to the Church. The Church is to be built by the Word of the Lord as well as by the Spirit of the Lord. The Spirit and the Word work together. The Book of Acts clearly shows the connection between the Spirit and the Word. This was to be so in relation to the Church, the Body of Christ.

1.   Jesus, the Word, gave commandments by the Spirit to the apostles (Acts 1:2).

2.   Jesus was THE WORD made flesh by THE SPIRIT (John 1:14-18; Matthew 3:15-21).

3.   The apostles would preach the word after the Spirit had come on them (Acts 1:8).

4.   The disciples spoke in tongues (words) as the Spirit gave them utterance (Acts 2:1-4).

5.   In the Last Days people would prophesy the word as the Spirit was outpoured on them (Joel 2:23-32; Acts 2:17, 18).

6.   Peter spoke the word with boldness by the Spirit to the Sanhedrin about healing of the lame man (Acts 4:8).

7.   The believers spoke the word with boldness after being filled with the Holy Spirit (Acts 4:31).

8.   The Spirit fell on the Gentiles as they heard the Word (Acts 10:44).

9.   The disciples at Ephesus spoke with tongues when filled with the Spirit (Acts 19:6).

10.   A Word of Wisdom and a Word of Knowledge is given by the Spirit (I Corinthians 12:8).

11. When the Spirit of truth is come, He will guide into the Word of truth (John 16:13; 17;17).

12. The Spirit moved and God spoke the Word in creation (Genesis 1:1-5).

D. The Holy Spirit and The Body of Christ (I Corinthians 12:13).

The importance of the Holy Spirit in relation to the Body of Christ must be recognized. It is the Holy Spirit who forms and fashions the Body of Christ and its various members.

In Acts 1, Christ, the Head and Builder of the Church returns to the Father God. In Him is all the Fulness of the Godhead bodily. In Him are all ministries, gifts, graces, spiritual fruit and the power of the Lord. This Fulness is to be manifested in the Church, His Body.

In Acts 2, the Holy Spirit descends from heaven to form the Church, the Body of Christ. It is by the Spirit that all the ministries, gifts, grace, power and fulness of the risen Head is to flow down to and through the Body. It is the same Spirit in the same Body, the spiritual Body of Christ.

Types which illustrate the relationship of "The Spirit" and "The Body" are considered in brief here. It is James who says, "The body without the spirit is dead" (James 2:26). Though referring to the natural physical human body, the truth is also applicable to the spiritual Body, the Church.

1. The First Adam

a. The Body (Genesis 1:26, 27; 2:7; Romans 5:14).

God's masterpiece was the creation of man. Man's body was formed out of the dust of the earth. Man was made in the triune image of God. God fashioned, formed, placed and set every member of Adam's body as it pleased Him. The human body has about 40 million members in it, all working harmoniously together to make a united body. The body of man is God's masterpiece in creation. His body was formed to be inhabited. When formed, Adam's body was as yet lifeless. Not one member could function or operate as God ordained until made alive. The body was complete, but lifeless.

b. The Spirit (Zechariah 12:1; Proverbs 20:27; James 2:26; Numbers 16:27).

The body without the spirit is dead. So God formed the spirit of man within him when he made the body. The spirit of man is the candle or lamp of the Lord. This lamp must be lighted. Light is life. God thus breathed into man the breath of life (lives) and man became a living soul (I Thessalonians 5:23). So the members of the body became alive, active and functioning. The same was true for the bride of Adam. This is all typical of Christ and His bride.

a. The Body

David in Psalm 139 speaks of the formation of the human body in the mother's womb. The language is also applicable to the Church as the Body of Christ. My substance was not hid from Thee (Acts 15:18; Matthew 13:10-13). God knows all. The body was curiously wrought in the lower parts of earth (Exodus 35:32). Made in secret in the mother's womb (Romans 16:25; Matthew 13:34, 35). God saw all my substance as yet unperfect. In His book all the members were written when as yet there was none of them (Hebrews 12:23). These were fashioned continually (Acts 2:46; 13:42; 14:22). Thus the human body is fearfully and wonderfully made. How much more is this applicable to the Body of Christ, His Church? Paul takes the natural body to be symbolic of the spiritual body. God sees every member of the Body of Christ before their existence, and He fashions and forms them to the image of His Son (Ephesians 1:1-11; Romans 8:28-32). The curious power of the Lord is seen in redemption.

b. The Spirit

I Thessalonians 5:23; Hebrews 4:12; Ecclesiastes 12:1; James 2:26. Man is a triune being; spirit, soul and body. The Word of God is the only thing that distinguishes between the triune parts of man. However, the body without the spirit is dead, lifeless. Death is the exit of the spirit from the body. The body returns to dust and the spirit to God who gave it. So the Body of Christ without the Holy Spirit is dead. It is the Spirit who causes every member to live, move, function and operate in their place in the body. The moment a baby is conceived, the spirit is there to give and maintain life.

3.   **The Tabernacle of Moses**

   a.   **The Tabernacle** (Exodus 25-40)

   The Tabernacle was built by the wisdom of God after the Divine pattern. It took approximately 9 months to complete. It was curiously made as to its vessels, curtains, structure. It is typical of the true Tabernacle, the Lord Jesus Christ (John 1:14-18).

   b.   **The Shekinah Glory**

   The Tabernacle was built for one purpose, this being, to house the Shekinah Glory of God. Without the Glory, the Tabernacle was incomplete. The Spirit of God in Shekinah Glory filled the Tabernacle, then the function of the sanctuary began to operate.

4.   **The Temple of Solomon**

   a.   **The Temple**

   II Chronicles 3-7 gives the account of the building of the Temple. It also was built after the Divine pattern, given by the Spirit to David. It was made by the wisdom and ability of God. The stones were quarried, fashioned, overlaid and then brought together noiselessly into one Temple as the work of God. It again pointed to the true Temple, Jesus Christ (John 2:18-22).

   b.   **The Glory of God**

   It was built for one purpose, to house the Glory of God. The presence and name of God dwelt there. His glory and His voice were there, without this Glory the Temple was incomplete. Ministry in the Temple could only continue under the Glory of God. Without it, all became a mere lifeless form, even as in the Tabernacle of Moses.

5.   **The Nation of Israel** (Ezekiel 37)

   a.   **The Body**

   The valley of dry bones teaches the same truth. The WORD of the Lord had to go forth first, this brought the bones and the body together. Bone came to his bone, and member to member. All found their proper place in the body. Flesh, sinews and skin came on them. All were ready to function. It can be used to symbolize the coming together of the Body of Christ. They had been a lifeless, scattered and divided body of people. The Word brought all together. But they were still lifeless.

   b.   **The Spirit**

   Note vs 8, 14. "But there was no breath in them." The Spirit of the Lord must move now. The whole House of Israel had come together, bone to his bone and member to his member, but still lacked life, the spirit of life. Then the Spirit entered into them and they stood up an exceeding great army. All this can become symbolical of the Church, as the army of the Lord, empowered by the power of the Spirit and the Word (Zechariah 4:6).

6.   **The Last Adam**

   Jesus Christ is the Last Adam, the begotten Son of God. We see the same revelation manifested in His life also.

   a.   **The Body** (Hebrews 10:5, 10; Colossians 1:22; Matthew 1:20-23).

This body was prepared for the Son of God in the virgin Mary. It was a body prepared to do the will of God. Incorruptible seed, and a perfect body was prepared for the Last Adam. The body of Jesus was curiously wrought by the Spirit over 9 months in the virgin's womb (Luke 1:35; Isaiah 7:14). Every member in this body was sinless, sickless, perfect, deathless and immortal. The Divine life of the blood of God was in the body of Jesus. The WORD was made flesh (John 1:14-18; I Corinthians 15:46, 47).

b.   **The Spirit** (Luke 1:35).

The Holy Spirit was involved in the formation of the body of Jesus by the over-shadowing of Mary, planting within her the seed of the WORD. He formed this sinless body for the incarnation (John 1:14-18). The body was prepared of God. Then later on at Jordan, the Holy Spirit filled this Tabernacle, this Temple with Himself (Matthew 4:16, 17; John 3:33, 34). He was the dwelling place of God, the habitation of His name, His presence, His words, His glory (John 1:14-18; 2:18-22). As Tabernacle and Temple were built according to the pattern by the wisdom and Spirit of God, so was Jesus Christ.

The begotten Word by the Spirit was after 30 years then the anointed Word by the Spirit.

7.   **The Church, the Body of Christ**

a.   **The Body**

Ephesians 4:4; I Corinthians 12:13; Hebrews 10:5; Ephesians 1:22, 23; Colossians 1:18, 24; James 2:26. The Church now is the spiritual body of Christ. What God did in the physical and natural body of Jesus, He desires to do in the spiritual Body, the Church. Every member will ultimately be sinless, sickless, deathless, immortal and incorruptible. They will be bone of His bone and flesh of His flesh. All will be according to the Divine pattern (I John 4:17). The Church is now God's Temple, his habitation. The believer individually and believers corporately are the Temple of God (I Corinthians 6:19, 20; II Corinthians 6:16-18; II Peter 1:13, 14; II Corinthians 5:1; Ephesians 2:20-22). The Church is to be indwelt by the Spirit. The Church Age is the "age of the Body" in formation. The Head is firstborn, the Body follows.

b.   **The Spirit**

Thus as each member is "born again", the Spirit enters them and they become a mystical member of this Body of Christ. Thus the 12, the 70, the 120, the 3000, the 5000 and multitudes were added to the Church unto this day (Acts 1:8; 2:1-4; I Corinthians 12:13; John 21-23; Luke 3:16). We see the two aspects of the Spirit's work in the members of the Body. Christ breathed on His disciples and they were "born of the Spirit". Then at Pentecost there was the rushing wind and they were "baptized with the Holy Spirit". This was individually and corporately. Christ was the Baptizer (John 1:32, 33).

They were personally baptized into the Spirit, and then corporately baptized into the Body by the Holy Spirit. Many members baptized into one Body. Thus through the Book of Acts (Acts 2, Acts 8, Acts 10-11, etc.) believers were born again and baptized into the Spirit and into the Body of Christ. They became living and active members of the Body. It was an immersion into the body of Christ.

Thus we have the importance of the Holy Spirit in relation to the Body (I Corinthians 12). It is a spiritual body. The Gifts, Fruit, Ministries, Operations and Functions of the Body of Christ are by the power of the Spirit. Without the Spirit all is lifeless, inactive, inoperative — dead indeed!

There are many, many lessons which can be learned from the natural human body which may be applied in principle to the Body of Christ. We conclude this chapter with some of these lessons.

★ In the human body, every member is active, operative, and each contributes towards the welfare of the body. Every member and cell has a function to carry out, also to live on out, as God gives them.

★ Every member is set in the Body as it pleases God.

★ Every member recognizes the other member.

★ Every member works with and for the other, not usurping authority over another.

★ Every member is subject to the head, or the nerve centre. None rebel.

★ Every member is connected to the other by the blood-life stream. I John 1:7.

★ Every member is connected by the breath of life. James 2:26; Genesis 2:7.

★ Every member functions at the direction of the head. I Corinthians 12:27.

★ Every member is interdependent on the other. I Corinthians 10:17.

★ Every member functions in their God-given place.

★ Every member has a unique God-given place.

★ Every member knows it is not the whole body.

★ Every member has a gift within it to make it a functioning member. i.e. The ear is a member, having the "gift" of hearing, otherwise it is deaf. The eye is a member but has the "gift" of sight, otherwise there is blindness. It is the "gift" in the member that makes it a useful and functioning member.

★ Every member works in the unity of the body also, to make it a harmonious body.

The human body is God's masterpiece in creation (Genesis 1:26-28; 2:7; Psalms 139: 13-17). With its untold millions (perhaps 30-50 million) cells, etc., its marvellous nervous system of communication, the blood, the skin, the arms and hands, the legs and feet, the heart, liver, kidneys, lungs, brains, head, eyes, ears, the protective structure of the bones (at least 246 bones in the body, 63 in the head, 24 in the sides, 16 in the wrist, 14 in the joints, 108 in the hands and feet), etc., and the wonder of all these working together in marvellous harmony and unity in the one body of man — all is indeed the marvel of the Divine creation.

If God did this in the old creation man, what shall He do in the new creation Man — The Body of Christ? He desires to relive His life in the Church which is His body. There are millions of unseen members in the natural body, as well as the seen. Yet all work together in harmony for a whole and healthy body. The unseen and invisible members and cells maintain the seen and visible in active health and life.

There are no "independent" members in the body. Every joint supplies (Ephesians 4:16).

All these lessons are evidently applicable to the members of the Body of Christ.

CHAPTER 15

CHURCH GOVERNMENT

Introductory:

Without doubt, one of the most controversial and, tragically, one of the most divisive areas is the subject of Church Government. All recognize that there must be some form of government, but what form it should take is a point of much contention and divergence.

Jesus said that every *city, house or kingdom* divided against itself will surely fall (Matthew 12:25, 26). The Church is likened to God's House, God's City and God's Kingdom. But it has certainly been divided as to its government. This is one of the reasons why the Church has not been able to stand against the Kingdom of Satan. Satan attacks all forms of government as ordained of God, because he is the lawless one, and wants to bring about a lawless society. Rejecting the government and the authority of God he sets himself up as government and authority. He who does not submit to authority sets himself up as authority. He who rejects God's government sets himself up as self-governing.

Satan led an angelic revolt against God's government in the eternities past (Isaiah 14:12-14; Ezekiel 28:1-19; John 8:44; II Peter 2:4; Jude 6).

He also brought the revolt of man against God's government in Eden (Genesis 3:1-6). There are a number of vital things relative to the subject of government which need to be considered before dealing more particularly with Church Government.

A. **Definition of Government**

The word "government" has been defined as:

★ The excercise of authority over an organization, institution, state, district, etc.; direction, control, rule, management.

★ A system of ruling, controlling, etc., an established system of political administration by which a state, district, etc., is governed.

★ Government involves (a) Territory, (b) People and (c) Leadership.

Thus we recognize that the Church as God's House, City and Kingdom needs government (Psalms 127:1; Isaiah 2:1-4; Joel 2:25-28; Acts 2:17).

Having defined the word we note that:

1. **Government is God-Ordained**

The powers that be are ordained of God. God has ordained that law and order be excercised and preserved in human society through appointed authorities (Romans 13:1-8). The powers that be are ordained of God.

I Corinthians 12:28. God has set in the Church governments (plural). i.e., Steering, piloting, directing.

Isaiah 9:6-9. The government shall be upon His shoulder: No end to it. Thus government means "rule, leadership, oversight, inspector, to go before, to guide, to captain, a governor."

Isaiah 22:22. The government shall be placed in the hand of Eliakim, which means "Resurrection of God".

II Peter 1:10. There are those who are presumptuous, self-willed, and not afraid to speak evil of dignitaries. They despise government.

Government in the universe is ordained of God.

2. **The Need of Government**

Without government lawlessness and anarchy prevail. There would be rebellion and chaos in the universe without Divine authority. Israel's history records that "there was no king in Israel and every man did that which was right in his own eyes" (Judges 18:1; 17:6; 21:25; 19:1).

Without some form of government, the spirit of lawlessness reigns with its resultant confusion. The mystery of iniquity is at work today to overthrow governments. Worlds are in collision without law and order in the universe. People are created to be governed.

3. **Divinely Appointed Realms of Government**

There are several major realms of government in the universe, touching both earth and heaven.

★   Government of Heaven, the universe, and the angelic realm (Psalms 145:10-13).

★   Government of the Home, involving husband, wife and children (Genesis 1:26-28).

★   Government of the Nation, involving the State and Human Government as established by God under the Noahic Covenant (Genesis 6-8; Romans 13:1-8).

★   Government of the Church (I Corinthians 12:28; Hebrews 13:7,17,24). The Church is a society within a society, a community within a community, a nation within the nations, and a Divinely governed institution within humanly governed institutions. It is His Kingdom — a Theocracy!

4. **Overthrow the Government**

II Peter 2:10; Isaiah 14:12-14; Matthew 6:6-9. There is law and order in the government of heaven. This *law—order* is demonstrated in the Godhead under headship (I Corinthians 11:1—3). However, Lucifer rose up in rebellion against this headship and constituted authority and caused the angelic revolt.

★   Satan was the leader of rebellion. He sought to overthrow the government of heaven. All freewill creations were tested at this point, as to whether they would serve God with their freewill or serve Satan. Thus it seems that a third part of the angels fell. Here the doctrine of existentialism was born. "Do your own thing." They followed Satan's challenge against the government of God and His authority. Satan thus fell from the position he sought to gain as the anointed cherub and guardian of the throne of God. He promised the angels who followed him positions of authority in his rival kingdom.

★   The same thing is evident in the fall of Adam and Eve. It was treason against God Himself. Eve was deceived. Adam sinned knowingly, but without realizing the full consequences on the unborn human race.

★   In Israel under Korah we also see rebellion against Divinely appointed authority of God as given to Moses (Numbers 16).

This has been the history of the human race. The challenge against God's authority and government has been challenged over the centuries. The Satanic power is behind it all. Church history shows the same conflict in the Church of Jesus Christ.

B. **Forms of Church Government**

Church history shows the various forms of Church government which have been tried out by the people of God. Much study has gone into this subject by the various writers of history. Some of the clues and indications from early Church history have been taken and used to formulate different systems of Church government. The pendulum seems to have swung back and forth between apparent extremes. Denominational forms of Church government have been made to maintain unity of doctrine, purity of life, this being done by strong government. However, this has never worked. Liberalism, Modernism, Apostasy and Heresy and death have all been manifest in the very Denominations who sought by strong centralized government to keep these things out. Generally speaking, if the denomination goes astray, then all of its churches under its jurisdiction follow suit.

Then the Independent Churches or local congregations have established forms of government. They have a greater measure of safety in the sense that, if Heresy arises, then it is more localized than spread through a whole Denomination. However, the same problems have manifested themselves on this local level as in the Denominational level.

The Church, like Israel of old, has followed world systems of government instead of God's system of government.

A consideration of New Testament revelation shows that there was a "threefold cord" manifested in Church government. Church history, both past and present show that various groups have taken one or the other of these cords and emphasized such, upholding it to be THE form of Church government. As will be seen, it seems that the answer is not one or the other of these cords but "*the threefold cord which cannot be broken*" (Ecclesiastes 4:12) that provides the necessary "checks and balances" needed in the delicate matter of Church government.

James Lee Beall, in "*Your Pastor, Your Shepherd*" (p.120) says that anthropologists tell us that basically there are 5 possible types of human government, these being:

★ Oligarchy — the government by an elite few

★ Monarchy — government by one man or woman

★ Gerontocracy — government by the old men

★ Democracy — government by a large portion of the people, usually through some form of representation

★ Theocracy (or Hierarchy) — government by God through appointed authorities. For the purpose of this chapter, we discover that these types of government may be classified under three basic systems. Robert S. Paul, in "*The Church In Search of Itself*" (p.31) in speaking of Church government says: "The three simple patterns that emerged paralleled the three basic systems of civil government known to the ancient world — Episcopal (monarchial), Presbyterian (oligarchic or aristocratic) and Congregational (democratic).

We see these systems manifest themselves in both civil and ecclesiastical rule.

1. **Monarchy**

   Monarchy is government by one person. It is an autocratic system of government. Autos = "self" and Kratos = "power".

   a. **Civil Rule**

   This can be seen in a Dictatorship, whether good or evil, benevolent or despotic. It is the rule of the one man, a form of government in which one person has supreme and absolute power above all others. The monarch can be independent and individualistic, excercising unlimited authority.

   Nebuchadnezzar was a king and illustrates this form of government, for "whom he would he slew, and whom he would he kept alive, and whom he would he set up, and whom he would he put down" (Daniel 5:19).

   Kingdoms of the world have illustrated this system of government; the Pharaohs in Egypt; the Kings of Babylon; the Emperors of Rome, as well as various nations today under a Dictatorship.

   b. **Church Rule**

   The monarchial rule is seen in the Church under the Papal and Episcopal forms of government. The Pope is called "The Bishop of Bishops". The Greek word for Bishop or Overseer is "episcopos" ("epi" = "over", and "skopos" = "to see or look"). The Bishop of the Church is the one man rule, the one who looks after and guards the flock of God. Authority is invested in him as the Church head, whether it be Pope, Bishop or Cardinal or other appointed Clergy.

The Churches which are governed by one man, whether he be called Bishop, Pastor, Minister or Presiding Elder, etc., illustrate the rule of the one man. He may be a good or bad ruler. He may be a benevolent or despotic Dictator. He may rule as a king over his kingdom and have the Nebuchadnezzar spirit (Daniel 15:19) or he may have a humble spirit. He may be a Godly Bishop or a hypocritical Bishop but he is a Monarchial Bishop.

Many times "Independent Churches" or "Autonomous Churches" come under this form of government. Diotrephes seemed to exemplify the independent spirit, loving the pre-eminence and rejecting or receiving whom he would as an autocrat (III John 9, 10).

The great danger relative to the rule of the one man, whether civil or ecclesiastical is that this person generally has no "checks and balances" for his own safety, as well as the safety of the people he rules over. False cults and their leaders have taken numerous people into slavery and death.

2. Hierarchy

The word "hierarchy" means "a group of officials" who together rule the people (Greek "Hieros" = sacred, and "Archos" = ruler). Hierarchy is Church government by a group of Priests or Clergy in graded ranks. Although this word does have religious connotations, the idea of "a group of officials" is seen in both civil and ecclesiastical forms of government. The following words illustrate such.

a. Oligarchy

"Oligo" means "few" and "Arche" means "rule". Oligarchy is government by elite few. Oligarchy is a form of government in which the supreme power is placed in the hands of a small executive class. Any one of these rulers is called an oligarch.

b. Gerontocracy

Greek "Geron" means "an old man" and "Kratos" means "power". Gerontocracy is simply the rule by old or aged men. It is a government controlled by old men. Certain nations had governments whose supreme magistrates were all over sixty years of age.

King Solomon took counsel with the old men while his son Rehoboam failed to do so and took counsel with the young men, his peers, who lacked wisdom that generally comes with the experience of years. The result was a divided kingdom that has never ever been united since that time (I Kings 12:1-24).

Churches who are governed by a group of "Elders" or "Bishops" come under this form of government, especially if the word "Elder" is taken in its stricter meaning as an "old man, or aged person."

c. Bureaucracy

Bureaucracy is defined as "government by departmental officials following an inflexible routine." It is governmental officialism, or the officials collectively. It is the concentration of authority in administrative bureaus. An example of bureaucratic form of government is seen in "The Party" in the countries under Communism or Socialism. It involves also Gerontocracy or the rule of the old men ("The Party" in Moscow illustrates this fact). Deacon Board control also illustrates this.

d. Hierarchy

The hierarchical form of government is the rule of the Priests or Bishops over God's people. These persons are not secular but sacred rulers as the word Hierarchy means (Greek "Hieros" = sacred, and "Archos" = ruler).

Hierarchical rule can include in itself "the rule of the few" (Oligarchy), "the rule of old men'' (Gerontocracy), and ''the rule of officials'' (Bureaucracy), except that, as noted, it is used more to refer to the sacred (Ecclesiastical) rule and not secular rule.

A hierarchy has the flavour of Nicolaitianism, or ''suppression of the laity'' thus creating ''clergy and laity'' (Revelation 2:6, 15).

The Roman Church recognizes the Pope as ''Bishop of Bishops'' and the Catholic Priesthood nullifies the priesthood of all believers. This is hierarchy! The Episcopal Church is the government of the Church by a Bishop whose authority is conferred on him by Bishops above him who comprize an ecclesiastical hierarchy.

The Presbyterian Church is the government of the Church by an Elder whose authority comes from ''the presbytery'' or ''session'', a group of elders of equal rank. These represent the people in District, State and National levels and in Sessions on through to the Assembly of Elders of the whole Presbyterian Church. There are widening degrees of authority in this Eldership, or presbyterial form of government.

Many local Churches have this form of government by the Elders in that locally governed Church. However, the great danger is that it can become an hierarchical form of government, and rob the congregation of their priestly ministry before the Lord, by the creation of ''clergy and laity''.

3. **Democracy**

The word ''democracy'' is made up of two words, ''Demos'' = ''the people'', and ''Kratis'' = ''to rule''. It means ''the rule of the people''. Democracy is government by the majority of the people. It is the peoples rights, the peoples voice, the peoples rule. It is government of the people, by the people, for the people by popular vote, directly or through representatives.

This form of government exists generally in the Western world as well as some of the other Democratic countries.

As far as Churches are concerned, the *Congregational, Baptist,* various *Churches of Christ,* some *Pentecostal* and other local Churches have the democratic system of government. It is the choice of the people to have who they will rule for them, subject to their authority. Thus we have the ''hire and fire'' pastoral system in operation so much.

It is worthy to note that Laodicea means ''mass rule'' or ''the rule of the people''. (Revelation 3:12-21). Christ, the Head of the Church, was sadly outside His own Church seeking admission.

The congregational form of government is democracy. It places the power and authority, and the government in the hands of the people, whereby they control the leadership of the Church.

Thus, under the Roman Catholic and Episcopal Churches authority is conferred by superiors in an ecclesiastical hierarchy.

Under the Presbyterian government authority results from the Session of Elders. Under the Democratic form of government authority is delegated by the people. In each case, authority comes from above or below. However, all forms of government go astray without God, for God can only govern *through men* when He truly governs *in men!*

Alex Rattray Hay in *''The New Testament Order For Church And Missionary''* (pp. 141-145) confirms the above comments, which we quote and adapt here.

He confirms the fact that among men there are three main types of government:
(1) Autocracy — absolute government by one man, and (2) Oligarchy — government by a privileged group, and (3) Democracy — government of the people by the people. Democracy is defined as ''A form of government in which the supreme power is vested in the people collectively, and is administered by them or by officers appointed by them.''

The whole Church is organized under one of these three forms, rejecting the theocratic form of government.

The autocratic form of government is found in the Roman Catholic Church and in Denominations with a government in which one man is given supreme control and in congregations where one man assumes a place of priestly privilege in the ministry of the Word.

The oligarchic form of government is seen in congregations where a group of Elders, in the appointment of whom the congregation has no say, undertake to find the will of the Lord for the congregation.

The democratic form of government is found in congregations organized on the congregational system. The responsibility is placed directly on the entire congregation. Decisions are made by vote and the opinion of the majority rules.

1   Where the responsibility is placed upon ONE MAN it is hoped he will know God's will and guide the congregation aright.

2   Where a group of ELDERS have that place it is expected that they will know His will and the congregation depends on them.

3   Where the congregation rules it is hoped that the decision of the majority will be Christ's will.

Thus human forms of government rob the people of priestly relationship to Christ and to God, as well as their responsibility as a congregation.

On page 350 of the same text the writer says: "The three main systems that have evolved as a result are the Episcopal, Presbyterial and Congregational. In each of these may be recognized a fundamental principle of the original order, although it has been modified to conform to human organization."

And again, "All have divided the Church into clergy and laymen, releasing the responsibility of the Word. Each system has the strength and the weakness derived from its order."

C.   The Government of God in the Old Testament

In viewing Divine government in Old Testament times we find that it falls into two major areas. There is government which is absolute and sovereign, and there is government that is of God through human instrumentality.

1.   Divine Or Sovereign Government

By Divine or Sovereign government we mean the rule and reign of God absolutely and directly over the affairs of mankind. We may say that this kind of government was manifested during the anti-diluvian era from Adam to Noah (Genesis 1-6). God Himself governed and judged Adam and Eve. It was God Himself who came and judged Cain for his rebellion and murder of Abel. It was God Himself who came to Noah and told him of the judgment by flood waters on a godless, violent and corrupt world.

Government was operated by God Himself in heaven upon the earth's inhabitants. God Himself ruled the affairs of world kingdoms, giving it to whomsoever He would (Daniel 1-7). God Himself ruled over Israel (Judges 8:22, 23).

2.   Human Government

It was under the Noahic Covenant that God introduced human government, the government of men by men. This was Divinely delegated and limited authority however. God was still soverign and supreme and His government universal. But here authority is placed by God into the hands of men to deal with men in the realm of murder and the taking of human life (Genesis 7-8-9).

These laws governing human lives were amplified more fully under the Mosaic Covenant as given to the chosen nation Israel. It was seen in measure when God raised up the deliverers in the time that the Judges ruled also (Acts 13:20). However, God's government is over all human government.

D. Theocracy in Israel

It is in the nation of Israel that we see more clearly Divine rule through human instrumentality. It is there that we see a true Theocracy — the rule of God under God, and thus through His chosen, appointed and anointed leaders. "Theos" = God, and "Kratien" = to rule. Thus Theocracy is "God-rule". But how did God rule in Israel? He ruled through instruments of His choice, His representatives, through His appointed officials or rulers.

Israel had this form of government under God and God raised up leaders to perform His will and exercise His rule, acting as His delegated authorities, under Divine unction and wisdom in total dependence upon Him.

These leaders were God-called, chosen and equipped. Sometimes the Divine choice was made sovereignly, by God Himself. Other times it was God's choice revealed through human instrumentality. The issue was that God rule was through human vessels of His choice.

1. Divine Sovereignty

a. Moses — sovereignly called and chosen of God to rule His people Israel (Exodus 3, Exodus 1-40).

b. Aaron — sovereignly called and chosen by God to be High Priest in Israel (Exodus 28, 29). Read Numbers 17 also.

c. Judges — The Judge — Deliverers were chosen of God sovereignly.

d. Elijah — sovereignly raised up as the prophet of God to Israel (I Kings 17).

e. Jeremiah — Jeremiah 1.

f. Ezekiel — Ezekiel 1-2.

g. Isaiah — Isaiah 6.

So it was generally with the Major and Minor Prophets. God sovereignly came to them and called them to act under His authority, to be His spokesmen to the people of God. All knew the sovereign call of God to the ministry. None were self-called, or man-called.

2. Human Responsibility Under God

On other occasions God chose men by using human vessels to confirm His choice. These men were not elected or voted in or out of office by people. They were God's choice.

a. Rulers — Exodus 18. By a word of wisdom from Jethro, Moses chose able and qualified men to be judges and rulers over God's people and share the load with him.

b. Joshua — Numbers 27. Joshua was chosen by God through Moses to be his successor to lead the people into the promised land and complete Moses ministry.

c. Saul — I Samuel 9-10. Even though Israel had rejected God's theocratic kingship and wanted a visible king like other nations, nevertheless, it was God who chose Saul through Samuel to be their king. Whose choice was Saul really? They chose a king. God chose their king for them.

d. David — I Samuel 16. It should be recognized that it was God's will for Israel to have a king, but not His time when Saul was chosen (Genesis 17). David was God's choice from His tribe, and chosen under Samuel in His time (Genesis 49:10).

e. Elisha — I Kings 19. Elisha, the prophet, was God's choice, but this was confirmed by the human instrumentality of Elijah and his mantle.

f. Levites — Numbers 1-4, 18.

The tribe of Levi was chosen by God through Moses and then given to Aaron as a gift for the service of the sanctuary. It was confirmed by the laying on of hands and they were appointed to serve the Tabernacle and the people of Israel (Acts 7:38).

Thus the choice of men originated with God Himself and was manifested directly or by human instrumentality. These men were chosen by God and called to rule over Israel, exercising Divine government in their midst. They acted for God as His delegated authorities. It is this that is meant by the use of the word theocracy here.

Theocracy is the rule of God directly or through his chosen, appointed and anointed authorities.

There were not:

1) SELF-called or chosen. As was Abimelech (Judges 9); Korah (Numbers 16); or Diotrephes (III John 9, 10).

2) MAN-called or chosen. As was King Saul, yet God permitted it and chose him for them (I Samuel 18, 9, 10; Numbers 14:4).

3.) But they were GOD-called and chosen, as was Moses, Aaron, Joshua, David Samuel, and the Prophets of God (cf. Hebrews 5:1-5).

They were not voted in or out by popular vote of the people. There was no bureaucratic or democratic choice of these people. These leaders were God-called and God-chosen leaders. This is THEOCRACY — the rule of God Himself, or His rule through His chosen vessels.

Israel was not a Democracy, even as the home is not a Democracy. Parents are the authority under God. The man is head of the house and is not voted in or out nor does he abdicate his throne. Human forms of governments have advantages as well as disadvantages, but the Church is not called to imitate these.

Government in the Church is a *gift* from God (I Corinthians 12:28; I Peter 4:10, 11). Government in the Church is not man-made like Israel saying "Make us a king like other nations" (I Samuel 8:7). God has His form of government for the Church. It is THEOCRATIC and not Democratic or Bureaucratic or Hierarchical or Monarchial! God's government of the Church must be through Divinely gifted people He has chosen. The development of this is from Christ the Head, then through the Twelve, and then on through Paul to the Eldership as laid out in the New Testament. This will be taken up in due time.

E. **The Headship of Christ**

Every Government has a HEAD. Without it, government could not function. This is true whether it speaks of government in the individual, the home, the Church, the nation, or the universe.

There must be HEADSHIP! Headship is government. Headship is authority!

It is Headship that co-ordinates all the members of the body, whether naturally or collectively in people.

The Scripture is clear that Christ is THE HEAD of the Church, and no other can usurp His Headship.

God has given Christ to be Head over all things to the Church, which is His Body (Ephesians 1:22). When we speak of Christ's Headship we speak of Lordship, Rulership, Authority, Government, Kingship. The GOVERNMENT is upon His shoulders (Isaiah 9:6-9). God has committed the key of David and the government of His kingdom into His hand (Isaiah 22:20-24).

Christ is the Headstone of the building (Psalms 118:21, 22; Mark 12:10; Matthew 21:42; Acts 4:11; I Peter 2:4-8).

The Scriptures also show that there is a Divine order of Headship in the universe, in the government of God both in heaven and earth.

1. GOD is the Head of Christ (I Corinthians 11:3).

2. CHRIST is the Head of the Church, His Body members, collectively and individually (Ephesians 4:15; Colossians 1:18; Ephesians 5:23-27).

   ★ Christ is the Head of every believer, individually (I Corinthians 11:3).

   ★ Christ is the Head of all principality and power (Colossians 2:10).

   ★ Christ is the Headstone which the builders, the religious leaders, rejected (Psalms 118:22; Zechariah 4:7; Matthew 21:42-44; Mark 12:10; I Peter 2:7; Acts 4:11).

   ★ Christ is the Fulness of the Godhead bodily (Colossians 1:19; 2:9).

3. The HUSBAND is the Head of his wife, as Christ is the Head of His Church (Ephesians 5:23-32).

4. Rulers were chosen to be "heads" over the nation of Israel (Exodus 18:13-26). They were not to usurp the headship of Moses under the headship of the Lord God, but only act as "heads" under "headship".

5. Ministries in the Church are not to act as "lords" over God's heritage, nor usurp the Headship of Christ (II Corinthians 1:24; I Peter 5:3). One can only and truly exercise headship as a husband or ruler if truly under the Headship of Christ (I Corinthians 11:3).

   Many time human headship and heads of denominations and organizations usurp the Headship of Christ bringing confusion and division into the Body of Christ.

6. **First the Natural, then the Spiritual**

   The Scriptures teach the principle that it is "first the natural, afterwards the spiritual" (I Corinthians 15:46, 47). Because of this there are some major lessons to be learned from natural headship of the human body.

   ★ The Head in the natural body is the seat of the mind, the seat of control and direction. Wisdom, knowledge and understanding are in the head. Christ is the Head of the spiritual Body, the Church. Therefore, He is the brains, the mind of God in the Church. He gives directions and exercises control.

   ill ★ The Head governs and directs every member of the natural body. By a thought from the head, every member obeys; every member submits and responds to the direction of the head.

   So every member of the Body of Christ should be submitted to the risen Head and obey His will and thought (Colossians 2:17-19; Ephesians 4:15).

   ★ The Head in the natural body is responsible for all food and nourishment being supplied to every member. Every member must receive from the head. So Christ the Head nourishes and cares for the Church, His Body; cleansing, purifying and nourishing the Body (Ephesians 5:27-32).

   ★ The Head holds the centre of the nervous system which connects the whole body to it in sensitiveness.

   Christ the Head is vitally connected to every member and the members to Him by the Holy Spirit, who is the Divine "nerve system" in the Church, His Body. There has to be sensitivity to His Spirit.

   ★ The Head is incomplete without the body, and the body is incomplete without the head. Each belong to the other. We cannot conceive of a bodyless head or a headless body.

   So Christ is incomplete without the Church, His Body, and the Body is incomplete without Him (Ephesians 1:22 23; 4:11-16; Colossians 2:17-19).

Christ, as THE HEAD of the Church, is perfect and infallible. He is the all-fulness of God

(Matthew 18:20; 28:18-20). Because of this He is able to govern the Church both locally and universally. This no man can do. This is why no one man can possibly or ever be the universal head of the Church. This is to usurp the Headship and place of Christ.

The Book of Acts reveals Christ the Head in heaven directing, controlling, governing, quickening the members of the Church, His Body, in the earth. By the Spirit He was able to send His thoughts, His will, His mind, His plans and purposes to the members of His Body (Acts 1-2; 8-10; 13:1-4, etc.).

The order of Headship is revealed. God is head over Christ, Christ is head over the Church by the Spirit. Every member of the Body must know this headship and hold the head, even Christ (Colossians 2:19). He is the Governor, the Director and God's authority is invested in Him. The Church, both universally and locally is under His headship. Rulers in the Church can only exercise headship as they are submitted to and governed by Christ's infallible Headship (Zechariah 9:7; 12:5-6; Genesis 45:26; I Peter 2:14; Matthew 2:6; Psalms 22:28; Genesis 42:6; Matthew 27:2-6; Galatians 4:2; II Peter 2:10).

F.   The Government of the Church

We come now to a consideration of the government of the New Testament Church, both universally and locally.

1.   The Government of the Church Universal

Government of the Church universal can only be under the Head and that is the Lord Jesus Christ.

The endeavours of men, of denominations and organizations, to set up a "World Church" with a "Central World Headquarters" is contrary to Scripture. It usurps the Headship of Christ. The Pope cannot be "Universal Head of the Church". How can any man or group of men effectively know the mind of Christ for the Church around the world? Countries and cultures may vary, needs of Churches in different localities around the world vary. There is great need for the "many-sided wisdom" of God in Christ. Only Christ, the infallible and Divine Head, whom God has given to the Body, can effectively govern and direct the Church universal.

There were no "Central Headquarters" for the Church in the Book of Acts. Jerusalem as the "Mother Church" did not try to control or govern every local Church established in the cities of the nations. Jerusalem was not "headquarters" or the governing body over Antioch or Corinth or any other Church in the cities. Neither did Rome control Corinth, nor did Ephesus control the Churches in Asia.

It is human nature that desires to set up some "Jerusalem" to be the governing head of Churches established around the world. This is not to be found in the Scripture. The only "Jerusalem" believers look to is "the heavenly Jerusalem" (Hebrews 12:22-24). The "Universal Headquarters" is also in heaven, which is Jesus Christ, the Head of the Church (Matthew 16:16-19; Ephesians 1:18-22). Christ alone is omnipotent, omnipresent, and omniscient and is thus qualified to be the Head of the Church. He alone is able to meet the needs of His people, everywhere, at all times (Matthew 18:15-20; 28:18-20).

2.   Government of the Church Local

Government of the Church local is also by Christ Jesus. But He Himself governs the Churches in various localities through local ministries.

One of the clearest revelations of Christ in the midst of His Church is the vision given to John on the isle of Patmos. Christ had already promised that "where two or three are gathered together in My Name, there I AM in the midst of them" (Matthew 18:15-20).

Now in Revelation 1:10-20 John sees the risen Christ "in the midst" of the seven golden lampstands which represented the seven Churches in Asia. Each of these were local Churches; Churches in cities as His light-bearers.

Christ addressed Himself to each of the "angel-stars", the messengers of each local Church. Each local Church received a distinct and separate letter. No letter was sent to "headquarters" or "Mother Church" to send out to the other Churches. Christ Himself spoke a word and ministered to each local Church in their respective city. These things were testified in the local Churches (Revelation 22:16).

No one Church had control over another Church. There was fellowship but no denomination formed out of these Churches. Each was under the sovereignty of Christ's Headship. Each was accountable to Him (Revelation 1-2-3). The same is true of every local Church in each city in the New Testament.

Each was locally governed. There was no central government. There was no central control. There was no earthly headquarters. Christ was THE HEAD of the Church, both universally and locally. He alone qualifies as the builder of His own Church. He alone is infallible and knows the need of each local Church, as well as the Church universally. How can any fallible man know such or be "head of the Church"?

The tragedy of Church History reveals how corruption set in and men as Bishops arose and took the place of Christ, usurping His authority and the sovereignty under Christ of the local Churches.

It would be profitable at this point to digress briefly into Church History and see how this corruption developed, both Biblically and Historically.

a. **Biblically — The Book of Acts**

1) **The Church at Jerusalem**

The original Church at Jerusalem was founded by Christ and the Twelve Apostles of the Lamb. Their names are in the foundation of the Bride City (Revelation 21:14).

There was multiple leadership, or plurality of leadership in the original Pentecostal Church order (Acts 2:14; 6:2). These Apostles were known as "the Twelve", twelve being the number of Apostlic government.

There were also Prophets at Jerusalem who ministered at Antioch (Acts 11:27-30).

There were also Elders in the Church at Jerusalem (Acts 15:6, 22; 21:17, 18). As the Church developed we see the Gospel spreading to both Jews and Gentiles and we see plurality of ministry at the various Churches.

2) **The Church at Antioch**

In due time the Gospel reached Antioch. Here we see a great Church established. Prophets and Teachers were in this Church, or, plurality of leadership (Acts 13:1-3).

From Antioch, Paul and Barnabas were sent forth and established Churches in the cities of the Gentiles. On their return visit these Apostles ordained Elders in every Church, by prayer, fasting and the laying on of hands (Acts 14:14, 21-23).

We note again the plurality of the eldership — not just one elder, but elders.

3) **The Church at Ephesus**

In the establishment of the Church at Ephesus, again we see multiple rule in the group of Elders. Paul, in Apostolic office, called for the Elders of the Church of Ephesus. He did not call for "the pastor", or "the bishop" or one ruling elder, but he called for the Elders!

Thus Biblical history shows that the Churches were under the rule and direction of multiple leadership, never just one person, never just one elder, whether he be called "Pastor", or "Bishop", or "Elder". It always involved plurality, or, a presbytery, which is a group of Elders.

b. **Historically — Church Decline**

The seeds of decline are seen in New Testament times and secular history gives evidence of the fruit in those seeds.

While the Twelve were alive, the Church maintained that plurality of Eldership, together ruling and caring for the flock of God.

It is the Apostle Paul who, in Acts 20, clearly saw the potential seeds of corruption and warned the Elders of Ephesus of the same. He also warned Timothy of the departure from the faith in the latter times (I Timothy 4:1).

In Acts 20:28-31 Paul forewarned the Elders of Ephesus of the twofold danger to the Church, the flock of God. He spoke of the wolves in sheep's clothing from *without*, and then of the dangers of Elders from *within*, who would seek to draw disciples after themselves, dividing the flock of God, and separating from the one fold.

Paul exhorted Timothy, who he had left at Ephesus, to warn certain Elders not to teach contrary doctrines (I Timothy 1:3, 4). He also told Timothy not to be in a hurry to ordain an Elder, to honour Elders but to rebuke those Elders before others if accusations of sin against them are justified (I Timothy 5:17-22).

It should be noted that Timothy is not a novice, but about 37-40 years of age at this time, as a study of his life will confirm. He is an Elder amongst other Elders.

It is the Apostle John who gives to us an indication of what was beginning to manifest itself in the Eldership at that period of Apostolic history, A.D.90.

History strongly suggests that John the beloved was at Ephesus in the last years of his life, after being released from banishment on the isle of Patmos. If this is so, then the significance of his third Epistle becomes weightier in the matter dealt with. This involved the commendation of two brethren, and the condemnation of one brother, named Diotrephes (III John 1-14).

It is evident that these brethren together had some position in the Church. The language is strong in denunciation of Diotrephes. He is characterized by the following:

★ He loved to have the pre-eminence amongst the brethren and in the Church.

★ He would not receive the apostles, or other travelling ministries.

★ He spoke against them with malicious words.

★ He forbad all others in the Church to receive any of these brethren.

★ He excommunicated from the Church any who did receive apostolic or other of the travelling ministries.

We might say that what happened here at "the Church" (III John 6, 9, 10) in Diotrephes shadowed forth that which happened in the history and decline of the Church after apostolic times.

Whereas Apostolic Churches had multiple rule, or plurality of Eldership, gradually ONE ELDER rose up, and, Diotrephes-like, assumed the pre-eminence in the Church over and above other Elders, and over that Church or over Churches. The Churches became ruled over by one Elder instead of a group of Elders.

Gradually there came a wrong distinction between the words "Bishop", "Elder" or "Presbyter", which is not to be found in the New Testament and which was not meant by the writers of the New Testament. Two distinct orders came into being during the second century.

Alex. Pattray Hay, in *"The New Testament Order for Church & Missionary"* (p.249), says:

"During the second century it seems to have become common for the Elders in a congregation to choose one of their number to preside over them, and to apply to him the designation of Bishop. Even then he was not considered as of higher rank, but simply "first among equals.""

Eusebius (A.D.300), writing of the time of the Apostles, used the terms Bishop and Presbyter interchangeably. This is the common writings of the early Fathers. However, with the subtle change of order and the change of meaning in similar words, we see the rise of the monarchial Bishop (spoken of a "monepiscopacy"), *above* and distinct from the Eldership. There came the rule of one Bishop in each of the congregations. He became the president over the other Elders. In due time, the ordinances of water baptism and the communion became invalid if such were not conducted by the Bishop.

The power of the Bishops over the Elders and congregation continued to expand in the third and fourth centuries. We see there not only the Bishop over a local congregation and over a city, but then the rise of metropolitan Bishops. These became Arch-Bishops, wielding great power over all and sundry.

As the Bishops took more power to themselves and became "Priests" of and for the people, believers lost their "priesthood ministry" and thus we have the creation of "clergy and laity", or a "priest-craft and people".

The Dark Ages, or, as Martin Luther aptly called it, "The Church's Babylonian Captivity", came into full focus for hundreds of years. Bishops were Priests, Elders were of lesser order or discounted and the congregations were robbed of priestly service to the Lord which was then done for them by a priest-caste. In principle, it was a horrible lapse back into the priesthood of the Old Covenant and Aaronic and Levitical order where only one tribe was allowed into priestly services and they did that on behalf of the other 12 tribes of Israel.

The New Covenant order is the priesthood of ALL believers, a royal priesthood after the Order of Melchisedek and not after the Order of Aaron (Hebrews 7; Revelation 1:5, 6; 5:9, 10; I Peter 2:5-9).

So the rise of the monarchial Bishop helped forward the subjugation of the priesthood of all believers, as well as the suppression of the ascension-gift ministries of Apostles, Prophets, Evangelists, Pastors and Teachers and New Testament Eldership.

Thus we see the failure in Church history in the fact that the Ecclesiastics made a distinction between "Bishops" and "Elders". The Bishops made themselves superior to the Elders and took the power over them and the local Churches. In time the Bishop of Rome became "the Bishop of Bishops", and then the local Churches were welded together under the One Holy Catholic Church, the Universal Church, under one Head, the Bishop of Rome. This is how the hierarchy came into existence.

As will be seen "Bishop" and "Elder" are one and the same (Philippians 1:1; I Timothy 3:1-2; Titus 1:5, 7). There is no Scriptural distinction between the "episcopos" and the "presbuteros". This pyramidal rise of power was contrary to Scripture. The word "Bishop" was of Greek City State origin. The word "Presbuteros" was of Jewish Synagogical origin (Luke 7:3). But both are one and the same person.

Each local Church was to be a completely autonomous unit, not subject to supervision of human agency be it Episcopal or Presbyterian. It is first of all subject to Christ THE HEAD, and then His delegated and appointed governmental gifts which He sets in the Church (I Corinthians 12:28).

Local Churches were welded into a Universal Church under the power of the city of Rome, and all Bishop/Elders were brought under the government of the Bishop and Church of Rome.

All of this was indeed contrary to the Scriptures and the revelation of the New Testament Church order.

How then were the local Churches governed by Christ? Our considerations bring us to the answer of this question.

G.   Government of the New Testament Church by Eldership

As has already been seen under Section B, concerning the Forms of Church Government, it seems that the Divine intention is to have the "three-fold cord" of Church government (Ecclesiastes 4:12). It is this which combines three Biblical points and provides for checks and balances in the government of any local Church. For the sake of orderly thought, we will consider (1) The Chief Elder, (2) The Multiple Eldership, and (3) Congregational relationships with the Eldership.

1.   The Chief Elder — First Among Equals

We submit this proposition for consideration.

"God's form of government is *theocratic in character*. That is to say, God *chooses, calls* and *equips* certain persons to be leaders and rulers over His people, investing and delegating them with *degrees of authority* according to His will. These persons are most commonly called *"Elders"*, and in any given group of Elders, God generally places *the mantle of leadership upon some one Elder*. This does not exalt this Elder above the other Elders but sets him in *responsibility* as *"First among equals"*.

a.   First the Natural

Nature itself, as also mankind, teaches the principle that some one must take the leadership. James Lee Beall in *"Your Pastor, Your Shepherd"* (pp. 109-118) says that setting up of government is seen even in the animal kingdom.

★   In the chicken yard, roosters establish leadership by subduing their opponents. It is called "the pecking order." The rooster who can outpeck all others is the undisputed head of the coop — that is until another arises who can outpeck him.

★   Animal with antlers, such as deer and moose, establish a horning order.

★   Sheep and goats have a "butting order" until leadership is established.

★   A flock of geese in flight always have a lead bird, the others following in formation accordingly. The lead bird takes the direction for the flock.

★   Sports and games which mankind plays always need leadership. Basketball, Football, etc. have to have organization, rules to govern, and leadership. Otherwise there is chaos and confusion, not sportsmanship.

Leadership is established in the animal kingdom in a beastly manner. Leadership is established among men in sports according to their ability to lead. People seek leadership. People select their own leaders. It is instinct to follow a leader. It reveals the need to be governed. If this need is not met then there is confusion and frustration. If men do not have leadership they will create it. Someone has to lead. Isaiah's times revealed this. When the mighty men had failed, they wanted to take someone to lead and be their ruler. The end result was that "children and women ruled over them". That is, immature and weak leadership took the lead (Isaiah 3).

People fear being left without direction (Ezekiel 13:7). Bad government is sometimes preferable to no government. Poor leadership is better than anarchy.

People will make their own leadership in order to be led. It is human nature to want government so bad that they will create their own. Human nature demands leadership of some sort.

Plato in *"The Republic"*, his great discourse on human government, describes the process of human government:

1) If there is no leadership, people select someone and nurse him to greatness.

2) In this time they call him their benefactor.

3) In time he changes from such to be a tyrant — self-serving now because of the deification by the people.

4) Tyranny now produces revolution.

5) People then pull him down from the pinnacle of power. The same society who nursed this leader to greatness will also pull him down.

This is what Jesus spoke about when He said the Gentiles have their "benefactors" who excercise authority upon them and lordship over them. But He said this was not the way it would be in the kingdom of God, among His leadership (Luke 22:24-27).

b. **Then the Spiritual**

Leadership in the Church is not arrived at by "the law of the jungle", i.e. "the survival of the fittest". This is not the way it is in the kingdom of God. Jesus reproved the disciples for the wrong motive and desire to exercise lordship and authority over the people as did the Gentiles (Luke 22:24-27; I Peter 5:3). It is because Christ Himself, as the risen Head of the Church, calls, equips and places His mantle of leadership on that person to lead the flock of God.

This person may be referred to as "bishop", or "chief elder" or "senior pastor", or "senior minister", or "presiding elder", "apostle", etc. But there must be leadership. We may say that "not every one can drive the bus, or the train." Final decisions for direction must be upon someone, otherwise there is confusion, frustration and lack of direction for the people of God.

We note this in the following:

1) **Christ The Chief Elder**

It is recognized that the Lord Jesus Christ is THE CHIEF ELDER above and among all other Elders (I Peter 2:25; 5:4). He is THE Chief Shepherd, and THE Bishop of our souls. He is THE sacrificial Lamb in the midst of the 24 Elders (Revelation 4-5). He is THE Apostle, Prophet, Evangelist, Pastor and Teacher. He is the fulness of the Godhead bodily. All the Divine nature, character, glory, attributes, grace and gifts are in Him in perfection (Colossians 1:19; 2:9; John 3:33-34). He is the Head of the Church, which is His Body.

2) **The Chief Elder in the Local Church**

Whilest recognizing that Christ is THE Chief Shepherd and Bishop, it is also evident from Scripture that, within a local Church, having plurality of Eldership, Christ will place a mantle of leadership upon some one elder to direct the people of God. This is done in conjunction with the multiple eldership, as the proposition presented at the beginning of this chapter shows.

★ Paul and Barnabas were spoken of as *"chief men among the brethren"* (Acts 15:22; 14:12). That is, they were both *leading* men, men of *command* with *official authority* (SC2233).

★ There were *"chief priests"* among the priesthood (Luke 9:22; 20:1).

★ There were *"chief* Pharisees" also (Luke 14:1).

★ There were *"chief* rulers of the Synagogue" (Acts 18:8, 17).

★ There were *"chief* apostles" also (II Corinthians 11:5; 12:11).

★ There were *"chief* musicians" in the Tabernacle of David who were also chief of the Levites (I Chronicles 15:22; Psalms 4, 5, 6 Titles).

★ Michael is called "*chief* archangel" amongst the angelic orders (Daniel 10:13).

So there should not be any problem in speaking of some one elder, upon whom God has placed the mantle of leadership, as "the chief elder", or "senior elder", etc. As long as this is not a "pride trip" in the person there should not be any problem, and as long as it is not a matter of giving a person "flattering titles" (Matthew 23:1-12; Job 32:21-22).

The thing that "the chief elder" has to beware of is that Diotrephes spirit and attitude, the desire to have the pre-eminence. He has to truly recognize that he himself is an Elder AMONG other Elders, and NOT an Elder ABOVE other Elders!

The thought of "*First among equals*" is illustrated in the very persons in the Godhead. The Father is the FIRST PERSON, the Son is SECOND, and the Holy Spirit is THIRD. However, Father, Son and Holy Spirit are equal as persons. For the purposes of creation and redemption, however, there is this order in the Godhead. The Father is indeed "first among equals". There is no competition, but recognition. Each person has distinctive function and ministry, yet are one in mind, will and judgment.

God has thus demonstrated in His own being the truth for man to follow. So it is with Christ. Christ is "the firstborn", "the firstbegotten", and, in relation to His brethren in the Church, He is indeed "first among equals". This is as to His humanity — not his Divinity. But He is the "firstborn among many brethren" (Romans 8:25-28).

a) **Old Testament Examples**

We note some examples from Old and New Testament as to "the chief elder" or the "first among equals", raised up and anointed by God to lead the people of God. These men may be used as types of Christ but even then we have THE LORD God, then "the set man" under Him, and the same continues in the New Testament, where we have THE LORD JESUS and "the set man" under Him.

★ Numbers 27:15-23. Moses, the leader of Israel, asks that God would "set a man" over the congregation of Israel so that they be not as sheep without a shepherd. There must be that "*set man*" appointed by God, that man with the mantle of leadership and direction upon him.

★ **Moses** and the Elders with him (Exodus 3:16-18; 4:29; 18:12-26; Deuteronomy 1:9-18).

★ **Moses** and Judges share burden (Exodus 18:17-26; Deuteronomy 1:14-17).

★ **Joshua** and the Elders with him (Joshua 7:6; 8:10, 33; 20:4; 24:1, 31; Judges 2:7-13). Joshua was "the set man" as Captain over the hosts of Israel. He was to bring them out and bring them in.

★ **Samuel** and the Elders (I Samuel 15:30). (Note — Not much record of Saul and the Elders under his reign!) (I Samuel 8:4). Samuel the Prophet and Eldership).

★ **Saul** and the Elders (What a failure in leadership!). I Samuel 15:30.

★ **David** and the Elders (II Samuel 5:3; I Chronicles 11:3; 15:25; 21:16). David was a King, Prophet-Priest, yet worked with the Elders as the Lord's anointed (Isaiah 55:1-3).

★ **Solomon** and the Elders (I Kings 8:1, 3; II Chronicles 5:2, 4).

★ **Josiah** and the Elders (II Chronicles 34:29).

★ **Ezra** and the Elders (Ezra 10:1, 8, 14). Ezra, the Scribe and Teacher Ministry.

★ **Ezekiel** the Prophet and the Elders of Judah (Ezekiel 8:1; 14:1; 20:1-3).

★ **The Chief or High Priest** and the Elders (Acts 24:1). The Jewish Sanhedrin consisted of 24 Priests, 24 Scribes, then 22 Elders, and then the one High Priest, making the Council of the Eldership. Thus Aaron, the High Priest, then the house of Aaron, and then the Levitical priestly tribe.

Thus in each case, we have various ministries of Prophet, Priest or King or Judge, and these men were "set men", raised up and anointed of God. Others recognized this mantle of leadership upon them. The safeguard was that the set men always worked in conjunction with other Elders, but each illustrate the principle of *"first among equals"*.

The Elders recognized this. The congregation recognized this also, but it was GOD who raised this "set man" up to leadership position.

b) New Testament Examples

The New Testament follows the same principle as set forth in the Old Testament relative to the "set man" and the plurality of the Eldership in the local Churches, even as exemplified in the local city Synagogues.

These men were "chief men", and recognized as leaders that had been "set in the body" as senior ministers.

★ **Peter** and the Elders (cf. Acts 1:15; 2:14, 38; 3:4-25; 4:8-12; 5:1-11). Peter was an apostle, but accepted as "first among equals". The keys of the kingdom were specifically given to him (Matthew 16:18, 19). In the Acts he is the one the Lord *first* used under the outpourings of the Spirit relative to both Jew and Gentile. Other apostles accepted it. There was no strife or lordship position or religious politics. Peter, as an Elder exhorts the other elders in his Epistle also (I Peter 5:1-4).

★ **James** and the Elders (Acts 12:17; 15:1, 2, 6, 13-22; 21:18 especially with Galatians 2:20). After Peter leaves, James becomes the senior shepherd at Jerusalem. James closes the council at Jerusalem over the Gentile problem.

★ **Paul** and the Elders of Ephesus (Acts 19:10-11; 18:11; 20:17-35). After being in Corinth for 18 months and Ephesus for 2 years, Paul calls for the Elders of the Church. They recognized the mantle of Paul's apostleship as leader.

★ **Timothy** and the Elders (I Timothy 3; Pastoral Epistles — Postscript). Timothy is spoken of as the first Bishop of the Church of Ephesus. There were Elders already at Ephesus. Timothy is left by Paul as "first among equals". He is not a novice, but a young man of about 40 years of age in this work.

★ **Titus** and the Elders (Titus 1:5; Postscript of Epistle). Titus, ordained the first Bishop of Crete, yet Paul told him to ordain Elders in every city and do the things he had left undone.
The same is true for Titus as for Timothy.

★ **Epaphroditus** with the Bishops and Deacons (Philippians 1:1; 2:25; 4:18). Epaphroditus was their "messenger" (apostle), and yet the Bishops and the Deacons were with him and addressed along with the saints at Philippi.

★ **Nymphas** and the Church in his house (Colossians 4:15). He was recognized as the leader and host with the House-Church.

★ **Aquilla and Priscilla** also had a House-Church (Romans 16:3, 4). These were recognized as teachers in the Body also.

★ **The Angel-Stars** of the 7 Churches in Asia (Revelation 1:11-20; with Acts 20:17). Revelation does not contradict Acts. There were Elders in the Church at Ephesus, yet the letter of John was addressed to "the angel-star" of the local Church.

★ **Christ,** the Chief Elder/Lamb in the midst of the 24 Elders around the throne, as "first among equals", ONLY as to the OFFICE of Eldership (Revelation 4-5).

(**Note** — Christ in His Sonship and Deity is above all and is the pre-eminent One, so we only speak of Him as "FIRST among equals" as to the office of a Bishop in His humanity).

Though no one man is especially designated "pastor" in Acts or the Epistles, yet some one person had the mantle of leadership and direction on them and worked closely with other Elders who provided checks and balances for him.

These were "chief men" (Acts 15:22). They were those who lead, who commanded, with official authority. They were chief men among the brethren. They were set men among the eldership and recognized as such.

3) **Plurality and Co-equality of Eldership**

Having seen that God does raise up leaders of His people in "the set man", what then is the safeguard against this man becoming a dictator or autocrat? What "checks and balances" does the Lord provide to prevent a monarchial Bishop from taking the pre-eminence as did Diotrephes (III John 9, 10)?

The answer is seen in the *plurality* or multiple eldership and the co-equality of such persons. These provide checks and balances for the "chief elder" who is "first among equals". He is first in leadership but certainly not exalted above the other elders.

The number of Elders in any local Church will depend on the enlargement of the flock of God. Smaller Churches may be governed by one Elder until the flock comes to increase. The number of Elders is basically determined by the need and by those who are qualified Scripturally to fulfil that office.

We consider both Old and New Testaments as to the plurality and co-equality of men called to be Elders. It should be noted that in relation to the New Testament local Churches the word "Elder" is always used in the plural form, even though no set number of Elders is mentioned. It is "Church" in the singular, not Churches. It is "Elders" in the plural, not Elder! The Old Testament shows this predominant plurality of Eldership in relation to the affairs of nations or the people of GOD whether Gentile or Israel.

The word "elder" in the Old Testament is used in plurality about 119 times and is used of "age" in *official* sense. Then the word "elder" used in singular about 24 times (elder, eldest) is used in *relational* sense.

The word "elder" is actually as old as the human race and the Bible itself and it is the most common and earliest known ministry of all.

a) **Old Testament Eldership — Plurality**

★ The Elders of Egypt (Genesis 50:7).

★ The Elders of Israel (Exodus 3:16, 18; 4:29; 12:21).

★ The 70 Elders of Israel (Exodus 24:1, 9, 14; Numbers 11:16-25).

★ The Elders of the Congregation (Leviticus 4:15).

★ The Elders of Moab (Numbers 22:4, 7).

★ The Elders of Midian (Numbers 22:7).

★ The Elders of the city (Dueteronomy 19:12; 21:2-6).

★ The Elders of the town (I Samuel 16:4).

★ The Assembly of the Elders (Psalms 107:32)

★ The Elders of Judah (Ezekiel 8:1).

★ The Elders, Scribes and High Priests (Matthew 15:2; 16:21; 26:3, 47, 57, 59; Mark 14; 43).

★ The Estate (Council) of the Elders (Acts 22:5).

★ The Elders who were patriarchs of the faith (Hebrews 11:2).

★ The Elders (Moral Law, Deuteronomy 4-5), the Judges (Civil Law; Exodus 18:13-26; Deuteronomy 12-16; 21:1-21), and the Priests of Israel (the Ceremonial Law, Deuteronomy 17-26).

Thus we have:

1) Elders of a House/Family (Genesis 50:7; Hebrews 11:2; II Samuel 12:17).

2) Elders of a Nation (Exodus 3:16-18; 4:29; 12:21; 17:5, 6; 18:12; 19:7; I Samuel 4:3).

3) Elders of the Sanhedrin (Exodus 24:1, 9, 14; Numbers 11:16-20).

4) Elders of the Congregation (Leviticus 4:15; Judges 21:16).

5) Elders of the Tribes (Deuteronomy 5:23; 31:28, 29).

6) Elders of the City (Deuteronomy 19:12; 16:18; 21:3-6, 19, 20; Judges 8:16; Ruth 4:2, 9-11; Ezra 10:14; I Samuel 16:4).

7) The Assembly of the Elders (Lit. "The Session, or Sitting"), Psalms 107:32. General use in New Testament speaks of the Sanhedrin (Matthew 27:3, 12, 41; Mark 14:43, 53; Acts 4:5, 8; 24:1; 23:14; 25:15).
See also Joel 1:14; 2:16.

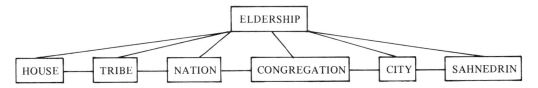

Thus all Elders had their areas of responsibility. The circle diagram may also be used to illustrate the Eldership responsibility according to enablements. The "Jethro Principle" certainly illustrates the need for and function of plurality of rulership in behalf of God's people (Exodus 18:13-27).

b) **New Testament Eldership — Plurality**

Of the approximately 69 uses of the word "Elder" in the New Testament, *twice* it is used in a *relational* sense (Luke 15:25; Romans 9:12), *seven* times it is used of an older person and/or elder in *official* sense (I Timothy 5:1, 2, 19; I Peter 5:1, 5; II John 1; III John 1), and about *sixty* times it is used in *official* sense in its plural form.

★ The relief money was sent to the *Elders* (Acts 11:30) in time of famine.

★ They ordained *Elders* in every Church (Acts 14:23).

★ The *Elders* in Jerusalem (Acts 16:4).

★ The *Elders* of Ephesus (Acts 20:17, 28).

★ The *Elders* of Jerusalem (Acts 21:17, 18).

★ The *Elders* are to rule (I Timothy 5:1, 17-21).

★ The *Elders* of the Church to anoint with oil and pray for the sick (James 5:14).

★ The *Elders* exhorted by Peter an Elder to oversee the flock of God (I Peter 5:1-5).

★ The *Elders* to be ordained by Titus in every Church and city (Titus 1:5).

★ Paul wrote to the *Bishops* and Deacons at Philippi (Philippians 1:1).

★ Believers are to obey *them* that have the rule over them (Hebrews 13:7, 17, 24).

★ Timothy was to make sure that *Elders* qualify for office (I Timothy 3).

★ The Lamb was in the midst of the 24 *Elders* (Revelation 4-5).
   This Priestly course was founded in the Tabernacle of David worship, as an order of Melchisedekian King-Priests unto God.

★ There were "prophets and teachers" at Antioch (Acts 13:1).

★ There were "prophets" at Corinth also (I Corinthians 14:29).

★ There were "prophets" at Jerusalem (Acts 11:27; 15:4, 6, 22).

★ There were "apostles and elders" at the Council concerning the Gentiles (Acts 15:1-5, 22, 23; 16:4).

★ A *presbytery* is a group of *Elders* in any given gathering (I Timothy 4:14). It is the order of Eldership.

Thus the New Testament Churches at Jerusalem, Antioch, Philippi, Thessalonica and Ephesus all show plurality of Eldership ministry and rule. Any given group of Elders in a local Church at any given gathering of Elders constitutes "the presbytery" at that place and time (I Timothy 4:14). The Greek word "presbuterion" used here means "Assembly of aged men, or Order of Elders".

It is "Elders" in the plural, and "Church" in the singular when dealing with the local Church.

The wisdom of God is seen in the plurality of Eldership because it:

1) Safeguards a Church from the rule of the one man, like Diotrephes, or a "monarchial bishop" (III John 9, 10), a spiritual dictatorship and autocrat;

2) Provides checks and balances in rulership, and

3) Makes a channel for the manifold wisdom of God to be released to the Body of Christ, the Church, and finally,

4) Provides multiple rule and feeding ministry in the local Church, as well as

5) Provides a covering and protection for all Elders.

c) **Co-Equality of Eldership**

Not only does the Old and New Testament show the *plurality* of Eldership, it also teaches the *co-equality* within that plurality of eldership. That is, no elder is to be exalted as a person above another elder. To do so is to violate God's own law and attitude to His people, for God is no respector of persons

(Romans 2:11; Acts 10:34; Deuteronomy 10:17; James 2:1-9). He does not show partiality or favouritism.

The New Testament writers recognized and accepted both *plurality* and *co-equality* amongst the Eldership. However, it is a co-equality of office and of elders as persons, but it is NOT a co-equality of Divine ability!

There is a variety of personality, degrees of spirituality and measures of God-given grace and ability within the Eldership. They are equal as persons, and equal as far as office. They are all Elders as persons! But there is difference of grace-gifts given to them by the risen Head, Christ.

We note this in the following:

★ Peter stood with the eleven as a co-equal apostle, at Pentecost (Acts 2:14).

★ Paul accepted Peter, James and John as three "pillars" in the Church at Jerusalem (Galatians 2:9) but did not exalt one above the other. They were fellow-apostles, fellow-elders.

★ Peter said he was an "elder" exhorting other "elders" (I Peter 5:1). He was a fellow-elder.

★ The 24 Elders in Revelation 4:4; 5:8-10 are all co-equal as fellow-elders and kings and priests unto God and all gathered around the Lamb in the throne of God.

★ Paul reproved the Corinthians for their carnality in exalting one ministry above another and glorying in men (I Corinthians 1:10-16; 3:21-23).

Thus all Elders are equal as persons and office. But there are differences of grace-gifts given to them which also have to be recognized.

Believers who see the *plurality and co-equality* of Eldership in the Church often let the pendulum swing to extremes on this matter and fail to recognize that amongst this kind of eldership God does set some elder as "first among equals".

They reject the concept of "chief elder" or "presiding elder" or "elder of elders" or "chief shepherd" through fear of depriving Christ of His place as THE Chief Elder and exalting some man above others. This fear can be healthy but needs to be balanced out by the Word of God on Eldership.

However, as noted previously, though there is co-equality as to office (all being "fellow-elders"), there is not equality as to *ability, responsibility, spirituality or grace-gifts!*

There will be different and various measures of the gifts of grace among the eldership as God wills (I Corinthians 12:1-31; Romans 12:1-8; Ephesians 4:9-16). The very fact that God has given a variety of ministry gifts, spiritual gifts and talents to the members of the Body of Christ confirms the truth of the same amongst the eldership. It is this fact that should be seen in the examples here of *plurality, co-equality* of eldership, yet an elder being *"first among equals"* by reason of Divinely given abilities and grace.

They were not set there as leaders of the rest because they were better than the others, but because GOD SET them there, equipping, anointing and enabling them to be "first among equals".

To whom much is given, more responsibility is upon them. To whom is given, of him will men require the more. He will be a responsible elder among elders (Luke 12:41-48).

The measure of *ability* is the measure of *responsibility*, which becomes the measure of one's *authority,* all of which is the measure of one's *account-ability* (Ephesians 4:6). One does not have authority or responsibility if there is no ability. One is only accountable for what one has.

The authority of an Elder is connected with his ability to feed the flock of God. The father in the home has authority as he is able to feed his family!

4.) The Relationship of Elders to Eldership

This matter will be dealt with more fully in *"Unity and Team Work of Ministries"* in a subsequent chapter. However, for the concluding sections of this chapter some thoughts need to be expressed as to the relationship of the chief elder and the other elders to each other.

For a plurality and co-equality of eldership to work and function as God intended, and also the chief elder among them, there must be principles in operation. Otherwise it will never work. These principles are manifested in the Godhead. Eldership must set the example before the Church of unity, teamwork, submission recognition.

★ Elders must have a personal relationship with the Lamb in the throne (Revelation 4-5).

★ Elders must have a personal relationship with each other as elders.

★ Elders must submit one to the other (I Peter 5:1-3).

★ Elders must maintain unity with others (Psalms 133). They must be joined together in the same mind, the same mouth, the same judgment (I Corinthians 1:10).

★ Elders must have the same spirit upon them as the chief elder (Numbers 11).

★ Elders must be examples to each other and to the flock of God (Acts 20:17, 31-35; I Peter 5:1-5). Paul was an example to the Elders of Ephesus.

★ Elders must take heed to themselves first (Acts 20:28-32).

★ Elders must watch that they do not draw disciples after themselves (Acts 20:28-36).

★ Elders must watch the spirit of lordship and abuse of authority among themselves (I Peter 5:1-3).

★ Elders must realize their safety is "in the cluster" (Isaiah 65:8).

★ Elders must be "joined in the spirit" (Numbers 18).

★ Elders must accept each other as to different personalities, etc.

★ Elders must be committed to each other.

★ Elders must maintain transparency, honesty and open communication.

★ Elders must maintain servant spirit (Mark 10:45).

★ Elders maintain recognition, not competition among one another.

★ Elders must be loyal to each other.

★ Elders must maintain a spirit of humility at all times (Philippians 2:1-11).

5) The Relationship of Congregation and Eldership

What then is the relationship of the congregation and the eldership? When Paul writes to the Philippian Church he addresses "the bishops and deacons WITH the saints" (Philippians 1:1). This constitutes New Testament Church order. Do the people have nothing to say in Church matters? Is all left to a "monarchial bishop" ("rule of one man"), or a hierarchy ("rule of the elders")? Or is there some part the congregation have as members of the priestly Body of Christ? The answer is in the affirmative. However, it needs to be clearly defined as to the part and areas that the congregation plays in the order of the local Church, otherwise all becomes a Democracy! The Church is not a democratic institution. It is not "the rule of the people". The Church is a Theocracy — "the rule of God through His appointed authorities".

It is because there has been the lack of checks and balances on leadership over the years that the democratic system of Church government arose. Hence, instead of government coming down from God through His leadership to the people, the people took the government into their own hands and appointed and thus controlled their own leadership.

a) **What the Congregation may not do**

According to the Scripture, the congregation may not do the following:

★ Appoint its own leadership by the democratic method, or "hire-fire" system.

★ Control the leadership as to the direction of the Church.

★ Control the finances of the Church as to its tithes and offerings. One could not see the Church in the Wilderness doing these things (Acts 7:38).

★ Take it into their hands to discipline leadership. This will be dealt with in the Chapter on "*Church Discipline*".

b) **What the Congregation may do**

According to the Scripture the congregation may do the following:

★ Pray for those who rule over them.

★ Submit themselves to their leadership and obey them as the leadership obey the Word of the Lord (Hebrews 13:7, 17, 24).

★ Consent and confirm matters of buildings/lands/extensions in the development of the Church property, especially as necessary for legal purposes.

★ Confirm the matters of Church discipline and excommunication on unrepentant members (Matthew 18:15-20; I Corinthians 5 are examples of such).

H. Overview of Forms of Government

Mr Jeff Harvey in "*The Biblical Church Pattern*" (pp.73-77, Un-Copyrighted Notes), in grappling with the three major forms of Church Government has set out an interesting comparison and contrast of each with what he understands to be the Biblical pattern of government. These comparisons set out here are worthy of consideration before the author's final SUMMARY of what he understands in the delicate balance in the "three-fold cord" of Biblical Church Government.

CHURCH GOVERNMENT

DENOMINATIONAL   OR   BIBLICAL

EPISCOPAL		BIBLICAL
1. The Elder becomes a priest or a clergyman. The Bishop becomes the ruler of the Elder.	—	1. The Elder and the Bishop are identical.
2. One Church with one Elder.	—	2. One Church with several Elders.
3. Pope, Cardinals, Archbishops etc., lead the whole Church.	—	3. The Five Ministries oversee the whole Church.
4. The Pope or Monarch, becomes the Head of the Church.	—	4. The Lord Jesus Christ is Head of the Church.
5. The Elder is ordained by the Bishop.	—	5. The Elders are ordained by the Presbytery.
6. Human system of government.	—	6. Divine order.

PRESBYTERIAL		BIBLICAL
1. Bishop and Elder identical.	—	1. Same.
2. Ordination by Presbytery.	—	2. Same.
3. Plurality of Elders.	—	3. Same.
4. Appointment from below.	—	4. Appointment from above.
5. Popular elections.	—	5. No popular elections.
6. Democratic.	—	6. Theocratic.
7. Distinction between ruling and teaching Elders.	—	7. No distinction: all Elders rule and teach.
8. Highest Court: appeal to man — General Assembly.	—	8. Highest Court: appeal to God.
9. General Assembly oversees the whole Church, i.e., that denomination.	—	9. The Five Ministries oversee the whole Church: no denomination.
10. Aaronic-style Priesthood.	—	10. Melchisedec Priesthood.
11. Human system of government.	—	11. Divine order.

CONGREGATIONAL		BIBLICAL
1. Bishop and Elder the same.	—	1. Same.
2. One man leadership.	—	2. Multiple leadership.
3. Popular elections	—	3. Eldership appoints.
4. Democratic.	—	4. Theocratic.
5. Ordination not required.	—	5. Presbytery ordains.
6. No outside interference permitted, as the Board has the final decision.	—	6. Open to Five Ministries for correction where necessary.
7. Each congregation sets its own doctrine, practices and standards.	—	7. Each congregation aligns itself to the Heavenly pattern.
8. Human Institution.	—	8. Divine order.

SUMMARY:

The "*threefold cord*" of (1) Chief Elder (or Bishop), and (2) Multiple Eldership (Presbytery), and (3) The Saints (or congregation) all working together in the Spirit of Christ is God's way of checks and balances in the government of the local Church.

It is recognized that the *Episcopal* (Monarchial Bishop), and *Presbyterial* (Council of Elders) and *Congregational* (Democratic) forms of government have worked in some measure or degree where the Spirit of Christ has been manifest. Government can never work with carnal people, only with spiritual people.

However, it is the Lord's desire that we aim towards the Divine ideal. But, even then, it is possible to have all the right form of government, as to the mechanics of it, and lack the life of the Spirit! It is possible to have organization and structure without organism, without life. Organization without organism makes all decent and in order — and dead!

With all our striving after the ideal, it is imperative that the Spirit of Christ, the spirit of grace, love and humility be manifested in every believers attitude. It is tragically possible to build "according to the pattern" and God never to put "the glory" there to seal it!

The government, after all, must be upon HIS shoulder (Isaiah 9:6-9).

In Conclusion:

1. The Presiding Elder or Bishop presents final decisions for the congregation and speaks as the voice of authority for the eldership as the "set man".
2. The group of elders confer and agree on the direction for the Church as the Church Council, the presbytery, acting as checks and balances.
3. The congregation consent, respond and confirm the major decisions of the eldership according to their area of responsibility.

This is how Church Government finds expression in the Local Church! The three valid streams or cords are brought together and "a three-fold cord is not quickly broken"(Ecclesiastes 4:12).

CHAPTER 16

THE OFFICE & MINISTRY OF AN ELDER

Introductory:

In our previous chapter we dealt with Church Government, especially as it is seen in the Local Church under God-ordained and Scripturally qualified Eldership. The Government is indeed upon "His shoulder" (Isaiah 9:6). But we see also that God has set in the Church governments (I Corinthians 12:28). The shoulder is part of the body, nearest the head. So government in the Church is nearest to Christ the Head. Government is a gift of God to certain individuals set in the Church. This has to do with Eldership especially who are called upon to rule in the Church (I Timothy 5:17; Refer Romans 12:8; Hebrews 13:7, 17, 24).

Government in the Early Church was first through Christ, then the Twelve, and then after that through Eldership and Deacons, as the need arose.

A study of the New Testament clearly shows that there are two offices set by God in the Church for the rule and service of His people. These two officers are ELDERS and DEACONS. The first pertains to ruling, the second to serving.

It should be recognized that there are basically two schools of thought pertaining to Eldership. One view holds that there are no Elders apart from or outside of the fivefold ministry of Ephesians 4:9-11. The other view holds that there are Elders who are not of the fivefold ascension-gift ministries. It holds that all ascension-gift ministries are Elders, but not all Elders are ascension-gift ministries. However, both schools of thought hold that ascension-gift ministries are Elders. All agree that these ministries should have the qualifications of Elders. Judas was a Bishop/Apostle, yet lost his ministry through transgression (Acts 1:20). Peter was an apostle yet also an elder (I Peter 5:1). The 24 Elders, or at least 12 of them are accepted, generally speaking, as apostles. Thus they are Elder/Apostles (Revelation 4:4). John the Apostle was also an Elder (II John 1:1; III John 1).

Many times people become "an offender for a word" (Isaiah 29:21). Words such as Bishop, Elder, or Deacon have been misunderstood and misapplied and associated with some bad experience and thus people are robbed of the truth of these words.

i.e. *Bishop*-Episcopalian Church/Order of the Bishops, Archbishops, or Pope, or Cardinals; Roman Catholic Church, or Episcopal Church.

i.e. *Presbyterian*-Eldership, with four Courts of Law, from (a) The Elders of the Local Congregation, and (2) Presbytery of Pastors only, and (c) The Synod and (d) the General Assembly of Elders.

i.e. *Deacon Board* Control with power to "hire and fire" and or else belittled in some Churches as to their ministry.

i.e. *Apostolic*-fivefold ministries of Ephesians 4:11.

Thus fear or failure rob God's people of accepting God's order in the New Testament. Hence the need of Jeremiah 1:10 in principle in order to receive ministry as God wants (Matthew 10:40-42). We bind those we do not receive as to the reward of their labour.

A. Definition of the Word

There are several words used in the Scripture which throw light on the meaning of the word "Elder" and also the ministry of an elder.

1. Old Testament

Hebrew *"Zaqen"* (SC2205) = "Old", translated "aged, ancient man, elder, eldest, old man, men and women, senator" (Genesis 10:21; 25:23; Deuteronomy 5:23; I Samuel 4:3; I Chronicles 11:3).

Chaldee, "*Siyb*" (SC7868) = "to become aged; old age", translated "elder" (Ezra 5:5, 9; 6:7, 8, 14).

The basic meaning of the word "Elder" as used in the Old Testament is referring to an older or old person, whether man or women. Therefore, it is not speaking of a young person, a novice in the wisdom of experience that generally comes with the years of time.

However, as will be seen, there is an interesting development of the role of elders even in the Old Testament used of the word.

2. **New Testament**

There are two especial words we need to consider when it comes to the definition of the word "Elder" in the New Testament. It should be remembered that the New Testament concept of eldership is basically a continuance of the Old Testament office, adapted to the local Church setting. These two words are "Elder" and "Bishop".

a. **Elder**

We note the Greek words and related words relative to Eldership.

1) **Presbuteros** (SC4245) = "elder, older person or a senior". Translated "Elder". It is applied several ways:

★ To an older person who is advanced in years, whether an older man or an older women, as senior (John 8:9; Luke 15:25; Acts 2:17; I Timothy 5:2; Philemon 9; Luke 1:18; Titus 2:2, 3).

★ To the Old Testament saints and patriarchs (Hebrews 11:2), and the Old Testament persons who formed the traditions which nullified the Word of God (Matthew 15:2; Mark 7:3-5).

★ To the official leaders of the Jewish people (Luke 7:3), whether of the local Synagogues or to the official Jewish Council called the Sanhedrin (Matthew 5:22; 10:17; 16:21; 21:23; 26:3, 47, 57, 59; 27:1, 3, 12, 20, 41; Luke 22:66; Acts 4:5-8; 6:12; 23:14; 24:1; 25:15; Mark 13:9; 14:55). Synagogue rulers are elders (Mark 5:22, 35; Luke 4:20; John 16:2; Acts 18:8).

★ To the officially ordained leaders of the New Testament Church or local Churches (Acts 14:23; 20:17, 18; I Timothy 5:1, 2, 17-19; Titus 1:5; James 5:14; I Peter 5:1).

This word appears 66 times in the New Testament, 12 of these being in the Book of Revelation.

2) **Presbuterion** (SC4244) = "Assembly of the aged men, or the Order of Elders".

★ It compares with Psalms 107:32 with the "assembly of the elders".

★ It is applied to the Council or Senate or Jewish Sanhedrin of the 70 Elders (Luke 22:66; Acts 22:5 [Estate of the Elders]).

★ It is applied to the group of elders in the local Church and is translated "Presbytery" (I Timothy 4:14).

It simply refers to any group of elders gathered together in session. The Presbyterian Church derives its name from this form of Church Government. This word occurs 3 times in the New Testament as seen above.

3) **Sumpresbuteros** (SC4850) = "fellow elders". Used only once in I Peter 5:1. Lit. A co-elder. Peter is an elder, a co-elder with the elders in the Church.

b. **Bishop**

We note the Greek related words concerning Bishops.

1) **Episkopos** (SC1985) = "an overseer, a superintendent, guardian". In the Greek it is compounded of two words. i.e., the preposition "*epi*" meaning "over",

and the word ''*skopos*'' meaning ''to look or watch, to peer about, to oversee'' (SC1909 and 4649).

The word is used 5 times in the New Testament and is translated:

★   Overseers (Acts 20:28).

★   Bishops (Philippians 1:1; I Timothy 3:2; Titus 1:7; I Peter 2:25).

It speaks of a Christian officer in general charge of a (or the) Church. Thayer says ''an overseer, a man charged with the duty of seeing that things to be done by others are done rightly, any curator, guardian or superintendent''. Vine says ''in the Christian Churches, those who, being raised up and qualified by the work of the Holy Spirit, were appointed to have the spiritual care of, and to exercise oversight over, the Churches.''

Wuest comments that ''the word came originally from secular life, referring to the foreman of a construction gang, or the supervisor of building construction, for instance.''

The Episcopal Church emphasizes this form of Government by its very name.

2) **Episkope** (SC1984) = the noun form of ''episkopos'' ''inspection (for relief); by implication, superintendence, specifically the Christian ''episcopate'' — the office of a bishop. It is translated:

★   Bishoprick (Acts 1:20)

★   Bishop (I Timothy 3:1).

★   Visitation (Luke 19:44; I Peter 2:12).

It has to do with inspection, visitation, investigation, the office of oversight.

3) **Episkopeo** (SC1093) = verb form of above, ''to oversee; by implication, to beware''.
Translated: ''looking diligently'' (Hebrews 12:15), and ''take the oversight'' (I Peter 5:2).

A careful study of these words in the following Scriptures show that there is a close connection between them and that they speak of one and the same office. Some have tried to make distinction between them, exalting one above the other and thus creating an unScriptural orders of Bishops and Elders.

Several of the Greek authorities show that ''Elder'' refers to the man, and ''Bishop'' refers to the office.

It has also been said that the word ''Elder'' has a Hebrew background whereas the word ''Bishop'' has a Greek background, yet both are descriptions of the same person with the same office. There is no thought of elevation one above the other in the use of these words.

These Scriptures confirm this fact.

★   Paul called for the ''elders'' (Greek ''presbuteron'') of the Church of Ephesus and said they were ''overseers'' (Greek ''episkopos''), Acts 20:17, 28, telling them to ''feed'' (Greek ''Poimaino'', shepherd, pastor) the Church of God.

★   Paul told Titus to ordain ''elders'' (Greek ''presbuteros'') in every city, and laid out the qualifications for these ''bishops'' (Greek ''episkopos''). Titus 1:5, 7.

★   Peter, who was an ''elder'' (Greek ''presbuteros'') spoke to the ''elders'' (Greek ''presbuteron'') and told them to ''feed'' (Greek ''poimaino'', shepherd, pastor) the flock of God, ''taking the oversight'' (Greek ''episkopeo'', Bishoprick). I Peter 5:2.

Hence an Elder is a Bishop and a Bishop is an Elder. The ELDER is the MAN, having maturity of experience, not being a novice. The BISHOP is the OFFICE or position he holds. SHEPHERDING or PASTORING is the WORK he does.

His status is Elder or Presbyter.

His duty is Bishop or Overseer.

His function and work is Pastor, Shepherd.

Vine says that the term "elder" indicates the mature spiritual experience of those so described; the term "bishop" or "overseer" indicates the character of the work undertaken.

Thus Elder, Bishop, Shepherd speak of one and the same person. It refers to the ministry of watching over, guiding, feeding, ruling, teaching and exerting protective care over the sheep by God's appointed leaders.

The *Elders* were to watch over as *Bishops* and tend and feed as *Shepherds* the flock of God.

B. Eldership in the Scriptures

1. Eldership in the Old Testament

This has already been mentioned rather fully in the Chapter on "*Church Government*" but we repeat some of those things again in this section.

The thought of eldership is very prominent in the Old Testament. A consideration of these following references reveal a progressive development of the concept of eldership from Patriarchal Eldership to Political and Ecclesiastical Eldership. These elders were men of age, of experience and of authority. Sometimes great men are not always wise, and younger sometimes are (Ecclesiastes 4:13; Psalms 119:99).

Thus we have:

a.   Elders of Pharaoh's Household (Genesis 50:7).

b.   Elders of the Land of Egypt (Political office) — Genesis 50:7; Proverbs 31:23.

c.   Elders of Moab and Elders of Midian (Numbers 22:7).

d.   Elders of Israel (Exodus 3:16, 18; 4:29; 12:21; 17:5, 7; 18:12; 19:7; I Chronicles 11:3; 15:25).

e.   Seventy Elders of the Elders of Israel (Exodus 24:1, 9, 14; Numbers 11:16-30; II Chronicles 19:8-11); shadowing forth the Sanhedrin.

f.   Elders of the Congregation (Leviticus 4:15).

g.   Elders of the Tribes (Deuteronomy 5:23).

h.   Elders of the Cities (Deuteronomy 19:12; 21:1-20; 22:15-18; 25:7-9; Judges 8:16; Ruth 4:2; II Samuel 19:11; Ezra 10:14).

i.   Elders of the Priests (II Kings 19:2; Isaiah 37:2).

j.   The Assembly of the Elders (Psalms 107:32).

It is evident that the Eldership here involved Patriarchal (Household), National (Israel, Moab, etc.), Tribal (Tribes), City Official (Cities), and Ecclesiastical (Priests) Eldership!

Eldership was involved in every area of the national and spiritual life of Israel. Israel was God's Kingdom, God's Church, and therefore it can be expected that God's government of Eldership should be seen (Exodus 19:1-6; Acts 7:38).

These things become types and shadows of the New Testament Church and New Testament Eldership also (I Corinthians 10:6, 11).

Though noted in the New Testament Gospels, the order of Eldership before the formation of the New Testament Church is still that of the Old Testament order. The Gospels refer to the Chief Priests, Scribes and Elders or the Council, which was the Jewish Sanhedrin who brought about the death of Messiah (Matthew 16:21; 26:3, 12, 20, 41; Mark 14:43, 53; Matthew 5:22).

The Sanhedrin consisted of 70 Elders plus a President or Presiding Elder. The order was as follows:

1) The High Priest — The Presiding Elder or President of the Council.

2) Twenty-four Priests — The redemptive ministry of the Temple, the heads of the 24 Courses of the Priests.

3) Twenty-four Scribes or Lawyers — The Official Interpreters of the Law.

4) Twenty-two Elders — Representatives of the people, the laity, from the local Synagogues.

Thus we have 70 Elders and the High Priest as Presiding Elder, "first among equals".

The tragedy of this Council was evidenced in the rejection and crucifixion of Prince Messiah, even as Christ Himself had foretold (Matthew 22:35; 23:1-33; Luke 5:30; 10:25).

The concept and function of Eldership is carried over from the Old Testament into the New Testament Church, with certain modifications, because of the emphasis on the locally governed Church, and not that of national government as under the Old Testament Israel of God.

2. **Eldership in the New Testament**

It is in the New Testament, especially in relationship to the Church that the thought of Eldership is more fully developed.

As the following references show, the concept of Eldership is similar to that of the Old Testament, but limited more especially to a local Church in a city.

There were:

a. Elders ordained in every Church (Acts 14:23; 20:17). Acts 14:23 is the first mention of Elders in a New Testament Church.

b. Elders ordained in every city (Titus 1:5).

Israel, as the Old Testament "Church in the Wilderness" (Acts 7:38) was one nation in Palestine for years. Because of this there were Elders of Cities, Elders of the Tribes, Elders of the Congregation and Elders of the Nation.

However, the New Testament Church is universal in its scope, yet local in its geographical expression. Hence the Elders in New Testament times were elders of a Church in any one city where a Church was established.

They were City-Church Elders. This constituted a Presbytery, the assembly or order of the elders (I Timothy 4:14).

It must be remembered that these elders were never elders *over* Churches but elders *in* local Churches. And there was never *one single* elder in or over a Church, but always *plurality* of elders acting as checks and balances against lordship. Together these elders "pastored" the flock of God. However, as already noted, someone must have indeed presided as "first among equals" (Acts 20:28; I Peter 5:2).

We note the Eldership in plurality in some of the following Cities and Churches.

★ **Church at Jerusalem**
Peter an apostle with the other eleven apostles — Acts 1:14.
They continued in the apostles doctrine — Acts 2:42. Plurality.

They laid money at the apostles feet — Acts 4:35.
The apostles and elders gathered together for counsel — Acts 15:2, 4, 6, 22, 23.
The apostles and elders wrote — Acts 16:4.
James and all the elders — Acts 21:18.

★ **Church at Antioch**
Certain prophets and teachers — Acts 11:19, 27; 13:1-4.

★ **Church at Ephesus**
Paul, Aquilla and Priscilla — Acts 18:18, 19.
Elders of Ephesus — Acts 20:17.
Elders that rule — I Timothy 5:17.

★ **Churches of Cilicia**
Ordained elders in all the Churches-Acts 14:23.

★ **Churches in Crete**
Ordained elders in every city — Titus 1:4, 5.

★ **Churches in Judea**
Barnabas and Paul sent with relief money to the Elders (Acts 11:29, 30).

★ **Churches of Pontus, Galatia, Cappadocia, Asia and Bithynia**
Elders to be ensamples to the flock (I Peter 5:1-5).

★ **Elders of Church** — Pray for sick (James 5:14).

★ **Twenty-four Elders** — Around the throne of God and the Lamb (Revelation 4:4).

★ **Them** — Obey, submit and salute them that have the rule over you (Hebrews 13:7, 17, 24).

Thus always plurality of Eldership in the Churches. Co-equality, plurality, authority, yet a first among equals in the eldership.

Thus Old and New Testament confirm the fact of plurality of Eldership and that Eldership was God's form of government over His people.

C. The Qualifications of an Elder

We come now to the important matter that makes an elder an elder. What is it that qualifies him to be an elder over the people of God?

The New Testament, especially the writings of Paul, clearly show that Elders must be qualified men before being accepted into public office. How much chaos and tragedy has ensued in the Church over its history because of having unqualified men in the office of an elder or bishop.

No one can expect the congregation to have confidence and respect for the Eldership unless these men qualify for this holy office. The emphasis is more on character than charisma, though both are necessary.

Although many of the qualifications may and should apply to all Christians, an Elder MUST have these qualifications. They are not optional. In Titus 1:7; and I Timothy 3:2, 7, the word *"must"* is used in connection with the eldership qualifications. The word means "it is necessary, or it is binding."

Ministry and offices in the secular world do not deal with or necessarily demand *moral or spiritual* qualifications. God does. Many firms may desire character and reputational references and academic qualifications. But God demands moral and spiritual qualifications for ministry in the Church. Ministry of Conservation, Ministry of Education, Ministry of Planning, Ministry for the Arts, Ministry for Consumer Affairs, Ministry of Housing, Ministry of Immigration and Ethnic Affairs, and Ministry of Water Resources and Supply can be unregenerate, immoral, etc., but not an Elder in the Church of Jesus Christ!

Other persons can be Doctors, Lawyers, Solicitors, Teachers, Educators, Managers, Members of Parliament and not be spiritual or moral. But one cannot hold office or ministry in the Church, God's Community, without certain qualifications laid down by the Lord Himself in His Word!

Church members should feel secure in qualified persons, who are examples to the flock of God. Husband, Wife and Children of Elders and Deacons households should be example houses to all others in the Church of God.

If any man *desire* (SC3713), "reach out after, long for, to covet, to stretch oneself" the office of a bishop, he should seek to qualify. It speaks of a deep inward drive or impulse to equip oneself for the ministry of an elder.

It is a "good work" (I Timothy 3:1). An excellent task. It is not a desire for a title or *office* position, but *WORK*! Cf. Matthew 23:1-12; Job 32:21, 22. Not flattering titles. The office is work! As long as one is functioning in the office and working he is such. It is not holding titular power, or power of a title.

Undoubtedly the lists given by Paul in Timothy and Titus are not exhaustive but they do cover implicitly in their definitions other related qualifications. It will be seen also that the qualifications of both Elders and Deacons are similar, hence all qualifications listed here are drawn from both, as also from that of the wives.

From the foundation of Christian experience laid down in the Gospels, and through the Acts on into the Church Epistles we note these qualifications.

The definitions of the words are taken from Greek Dictionaries as well as various translations and recognized English Dictionaries (Webster's, Westminister and Collins English Dictionaries).

For the sake of convenience, these qualifications are grouped into four major categories. However, it should be recognized that such cannot be held in any hard and fast manner as Paul flows them into each other. Any person desirous to excel in office as an elder will certainly seek to qualify in every way.

* We have what Paul says about Elders in Acts 20:17-32; I Timothy 3; Titus 1.
    * We have what Peter says about Elders in I Peter 5.
        * We have what James says about Elders in James 5:14, 15.

The qualifications will cover the following order:

1. Spiritual qualifications — check on spiritual life.
2. Character qualifications — check personal and secular life.
3. Domestic qualifications — check married life, wife, children and home life, and neighbours.
4. Ministry qualifications — functional life in the Church.

The Character, Charisma and Conduct of an Elder must be related, otherwise his witness and ministry is nullified.

It is worthy to note other translations of these qualifications as listed in the given Scriptures.

a. Spiritual Qualifications

The following qualifications should hardly have to be mentioned. However, many Denominational groups ordain Elders (and Deacons) without these spiritual qualifications, doing it on the basis of good character, reputation or business ability. There are certainly unregenerate people who have certain good character qualities as well as moral, but they have not been born from above. As such they are disqualified from holding office in the Church in God's mind.

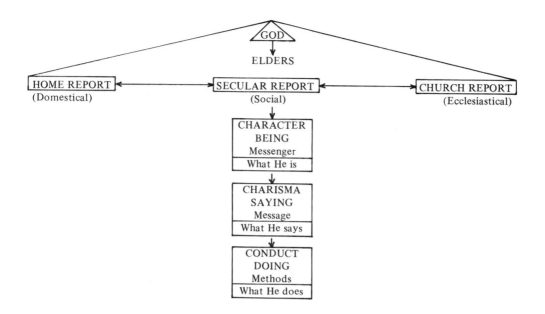

1)   An elder *must* be born again, born of the Spirit, born from above (John 3:1-5).

2)   An elder must have followed the Lord in obedience to His Word in the waters of baptism (Mark 16:15-20; Acts 2:37-47). He cannot lead others in obedience to the Word that he himself has not obeyed.

3)   An elder must be baptized and filled with the Holy Spirit (Acts 2:1-4; Ephesians 5:18). How can an elder lead and direct the Church without the continual filling of the Holy Spirit?

4)   An elder must be *made* an overseer by the Holy Spirit. Ministry and people will recognize this fact and confirm it (Acts 20:28).

These spiritual qualifications are foundational experiences that place one in the Church. One can be a member of a denomination without these things, but one cannot be a member of the New Testament Church without such. One must be ''added to the Lord'' first, then ''added to the Church'' (Acts 5:14; 11:24; 2:41, 47).

b.   **Character Qualifications**

The character qualifications listed here should be evident in all believers. But for the Elder and Deacon these things *must* be evident in order to qualify for office.

1)   **An Elder must be blameless** (I Timothy 3:2; Titus 1:6).

Having unquestionable integrity, irreproachable. Not able to find fault with, or deserving of censure. The conduct of an elder must be an example to the flock of God and free from the taint of scandal and accusation. He is to be above reproof, rebuke or reprimand (Galatians 2:11; Philippians 2:15; II Peter 3:14; II Corinthians 6:3). No charge should be brought against him, no guilt laid on him because of his Christian life.

Amp. Give no grounds for accusation, but must be above reproach.
Phillips — Must be of blameless reputation.
Knox — Must be one with whom no fault can be found.
Might and possibly will be blamed but must not be guilty (Matthew 27:12, 24; Mark 14:56; Luke 23:14).

2) **An Elder must be of Good Behaviour** (I Timothy 3:2).

Modest, orderly, disciplined, respectable life-style. Honourable, dignified, decorous, good deportment, not forward, boastful, arrogant, presumptuous (I Timothy 3:15). Well behaved.

Adam Clarke — orderly, decent, grave and correct in the whole appearance, carriage and conduct.

3) **An Elder must be Vigilant** (I Timothy 3:2)

Wide awake, watchful; not careless, sleepy, indifferent, lethargic. Think of a Watchman (Ezekiel 3:17-21; I Peter 5:80. Greek Lit. To be sober, abstinence in respect to wine, wary, cautious, circumspect and clear headed as opposed to the effects of alcohol on a man (sleepiness, numbness, unclear thinking). A thoughtful person.

4) **An Elder must be Temperate** (Titus 1:8)

Denotes keeping oneself in hand, self-controlled, disciplined, self-restraint, able to govern oneself in all respects, in passions, in spirit (Galatians 5:23). Self-controlled over appetites and affections. Strong in a thing, masterful, free from extremes and excesses, moderation. (Romans 12:14; I Corinthians 9:25; I Timothy 3:2).

A man not in bondage to himself or desires of the flesh.

5) **An Elder must be Sober** (Titus 1:8; I Timothy 3:2)

That is, sober-minded, prudent, sensible, discreet, having a sound mind. Not given to fanciful thinking or emotional irrationality. Using sound judgment. A disciplined mind. Gravity without sadness (Titus 2:2; 6:4, 12; I Peter 1:13; Romans 12:3; I Peter 4:7; 5:2; I Thessalonians 5:6; Acts 26:25).
Sane, subdued, thoughtful, not irrational, cautious.
Orderly, discreet, prudent.

6) **An Elder must be Just** (Titus 1:8)

Righteous, equitable, upright, straight, exact, conscientious, impartial in all his dealings, as a Judge in court. Not only being in right standing before God but also doing right before God in dealings with other people. Right conduct. Fair and impartial. Able to make objective judgments based upon principle.

7) **An Elder must be Holy** (Titus 1:8)

Being devout, pious, pleasing God and set apart for His services as opposed to being carnal and not totally dedicated to God.

Not abusing the grace of God, but believes, teaches and practices holiness of life, without which no man can see the Lord. Holy in thought, word, and deed, as He is holy (I Peter 1:15, 16; Hebrews 12:10, 14).

Devout, separated from sinful lifestyle.

8) **An Elder must be a Lover of Good** (Titus 1:8)

Lover of good things, persons, truth, righteousness, activities; not of evil or questionable things, etc.

Philippians 4:8. Whatsoever things are good . . . Promoter of virtue.

9) **An Elder must be Hospitable** (I Timothy 3:2; Titus 1:8)

Fond of guests and kind to people who they receive into their houses. A help to strangers (Hebrews 13:2; I Timothy 5:10; Matthew 25:34-40). Receiving and entertaining strangers without reward. Generous, liberal, bountiful; not niggardly or unsociable.

Fond of guests, enjoys the company of others, especially believers (Mark 6:31; Proverbs 25:17). Willing to receive strangers (I Peter 4:9).

10) **An Elder must be Patient** (I Timothy 3:3)

Gentle, kind, considerate, forbearing, longsuffering, quality of endurance, perseverance (I Thessalonians 2:7; 5:14).

Mild disposition, ability to remain calm, tolerant, forbearance, possessing quiet endurance under stress or annoyance. Tranquil (II Timothy 2:24).

11) **An Elder must not be a Brawler** (I Timothy 3:3)

Not quarrelsome, not contentious, but peaceable. Does not strive, not argumentative and not a fighter (Titus 3:2; Proverbs 21:9; 25:24).

Kind, conciliatory, uncontentious.

12) **An Elder must not be soon Angry** (Titus 1:7)

Not prone to anger or quick tempered, cranky, or irritable. Not contentious, provoking to dispute, petty fights, wrangle, wrath, rage, fury, wild, irascible. One can be angry and sin not if of Divine origin (Ephesians 4:32).

One who can control his own spirit, not quarrelsome, not selfish argumentation.

13) **An Elder must not be a Striker** (I Timothy 3:3; Titus 1:7)

Not violent, combative, or pugnacious. Does not revile or smite, hit or lash back with hand or mouth. Not a quitter (I Peter 2:23).

Not pugnacious, but gentle. Not given to physical violence, but one characterized by forbearance and tenderness. Not a fist fighter. Not belligerent.

14) **An Elder must not be greedy of Filthy Lucre** (I Timothy 3:3; Titus 1:7)

Not after money as an hireling, thief or robber (I Timothy 5:17, 18; 6:9-10; I Peter 5:2; Acts 20:17-25). Not after financial gain. Not acquiring money by dishonest means or acquiring dishonest money by any means. Not having a Judas spirit, Ananias or Sapphira, or Simony spirit — examples of judgment for greed of filthy lucre (Matthew 27:3-5; Acts 5:1-10; 8:18-24). Not the Achan spirit (Joshua 7:21).

Free from the love of money (Psalms 119:36). Not fond of sordid gain, or stingy with material blessings.

15) **An Elder must not be Covetous** (I Timothy 3:3)

Not controlled by unlawful desires or lusts, not avaricious. Not greedy. Covetousness is the root sin (Romans 7:7; Exodus 20:17; Deuteronomy 5:21; Acts 20:33). Can covet money, position, power. Covetousness is idolatry (Ephesians 5:3; I Corinthians 5:9-11).

Not a lover of money — insatiable desire for wealth and ready to obtain it by questionable means. Amp. New Testament.

Money in the ministry must never be the motivation or the major factor upon which you base your decisions (Matthew 6:33; I Timothy 6:6-11). Not crave to be rich. Hireling spirit.

16) **An Elder must not be Self-willed** (Titus 1:7)

Self-willed, given over to ones own will, not willing to surrender to anothers will. Self-will caused Lucifer to fall (Isaiah 14:12-14). Angels fell through self-will (II Peter 2:4). Adam and Eve also. Root and essence of sin is self-will. Man's freewill must be surrendered to God's good and perfect will (Romans 12:1, 2; II Peter 2:10; Daniel 11:36; Ephesians 5:17). Take heed to self (Acts 20:28).

Not arrogant, stubborn, overbearing, self-pleasing, self-conceited, ego-centric, but one who is in submission to God's authority and seeks harmony with the will of other Elders submitted to God's will.

Not headstrong, obstinate, disregard for other, unyielding, insistent. It includes self-love, self-seeking, making self the centre of all. Set on having ones way, inflexible. Not an insensitive person, forcing his own ideas and opinions on others.

17) An Elder must not be given to Wine (I Timothy 3:3)

Lit. Not tarrying at wine or staying near wine, and quarreling as drunks do (Titus 1:7). Not addicted to wine, not a drunkard, not a winebibber, prone to intemperance. Not actual intoxication (Proverbs 20:1; 4:7; 21:17; 23:29-35; 31:4-6; 23:20; Ephesians 5:18).

To drink (liquor) repeatedly in small amounts (especially strong drinks) = tipping. Not addicted to wine.

Note — The total Biblical revelation is negative against drinking of wine.

18) An Elder must be of Good Report (I Timothy 3:7)

Having an excellent testimony and reputation with those outside of the Church (i.e. the non-Christian community). This includes the areas of business, community relations and secular and civil law. An elder must be a respected person in his secular work, as well as neighbourhood and Church work. Outsiders should think well of him. He should have a good witness, a good record. An example to and in the community. Good reputation with those outside the Church. Unbelievers should respect his character and integrity.

19) An Elder must be Grave (I Timothy 3:8, 11; Titus 2:2, SC 4586).

Venerable, i.e., honourable; honest.

20) An Elder must not be Double-tongued (I Timothy 3:8)

Not twofold, acting two parts, saying one thing to the face and meaning another thing behind the back. Linked with double-dealing, double-faced, double-minded, two-tongued. Unstable, unsettled in mind and word, unwilling to stand by his word.

21) An Elder must not be a Slanderer (I Timothy 3:11)

Greek "Diabolis", like the Devil who is a slanderer of God and His people. Slander = To give false report, to injure another by uttering falsehood, to defame, villify, scandalize.

"To tell the truth in such a way as to give the lying (false) impression" Charles Finney.

22) An Elder must be Faithful in all things (I Timothy 3:11)

Reliable, trustworthy, honest, dependable. Opposite to faithlessness, dishonesty, hypocrisy.

Old Testament Elders were men of faith (Hebrews 11:1, 2, 39).

23) An Elder must be a Steward of God (Titus 1:7)

A steward is a manager of a household (Greek "Oikonomos"). An elder is a manager of God's household, a servant employed to manage the affairs of God (I Corinthians 4:2; Luke 12:42; 16:1, 3, 8; Romans 16:23; Galatians 4:2; I Peter 4:10). This must be seen in his own house *first*, then God's house!

24) An Elder must desire this Office (I Timothy 3:1)

That is, not in a covetous way as struggling and striving for position and recognition, but to stretch after it, be zealous to qualify for it and willing to face the responsibility thereof.

Taking office is accepting the oversight work of the flock of God (I Peter 5:2).

25) An Elder must not be a lord over God's people (I Peter 5:1-3)

Not to be domineering, or dictatorial over God's people, exercising spirit of "lordship" as the Gentiles do over their people.

Not to control, subjugate, exercise dominion in overbearing way (Mark 10:42-45).

26) An Elder must be an Example to the flock of God (I Peter 5:3)

A specimen, a pattern, follow by practising what one preaches (I Corinthians 11:1; Philippians 3:17).

Tupos = a die (as struck), i.e., by implic. a stamp. A model for imitation, a style or pattern (I Timothy 4:12; I Peter 2:21; Ephesians 5:1).

c. Domestic Qualifications

We come to the qualifications of the home life of an Elder (and/or Deacon). These have to do with the household, the wife and the children and we set them out accordingly.

1) The Husband

a) An Elder must be able to Rule his own house well (I Timothy 3:4)

An elder must preside over and manage his own household in an excellent manner. The ruling aspect includes the concept of concern, caring, management of family members, finance, material possessions, etc. It is the good conduct of the affairs of the family and their overall direction. Should be a household of faith. How can he preside and manage the affairs of the house (Church) of God unless he can his own house, which is a type of the Church (I Timothy 3:4, 5:15). His house must be in order to have the Church in order and vise versa.

To rule is to direct, manage, lead, and give aid as superintendent. It means to preside, maintain, be over. The order of ones house in the areas of neatness, cleanliness, orderliness and harmony. Head and governor of his own house. "If a man know not . . ." vs 5.

A man's household can disqualify him for this high and holy office.

b) An Elder must be the Husband of One Wife (I Timothy 3:3; Titus 1:6)

Not necessarily to be married, but if married, an elder must be married to one wife. Not a bigamist, or polygamist. One-wife sort of husband. This includes in itself Christian morality; no fornication, or adultery or any immoral behaviour.

(Note — It does not specifically involve divorce and/or remarriage).
An elder's house needs to be in order as he is to be given to hospitality. It then becomes an example household. One who supervises, manages, governs as a father presiding in his home.

2) The Wife

a) An Elder's wife must be Grave (Titus 2:2; I Timothy 3:8, 11)

i.e. Venerable, honourable, honest, grave. The wife can disqualify her husband from office. A Deacon's wife must have these qualifications; so it is implied that the Elder's wife also qualify.

b) **An Elder's wife must not be Slanderous**

Greek "Diabolis". Like the Devil, slanderer of God and His people. Slander = to give a false report, injure another by defaming, uttering falsehood, villify, scandalize. Charles Finney. "To tell the truth in such a way as to give the false (lying) impression."

An elder's wife has to watch her tongue also.

c) **An Elder's wife must be Sober** (I Timothy 3:2; Titus 1:8)

Discreet, sober minded, sensible, sound mind. Not given to fanciful or emotional irrationalities. Sound judgment. Disciplined mind. This is the kind of wife an elder needs.

d) **An Elder's wife must be Faithful in all things**

Reliable, trustworthy, dependable; opposite to faithlessness, unreliable, not dependable (I Timothy 3:2, 11).

3) **The Children**

Children are a reflection of their parents. "My parents do this . . ." Children follow the parents they admire, and do what they do, more than what they say. The qualifications for an elder's children are laid down in I Timothy 4:4, 5, 12; Titus 1:6. Children can disqualify their parents from office also.

a) **An Elder's children must be in Subjection** (I Timothy 3:4, 5)

Family life is open for inspection. Minister's children, often are the worst behaved children and bring reproach on the elder and the Church as well as on Christ Jesus.

Subjection = Holding or keeping his children under control, in obedience, submission, subordination. "Keeping his children under control, with true dignity, commanding their respect in every way and keeping them respectful. Amp. New Testament.

The children must respect their father and accept him as leader of his household.

b) **An Elder's children must have Gravity** (I Timothy 3:4, 5)

Gravity = seriousness without sadness, true dignity, respect, reverence, venerableness.

c) **An Elder's children must be Faithful** (Titus 1:6)

Believing children, or children who believe in Jesus Christ as their own personal Saviour. Elder's children should be Christians. "Whose children are (well trained and are) believers." Amp. New Testament.

Trustworthy, trustful children, reliable, believing children, dependable, inspiring trust or faith (Acts 16:1).

d) **An Elder's children should not be accused of Riot** (Titus 1:6)

Riot = unrestrained behaviour, uproar, disturbing the peace, highly excited, rowdy, behaving wildly, debauchery, abandoned to vice; the opposite to peace and quiet.

Elder's children should not be open to the charge of being wild or loose in morals or conduct, but should be examples to other children. They should not be accused or have a criminal charge against them.

There should be no reason to excuse their conduct.

e) **An Elder's children must not be Unruly** (Titus 1:6)

Unruly = lawless, disorderly, insubordinate, rebellious, uncontrollable, badly behaved, not subject to, without rule.

An elder's children should not be undisciplined, disobedient, independent, unsubdued or rebellious. They should be obedient, and respectful to proper authority whether it be Civil or Church authority. This should be seen in their home life under their parental authority. Children who obey quickly and quietly.

d. **Ministry Qualifications**

The function and ministry of an Elder will be covered more fully in time but sufficient for the moment is to note those qualifications mentioned in Timothy and Titus and Acts.

1) **An Elder must be called by the Holy Spirit** (Acts 20:17, 28)

Unless the Spirit calls, it is no use man striving or man calling. Paul said to the Elders of Ephesus that the Holy Sprit had made them overseers of the flock of God. They were not self-appointed or man-appointed Elders. The ministry and congregation accept and confirm those whom the Holy Spirit makes Elders.

2) **An Elder must hold fast the Faithful Word as he has been taught** (I Timothy 3:9; Titus 1:9).

He must hold the mystery of the faith. That is, not to be shaky in doctrine, but stedfast in the Word of God, the faith once delivered to the saints, the apostles doctrine (Jude 3; Acts 2:42). He must cling to, be devoted to the faithful Word.

3) **An Elder must be able to Teach** (I Timothy 3:2)

Skilled in teaching, instructive. Having been taught an Elder must be able to teach and instruct others. He must teach the apostles doctrine (II Timothy 2:2). Apostles and Elders together settled the doctrinal disputations in the Book of Acts (Acts 15:4, 22).
Apt to teach = "able to teach, to teach in a skilful manner."
"To be a capable and qualified teacher" (Amp New Testament).
Able = to be powerful, strong and mighty in teaching the Word.
Thus he needs to know the Word if he is to teach others.

4) **An Elder must be able to Exhort and Convince** (Titus 1:9)

An Elder should be able to exhort = to admonish, encourage, summon, appeal to, by sound doctrine and also to convince = convict, reprove, correct and convince those who oppose and speak against true teaching.

"Able to give stimulating instruction and encouragement in sound (wholesome) doctrine and to refute and convict." Amp. New Testament. (John 3:20; 16:8; Ephesians 5:11, 13; I Timothy 5:20; John 8:9, 46).

5) **An Elder must not be a Novice** (I Timothy 3:7)

Greek "Neophyte", or newly planted one. Not a beginner, a probationer, not a new convert, a young convert or newly one come to the faith.

Novice in knowledge, wisdom, understanding and inexperienced in the things of the Spirit and Word and dealing with people. Great danger of pride and self-exaltation in novices (I Timothy 3:6; Proverbs 18:16; 13:10; 16:18). It is worthy to note that in the Old Testament the ages for the call and the ministry of God ranged from 20 years (Warfare), and 25 years, and 30 years (Joseph, David, Priests, Ezekiel, Jesus), and then in the New Testament Timothy and Titus as young men (about 40 years when Paul wrote to them in Epistles).

6) **An Elder must be able to Shepherd the flock of God** (Acts 20:28).

This will be spelled out in more detail under **The Ministry & Function of an Elder.**

D. **The Probation of Elders**

A consideration of I Timothy 3:8, 10 shows the similarity of qualifications of Elders and Deacons. The elders must be qualified according to verses 1-7, AND *"likewise"*, or in like manner the deacons must be qualified as in verses 8-13. Concerning deacons, Paul say, "And let these *also* first be proved", *then* let them use the office of a deacon (vs 10).

Just as there is a period of probation — a proving time — for the deacons, it is implicit that there be a period of probation *also* for prospective elders. It takes a period of time to prove people.

Probation = tried by experiment, tested as to genuineness before using the office. Investigated, proving time. Amp. New Testament.

Elders could be "proven" in Deaconship. Philip the Evangelist (Eldership) first served as a Deacon in Jerusalem in the early Church (Acts 6:1-8). The principle here is worthy of consideration, for, how can a person *rule as an elder* who has not *first served as a deacon?* They rule best who have learned to serve first! God's first principle is generally to prove those He uses. i.e.,

Joshua proved himself as a servant under Moses.
Elisha proved himself as a servant under Elijah.
Timothy proved himself as a servant under Paul.

Note also Judges 7:4; Deuteronomy 8:1-3, 15-17; Exodus 15:25; Psalms 17:3; 81:7; 95:9; II Corinthians 8:22; I Thessalonians 5:21.

Elders and Deacons should be proved, tried by experiment, tested as genuineness before using the respective offices.

E. **The Term of Office for Eldership**

Elders were never voted in or out by the people as in a democracy. They were not in office for one or more years. Their term of office for eldership is for life unless they Scripturally disqualify themselves, or resign or die. If unable to be active, then their wisdom is always available to the Church.

F. **The Ordination of Elders**

Paul and Barnabas "ordained elders in every Church" they had established (Acts 14:23).

Paul also told Titus to "ordain elders" in every city as he had appointed him (Titus 1:5).

Paul also told Timothy "Never be in a hurry to ordain a presbyter" (I Timothy 5:22, Moffatt's).

Ordination means "the public setting apart of a man to the ministry, or the solemn induction by the Church into the pastoral office the one chosen to be the pastor" (H. A. Kent).

False concepts of Ordination teach that the person receives superior ecclesiastical authority or power and special rights to exercise the ministry. The Bible concept is that the person is set aside for the office of Christian ministry according to:

1. Divine Sovereignty — The call of God on a man. It is God who ordains through Christ, otherwise ordination is null and void.

2. Human Responsibility — The ministry and the Church recognize this call and confirm this before the Church in the Scriptural manner.

3. The word "ordain" means "to place down (SC 2525) permanently; to designate, to constitute (Hebrews 5:1; 8:3; I Corinthians 9:14; Galatians 3:19; Acts 1:22; 10:42; 13:48; 16:4; 17:31).
    ★ Jesus ordained the Twelve before sending them out to preach (Mark 3:14; John 15:16. SC 5087). He made them apostles by appointing them to this office.
    ★ Paul was ordained a preacher and teacher (I Timothy 2:7. SC 5087). God placed or set him into the ministry.

★ Paul and Barnabas ordained elders in every Church (Acts 14:23. SC 5500). The Greek thought is "to vote by stretching forth or out the hand." Appointment by uplifted hand. Handstretcher, Reacher.

Congregation can stretch forth their hand in confirmation — not in the sense of voting by democratic vote, which is unScriptural.

★ Titus was told to ordain elders (Titus 1:5, SC2525. "To put, set, or appoint").

Thus Divine sovereignty and human responsibility is involved in the ordination of Eldership to office.

4. The Ordination Service may take the following suggested order:

a. **Devotional Word**

The Elder is receiving "a charge" before the Lord. Greek "Parangelia", a mandate (SC 5853). It means "to transmit a message, by implic. to enjoin." It is from the base of SC 32 "angelos" — to bring tidings, a messenger. Thus Joshua was given "a charge" before Israel and inducted to Office (Numbers 27:11, 19, 23; Deuteronomy 1:16, 18).

Paul gives Timothy various "charges" in his Epistle also (I Timothy 1:3, 18; 4:11; 5:7, 21; 6:13, 17; II Timothy 4:1).

The charge was before (1) God the Father, and (2) The Lord Jesus Christ, the Son, and (3) The Elect Angels, (4) The Presbytery, and (5) The Congregation (I Timothy 5:21; 6:13; II Timothy 4:1; I Timothy 4:14, 16).

b. **Fasting**

Elders were men who sought God in fasting times (Acts 14:23) and were ordained during such time. An Elder should be a fasting person, keeping the body under subjection and in strong spiritual relationship with the Lord for his responsibility.

c. **Prayer**

Accompanied with fasting Elders were ordained in prayer (Acts 14:23). The importance of prayer is seen in Acts in all of the activities of the Church.

d. **Imposition by Laying on of Hands of Apostles** (Acts 14:23)

Not voted in by the Church, or chosen by people as Deacons, but Church recognizes and confirms them by outstretched hands.

Laying on of hands is both Old and New Testament order. Identification, devotion to God, setting apart for service to God and the people of God is involved in this service. Leviticus 3:2, 8, 13; 4:4, 29; 16:21; Numbers 8:12; Mark 5:23; 16:18; Acts 8:17-19; 13:2-3; 19:6.

★ Jacob blessed his sons by laying on of hands (Genesis 48-49).

★ The Israelites laid hands on the sacrifices (Leviticus 1-7).

★ Aaron and his sons were ordained to ministry by imposition of hands (Exodus 29; Leviticus 8; Numbers 18; 8:5-22). So also the Levitical tribe by the laying on of hands of the twelve tribes.

★ In the Day of Atonement offering also hands were imposed (Leviticus 16:21).

★ In the execution of offenders and capitol punishment hands were laid upon the guilty one (Leviticus 24:14).

★ Moses appointed Joshua as his successor by imposition of hands (Numbers 27:18-23).
Joshua is set before Moses, before the Priest, before the Congregation, as hands are laid upon him and he is given a charge.

★ Jesus blessed children (Matthew 19:13-15).

★   Healing of the sick by hands laid on them (Matthew 9:118; Acts 5:12).

★   The reception of the Spirit by imposition of hands (Acts 8:17-19; 19:6).

★   In the appointment of Deacons (Acts 6:6).

★   In the impartation of spiritual gifts (I Timothy 4:14; II Timothy 1:5).

★   In the ordination of Elders (Acts 14:23; Titus 1:5).

★   Upon the Apostle Paul (Acts 9:3-17; 22:7-16; 13:1-4).

★   Upon Timothy (I Timothy 4:14-16; Acts 16:1-3; II Timothy 1:6; I Timothy 1:18-20).

e.   **Presentation and Acceptance by Congregation**

Numbers 27:15-23. So did Moses as he laid hands and charged Joshua to be the shepherd of the flock of God. Joshua would lead the people in and out, and go before them into the land of promise.

G.   **Relationship of Elders and Ministries**

It is important that Local Church Elders understand their relationship to any travelling or visiting ministries also and vice versa.

1.   **Apostles and Elders**

In the early Church, the 12 Apostles were the governmental and foundational ministries. In due time the government was turned over by the Apostles to the local Elders.

Thus in Acts we see ''the Apostles and the Elders'' working together in harmony by the Word and the Spirit. Apostles were also Elders but were the chief ministries among the Eldership. Acts 15:2, 4, 6, 22, 23; 16:4; 21:18.

Paul was a founder-apostle-elder, yet he turned the Churches over to local Elders and then worked through and with them in due time (Philippians 1:1). Apostles are Elders when in the local Church, but when sent forth by the Eldership they fulfill their Apostleship from this local Church (Acts 13:1-4; 14:4; I Peter 5:1; II John 1; III John 1). Thus Peter was an Apostle/Elder; John was an Apostle/Elder, and so was Paul.

2.   **Elders and Apostles**

As noted, in due time, the government of the Church under the original 12 Apostles, and also Paul, was turned over to the Eldership. The Elders from then on pastored the flock of God. The Elders could refuse an Apostle entry to their local Church at any time, to their gain or loss.

The Lord actually commended ''the angel'' of the Church of Ephesus for trying those who said they were Apostles and finding them liars (Revelation 2:1-6).

Even Paul the Apostle depended, not on his external control of the Church or Churches, but on the Corinthian believers themselves as a congregation to deal with the fornicator (Cf. I Corinthians 5:13).

And when he came to Ephesus he called for the Elders of the Church (Acts 20:17).

Thus Apostles, or other visiting ministries, work with the local Elders and the local Elders work with proven ministries the Lord sends to them.

H.   **Relationship of Elders and Deacons**

Paul wrote to the saints at Phillipi greeting the Bishops and Deacons. It shows that there was a good relationship between these offices (Philippians 1:1). There can be nothing more devastating to a local Church than a competitive spirit between these two offices of Eldership and Deaconship.

These things destroy a Church. For, if there is not a spirit of love and unity evident in action amongst the Elders and Deacons, how can it ever be in the Body of Christ. The example should be here. Both Elders and Deacons, whether ruling or serving should have the people of God at heart, to serve and bless them. The same principles as seen in "*The Relationship of Elders to Eldership*" in Chapter 15 on "Church Government" are applicable here in the relationship of Elders and Deacons.

The ruling and serving ministries are there for the people of God, not for the office or position of power for themselves.

I. **The Ministry and Function of the Eldership**

1. **Old Testament Eldership**

   The responsibilities of Elders in the Old Testament seemed to fall into two major categories; that belonging to the Elders who handled *legal and social* matters, and that belonging to the Elders who handled *spiritual and ceremonial* matters.

   a. **Elders over Legal and Social Affairs**

   Recorded laws of Israel show that the duties of these Elders included:

   1) Bringing murderers to trial (Deuteronomy 19:12; 21:1; Joshua 20:4).

   2) Punishing by death stubborn and rebellious sons (Deuteronomy 21:19).

   3) Punishing a person guilty of slander (Deuteronomy 22:15).

   4) Penalizing a man for non-compliance with the Levirate marriage law (Deuteronomy 25:7).

   5) Enforcement of the law (Deuteronomy 27:1).

   6) Conducting a service in expiation of unwitting violation of the law (Leviticus 4:13).

   7) Choosing and counselling of kings (II Samuel 3:17-21; I Kings 12:6-8, 13).

   8) Ratifying covenants (II Samuel 15:3).

   9) Legislation of reforms (Ezra 10:8-14).

   In the time of Christ the members of the Sanhedrin or Council of Elders handled both legal and spiritual matters, although Rome limited their power to execute the death penalty.

   These duties have since passed into the hands of the Civil Government and associated authorities in our society.

   b. **Elders over Spiritual and Ceremonial Affairs**

   The Scriptures also show that there were Elders who concerned themselves with the spiritual and ceremonial affairs of the people.
   Their duties involved the following:

   1) Teaching and instruction of the Scriptures (Deuteronomy 33:8-11; Malachi 2:1-10). The Levites were the teaching priests (II Chronicles 15:3).
   In later times there were Elders of the Synagogues who read and instructed the people out of the Scriptures.

   2) Prayer for the people, dedication of children and also priestly blessings (Numbers 6:24-27).

   3) Receiving tithes and offerings for the Temple priests, the Temple tax for upkeep of buildings, and offerings for distribution and support of the priesthood.

   4) Receiving and offering of gifts, sacrifices and oblations of the people upon the altar of God and making the reconciliation for the sins and the trespasses of the people.

   The ceremonials of the law, and the order of the Aaronic and Levitical Priesthood have been fulfilled and abolished, but the ministry continues on into the New Testament Church in the spiritual order of Melchisedek.

2. **New Testament Eldership**

Paul says that ''if a man desire the office of a Bishop, he desireth a good *work.*''

The work of the Elders in any Local Church may be seen in the following things. All will function according to the measure of the gifts and/or talents of eldership given to them by Christ, the Head of the Church (Matthew 25: 14-30; Luke 12:41-48; 19:11-26).

a. **Ruling the flock of God** (Hebrews 13:7, 17, 24; I Timothy 3:4, 5; 5:17; Romans 12:8; I Thessalonians 5:12-14; I Peter 5:2, 3).

b. **Teaching the flock of God** (Hebrews 13:7; I Timothy 5:17; Titus 1:9; I Timothy 3:2; II Timothy 2:2).
    Labouring in the Word and doctrine (I Corinthians 16:16; I Thessalonians 5:12).

c. **Shepherding the flock of God** (Acts 20:17, 28; I Peter 5:2; John 21:15-17).

    It is to guard and protect the sheep from wolves, feed them green pastures, lead beside still waters and lay down one's life for the sheep (John 10 with Ezekiel 34).

d. **Overseeing the flock of God** (Acts 20:28; Titus 1:7; I Peter 5:2, 3).

    To take the leadership, direction, watch over, care for, and superintend the flock of God. Watch for wolves from outside, and the ''Diotrephes'' spirit from inside among the Eldership.

e. **Caring for the flock of God** (James 5:14, 15; Ezekiel 34; Jeremiah 23:1-5).
    Care for the sick, healing, lost, straying, wandering, bruised sheep.

f. **Governing the flock of God** (I Timothy 5:17; I Corinthians 12:28; Isaiah 9:6; II Peter 2:10).
    Government of the local Church needed by Eldership. Responsible for the souls of the people, and that God's house is well governed.
    Watch for divisionary things (Romans 16:17, 18; Colossians 2:8, 18; I Corinthians 1:10-16; Acts 15:22-31).

g. **Living for the flock of God** (John 10; Ezekiel 34; Jeremiah 23:1-5).
    The shepherd lays down his *life* for the sheep. It is not just a job, but a life calling.

h. **Safeguarding the flock of God from False Ministries** (Acts 15; Revelation 2:2; Acts 2:42; 16:4, 5; I Timothy 4:1).
    Many false ministries travel around seeking sheep to devour. The true Eldership will guard the flock from false ministries and prove any they allow in to minister to their people first. Beware of mixture of seed in the vineyard of the Lord (Leviticus 19:19; Deuteronomy 22:11).

Thus the Eldership have their work before the Lord and will have to give an account to the Lord for the sheep He entrusted to them. They desire to do this with joy and not with grief (Hebrews 13:7, 17).

J. **Responsibility of Congregation to Eldership**

Although Elders are not perfect, yet they are God's established authorities over His people. Elders have their responsibility to the people and people have their responsibility to the Eldership also. If Elders need discipline, then it will be carried out in God's way according to I Timothy 5:19, 20. People can ''make'' or ''break'' their Eldership according to their attitude and reception of them in their God appointed offices.

1. The congregation should know and should have proved them (Revelation 2:2).

2. The congregation should appreciate them highly in the Lord (I Thessalonians 5:12, 13).

3. The congregation should honour and reward them. If possible they should be supported by tithes and/or offerings.

    In the Old Testament the Levites were supported by the tithes and offerings of the people (Genesis 14:20; Leviticus 27:30-33; Numbers 18:21-24, 25, 26; 27:30; 10:15).

    The tithing system was before the Law, confirmed under the Law, and also under Grace by Jesus (Matthew 23:23).

    The ox that treads out the corn should not be muzzled. i.e., The Elder who treads the corn of the Word should not be robbed (Deuteronomy 25:4; Malachi 3:9, 10). At times a minister supports himself by his own hands, as did Paul (I Corinthians 9:1-19; I Timothy 5:17-18).

4. Do not accept accusations against an Elder without witnesses (not just accusers) I Timothy 5:19.

5. Obey them and submit to them in the Lord (Hebrews 13:17).

6. Call for them when sick (James 5:14, 15).

7. Continue stedfastly in the doctrine they teach (Acts 2:42).

8. Pray for them (Ephesians 6:18-20).

9. Expect those who sin to be disciplined openly by the ministry (I Timothy 5:20). Leave the judgments to the Lord and the ministry. Do not criticize them. Remember Miriam (Numbers 12), and Korah (Numbers 16; Psalms 106:32, 33). (The subject of "*Church Discipline*" is dealt with in a separate chapter and deals with discipline of members and ministries).

CHAPTER 17

THE MINISTRY AND FUNCTION OF THE DEACON

Introductory:

The second office in the Church, along with the Eldership, is that of the Deacon. Paul writes "to all the *saints* in Christ Jesus which are at Philippi, with the *bishops and deacons.*" Philippians 1:1.

The New Testament knows no other offices than these two. The three groupings of God's people spoken of here are "Saints", with "Bishops" and "Deacons", ruling and serving the Body of Christ.

"They that use the office of a Deacon . . ." (I Timothy 3:13).

There is much confusion about this office, as to qualifications and responsibilities. Some have them as Ministers of the Gospel, others have Arch-Deacons, some as Board of Directors, or over Almsgiving. This office has been taken to extremes by under-rating or over-exalting it.

The Roman Catholic Church looks upon Deacons as inferior ecclesiastic, second in the sacred order, and with the Bishops permission may preach and even baptize. The English Church look upon such as clergymen, the lowest grade, who may perform all the offices of priests, except consecration of the sacred elements and pronouncing absolution.

German Protestant Churches have an assistant minister called Deacon; if there is two then the first is called the Arch-Deacon.

In the Presbyterian Church this office is commonly merged with the ruling Elder, thus Deaconship is mostly disused.

In the Methodist and Episcopal Church in the U.S.A., it is basically the same as the English Church.

In the Baptist Church, the Deacons are the Board of Directors and control the secular affairs of the Church, and most times "hire and fire" the Pastor. However, as will be seen, most of this is absolutely contrary to the Scriptures and the original intention and institution of the diakonate as in the Book of Acts.

A. **Definition of the Word**

There are several Greek words transliterated in the Bible which shed light on the meaning of the word "deacon".

1. **Diakonos** = "A servant of the people, a waiter, attendant, servant or a minister." (Noun used 30 times in Greek Text).
    It is translated:
    Deacon, 5 times; Servant, 7 times. (Matthew 22:13; 23:11; Mark 9:35; John 2:5, 9; 12:26; Romans 16:1).
    Minister, 20 times. (Matthew 20:26; Mark 10:43; Romans 13:4; 15:8; I Corinthians 3:5; Galatians 2:7; Colossians 1:7, 23. etc.).

2. **Diakonia** = "A service or ministry to the people" (Noun used 34 times in Greek Text). The Service. "Service or attendance as a servant".
    K.J.V. translates this word: ministry (16), ministration (6), ministering (3), serving (1), relief (1), office (1), service (2), administration (2), do service (1), to minister (1).

    Refer to Luke 10:40; Acts 1:17, 25; 6:1, 4; 11:29; 12:25; 20:24; 21:19; Romans 11:13; 12:7; 15:31; I Corinthians 12:5; 16:15; II Corinthians 3:7-9; 4:1; 5:18; 6:3; 8:4; 9:1, 12, 13; 11:8; Ephesians 4:12; Colossians 4:17; I Timothy 1:12; II Timothy 4:5, 11; Hebrews 1:14; Revelation 2:19.

3. **Diakoneo** = To serve the people, to be an attendant, to wait upon (Verb, 37 times in Greek Text). The Act of serving.

K.J.V. translates this word: minister unto (15), serve (10), minister (7), administer (1), use the office of a deacon (2), minister to (1).

Matthew 4:11; 8:15; 20:28; 25:44; 27:55; Mark 1:13, 31; 10:45; 15:41; Luke 4:39; 8:3; 10:40; 12:37; 17:8; 22:26-27; John 12:2, 26; Acts 6:2; 19:22; Romans 15:25; I Corinthians 3:3; 8:19-20; I Timothy 3:10, 13; II Timothy 1:18; Philemon 13; Hebrews 6:10; I Peter 1:12; 4:10-11.

These words basically mean "servitude to others", "to act as a ministrant, a servant, to wait, an attendant."

The word is used in an *unofficial sense* of household servants and of the many ways that people minister and serve one another. And it is used in an *official sense* of those appointed specifically to "the Church office of a deacon" (Philippians 1:1; I Timothy 3:10, 13).

B. The Spirit of a Deacon

Jesus Christ, as the Head of the church, gave us the supreme example of Deaconship. This was because he had the *spirit* and attitude of a Servant. Christ is THE DEACON, THE SERVANT one amongst us. He came not to be ministered unto but to minister and give His life a ransom for many. He came to serve and act as a Deacon (Mark 10:42-45; Romans 15:8).

He said to the 12 apostles that they would be great if they *served* one another. "Whosoever will be great among you, let him be your *minister* (deacon)" (Matthew 20:25-28).

All members of the Body of Christ, regardless whether they be Elders or Ascension-gift ministries, Deacons or Saints, should have a *servant attitude*, the *spirit* of a servant (I Kings 12:6, 7).

By love serve one another (Galatians 5:13; Ephesians 4:12).

Thus we (1) Serve the Lord (Hebrews 12:28), and (2) Serve one another (Galatians 5:13).

All should have the *spirit* of a deacon, though all will not have the *office* of a deacon. The Body of Christ is primarily a serving Body, ministering as priests to the Lord and to one another.

C. The Office of a Deacon (I Timothy 3:10, 13).

We note the word "office" used of both elders and deacons in verses 1, 10, 13. Funk and Wagnalls define the word "office" as "A particular duty, charge or trust; an employment undertaken by commission or authority; a post or position held by an official or functionary; specifically, a position of trust or authority under a government."

Such is the office of a Deacon in the Church.

D. The Qualifications of a Deacon

The qualifications of a Deacon are very similar to those of the Elder. These are listed from Acts and Timothy again here, in brief, with several additional thoughts. However, the reader should refer back to the qualifications of the Elder for fuller amplification of these qualities.

We consider these in the following order:

★ Spiritual Qualifications
★ Character Qualifications
★ Domestic Qualifications

1. Spiritual Qualifications

a. A Deacon must be born again, born of the Spirit (John 3:1-5).

b. A Deacon should have followed Christ in baptism (Acts 2:38).

c. A Deacon should be filled with the Holy Spirit (Acts 2:1-4; 6:3; Ephesians 5:18). Not only the baptism but continually filled with the Spirit.

d. A Deacon should hold ''the mystery of the faith'' in a pure conscience and maintain a clear conscience before God and man (I Timothy 3:9, 13).

e. A Deacon must be full of wisdom (Acts 6:3). It is needed continually.

f. A Deacon must be full of faith (Acts 6:3).

Note that Stephen and Philip surfaced out of the diakonate to be ministry and evangelist with a signs-following ministry (Acts 6:8; Acts 7-8).

Unbelief has no place in the diakonate.

2. **Character Qualifications**

a. A Deacon must be grave (I Timothy 3:8, 11).
Venerable, reverent, dignified, sincere in spirit, serious minded (Titus 2:2, 7).

b. A Deacon must not be double-tongued (I Timothy 3:8).
James 1:8; 4:8; I Chronicles 12:33; Psalms 12:2. He must not be given to talk in twofold manner by gossip, saying one thing to one person and then another to someone else. Dangerous if tongue not under control (James 3).

c. A Deacon must not be given to wine (I Timothy 3:8).
Not a drunkard or given to excesses.

d. A Deacon must not be greedy of filthy lucre (I Timothy 3:8).
Titus 1:7, 11; I Timothy 3:3; I Peter 5:2. Beware of covetousness or love of money, in handling tithes and/or offerings, etc.

e. A Deacon must be blameless (I Timothy 3:10).
Nothing to accuse, above reproach (I Timothy 5:7).

f. A Deacon must be of Honest Report (Acts 6:3; 16:1-2).
Timothy was well reported of by the brethren. Deacons should have good report of neighbours, employees and business world.

3. **Domestic Qualifications**

a. **The Husband**

1) A Deacon must be the husband of one wife (I Timothy 3:12). Not a bigamist. Not an immoral person in any way.

2) A Deacon must be able to rule his own house well (I Timothy 3:12, 15). How can he serve in the house of God if his own house is not ruled?

b. **The Wife**

1) A Deacon's wife must be grave (I Timothy 3:11). That is, reverent.

2) A Deacon's wife must not be a slanderer (I Timothy 3:11).
Applicable to Deaconness also. Not ''Diabolis'', devilish, evil account, accusers like Satan (Proverbs 10:18; Psalms 101:5). Satan is a whisperer, a gossiper, against God and His Word, and brought about the Fall of Eve. Wives can disqualify their husbands from office.

3) A Deacon's wife must be sober (I Timothy 3:11).
That is, sound mind and judgment, sensible, self-controlled, watchful, of a disciplined mind.

4) A Deacon's wife must be faithful in all things (I Timothy 3:11).
Faithfulness is required. Reliability, dependableness.

c. **The Children**

1) A Deacon and wife must be able to rule their children well (I Timothy 3:12). How can they teach other children in the Church if not so?

2) A Deacon and his wife must have their own house in order before taking office in the house of the Lord (I Timothy 3:12, 15).

The reader is referred to the qualifications of Elders for fuller treatment of these words, along with other qualifications listed there.

E. The Probation of a Deacon

Paul is clear on the fact that Deacons should "also first be proved" (I Timothy 3:8, 10).

Proving takes time! There should be a probationary period for both Elders and Deacons. As already mentioned, all Elders could serve as Deacons first. Out of the Deaconship will surface Elders, although all Deacons will not become Elders. The word "prove" means "to test, examine, scrutinize to see whether a thing is genuine or not." A Deacon must not be a novice.

Stephen and Philip both served as Deacons first, yet rose to ministry out of such, especially Philip the Evangelist (Acts 6:1-6; 7; 8; 21:8).

F. The Ordination and Appointment of Deacons

In the appointment of the original Deacons in the early Church, we see a beautiful co-operative choosing of men to this office. The Apostles and the Church co-jointly appointed these Deacons to office.

Here we see how Deacons were chosen (Acts 6:1-6; I Timothy 5:21-22; Hebrews 6:1-2). There are foundational lessons for all Churches to be seen here.

1. The Need (Acts 6:1, 2, 4)

The disciples multiplied and the widows were neglected in the daily "ministration" (Greek "Diakonea"). The Apostles could not leave the ministering of the Word of God to "serve" tables. It was not because they would not!

2. The Apostles Word (Acts 6:2-3).

The Twelve called the multitude together and told them to "look ye out from among you" seven qualified men to be appointed over this business. The Apostles laid out the qualifications for these men to be appointed. These men were not position seekers (Psalms 75:5-7; Jeremiah 45:4; Matthew 23:1-12; Mark 10:35-45). Their gift made room for them (Proverbs 18:16).

They were members of the local Church at Jerusalem. The people did not act on their own. It was at the suggestion of the Apostles, the leadership.

3. The Response of the Multitude and their Choice (Acts 6:5, 6).

The saying pleased the whole multitude, and "they chose" seven men, "whom they set" before the Apostles for this appointment. The multitude knew these men, had confidence in them, and saw the required qualifications. The Church approved of them.

The congregation made the choice under the leadership of the Twelve.

NOTE — In Old and New Testament men were called and chosen in God's sovereignty at times (Exodus 3; I Kings 17; Acts 9; Matthew 10). i.e. Moses, Elijah, Paul and the Twelve, etc.

Other times the Lord used men to confirm His call on others. So Moses and Joshua (Numbers 27), and Elijah and Elisha (I Kings 19), and Paul and Timothy (Acts 16:1-4), and Elders (Acts 14:23).

Then God used men to confirm His call. Thus we have the Levitical Tribe set apart as the "servant tribe" for Israel (Numbers 1-2-3-4; Numbers 18).

Then here we have the Deacons chosen by the Church under Apostolic leadership. Israel was the Church in the Wilderness (Acts 7:38).

4. The Appointment of Deacons Acts 6:4-6).

The Apostles, as the presbyters, appointed (SC 2525. "Kathistemi") these men to serve as Deacons by prayer and the laying on of hands (I Timothy 4:14). They were elected by the congregation, and appointed by the ministry.

Thus, because of the need, and at the word of the Apostles, the people chose qualified men and brought them before the Apostles. The Apostles were satisfied with their choice and laid hands on them, setting them aside to this appointment by prayer.

The principles laid down here are suitable for any local Church today!

In Summary:

★ The Apostles acted together. Peter did not act on his own.

★ The Apostles took the initiative and called the Church together suggesting Deacons be chosen from among them.

★ These chosen were to be qualified:
  — Members of that local congregation.
  — Men of good report.
  — Men filled with the Holy Spirit.
  — Men of wisdom.
  — Men full of faith.

★ The whole congregation made the choice of men.

★ The Apostles approved, prayed, laid hands on them, and appointed them to office.

We see that:

The Church at Jerusalem had qualified Deacons (Acts 6:1-6).

The Church at Philippi had Deacons (Philippians 1:1).

The Church at Ephesus had Deacons (I Timothy 3:1-13), where fuller qualifications are given here.

G. The Authority of a Deacon

Many Churches today have failed to realize what and where the authority of the Deacon is. Thus they have "Deacon Boards" who "hire and fire" their pastor or minister, and who control the finances of the Church. In fact, the Deacons become the controlling power of the Church and of the ministry. This is unScriptural! The government of the Church belongs to the ministry or the Eldership. The Deacon's authority is delegated and limited as:

Deacons were *delegated* by the Apostles (Bishops, Elders) of the early Church (Acts 6:3).

Deacons were *under the authority* of the Elders (Acts 6:3). "Whom we may appoint over this business." They act under authority. They handled the temporal affairs for the widows here; Alms for the poor — NOT the tithes for ministry.

Deacons are the servants of the ministry and the people in the designated areas assigned to them.

Thus the Deacons authority is delegated and limited. Their authority comes by the appointment of men to do designated and specific areas of work in the Body of Christ.

The measure of their responsibility is the measure of their authority which is given to them by the Eldership.

Deacons are NOT necessarily called to preach or minister the Gospel, though this is possible to surface as in the case of Stephen and Philip.

Deacons are NOT called to rule in the Church, though they serve with those who do rule, that is, the Eldership. The major distinctions between Eldership and Deaconship have to do with *teaching* and *ruling*.

H. The Term of Office of a Deacon

In contrast to that of the Elder, whose term of office is for life, unless he disqualifies himself, the terms of office for a Deacon may be limited. That is, one could be a Deacon for life, but if he is not *functioning* as a Deacon, then he no longer holds the *office* of a Deacon. Deaconship is not merely a *title*, or an *office*, but a *function!*

If a person was a Deacon over the widows and in charge of the daily ministration of such, he would function in the office of a Deacon. However, if he ceased to act responsibly in that area, he would cease from the *office* of a Deacon. Otherwise, all he has is a functionless title!

However, though a person may cease to function in the *office* of a Deacon, he should maintain the *spirit and attitude* of a Deacon, as every member of the Body of Christ should have.

Thus authority for the office of a Deacon comes from the office of a Bishop. It is man-made and God-confirmed. The Deacon's office is man-appointed and functions as long as the responsibility is being fulfilled.

I. The Ministry and Function of a Deacon

As in all the ministries there is "the cluster" and there is "the measure of the gift" of Christ and "a measure of grace" given by the Lord, so in the Diakonate (Romans 12:3, 6, 7; Ephesians 4:1-6).

Various Deacons will have differing grace and gift, which need to be discovered and used accordingly for the needs of the Body of Christ.

The Deacon must "wait" on his ministry (Romans 12:7). A job description is always helpful to give to the Deacons in their particular area.

1. Old Testament Deacons (Numbers 1-2-3-4; Numbers 18)

The Old Testament Israel was spoken of as "The Church in the Wilderness" (Acts 7:38).

We may take the Tribe of Levi as being the "servant tribe" or the Diakonate Tribe, for they were chosen from among the tribes to serve the tribes, as well as to serve the Aaronic Priesthood (the ministry).

Their duties consisted of the following:

a. Service to the Lord.

b. Service of the Tabernacle, whether in journeys or operation.

c. Service of the Priests, that is, Aaron and his sons.

d. Service of the sacrifices of the altar that the people brought.

e. Service of the 12 Tribes; distribution of freewill offerings, etc., to the widows, the orphans, etc.

f. Service of the law of the Lord and His statutes to the people.

2. New Testament Deacons

We follow a similar pattern in the New Testament Church in spiritual sense as also material things as shadowed by the Levitical Tribe.

a. Deacons were servants to Christ (Matthew 25:44). As much as ye did to the least of these little ones, ye did it to me.

b. Deacons were servants to the ministry (Acts 20:4; Colossians 1:23-25).

c. Deacons were servants to the Local Churches (Romans 16:1-2).

d. Deacons were servants to the Congregation (Acts 6:1-6), especially here to the widows in need.

J. Deacons and Deaconesses

The New Testament mentions a number of people who are referred to as servants in one way or other. These may be spoken of as Deacons. And then again there were women involved in serving the Lord or His people, and it is evident that there was a number of women who were

Deaconesses in the early Church. We note a list of those spoken of as "servants" or "ministers" which can be pointing to the Diakonate. Temporal and spiritual things are involved.

1. **Deacons**
   ★ Christ is THE Servant of Servants, the example Deacon. He humbled Himself and took upon Himself the form of a Servant (Philippians 2:1-8; Luke 22:26, 27). Refer also Romans 15:8.
   ★ Angelic beings ministered to Christ at His temptation (Mark 1:13; Matthew 4:11).
   ★ Angels are also ministering spirits to the heirs of salvation (Hebrews 1:14).
   ★ Civil Rulers are servants, ministers of God also (Romans 13:3, 4).
   ★ These seven men were named as the first Deacons in the early Church, and of note among them were Stephen and Philip (Acts 6:1-6).
      Stephen, Philip, Prochorus, Nicanor, Timon, Parmenas, Nicolas.
   ★ Paul said that he and Apollos were servants through whom the Corinthians believed. They were able ministers of the New Covenant (I Corinthians 5:5; I Timothy 4:6; II Corinthians 3:6; 6:3, 4).
   ★ John Mark ministered to Paul and Barnabas for a while (Acts 13:5).
   ★ Apostles have part of this ministry (Diakonate) (Acts 1:16, 17, 24, 25).
   ★ Tychicus was a faithful minister to the Church of Ephesus (Ephesians 6:21, 22; II Timothy 4:12; Titus 3:12) and Colosse (Colossians 4:7).
   ★ Timothy also was a minister and served the Church (I Thessalonians 3:2).
   ★ Epaphros was a faithful servant of Christ (Colossian 1:7, 8).
   ★ Archippus is told to take heed to the ministry he had received in the Lord and fulfill it (Colossians 4:17).
   ★ Timothy and Erastus ministered to Paul as young ministries coming up (Acts 19:21, 22).
   ★ Onesiphorus ministered to Paul in many ways and many times acted as a Deacon to Paul (II Timothy 1:16-18).
   ★ The household of Stephanas was devoted to the service of the saints (I Corinthians 16:15).

It is clear that it is the Spirit of Christ to serve one another. The Lord Jesus is the supreme example. The Ministry of a Deacon is Christ re-living His life and ministry in and through the members of the Body.

Servanthood touches Divine, Angelic, Ecclesiastical, Political, Spiritual and Temporal beings and things. This is the broadest use of the word.

Many of the men above served as Deacons to the Churches, proving themselves in the local Churches before coming to their ministry-gift Christ had given them.

They travelled at times with the Apostles, and also from Church to Church. They took messages and reports of the welfare of the Churches and the ministry, etc. They were servants to the Churches, ministering in the distributions of freewill offerings to the needy, the poor, as well as ministering in other temporal areas.

2. **Deaconesses**

It is evident from Church History that there were also certain women chosen to be Deaconesses to the Churches. Some expositors suggest that the qualifications laid down in I Timothy 3:11 could also be speaking of an order of Deaconesses in the Church. "The women" could mean "the wives" or just "the women" who are Deaconesses. Either way, the truth is consistent with Scripture and Church History.

R.B.C. Howell in *"The Deaconship"* (pp. 115-117) comments on the historical evidences of Deaconesses.

Female assistants to the deacons, usually called Deaconesses, existed in the primitive Church. They were ladies of approved character and piety; and their duty required them to minister to females, under circumstances in which it would have been manifestly improper that the other sex should have employed. Their services were regarded as of very great importance, if not entirely indispensable. Ecclesiastical historians, the early Fathers, and other writers refer to them frequently and familiarly.

Mosheim, for example, in his "*History of the First Century*", introduces them thus: "The Eastern Churches elected *deaconesses,* and chose for that purpose, matrons, or widows, of eminent sanctity, who also ministered to the necessities of the poor, and performed several other offices, that tended to order and decency in that Church."

Early Church Fathers confirm the fact that Deacons played a certain role in the Church of the first few centuries.

Ignatius, a contemporary of the Apostle John speaks of Deacons being more than just servers of meat and drink.

Irenaeus also saw a pattern in Acts 6 and believed that the Church should be under the direction of not more than seven men.

In AD 315, the **Council of Neo-Caesarea** set seven as the number of men to administer in the affairs of the Church.

Clemens of Alexandria of the second century confirms the same, using Paul as authority on the matter.

Jerome of the fourth century also speaks of them.

Documents of the Early Church (p.5) speak of two maidservants who were tortured, who were called *Deaconesses.* In the SYRIA DIDASCALIA from the late third century we are told that:

★ Deaconesses were to assist women in baptism.

★ Deaconesses were especially used in the "art of anointing and to go into the houses of the heathen where there are believing women, and to visit those who are sick and to minister to them in that of which they need, and to bathe those who have begun to recover from sickness."

Some expositors also suggest that I Timothy 5:9-10, when speaking of "widows being *taken into the number*" refers to the Order of Deaconesses and the necessary qualifications for them to be supported by the Church.

Their age, of course, prohibits the idea of heavy active service, so it is suggested that they, being of great age, should be supported by the Church because of the many years they have ministered to the saints, washed feet, and given hospitality — or, in other words, served as DEACONESSES!

A second passage which some expositors use is that in Philippians 4:3. Here Paul speaks of "those women who laboured with me in the Gospel". Perhaps these women also were Deaconesses and helped the ministry.

They were recognized as "these women" by Paul.

A third passage, which we have already referred to, is that of I Timothy 3:11 where some expositors say that "Even so must their 'wives' " can be more especially referring to "the women", i.e., the deaconesses qualifications, NOT to the wives of deacons! Deaconesses must be grave, not slanderers, sober, faithful in all things. However, both could be accepted as true.

We note a list of women who served or ministered to the people of God, and can be recognized as deaconesses.

★ The Shunamite women ministered to Elisha (II Kings 4).

★   Martha served (Greek 'Diakonea') the Lord and His disciples (Luke 10:38-42; John 12:2, 26).

★   Peter's wife's mother was healed and then ministered to Jesus (Matthew 8:14, 15; Mark 1:31).

★   Certain women ministered to Jesus; Mary Magdalene, Mary the mother of James and Joses, and the mother of Zebedee's children (Matthew 27:55, 56).

★   Joanna, the wife of one of Herod's stewards, and Susanna and many others also ministered to Jesus (Luke 8:1-3).

★   Dorcas ministered to the necessity of the poor (Acts 9:36-40).

★   Phebe (Romans 16:1-2) was a deaconess, a servant of the Church at Cenchrea.
Paul asks the local Church at Rome to assist her in whatever business she needed and to act like saints in doing so.
It is evident that there are certain services that are best handled by women who would be deaconesses.

Other areas of Deaconship in the local Church could be:

★   Deacons over 'house-church-meetings' or home fellowship groups.

★   Deacons who are ushers at the Church gatherings and meetings.

★   Deacons over the nursery and care for the young of the flock.

★   Deacons over the welfare and care of the widows (Harvest Festival Seasons).

★   Deacons over the Commissary, or Saints Relief Fund.

★   Deacons over the Janitorial work of Church buildings.

★   Deacons over maintenance of Church property.

★   Deacons to serve and host visiting ministry.

★   Deacons over errands for the local Eldership.

★   Deacons over the orphans in the Church.

★   Deacons over the Communion Table and Service.

★   Deacons over baptismal services (men for men, women for women).

★   Deacons for visitation of sick in home or hospital.

★   Deaconesses for women's need.

★   Deacons for secretarial work, or deaconesses.

★   Deacons over wedding preparations.

★   Deacons over Hospitality.

If there are husbands and wives who qualify, then there can be husband/wife team in the deaconship, according to abilities and areas they excel.

K. Relationship of Deacons to Eldership and Congregation

Deacons must always maintain the servant spirit of Christ knowing that they first serve the Lord Jesus Himself.

★   Deacons must maintain a servant spirit to the Eldership, as unto the Lord.

★   Deacons must maintain the spirit of a servant, and love to the members of the congregation they serve.

By constant remembrance that "as much as they do it unto the least of these My brethren, ye do it unto Me", then service will be delightful and rewarded with "Well done, thou *good* and *faithful servant,* enter into the joy of the Lord" (Matthew 25:14-30).

CHAPTER 18

THE ASCENSION-GIFT MINISTRIES

Introductory:

The Epistle of the Ephesians, called "The Epistle of the Church, the Body of Christ" speaks of five ministries that are given to the Body of Christ for a specific time and a specific purpose.

"When He ascended up on high, He led captivity captive, and gave gifts unto men . . . And He gave some, apostles; and some, prophets; and some, evangelists; and some pastors and teachers; for the perfecting of the saints, for the work of the ministry, for the edifying of the body of Christ: Till we all come in the unity of the faith, and of the knowledge of the Son of God, unto a perfect man, unto the measure of the stature of the fulness of Christ . . ." (Ephesians 4:8, 11-13).

There are some important points to be noted before proceeding to a more detailed study of each of these ministries in succeeding chapters.

A. The Godhead Involved

In the building and operation of the Church, the Godhead, as Father, Son and Holy Spirit, is involved. God is a giving God, and all the power and fulness of the Godhead is made available to the people of God to bring the Church to all that God intends it to be.

God's redemptive purposes involve the Church.

1. The Father God

The Father gave His Son to be head over all things (Ephesians 1:20-22). The Father gave His Son to be the Saviour of the world (John 3:16; II Corinthians 5:18, 19). Love motivated the Father to give all in His blessed Son. The Father's burden was the whole world. The Father's gift was His only begotten Son. It is the Father God who gives the power to operate and work all things in the Body of Christ. It is God that worketh all and in all (I Corinthians 12:6).

2. The Son of God

The Son of God gave Himself for the Church (Ephesians 5:23-27). He prayed not for the world but for His own (John 17:9). The Burden of the Son was for a glorious Church.

The Son not only gave Himself but He also gave the Holy Spirit (Acts 5:32; John 16). And then He also gave ministry-gifts to perfect the Church. After His death, burial, resurrection, ascension and glorification, He gave the five-fold-ministry mentioned in Ephesians 4:9-11. These ministries are actually extensions of Himself, His own ministry flowing into the many-membered Body of Christ, the Church. Because they were given after His ascension, they are called "post-ascension-gift ministries" (I Corinthians 12:5; Ephesians 4:8-16).

These are His instruments for the perfecting of the Church in earth. Thus the Son's burden is the whole Church. The Son's gifts to the Church are the Holy Spirit, and the five ascension-gift ministries.

3. The Holy Spirit

The Holy Spirit is God's gift through Christ to believers individually and corporately to the Church. He works with the Father and with the Son. He also is a giver of gifts. He gives the spiritual gifts mentioned in I Corinthians 12:4, 7.

Thus we have "diversities of gifts, but the same Spirit" — The Holy Spirit.
And we have "differences of ministries, but the same Lord" — The Son.
And we have "diversities of operations, but the same God" — The Father.
The burden of the Holy Spirit is the individual believer, and also the whole Body of Christ, the Church, seeking that all flow in their place and function in the Body.

Thus, Father, Son and Holy Spirit — the eternal Godhead — are vitally involved in the eternal purpose concerning the Church. The Godhead is a giving God!

IN SUMMARY DIAGRAM we may view it as follows:

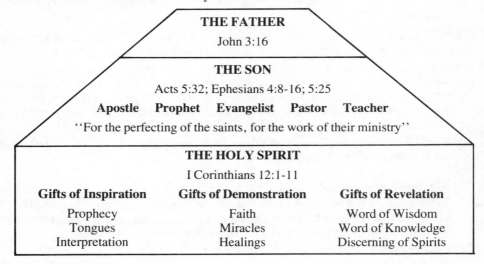

THE FATHER

John 3:16

THE SON

Acts 5:32; Ephesians 4:8-16; 5:25

Apostle   Prophet   Evangelist   Pastor   Teacher

"For the perfecting of the saints, for the work of their ministry"

THE HOLY SPIRIT

I Corinthians 12:1-11

Gifts of Inspiration	**Gifts of Demonstration**	**Gifts of Revelation**
Prophecy	Faith	Word of Wisdom
Tongues	Miracles	Word of Knowledge
Interpretation	Healings	Discerning of Spirits

B. Ascension-Gift Ministries

As noted already, these five ministries are spoken of as "ascension-gift" ministries. The reason is this. It was AFTER Christ's descending and ascending ministry that He gave these gifts to the Church. A number of Scriptures speak of Christ's "ascending and descending" to earth and heaven (Genesis 28:12; Proverbs 30:4; Romans 10:6, 7; Deuteronomy 30:12-14; Judges 5:12; John 3:13; Psalms 68:18; John 1:51; Ephesians 4:1-16).

He descended from heaven to earth to redeem us. He ascended from earth to heaven to glorify us. The five ministry-gifts were given for this purpose also. It is worthy to note that Christ did not choose a prophet, evangelist, pastor or a teacher of the fivefold type BEFORE His ascension. He chose TWELVE APOSTLES AS THE FOUNDATION of the New Testament Church. Thus these five are "post-ascension gift ministries."

C. The Gifts of Grace

These ministries are five. Five is the number in Scripture that God links with grace, atonement, life. It is in and through these five gifts that the Lord's power, grace and life and truths of the atonement flow.

They are "grace-gifts" (Ephesians 4:7, 11; Romans 12:3, 6), from the risen Christ. They are His gifts to the Church. They are expressions and channels of His grace. Paul received "grace and apostleship" (Romans 1:5; I Corinthians 3:10; Romans 15:15, 16; Galatians 2:9; I Corinthians 15:9, 10).

The grace of Christ flows through these gifts. We may say that each of these ministries are an expression of Christ — "Christ in you, the hope of glory" (Colossians 1:27).

★   The fruit of the Spirit — His nature and character.

★   The gifts of the Spirit — His power.

★   The ministry gifts — His offices.

Christ gives Himself back to the Church through His ministries. Because He is the fulness of the Godhead bodily, He flows that fulness through the ministries into the many-membered Body of Christ, His visible expression in the earth (Colossians 1:19; 2:9; John 1:14-16). Thus "of His fulness have all we received and grace for grace".

D. **The Fivefold Ministry**

These ministries specified are the Apostle, Prophet, Evangelist, Pastor and Teacher (Ephesians 4:11).

(**Note**: Some expositors combine the Pastor-Teacher as one, so making only four ministries. Experience shows that some Pastors are not Teachers and some Teachers are not Pastors, though ''teaching the word'' is involved in measure in both of these ministries. The writer holds to the general view that there are five ministries listed here).

There are about 81 references to Apostles; 14 references to Prophets; 10 references to Teachers (though Scribe is mentioned many times, 47 times, meaning Master); 3 references to Evangelist; 1 reference to Pastor, plus about 16 to Shepherd (same Greek word).

E. **The Purpose of the Fivefold Ministry**

The purpose for which these five ascension-gift ministries are given is seen clearly in Ephesians 4:12. They were given: *continue ministry of christ*

1. FOR the perfecting or maturing of the saints,

2. FOR the work of the ministry, i.e. to bring the saints into the work of their ministry,

3. FOR the edifying or building up of the Body of Christ.

   We may also say that these five ministries are given FOR the balance of each other as well as balance in the Body of Christ.

F. **The Consummate Ministry of the Ascension-Gifts**

The end result of these ministry gifts is found in Ephesians 4:13-16.

1. To bring the Church to the *unity* of the faith, unto the knowledge of the Son of God.

2. To bring the Church unto a *perfect man*, a full grown man, maturity.

3. To bring the Church unto the *measure of the stature of the fulness of Christ*. Having arrived at that standard the Lord will be able to present to Himself a glorious Church, without spot or wrinkle, but holy and without blemish (Ephesians 5:23-33).

G. **Time Limit**

We may ask what is the time limit or duration of these ministry gifts, that is, the five of them?

These ministries are given UNTIL the purpose is accomplished as laid out in Ephesians 4:12-16. The fivefold ministry has not always been accepted by the Church as a whole. The ministries of Evangelist, Pastor and Teacher have generally been accepted. However, the ministries of Apostles and Prophets have been relegated to the past history of the Church, to its foundation and its inception.

But the word is that these five ministries were given by Christ until the consummation. This has not yet been reached, hence the necessity for *all* of the fivefold ascension and gifted ministries. Each have a part to play in the whole of the purposes of God.

H. **Types of the Fivefold Ministries**

There are many types of the fivefold ministries, especially as is seen in the use of the number five. Of these we will note only a certain number.

1. **Old Testament Israel Ministries**

   Israel is called ''The Church in the Wilderness.'' Acts 7:38. Many things in Israel's history foreshadow the history of the New Testament Church. This is seen in the matter of the Old Testament ministries manifested in Israel's history, as the type, and consummated in New Testament Church history, the antitype.

Old Testament Israel — The Type	New Testament Church — The Antitype
Moses, Old Covenant mediator	— Jesus, New Covenant mediator
The 12 leaders, princes	— The 12 apostles, princes
The 70 elders of Israel	— The 70 others sent out
The Passover Feast	— The Gospels
The Pentecost Feast	— The Book of Acts
Old Testament 'fivefold ministries'	— New Testament 'fivefold ministries'
(1) Priests	— Apostles
(2) Judges	— Prophets
(3) Kings	— Evangelists
(4) Prophets	— Pastors
(5) Pastor/Shepherds	— Teachers

(**Note**: the important point of correspondence is the number five, not necessarily correspondence of these ministries, though there is that in measure, as is evident by comparison).

Sad to say Priests became corrupted and precipitated the rise of the Judges. Then the Judges were failures often, and precipitated the rise of the Kings. Then the Kings were often wicked and thus precipitated the ministry of the Prophets. Many times the Pastor/Shepherds also failed. However, there were always true ministries even under Old Testament times. The same failure and God's revelation of grace is revealed in the fivefold ministries of the Church in our history.

2.   **The Bars of the Tabernacle of Moses**

Exodus 36:31-34. The Tabernacle of the Lord had five bars which bound the whole structure together as ONE Tabernacle. The individual boards stood in sockets of silver, but to stand upright, or alone, would not have constituted the Lord's Tabernacle. As they were united to each other, and structured together by the five boards, so is the Church. The believers individually and corporately are bound to each other and together as ONE Church by the five ministries.

3.   **Aaron and his Sons** (Exodus 28-29).

Between the tribes of Israel and the Lord were Aaron and his 4 sons, thus making fivefold ministry here. Cf. Hebrews 3:1. Christ is THE Apostle and High Priest of our confession. So the High Priest is also The Sent one, and the 4 sons typify the four other ministries.

4.   **The Cloud the size of a Man's Hand** (I Kings 18:41-46).

In time of famine, there came time of rain. The cloud the size of a man's hand was manifest after the 7 times praying of Elijah. The hand consists of the number five. The cloud came out of the 'sea', symbolic of peoples, nations and tongues. Draw the hand, and symbolize each of the fivefold ministries in the thumb and fingers. Thumb and pointer work together, as apostle and prophet. The longest finger is the evangelist in outreach. The 'ring' finger is the pastor, and the small finger is the teacher. The thumb (apostle) can touch all others, yet the five work together for the whole body. The fivefold are the 'hand' ministry.

5.   **The Five Restoration Ministries**

In the restoration from Babylon we see five ministries for the people of God with the same message and distinctive ministries.
Zerruabbel the apostle, laid the foundation.
Joshua, the high priest and intercessor, pastoral care.
Haggi and Zechariah — the prophets; also Malachi.
Nehemiah — Governor and overseer.
Ezra — the Scribe, Teacher and Hermeneutician of the Law of God.

6. **The Five Senses**

God has set five senses in the human body for the protection and care of the body. So he has set five ministries as the 'spiritual senses' of the Body of Christ for its protection and care.

Many other 'fives' could be mentioned. We note some of these here which may be expanded in their spiritual application.

★   The five loaves which Christ used to feed the multitude (Matthew 14).

★   The five pillars of entrance into the holy place of Moses' Tabernacle (Exodus 26:36).

★   The five articles of furniture in the Tabernacle, The Ark of the Covenant being the symbol of Christ (Exodus 25-40). Superimpose the Christ over the fivefold furniture and the ministries. The articles each have their distinct ministry as seen in the fivefold ministry.

★   Moses, Apostle; Aaron, the Prophet; Bezaleel and Aholiab, the Teachers. Wise women were involved in building the Tabernacle of the Lord.

I.   **Warnings against Hierarchy**

One of the great dangers to watch against is that which most denominations fall into. That is, depriving the people of the priesthood of all believers. Churches who accept and recognize the fivefold ascension gift ministries need to beware that these fivefold ministries do not become a 'priestcraft' which rob the believer of his priestly worship, and responsibilities before God.

Jesus warned about this in Revelation 2:6. It was called the doctrine of the Nicolaitans, which is "to conquer the laity". Nico = To conquer, and Laos — which is interpreted to mean — "the people, or laity". Thus Church History shows the rise of "clergy and laity" and the "priestly assumption" of ministries which snuffed out the priesthood of all believers.

Then again it is possible for one of these ministries to become a spiritual autocrat, a dictatorship, independent, autonomous, arrogant, domineering, despotic and arbitrary. Thus one-man-rule can usurp the place of Christ and also rob the believer of his priesthood.

This can be done through rule of the plurality of eldership also. The whole sum of the matter is that any ministry, singular or plural, can become a hierarchy, a priest-class and rob the members of the Body of Christ of their responsible priestly functions.

There is only ONE Mediator between God and man, and that is the Man, Christ Jesus. No man or group of men, ministries or officials, dare usurp the place of Christ's mediatorial ministry. Whether ministries or members, all together are members of the priestly company, with varying responsibilities and functions under Christ, the Great High Priest. (Revelation 1:6; 5:9-10; Hebrews 5-6-7.)

CHAPTER 19

THE MINISTRY OF THE APOSTLE

Introductory:

``And He gave some, *apostles* . . .'' (Ephesians 4:11).

``God hath set in the church firstly *apostles* . . .'' (I Corinthians 12:28). ``Are all *apostles*?'' (I Corinthians 12:29).

The ministry of the apostle is one that is much misunderstood. It is a ministry that has been limited to the period of transition from the Old Covenant to the New Covenant. It has been relegated to the period of the Book of Acts and early Church history. With the death of the apostle John and the completion of the Old and New Testament canon of Scriptures, it has been taught that the apostolic ministry was no longer required. However, the Ephesian Epistle distinctly says that Christ, *after* His ascension, gave gifts to men, and ``He gave some, apostles.'' This ministry, along with the others, was given for a certain period of time, ``*until*'' the Church comes to unity and maturity. This has not yet come to pass. Therefore the Church needs the apostolic ministry today. We consider the ascension-gift ministry of the apostle.

A. Definition of the Word

It is worthy to note the change and development of this word from secular language to what it came to mean in the Church. It seems that this word, as other words, took on a new and fuller meaning in the Church than it did even in secular use.

1. Ancient Greek Usage

The word ``*APOSTOLOS*'' rarely has in classical Greek anything like the meaning which it has in the New Testament (Karl H. Rengstorf in ``*Apostleship*'').

In Classical literature it had various usages:

a. A Naval expedition, a cargo ship, a fleet of ships sent with a specific objective;

b. The admiral or commander of a naval expedition or fleet of ships;

c. The colony which was founded by the admiral; a group of colonists sent overseas;

d. A personal envoy, or emissary or ambassador, a delegate.

(Arndt and Gingrich and Dictionary of New Testament theology. Vol. I, Colin Brown). Kittel's Theological Dictionary (Vol. I, p. 407) says ``If a fleet of ships was sent by Rome to establish a new colony elsewhere, all these were called 'apostles' — i.e. the fleet, the admiral and the newfound colony.''

The usage of the word connects *the sender* and *the one who is sent*. Jesus said: ``Verily, verily, I say unto you, the servant (slave) is not greater than his lord; neither he that is sent (a sent one, apostle) greater than he that sent (Christ, the sender) him'' (John 13:16).

Even in this ancient usage, the dominant thought is that of someone being SENT!

2. Hebrew Usage (SC 7971)

The Rabbis applied the term ``*Shalach*'', ``to send away'', to the one who was commissioned and authorized by God.

Isaiah the prophet, therefore, was ``a sent one'' (Isaiah 6:8), the authorized representative of God, the sender being one with Him who sent him.

The Rabbis had two groupings especially; these being, the priesthood, and several of the great prophets, such as Moses, Elijah, Elisha and Ezekiel, because of special acts of God done through them (Kittel, p. 419).

According to Colin Brown in "*Dictionary of New Testament Theology*" (Vol. 1, p. 27) the LXX (The Septuagint, or Greek Translation of Hebrew Scriptures), the words "apostello" and "exapostello" are used some 700 times. They are used almost exclusively to render "Shalach", stretch out, send. It meant the authorization of the messenger (Cf. Joshua 1:16; II Kings 19:4; Jeremiah 34:3).

The noun "*apostolos*" is found only in I Kings 14:6. Here Ahijah the prophet is sent, or *commissioned and empowered* with a hard word for Jeroboam's wife. The emphasis here is "not" the institutional appointment of someone to an office, but the authorization of him to fulfil a particular function or a task which is normally clearly defined. "The stress is laid on the one who gives his authority to the one he sends or take into his service." (Colin Brown, p. 127, 128).

3. **Koine Greek Usage**

Brown continues to say (p. 128), in contrast to the LXX, the frequent occurrence of the noun *APOSTOLOS* is something new. The word is used six times in Luke; twenty-eight in Acts; thirty-four in Paul's writings, once in Hebrews, three times in Peter, once in Jude, three times in Revelation, and Matthew, Mark and John use it once each.

In striking contrast with classical Greek, *apostolos* is used in the New Testament only in the general sense of messenger, and particularly as the fixed designation, a definite office; the primitive APOSTOLATE!

The one sending is represented in the one sent. Jesus said, "He that receiveth you receiveth Me, and he that receiveth Me receiveth Him that sent Me" (Matthew 10:40). The Father sent the Son (The Apostle), and the Son sent the Twelve disciples (The Apostles) (John 13:16; Luke 10:11; 6:13).

The Greek word "apostolos" from which we derive the word "*apostle*" literally means "*one who is sent forth*".

Various expositors add:

★ "A delegate, messenger, one sent forth with orders" (Thayer).

★ "One sent forth" (Smith's Dictionary).

★ "One sent as a messenger or agent, the bearer of a commission, messenger" (Analytical Greek Lexicon).

★ A title denoting a commissioned messenger or ambassador. It occurs 79 times in the New Testament with various shades of meaning, both of precise and of a general character (Interpreter's Dictionary).

★ "Delegate, envoy, messenger, missionary" or "one especially commissioned" (Arndt and Gingrich).

EXAPOSTELLO means "to send forth, to send away; to send away from one's self; to dispatch on a service or agency" (Thayer, p. 68). It is used 13 times in the New Testament (Luke 1:53; 20:10, 11; Acts 7:12; 9:30; Luke 24:49; Acts 11:22; 12:11; 13:26; 17:14; 22:21; Galatians 4:4, 6).

Taken together, the word "*apostle*" simply means "a sent one, an ambassador, a delegate, one who is sent forth, one commissioned and authorized by another to represent another and carry out his will and purposes. The sent one is one with the one who sent him.

B. **Orders of Apostles**

The New Testament shows that there were several ranks or levels of the apostolic order.

1. **Christ, THE Apostle** (Hebrews 3:1).

Christ is spoken of "THE Apostle and High Priest of our confession." The Rabbis applied the term apostle to the priesthood as well as to some of the prophets, as already noted.

Perhaps the writer to the Hebrews had this thought in mind when he combined both offices of PRIEST and APOSTLE in Christ as our Apostle and High Priest.

Jesus Christ is indeed "THE Sent One". He is THE Apostle, the only infallible apostle and all other and lesser apostles seek to follow and emulate Him and will be judged by Him.

As Head of the Church, as the God-Man, He stands unique among and above all. In all things He takes the pre-eminence (Colossians 1:18, 19).

The Gospel of John could well be called the Gospel of Christ's apostleship. He was "The Sent one", sent forth by the Father, one with the Father, representing the Father and fulfilling His will and purposes as the faithful apostle and high priest of our confession (John 3:17, 34; 5:36-38; 6:29, 57; 7:29; 9:7; 10:36; 17:3, 8, 18, 21-25; 20:21).

The character, nature, grace, revelation and signs of an apostle were perfectly manifested in Him.

2. **The Twelve Apostles of the Lamb** (Revelation 21:14)

    We note some of the most prominent points about this rank of apostles.

    a. The twelve apostles were chosen by Christ after a night of prayer (Luke 6:12, 13).

    b. There are four listings of the name of these twelve (Matthew 10:2-4; Mark 3:16-19; Luke 6:12-16; Acts 1:3). Their names are:
        Peter, James, John, Andrew,
        Philip, Nathanael, Thomas, Matthew,
        James (Son of Alphaeus), Simon (the Zealot),
        Judas (or Thaddeus), and Judas Iscariot.

        It is significant that each listing mentions Peter first, and Judas the traitor last.

    c. Paul speaks of "The Twelve" (I Corinthians 15:5). Paul also speaks of those who were "the most eminent apostles" (II Corinthians 11:5; 12:11. NAS). The marginal of NAS says "the super apostles" while the A.V. says "the chiefest apostles".

        Although there is difference of opinion as to the replacement of Judas Iscariot, it does seem that Matthias is the one chosen to complete "The Twelve" between Passover and Pentecost. This is seen in the following references.

        In Acts 1:15-26, after prayer and the casting of lots, at the suggestion of Peter, Matthias is chosen to complete the twelve apostles. Matthias was numbered with "the eleven apostles" (Acts 1:26).

        The casting of lots was a pre-Pentecost act and it was confirmed by the Lord as to the choice (Leviticus 16:8, 9; Proverbs 16:33). Matthias was not chosen directly by the Lord but by the eleven in prayer.

        H. B. Hackett in "*Smith's Dictionary of the Bible*" (p. 127, 128) says: "The original qualifications, as stated by Saint Peter, on the occasion of electing a successor to the traitor Judas, a fallen apostle, was, that the person should have been personally acquainted with the whole ministerial course of our Lord, from the baptism of John until the day when He was taken up into heaven. He himself describes these as they that had continued with Him is His temptations" (Luke 22:20; Acts 1:21).

        On the Day of Pentecost "Peter, standing with the eleven" (Acts 2:14) gave the Pentecostal sermon with its attendant results.

        "The Twelve" are also mentioned in Acts 6:2.

        Then Paul says that the risen Christ was seen of "The Twelve", not "The Eleven" (I Corinthians 15:5).

        Hence Matthias is recognized as one of "The Twelve":

        1) Before Pentecost (Acts 1:26),

2) At Pentecost (Acts 2:14),

3) After Pentecost (Acts 6:2),

4) And by the apostle Paul himself (I Corinthians 15:5).

d. The number twelve is the number of government, of apostolic foundations. It is prominent in Israel's history as a nation and very prominent in the New Jerusalem, the city of God (Revelation 21-22).

★ The 12 sons of Jacob were the foundation sons of Old Testament Israel (Genesis 48-49).

★ The 12 wells of water symbolized the twelve apostles (Exodus 15:27).

★ The 12 pillars at Mt Sinai symbolized the 12 apostles (Exodus 24).

★ The 12 princes and their offerings for the dedication of the brazen altar also symbolized the 12 apostles (Numbers 7).

★ The 12 stones with the 12 names of the 12 tribes in the breastplate of the High Priest pointed to such (Exodus 28-29).

★ The 12 loaves of shewbread on the Table pointed to the same (Exodus 25:23-30).

★ The 12 lions on Solomon's throne (I Kings 10:20), and the 12 oxen upholding the molten sea in the temple courts pointed to the same truth (I Kings 7:25, 44), and the 12 porters at the gates of Jerusalem also (I Chronicles 26:13-19).

The city of God has 12 gates, 12 foundations, 12 names, 12 manner of fruits, 12 gates of pearl, etc. All point to foundational ministries, apostolic government, the authority of God manifested in the number twelve.

None can add to ''The Twelve'' foundation apostles.

Many others could be mentioned. The consummation of the number twelve is seen in the city of God. There we see the names of ''The Twelve Apostles of the Lamb'' on the foundations (Revelation 21:14).

It is a unique place, reserved especially for those apostles who were with the Lamb in His earth walk, reaching from His baptism to His ascension, over a period of 3½ years ministry.

They were each chosen (except Matthias in his replacement) by the Lord on earth and before His ascension. They were pre-ascension apostles.

e. The Twelve were especially sent to the House of Judah in a period of transition from the Old Covenant economy to the New Covenant economy. They ministered at the over-lapping of dispensations. They were more distinctly ''The Jewish Twelve'' (Matthew 10:2; Mark 3:14; Luke 22:14). Peter, in time, opened the door of faith to the Gentiles (Acts 11:17), but he was the apostle of the circumcision (Galatians 2:7-9). They were sent ''to the Jew first'' (Romans 1:16; 2:9).

The Old Testament age was the age of the Prophets. The New Testament opens with the ministry of the Apostles (Cf. II Peter 3:1-2).

f. The reward of the Twelve is to sit on 12 thrones in the regeneration and rule over the 12 tribes of Israel (Matthew 19:28).

g. The Old Testament Scriptures were written primarily by the inspired prophets. The New Testament Scriptures were written primarily by the inspired apostles, but both confirmed each other. The New Testament apostles saw the fulfilment of the word of the Old Testament prophets (II Peter 3:2; 1:20-21; I Peter 1:10-12).

h. It should be noted that the first ministry chosen by Christ in His earthly walk was that of apostles. No prophets, evangelists, pastors or teachers were expressly chosen until after His ascension. This shows a distinct change of order from the Old Testament prophets to the order of New Testament apostles.

In Summary:

Alex, Rattray Hay, in *"The New Testament Order For Church And Missionary"* (pp. 214-217) says this of The Twelve, and which we condense and adapt for our summary:

★ The Twelve had a special position and a special mission.

★ The Holy Spirit, through them, laid the doctrinal foundation of the Church, called the apostles doctrine (Acts 2:42).

★ Through them the structural foundation of the Church was revealed and laid. This included the Keys of the Kingdom, opening the door to Jews and Gentiles (Matthew 16:16-19; 18:15-20).

★ They form the link which joins the old Dispensation with the new. Through them the unity and continuity of God's purpose is preserved. Their roots are in the glorious Dispensation that has ended; their ministry is in the more glorious new Dispensation.

★ These Twelve were called and appointed by the Lord in the flesh prior to the cross; they were trained by Him and were His companions during His ministry on earth. They were eye-witnesses of His life, crucifixion and resurrection.

★ All were Jews born in Galilee or Judea. They were of the House of Judah.

★ Their authority was delegated and limited. Their authority was in Christ and the Word and Spirit he gave them. They were not High Priests or a Sanhedrin.

The very fact that these are called "The Twelve Apostles of the Lamb" show that they hold a unique place in the redemptive plan of God both in time and eternity.

3. Paul, the Apostle to the Gentiles

There is absolutely no doubt that Paul stands as unique among other apostles mentioned in the New Testament, apart from the twelve apostles of the Lamb. For this reason, we devote this section to the uniqueness of his apostolic ministry. He is spoken of as apostle extra-ordinary to the Gentiles. We consider come of the important factors involved in Paul's apostleship.

a. Paul was not one of "The Twelve"; that is, of the original twelve. He himself felt that he was "one born out of due season" (I Corinthians 15:5, 8).

b. Paul was a "called apostle" (Romans 1:1; Galatians 1:1, 15; I Corinthians 1:1; Ephesians 1:1; II Corinthians 1:1; Ephesians 2:8; Colossians 1:1; I Timothy 1:1; 2:7; II Timothy 1:1, 11; Titus 1:11).

Paul humbly but consistently attests to his calling as an apostle in most of his Epistles. He is first spoken of as an apostle, along with Barnabas in Acts 14:14.

Note: It is worthy to see that Paul calls himself "An apostle", never "THE apostle". Paul was "A father" but not called "Father Paul". Thus he was not a title-conscious man, but did specify his office (I Corinthians 4:15; Matthew 23:8-10). He was not after flattering titles.

c. Paul was a "post-ascension apostle". That is, he was called personally on the road to Damascus by the heavenly and risen Christ after his ascension (Acts 9:1-20; 22:1-22; 26:1-23).

d. Paul had "seen the Lord" which was counted then as an important qualification for apostleship (I Corinthians 9:1-2; 15:9; II Corinthians 11:4, 5).

e. Paul was directly commissioned by Christ to minister to both Jews and Gentiles but especially to the Gentiles. He was the apostle of the uncircumcision (Galatians 2:7-8; Acts 9:15; 26:15-18; Romans 11:13; 15:15-20; Galatians 1:15-17; I Timothy 2:7).

f. Paul's apostleship was confirmed by miraculous signs and wonders (Acts 14:27; 15:3-12; II Corinthians 12:12).

g. Paul suffered much as an apostle (II Corinthians 11-12).

h. Paul's apostleship was sealed by the fruit he had; the founding and establishing of Churches in the cities the Lord sent him to (I Corinthians 9:2; I Corinthians 3:9-10). Paul was a "wise master-builder", and he was also a "father" to the Churches (I Corinthians 4:15).

i. Paul's apostleship was not inferior to that of the Twelve. He says he was not one wit behind the chiefest of apostles (II Corinthians 11:15; 12:11-12).

It is significant to note that Peter and Paul were the two major apostles in the Book of Acts. Acts 1-12 centres around Peter, the apostle to the circumcision, and the Church at Jerusalem. Acts 13-28 centres around Paul, the apostle to the uncircumcision, and the Church at Antioch.

Because the Lord foresaw the ensuing carnal comparison of Peter and Paul by believers (I Corinthians 3:1-8, 21-23; Galatians 2:7, 8; I Corinthians 15:1-10), it seems as if He equipped them both for their distinctive apostolic roles, as the following comparison shows.

Peter		Paul
Apostle to Jews, Circumcision	—	Apostle to Gentiles, Uncircumcision
Foundation ministry	—	Foundation ministry
Apostolic revelation to the Church	—	Apostolic revelation to the Church
To the Jew first	—	To the Synagogues first
Then to the Gentiles	—	Then to the Gentiles
Lays hands on Samaritans	—	Lays hands on the Ephesians
Outpouring of Holy Spirit	—	Outpouring of Holy Spirit
Healed a lame man	—	Healed a lame man
Raised a person from the dead	—	Raised a person from the dead
Signs and wonders	—	Signs and wonders
Deals with a sorcerer	—	Deals with a sorcerer
Witnessed before the Sanhedrin	—	Witnessed before the Sanhedrin
Seven addresses recorded in Acts	—	Seven addresses recorded in Acts
Established local churches	—	Established local churches
Imprisoned for witnessing	—	Also imprisoned for witnessing
Angel of Lord delivers from prison	—	Angel of Lord sends earthquake
Arrested in the Temple	—	Arrested in the Temple
Chains fell off	—	Chains loosed
A man of heavenly visions	—	A man of heavenly visions
Religious and political opposition	—	Religious and political opposition
Beaten for the name of Jesus	—	Beaten and stoned for name of Jesus
Jerusalem, Judea, Samaria	—	The Uttermost parts of the earth
Writer of two Epistles	—	Writer of 14(?) Epistles
Centre — Jerusalem	—	Centre — Antioch

Paul seemed to be an apostle who functioned in each of the fivefold ministries, and also other functions and also in the gifts of the Spirit. He is seen as apostle (Ephesians 1:1), teacher (II Timothy 1:11), and prophet, and evangelist (Acts 17:2-4), and pastor (Acts 18:9-10; 19:10). He worked miracles, had gifts of healing, discerning of spirits, governments, faith, words of wisdom and knowledge, etc. He was indeed apostle extra-ordinary in his time.

j. Paul, as seen already, wrote 13 (or 14, if Hebrews) of the 27 books of the New Testament — Apostolic revelation was given to him comparable to none except the apostle John. Even Peter said Paul wrote things hard to be understood, but accepted his writings as inspired Scripture (II Peter 3:15, 16). He could say "I have received of the LORD that which I delivered unto you'' — NOT of the other apostles, who added nothing to him as far as apostolic revelation was concerned (I Corinthians 11:23; 15:3; Galatians 1:11, 12; 2:1-9; Ephesians 3:1-12).

Thus Paul, the apostle to the Gentiles, stands unique among all other apostles. He was indeed a ''super-apostle'' by reason of the grace of apostleship upon him. He was the FIRST post-ascension apostle chosen directly from heaven by Christ Himself, the Head of the Church.

So unique and distinct is Paul's apostleship, that some Bible expositors believe that he was the Lord's choice to replace Judas, the fallen one of the Twelve, and not Matthias. Matthias was *chosen by lot* before the outpoured Spirit at Pentecost under Old Testament custom. Paul was *chosen by the Lord,* after Pentecost, under New Testament dispensation of the Spirit.

There is much value in this thought. The following ''*General Bible Theme*'' is adapted from Rev. W. W. Patterson's notes and well worthy of consideration.

Truth as Revealed in Type and Fulfilment

Old Testament Type and Prophecy	—	New Testament Antitype and Fulfilment
GOD revealed to *Natural* Israel	—	GOD revealed to *Spiritual* Israel
The Church in the Wilderness (Acts 7:38)	—	The Church in the New Testament
		The Church of firstborn (Hebrews 12:23)
Exodus 3:15-16. The LORD GOD of your fathers:	—	Matthew 3:16-17; 28:19. In THE NAME of
(1. Abraham		(1. The Father, and of
The God of (2. Isaac	—	Godhead (2. The Son, and of
(3. Jacob		(3. The Holy Spirit (I John 5:7).
The *12 sons* of Jacob (Genesis 48).	—	The *12 apostles* (Matthew 10:1-4).
Then the *70 souls* of Jacob's house who went down into Egypt.	—	The *70 others* sent forth by Christ (Luke 10:1).
Then the *innumerable hosts* of natural Israel (Genesis 22:17).	—	The *innumerable* hosts of redeemed spiritual Israel (Revelation 7:9)
''As the sand upon the seashore'' (Hebrews 11:12; Romans 9:27).		''As the stars for multitude'' (Hebrews 11:12).
Rueben, *one of the 12 sons* of Jacob sinned, lost or forfeited birthright. (Genesis 35:22; 49:4; I Chronicles 5:1)	—	Judas, *one of the 12 apostles* sinned, and lost his Bishoprick (John 6:71; Matthew 26:21-25, 47-49; 27:3-5; Acts 1:16-20).
Jacob adopted the two sons of Joseph:	—	The New Testament 'Adopts' two apostles:
1. *Manasseh,* the elder, to become a great people (Genesis 48:19a)	—	1. *Matthias,* chosen by lot (Acts 1:21-26; 2:14; 6:2; I Corinthians 15:5)
2. *Ephraim,* the younger, to become a multitude of nations (Genesis 48:19b)	—	2. *Paul,* chosen by the Lord and is apostle to multitude of Gentile nations (Acts 9:1-18; 22:6-21; 26:12-23)
Ephraim is *set before* Manasseh	—	Paul is *set before* Matthias
and receives a *Double Portion*	—	and takes the lead in Acts.
Genesis 48:22; Jeremiah 31:9.	—	Receives a *Double Portion* of the Spirit
Ephraim now becomes the *Firstborn*	—	The portion of the *Firstborn* II Kings 2:9
Ephraim is listed among the	—	Paul's name is thus possibly (?)
twelve tribes. Tribal name.		in the Foundations of the City of God.
This makes 13 Tribes in Israel	—	Matthias and Paul make 13 Apostles

Eternity alone will reveal whether the name of Matthias or Paul is in the foundation of the city of God (Revelation 21:14).

Paul, however, was certainly a wise master-builder who laid "THE foundation" — Christ Jesus, and warned all others to take heed how they built (I Corinthians 3:9-16).

4. Ascension-Gift Apostles

Although Paul was the first ascension-gift apostle chosen, he stands unique among all other ascension-gift apostles. No other apostle mentioned in the New Testament has their apostolic ministry attested to like the apostle Paul. All others mentioned are lesser apostles, none having the measure of the grace or gift of apostleship bestowed upon Paul by the Lord Jesus Christ.

Altogether there are over 80 references to apostles, amongst these there are about fifteen other persons mentioned or designated as apostles besides the original Twelve Apostles of the Lamb. These were named *after* Christ's ascension.

★ Matthias (Acts 1:26).

★ James, the Lord's brother (Acts 1:14; I Corinthians 15:7; Galatians 1:19; 2:9).

★ Paul (Acts 14:14; 22:21).

★ Barnabas (Acts 4:36; 11:22-30; 14:1, 4, 14; I Corinthians 9:6).

★ Apollos (I Corinthians 4:6-9).

★ Andronicus (Romans 16:7).

★ Junia (Romans 16:7).

★ Epaphroditus (Philippians 2:25, Messenger = Apostle).

★ Titus (II Corinthians 8:23, Messenger = Apostle).

★ Two unnamed brethren (II Corinthians 8:23).

★ Timothy (Acts 19:22; I Thessalonians 1:1; 2:6).

★ Judas (Acts 15:23; I Thessalonians 2:6).

★ Silas/Silvanus (Acts 15:23; I Thessalonians 2:6; 1:1).

★ Erastus (Acts 19:22).

★ Tychicus (II Timothy 4:12).

God has set in the Church, firstly apostles (I Corinthians 12:28). These are the gifts of Christ to His Body (Ephesians 4:11). In totality we have about 28 persons mentioned in the New Testament as apostles.

A study of the lives and ministries of these mentioned as apostles (except Paul), show that none of these compared with Paul as to revelation, signs and wonders or the apostolic ministry given to him. Yet they were called apostles, but undoubtedly apostles of lesser order and grace.

So has it been through Church history. None can compare with the original Twelve, nor with the apostle Paul, but many can be compared and spoken of as lesser apostles, though they are apostles, Church history evidences men, too numerous to name, who could indeed be designated as lesser apostles, who did apostolic work. Many missionaries and ministries in modern times also qualify as lesser apostles. It must be remembered that Christ gives this ministry according to the measure of grace and the measure of the gift that He desires to manifest in and through them (Romans 12:1-6; Ephesians 4:7). Only as this fact is recognized will we cease to measure every apostolic ministry by the Twelve or by Paul.

Rev. Earnest Gentile writes in some notes:

"There is a theoretical teaching that in the last days, the Church will again be led by twelve apostles, one of whom will 'fall away' (like Reuben of the 12 sons, and Judas of the 12 apostles) to become the last-day Antichrist. Such an apostolic college would be composed of Gentile apostles of various races. Such teaching is based on the symbolism of the 12 stars crowning the last-day Church (Revelation 12), and the meaning of the 24 Elders of Revelation (12 Early-day, and 12 Last-day apostles). Obviously, we will need thousands of apostles to complete the perfection of the Church and the evangelization of the world. But it is also great and very exciting to contemplate that just as the Church Age began with 12 Jewish Apostles leading a basically Jewish Church, the Age will end with 12 (or a representative number of) Gentile Apostles leading a mainly Gentile Church. Such apostles would be a special category of their own, and could only be brought together by God Himself.''

If this is so (and the patterns of Scripture seem to confirm it to be so), then undoubtedly these last day apostles will be men like Paul. They will have the character, qualifications, revelation and ministry that Paul had. Paul was set forth to be a pattern to those who would afterwards believe on Christ (I Timothy 1:12-16). Perhaps there is some implication in the fact he was an apostle ''born out of due season'', for he typifies the last day apostles!

5. **Apostolic Companies**

In the early Church there were ministry-teams ''sent out'' to various places who could be referred to as ''apostolic teams'' or ''apostolic companies''. It was not that all on these teams were apostles but they were ''sent ones'' to fulfil certain tasks in either pioneering or establishing Church.

Christ sent out the seventy two by two (Luke 10:1-20). Their commission was similar to that of the Twelve sent out. However, though they were ''sent ones'' (Greek ''Apostella'', to send), they were not ''apostles''.

So we may say that there are apostolic companies today though all among them are not apostles. In this manner we could speak of all of the fivefold ministries as ''apostolic'', in the sense that they are all ''sent ones'' by the risen Christ. Apostolic companies were formed by the Spirit: ''The Spirit said . . . .'' Christ sent the Twelve in twos, as He knew they would balance each other, working together.

Following are some of the most outstanding ''apostolic companies''.

★   Peter and John sent to Samaria (Acts 8:14) to Philip the evangelist.

★   Barnabas, Saul and Mark (Acts 13-15). Apostles and Deacon.

★   Paul and Silas (Apostle and Prophet) (Acts 15:40).

★   Barnabas and Mark (Apostle and Deacon). Acts 15:37-39.

★   Paul, Silas, Timothy and Luke (Apostle, Prophet, Deacon, Physician). Acts 16:9.

★   Paul, Silas, Timothy, Luke, Aquilla, Priscilla and Apollos (Apostle, Prophet, Deacon, Physician, Teachers). Acts 18:2-24.

★   Paul, Silas, Timothy, Luke, Erastus, Gaius, Aristarchus (Apostle, Prophet, Deacon, Physician and ministry in training). Acts 19.

★   Paul, Silas, Timothy, Luke, Sopater, Aristarchus, Secundus, Gaius, Tychicus and Trophimus (Apostle, Prophet, Physician and other ministries in training) Acts 24.

★   Judas and Silas, as prophets, sent with the Epistle (Acts 15:27).

★   Barnabas and Saul bring relief money to Jerusalem (Acts 11:30).

A careful study of the Book of Acts and these apostolic teams show that they were involved in the planting, instruction, correction and establishing of the Churches (Acts 13-20). No apostle was a ''loner'' or ''independent'' of other Churches or ministry.

C. **Calling, Qualifications and Ministry of an Apostle**

In the light of the New Testament, there are certain basic things by which apostolic ministry can be recognized. It is not that all apostles will be exactly alike or have the same measure of the grace-gift of Christ, but there will be enough of the evidences that confirm that person is an apostle. There should be definite Calling, Qualifications and Ministry manifest in a genuine apostle.

1. **Calling of an Apostle**

   An apostle, as any other ministry, must have a distinct calling of the Lord and he must know this calling.

   ★ The Twelve were called and ordained by the Lord Jesus Himself (Mark 3:13-15; John 15:16).

   ★ The Seventy were called also by the same Lord (Mark 6:7-13).

   ★ Paul was called by the risen Lord and was deeply conscious of his calling to apostleship (Colossians 1:1; I Timothy 1:1; Titus 1:1; Romans 1:1; I Corinthians 1:1; II Corinthians 1:1; Galatians 1:1; Ephesians 1:1).

   Paul could say of his calling:

   a. He was not an apostle by the will or call of man or by men.

   b. Paul knew THE apostle had called him (I Timothy 2:7; Hebrews 3:1).

   c. Paul knew he was separated by God the Father to this calling.

   d. Paul had his calling also confirmed by other ministries too.

      ★ It was revealed to Ananias (Acts 9:1-20).

      ★ Something must have been revealed to Barnabas that caused him to seek Saul out from Tarsus and bring him to Antioch (Acts 9:27).

      ★ The Holy Spirit confirmed his calling with Barnabas in due time at Antioch from whence he was sent out as an apostle (Acts 13:1-4; 14:14).

      ★ Peter accepted Paul as an apostle (Galatians 2:17-19).

      ★ The Church at Jerusalem recognized Paul as an apostle to the Gentiles (Galatians 2:1-9).

   Paul's calling and election in eternity was confirmed in time by the Lord and other ministries in the body of Christ. The Lord had put him into the ministry (I Timothy 2:7; 1:12-16).

   Thus Paul was called by the Lord. His calling was confirmed at Damascus, at Antioch and at Jerusalem. It was foreordained in eternity and confirmed in time by the Lord and by other ministries.

   Timothy and Titus were lesser apostles, and their calling was confirmed by the laying on of hands of other apostolic ministries (Acts 16:1-3; 19:22; Romans 16:1; I Corinthians 4:17; Philippians 2:19-24; I Thessalonians 3:2; I Timothy 1:1; II Timothy 1:2).

   An apostle must know his calling to this office. The Lord can and will confirm that calling to and through other ministries.

   An apostle will know that he is ''a man sent from God'', for an apostle is also a sent one.

   Jesus was sent by the Father. The Gospel of John confirms this.
   The Twelve were sent by the Son, especially to the Jews (Luke 22:30).
   Paul was sent by Holy Spirit (Acts 13:1-4) to the Gentiles.
   Paul and Barnabas together were sent by the Church (Acts 13-14).

   We may illustrate the Apostolate with Christ, the Head, and the Twelve as the Shoulders (Isaiah 9:6, Government on His shoulder), and the Post-ascension apostles, the many, as the Body of the Apostlate. The many are Body-building apostles.

2. **Qualifications of an Apostle**

Apostles, as any of the fivefold ministry, must be qualified persons.

a. **An Apostle must have the character qualifications of an Elder**

Qualifications of Elders have already been dealt with. Apostles are elders, though all elders are not apostles.

Peter spoke of himself as an elder among elders (I Peter 5:1-5).
John the apostle spoke of himself as an elder (I John 1:1; III John 1).

Most expositors hold that 12 of the 24 elders in Revelation 4:4, and 5:8 are 12 apostles of the Lamb.

An apostle is also spoken of as holding the office of a bishop (Acts 1:15-16). Judas, an apostle, fell from his bishoprick.
An apostle will be a qualified elder (I Timothy 3; Titus 1).

b. **An Apostle will have a Servant spirit**

Paul, James, Peter and John, though apostles, all spoke of themselves as being "slaves of Jesus Christ". That is, they were bond-slaves, love-slaves to His will (Titus 1:1; Philippians 1:1; Romans 1:1; James 1:1; II Peter 1:1; Revelation 1:1). They had a servant spirit (Mark 10:35-45), Apostle-Deacons! Perhaps some of the greatest words concerning apostleship were spoken by John Alexander Dowie, before his spiritual decline in "*The Life of John Alexander Dowie*", by Gordon Lindsay, when Mr Calverly, looking to Dr. Dowie, said, amidst great applause, "But I think I can see an apostle".

"I have not the slightest idea but that our dear brother Calverly spoke with that perfect honesty which has always characterized him, and that he would not have been guilty for a moment of flattery. But I am too perfectly honest when with no mock humility I say to you from my heart, I do not think I have reached a deep enough depth of true humility, I do not think I have reached a deep enough depth of true abasement and self-effacement for the high office of an apostle, such as he who had reached it could say, and mean it too, 'I am less than the least of all saints, and not worthy to be called an apostle.' "

But if my good Lord could ever get me low enough, and deep enough in self-abasement and self-effacement to be truly what I want to be and hope in a measure I am, "a servant of the servants of the Lord," why, then I should become an apostle by really becoming the servant of all.

In becoming an apostle, it is not a question of rising high, it is a question of becoming low enough. It is not a question of becoming a "lord over God's heritage", but it is a question of if a man shall be called to be an apostle whether he can get low enough, low enough to say from the depths of his heart, the words of the apostle Paul, "It is a faithful saying, and worthy of all acceptation, Christ came to save sinners of whom I am (not I was) chief."

I do not know if any persons here have a notion in their minds that the apostolic office means a high pompous position, wearing a tiara, and swaying a sceptre. If so, they are entirely wrong. It means a high position truly, but the power of one that can take the lowest place. I think some of you have got a very false conception of power in the Church of God. Power in the Church of God is not like power in the Government of the U.S.A., where a man climbs to the top of the pyramid of his fellows to the acme of his ambition, and there makes it fulfil his personal pride and purpose. Power in the Church is shown in this, that a man gets lower and lower and lower and lower, until he can put his very spirit, soul and body underneath the miseries and at the feet of a sin-cursed earth and a diseased and smitten humanity and live and die for it and Him who lived and died for it. That is what I understand by the apostleship."

c. **An Apostle will have Spiritual Authority**

This authority is spiritual authority. It is not dictatorship or lordship over God's heritage. It is not assumed authority. Jesus spoke with authority, not as the Scribes. He had authority because He was under authority.

Neither Peter nor Paul excercised any dictatorial authority as apostles. Paul would not use his authority for their destruction but for their edification (II Corinthians 1:24; 10:8; I Peter 5:1-5; I Thessalonians 2:1-8; Luke 22:24-27; I Corinthians 4:21; II Corinthians 13:2, 10). Paul did not excercise authority in Churches he did not found.

Paul excercised a spiritual authority among his Churches and workers but not an official authority, controlling them and their movements.

He would "send" and "leave" and "persuade" and "encourage" his workers to do certain things for the Gospel, but he did leave it to their knowing the will of the Lord (Acts 16:1-4, 9, 10; 17:15; 20:3-5, 13-14; I Corinthians 16:10-12; 8:6; II Corinthians 8:16-18, 22; Ephesians 6:21, 22; Ephesians 6:21, 22; Philippians 2:25; Colossians 4:7, 14-17; I Thessalonians 3:1-2; II Timothy 4:9-13; Titus 1:5; 3:12-13).

d. **An Apostle will be a Spiritual Father**

I Corinthians 4:15-21; 11:34. Though there are many instructors, yet there are not many fathers. An apostle will be a spiritual father in the Lord, though he will not be called "father" (Matthew 23:1-12; I John 2:12-14). Paul was gentle as a nursing father (Numbers 11:12; I Thessalonians 2:6-11; Philippians 2:22; Ephesians 6:4).

e. **An Apostle must be sound in Doctrine**

An apostle will be sound in the apostles doctrine once delivered to the saints (Acts 2:42; Romans 16:25, 26).

He will have apostolic revelation, insight, understanding and wisdom of the Word, of both Old and New Testaments (Galatians 1:12; Ephesians 3:5; I Corinthians 14:26; Matthew 16:13-18).

He will be able to make apostolic decisions on doctrinal issues (Acts 15).

f. **An Apostle will be clothed with Humility**

Although all believers should be clothed with humility, an apostle must be characterized by this quality. Jesus, THE apostle was humility personified. The greatest must be the humblest. Humility is a necessary attitude because of this high calling of apostleship.

The Lord gave Paul a thorn in the flesh to keep him humble because of the abundance of revelations given to him and lest he should be exalted above measure (II Corinthians 11-12; Acts 20:19; II Corinthians 10:2, 18). An apostle will not be given to self-glory or want the pre-eminence (I Corinthians 4:9; John 5:44; III John 9, 10). There will be no self-deification as manifested in Lucifer (Isaiah 14:12-14).

g. **An Apostle will be noted for Patience (II Corinthians 12:12).**

Patience and/or endurance will be a characteristic of apostolic ministry. Paul is certainly a pattern apostle of this quality. It is needed with the people of God who may be slow in their spiritual development. Endurance is also needed for the work of the ministry.

h. **An Apostle will be exemplary as a leader to follow** (I Corinthians 11:1)

Paul said to follow him as he followed Christ. The safeguard is that we may follow any ministry so long as he follows close to Christ. If he ceases to follow Christ, then we do not follow the leader but Christ. An apostle must approve himself as the minister of Christ (II Corinthians 6:3-10).

i.   **An Apostle should manifest the qualities of Divine love**

I Corinthians 13; II Corinthians 12:15. Love is kind, gentle, long suffering, patient, hopeful, faithful and God-like. An apostle need Divine love qualities.

3.   **Ministry of an Apostle**

The following material is gathered from the ministries of the major apostles of the New Testament. However, it should be remembered that everyone of these things cannot be laid on all, but all will operate in their apostolic ministry according to the measure of the grace-gift the risen Christ gives to them.

a.   Apostolic ministry, as the fivefold ministry, is given to the Body of Christ for:

1)   The perfecting and maturing of the saints,

2)   The work of the ministry, to bring saints into the work of their ministry,

3)   The edifying, or building up of the Body of Christ,

4)   The bringing of saints into the unity of the faith,

5)   The bringing them to the knowledge of the Son of God, to a perfect man,

6)   To bring them to the measure of the stature of Christ's fulness,

7)   To bring them out of childhood unto adulthood.
Ephesians 4:11-16; Colossians 1:25-29; Hebrews 6:1-2.

b.   Apostolic ministry involves founding and/or establishing New Testament local Churches on the sure foundation, Christ Jesus.

I Corinthians 3:9-16; Romans 16:20; I Corinthians 9:1; Ephesians 2:20-22.

The Church is built on the foundation laid by the apostles and prophets. Other builders are to take heed how they build. Apostles are foundational ministries.

(Note — A study of the list of apostles show that not all pioneered or founded Churches, but all were involved in establishing them in the faith once delivered to the saints; foundational truths).

c.   Apostolic ministry involves preaching and teaching the Word of the Lord.

I Timothy 2:7; II Timothy 1:11.

Each of the fivefold ministries are ''WORD Ministries'' but there is a distinctiveness about the ministry of the Word in apostolic preaching and teaching. There is insight and illumination relative to the Scriptures.

d.   Apostolic ministry involves, as the Spirit wills, signs and wonders. Certain gifts of the Spirit belong to this ministry gift of Christ. Healing, exorcism, raising the dead, miracles, etc., as the Lord willed (Acts 4:23; 5:12; II Corinthians 10:18; 12:12; I Corinthians 4:19-20; Romans 11:13; 15:18, 19; Acts 3:1-8; 9:36-43; 16:18).

e.   Apostolic ministry involves ordination and appointment of ministries. Deacons chosen by the congregation were approved and appointed by the apostles to that service (Acts 6:1-6).

Paul and Barnabas ordained elders by the laying on of hands with prayer and fasting in the Churches they established (Acts 14:23).

Paul was invoived in the presbytery and impartation of spiritual gifts in the ordination of Timothy to ministry (I Timothy 1:18; 4:14; 5:22; II Timothy 1:6; 4:6; Romans 1:11).

f.   Apostolic ministry involves the baptism of the Holy Spirit.

Acts 8:14-18; 10:1-16; 19:1-6. Peter and Paul both saw people coming into the baptism of the Holy Spirit evidenced with speaking in tongues. However, this is not limited to apostolic ministry.

g. Apostolic ministry involves preparation and placing of other potential ministries.

II Timothy 2:2. Paul taught faithful men who would also teach others. Paul trained Timothy (Acts 16:1-4). Barnabas chose Mark and in time developed him (Acts 13:5, 13).

Paul sent Timothy and Epaphroditus and others as messengers to the Churches for report and instruction (Philippians 2:19-25; Titus 3:12; I Thessalonians 3:1-2; II Timothy 4:10-13, 21; Romans 16:1-2; Colossians 4:7-12; Acts 15:36). The Spirit led and confirmed in these things.

h. Apostolic ministry involves Church judgments and disciplines.

This involves ''binding and loosing'' ministry given to apostles (Matthew 16:16-19; 18:15-20; Isaiah 26:9; 4:4; I Peter 4:7). It is judgment at the house of God.

1) Sapphira and Ananias were judged by the Lord through the word of the apostle Peter for lying to the Holy Spirit (Acts 5:1-11).

2) Elymas, the Jewish sorcerer and false prophet was blinded by the Lord through the apostle Paul for resisting the Gospel (Acts 13:11).

3) The Corinthian fornicator was disciplined under apostolic instruction (I Corinthians 4:21; 5:1-13; II Corinthians 2:6-11; 13:2, 10).

4) The apostle John said he would deal with Diotrephes when he came for his arrogance (II John 9, 10).

5) Paul dealt with others for their false doctrine (I Timothy 1:20).

6) Church discipline was placed on divisionaries (Romans 16:17).

Thus the keys of the kingdom and the binding and loosing ministry promised by Christ to the apostle Peter and the Church is involved in these apostolic judgments and disciplines (Matthew 16:16-19; 18:15-20; I Peter 4:17; James 5:9; Proverbs 19:29; 13:23).

i. Apostolic ministry has vision for the whole Body of Christ.

Ephesians 3:1-9; 4:1-16. Apostles cannot be sectarian but they must have a vision for the whole Body of Christ. They are given to the Body, for the Body. Local Churches may either accept or reject apostolic ministry to their gain or loss (Revelation 2:1-6).

j. Apostolic ministry will especially care for the Churches he founds.

II Corinthians 11:28. Paul had the care and concern of all the Churches.

These Churches he founded were the seal of his apostleship (I Corinthians 9:1-2; 7:17; 11:34; II Thessalonians 3:14).

k. Apostolic ministry is willing to sacrificially suffer for the Church.

A study of the pattern apostle, Paul, shows how he willingly suffered for the Church, the Body of Christ. He was willing to lay down his life for the flock of God. (Acts 5:18-40; 7; Colossians 1:23-29; I Corinthians 4; II Corinthians 6:3-10; II Corinthians 11-12 chapters).

l. Apostolic ministry will be willing to be tested and proven true.

True apostles will be willing to be tried and tested by the Word of God and be willing to submit to other ministries. Cf. Revelation 2:2; Galatians 2:11-13; Acts 17:10-12. To try is to test, prove, examine. The Bereans were willing to test Paul's word out by the Scriptures. Apostolic ministry is not infallible and no true apostle is afraid of being tested out as to the revelation he brings. There are false and self-made apostles (II Corinthians 11:13-15).

m. Apostolic ministry will be characterized by wisdom.

II Peter 3:15, 16; I Corinthians 1-2-3. Moses and Solomon had God-given wisdom.

So should apostles in the building of God's house, the Church.

Apostolic ministry especially is noted for "word of wisdom" (I Corinthians 12:8).

n.   Apostolic ministry may apparently minister in other of the fivefold ministry, as the Lord wills and the need arises, although he majors in one.

Paul was an teacher/apostle (II Timothy 1:11).
Paul and Barnabas were listed among the prophet/teachers at Antioch (Acts 13).
Peter was a pastor/apostle (John 21:15-17).
Timothy could have been an evangelist/apostle (II Timothy 4:5).

Old Testament ministries seem to overlap also. Jeremiah was a pastor/prophet. Isaiah was an evangelist/prophet.

So at times there seems to be an overlapping of ministry in ministries according to the need and God's purposes. It is apostolic ministry that reveals the "pastoral/teacher" ministry, as well as the prophetic in the New Testament Epistles. The Lord and the Spirit gives *gifts* to *persons* and these persons themselves are gifts to the Church (I Corinthians 12:8-10; Ephesians 4:9-11).

o.   Apostolic ministry will set God's house in Divine order.

Note the use of the word "order" in these verses concerning Paul's ministry. I Corinthians 11:34; 7:17; 16:1-2; II Thessalonians 3:14; Colossians 2:5.

p.   Apostolic ministry should be identified with a Local Church.

Though Paul said he was "free from all to be servant of all" (I Corinthians 9:19), he was not a law to himself. And though he founded Churches, yet he himself was part of the local Church at Antioch for years and reported to them periodically (Acts 13-14).

It is a good safeguard for all ministries to have the covering of a local Church and other ministries.

q.   Apostolic ministry has the ministry of governments also (I Corinthians 12:26-29).

4. **Recognition of Apostolic Ministry**

The principle used here is applicable to any and all of the fivefold ministry. That is, the recognition and acceptance or rejection of ministry in the members as well as the ministries in the Body of Christ.

Jesus said if we receive a prophet in the name of a prophet we receive a prophet's reward (Matthew 10:40-42). And to receive those who have been sent by the Lord is to receive the Lord who sent them. To reject those sent is to reject the One who sent them (Matthew 10:11-14; John 13:20; Matthew 25:40; Luke 10:16; I Thessalonians 4:8; John 5:22, 23).

If a person has a true ministry gift, and is a tried and true apostle (Revelation 2:2), then the Church should receive such. Receiving them releases their ministry and the Church receives the reward of that ministry's labour in the Word of the Lord. To do otherwise is to bind that ministry, so that there is no release of the Word of the Lord.

D. **Warnings Against False Apostles**

As with every other ministry there is true and false, so it is with apostles. The Scriptures warn against false apostles.

II Corinthians 11:13; 12:11; Revelation 2:2. They are false, not because they claimed apostleship but because of the false doctrines they bring, leading people astray from the truth of the Gospel.

It is John, the last living apostle, who commended the Church at Ephesus for trying out those who said they were apostles and found them liars and deceivers.

CHAPTER 20

THE MINISTRY OF THE PROPHET

Introductory:

"And He gave some, *prophets* . . ." (Ephesians 4:11).

"God hath set in the Church . . . secondarily, *prophets* . . ." (I Corinthians 12:28).

"Are all *prophets*?" (I Corinthians 12:29).

Along with the ministry of the apostle, the ministry of the prophet is one that is much misunderstood. It too has been limited to the transitionary period of the early Church from the Old Covenant to the New Covenant economy. The ministries of "apostles and prophets" have been counted temporary and transitional ministries until the completion of the New Testament canon of holy Scripture.

And on the other hand, there is much misunderstanding and confusion over the ministry and function of the New Testament prophet when compared with that of the Old Testament prophet.

Both the Pauline Epistles of Corinthians and Ephesians clearly show that God has *set* in the Church "apostles and prophets" UNTIL the Church comes to unity and maturity. It is inconsistent to take the ministries of Evangelists, Pastors and Teachers and say they are still in the Church today and to relegate the foundational ministries of Apostles and Prophets to the early Church era.

The Church needs the prophetic ministry today. One of the signs of the last days is the prophetic word coming as a result of the outpouring of the Holy Spirit on all flesh (Joel 2:28-32; Acts 2:14-21).

Because of the predominance of the ministry of the prophet in Old Testament times, a rather complete consideration is given to such here. This is necessary in order to help us understand the distinction and differences between the Old Testament and the New Testament prophets.

We consider therefore, the ministry of the Prophet.

A. **Definition of the Word**

Webster's Dictionary defines prophecy as: "Prediction of the future under the influence of Divine guidance; act or practice of a prophet; something predicted." There are several words in Scripture used to refer to prophecy:

1. **Old Testament Hebrew**

   Chazah = "to gaze at; mentally to perceive, contemplate (with pleasure); specifically to have vision of; to see, behold with the eye; to see as a seer in the ecstatic state."

   Translated:
   behold — Job 23:9; Psalms 17:2; 27:4
   look — Isaiah 33:20; Micah 4:11
   prophesy — Isaiah 30:10
   provide — Exodus 18:21
   see — Isaiah 1:1; 13:1; Ezekiel 13:6-8; Habakkuk 1:1; Zechariah 10:2.

   Massa = "a burden; specifically tribute, or abstractly porterage; figuratively an utterance, chiefly a doom, especially singing; mental desire."

   Translated:
   burden — Isaiah 13:1; 15:1; 17:1; 19:1; Jeremiah 23:33, 34, 36; Habakkuk 1:1
   carry away — II Chronicles 20:25
   prophecy — Proverbs 30:1; 31:1

song — I Chronicles 15:22, 27
tribute — II Chronicles 17:11

Naba = "to prophesy; i.e., speak (or sing) by inspiration (in prediction or simple discourse); prophesy under the influence of Divine spirit, in the ecstatic state."

Translated:
prophesy — I Samuel 10:11; Jeremiah 2:8; 26:11; Ezekiel 37:7; Joel 2:28; Amos 3:8
make self a prophet — Jeremiah 29:26, 27

Nebuwah = "a prediction (spoken or written)."

Translated:
prophecy — II Chronicles 9:29; 15:8; Nehemiah 6:12.

Nataph = "to ooze; i.e., distill gradually; by implication to fall in drops; figuratively to speak by inspiration; prophecy, discourse."

Translated:
drop — Judges 5:4; Ezekiel 21:2; Amos 7:16
prophesy — Micah 2:6, 11

Thus in these Hebrew words we see prophecy as an ecstatic vision, a burden, a Divinely inspired utterance, a written or spoken prediction, and a dropping down of inspired speech.

The prophet was one who spoke for God as His mouthpiece (Jeremiah 15:19; Exodus 7:1; 4:16; II Peter 1:20, 21; II Kings 17:13; 21:10; 24:2). He was to "boil or boil forth like a hot spring or fountain", "to bubble up, burst forth with violence", or "to speak utterance in an exalted and excited manner by the Spirit of God."

2.   **New Testament Greek**

Propheteuo = "to foretell events, divine, speak under inspiration, excercise the prophetic office; to proclaim a Divine revelation, prophesy, to foretell the future; to speak forth by Divine inspiration; to break forth under sudden impulse in lofty discourse or in praise of the Divine counsels."

Translated:
prophesy — Matthew 15:7; Luke 1:67; 22:64; John 11:51; Acts 2:17, 18; 21:9; I Corinthians 14:1, 3-5; I Peter 1:10; Jude 14; Revelation 1:3.

In Koine Greek the concept of prophecy was solidified to the point that only one word was used to encompass it. In the New Testament prophecy meant to proclaim a Divine revelation, to foretell the future, and to break forth under sudden impulse into inspired discourse.

B.   **The Nature of Prophecy**

The nature of prophecy is basically twofold: forth-telling and fore-telling. There are as well, different degrees of prophetic inspiration.

1.   **Prophecy as forth-telling:** This form of prophecy is in the realm of preaching: the prophet speaks for God to the people, communicating the mind of God for the present. Often the past will be used to deal with the present. This will include such things as exhortation, reproof, warning, edification and comfort.

2.   **Prophecy as Fore-telling:** This aspect of prophecy is in the form of prediction: the prophet speaks for God, communicating His mind for the future. Often both the past and present will be used to deal with the future. Many times the purpose of prophetic prediction was to produce present godliness.

C.   **Degrees of Prophetic Inspiration:** Scripture reveals that there are varying degrees of prophetic funtion. These are:

1. **The Spirit of Prophecy** — This is defined in Revelation 19:10. "The testimony of Jesus is the Spirit of prophecy." The Spirit of prophecy is the Holy Spirit's ability to come upon men and cause them to speak forth inspired utterances.

   The Spirit of prophecy was evident in the Godly line from Adam to Moses.

   a. Adam prophesied concerning his bride and the marriage estate (Genesis 2:20-25).

   b. Enoch prophesied of the second coming of Christ (Jude 14, 15).

   c. Noah was a preacher of righteousness because the Spirit of Christ was in him (II Peter 2:5; Hebrews 11:7; I Peter 3:20).

   d. Abraham was spoken of as a prophet (Genesis 20:7).

   e. Isaac and Jacob had the Spirit of prophecy upon them as they blessed their sons (Genesis 27; 48; 49; Hebrews 11:20, 21). Note also Psalms 105:9-15).

   f. Joseph prophesied of the Exodus from Egypt (Genesis 50:24; Hebrews 11:22).

   At times the Spirit of prophecy fell upon groups of people. In Numbers 11:24-30 the Lord took of the Spirit that was upon Moses and placed it upon seventy of the elders of Israel and they prophesied. In I Samuel 19:20-24; 10:10 the Spirit of prophecy fell upon several groups of messengers, as well as upon King Saul. However, Saul was not among the prophets, but came under the Spirit of prophecy. Prophecy was the evidence of the Spirit coming on people in the Old Testament. So the Spirit of prophecy falls in meetings at times on New Testament believers.

2. **The Gift of Prophecy:** This is mentioned in I Corinthians 12:10; Romans 12:6; Acts 2:18 as one of the gifts of the Spirit. It can be defined as the God given ability to speak forth supernaturally in a known language as the Spirit gives utterance. It is seen as being an operation of the Spirit in the New Testament Church which must be excercised within Divine guidelines (I Corinthians 14:3, 25, 31; I Thessalonians 5:20). Philips's four daughters are an example of this gift, in that the Scripture states they prophesied (Acts 21:8-14, 9). However, they were not prophetesses, for Agabus the Prophet spoke to Paul (I Corinthians 14:31). That is, all may prophecy but not all are prophets!

3. **The Office of a Prophet:** In Hosea 12:10 and Hebrews 1:1 it is stated that God spoke to His people by the ministry of the prophets. A prophet was a person who was given the distinctive ministry of representing God before man. He did so by moving under the "prophetic mantle" that came upon him. The prophet was God's mouthpiece, or spokesman, through which the Word of God flowed, whether forthtelling or foretelling. There were many men of God throughout the Scriptures who held this office. These will be dealt with in the following section. "Would God all His people were prophets", said Moses (Numbers 11:29).

4. **The Prophecy of Scripture:**

   In II Peter 1:19-21 the expression "prophecy of Scripture" is used to refer to the prophetical books of the Old Testament. Because the Scriptures are the inspired Word of God, the prophecy therein must be regarded as inspired and infallible revelation (II Timothy 3:15, 16). This then is the highest degree of prophecy and requires the most careful and systematic interpretation. Each of the previous three must be judged by this fourth. The first three are fallible, the fourth is infallible. This type of prophecy is no longer given today as the 66 Books of the Bible are completed. Nothing is to be added to this completed Word (Revelation 22:18, 19).

D. The Ministry of the Old Testament Prophets

1. Designations of the Prophets

In all of the various periods of Israel's history in the Old Testament, there appears to be no greater or grander ministry than that of the prophets. The prophets were noble and holy men of God. They were the representatives of God to Israel, declaring His word, His mind and His will to the nation in times of prosperity or adversity. The ministry of the prophet is seen to be distinct from the ministry of the priest. The priest was man's representative before God by prayers and sacrifice. The ministry of the priest was from man into God. The prophet, on the other hand, was God's representative to man. He was God's ambassador who was sent from the presence of God with the words of God. His ministry was from God out to man. The prophet was the one who stood in the inner counsels of the Lord God. He received a particular message for his time, situation, generation and group although often such reached over to our generation (I Peter 1:10-12; I Kings 17:1; Jeremiah 23:16-22).

These prophets were known under the following designations:

a. **The Man of God** — I Samuel 9:6; I Kings 12:22. Morally and ethically, the prophets were indeed men of God, following, declaring and upholding the ways of God.

b. **The Seers** — I Samuel 9:9; II Chronicles 33:18; 35:18; II Samuel 24:11; Amos 7:12; Isaiah 29:10. The prophets were first called seers because of the visions, insight and foresight which they received from the Lord for the people. There were false prophets who "have seen nothing" (Ezekiel 13:3).

c. **The Interpreters** — Isaiah 43:27. The word "teachers" means "interpreters." The prophets were the interpreters of the Law of the Lord. They interpreted the history of the nation in the light of the Word of the Lord.

d. **The Messengers of the Lord** — Isaiah 43:19; Malachi 3:1. The prophets were the Divine messengers, sent by God, bearing the messages of the Lord to the nation. They delivered the messages faithfully.

e. **The Servants** — Haggai 2:3. The prophets were also called the Servants of Jehovah. They were His slaves; love-slaves to the will and service of God.

f. **The Prophets** — Hosea 12:10. The most common designation is that of prophet. These men who were prophets were public expounders and preachers of the Word of the Lord. They spoke under inspiration of the Spirit. "Holy men of God spoke as they were moved of the Holy Spirit" (II Peter 1:21). They prophesied through both preaching and prediction. They represented God's Word to Israel. They upheld the righteousness of the Law, the holiness and mercy of God, Divine sovereignty over the nations, and reproved the sinfulness of men.

E. **The Development of the Prophetic Office**

It is important to see the rise and development of the prophetic office. Two focal points are seen in the prophets Moses and Samuel.

1. **The Prophet Moses — The Letter of the Law**

Moses stands unique among the Old Testament prophets because of that which he represents before God and the nation of Israel. Moses was the prophet who received the Law of God on Mt Sinai. He actually became the *foundation ministry* and all succeeding prophets were tested by the Law given to Moses.

He is the "Paul" of the Old Testament (Numbers 12:6; Deuteronomy 34:10; 18:15-18; Exodus 33:11; Luke 16:29; Deuteronomy 13:1-5; Isaiah 8:16-20).

The Lord communicated with Moses face to face and he becomes a type of the Messiah who would be "like unto him" (Acts 3:22-33).

2. **The Prophets Samuel to Malachi — The Spirit of the Law**

It is under Samuel that we see a distinct development of the prophetic office. The Scriptures clearly mark Moses and Samuel as being key men in the prophetic ministry:

"For *Moses* truly said . . ." (Acts 13:22).

"Yea, and all the prophets from *Samuel* and those that follow after . . . ." (Acts 3:24).

"And after that he gave them judges about the space of 450 years, until *Samuel* the prophet . . . ." (Acts 13:20; Hebrews 11:32).

Samuel was the *last* of the Judges and *first* of the line of prophets. Thus, from Samuel to Malachi we have the ministry of the prophets. It seems evident from the Scriptures that Samuel, under direction of the Lord, gathered together young men who were hungry after God into "schools of the prophets." Here they received education and instruction out of the Law of Moses and were taught how to respond to the Spirit of the Lord in worship and prophecy (I Samuel 9:20).

The Scriptures speak of these centres, where the sons of the prophets would gather together in preparation for ministry. These men became known as "sons of the prophets" and there seemed to be schools of the prophets in these places.

★　Ramah — I Samuel 19:18-24.

★　Bethel — II Kings 2:3.

★　Jericho — II Kings 2:5, 7, 15.

★　Gilgal — II Kings 4:38; 2:1.

The dominant purpose in the establishment of these "schools of the prophets" was to maintain the spirit of the Law.

If Moses stood for the *letter* of the Law, the prophets indeed stood for the *spirit* of the Law. The true prophets of God never contradicted the letter of the Law; they upheld it. But when it degenerated into a dead form and mere ritual, the Holy Spirit came upon them to inspire and revive the spirit of the Law. Thus we have the Major and Minor Prophets, then 400 silent years unto John the Baptist (Luke 7:26-28).

F.　Old Testament Prophets in Relation to Kings

Not only do we see the beginning of the prophetic office in Samuel, we also see the beginning of the kingly office, or the monarchy in Israel. It was the prophet Samuel who anointed both Saul and David to their kingly ministry. From this period until the Captivities of the House of Israel and the House of Judah, there is a distinct relationship between the prophets and the kings. Most of the kings of Israel and Judah had a prophet of God sent to them. God's purpose was to influence the government of the nation as a whole through the king by means of the prophetic word. The prophet represented the Word of the Lord to the kings, and the kings were judged according to their acceptance or rejection of the prophetic word.

In previous periods, men inquired of God through the Priest, but now inquiry of God was primarily through the Prophet. Thus, most of the kings were privileged to have the ministry of the Word of the Lord through the prophets.

★　Saul and David had the ministry of Samuel (I Samuel 9, 10, 16).

★　David had Nathan and Gad also as prophets (II Samuel 12; 24:11).

★　Solomon had the prophet Nathan (I Kings 1:38).

★　Rehoboam had the prophet Sheminiah (I Kings 12:21, 22).

★　Ahab had Elijah and Elisha (I Kings 17:1; 19:16).

The kings of the House of Israel and Judah had prophets sent to them. These are referred to as the Major and Minor Prophets, and are spoken of in the opening verses of the Major and Minor Prophets. Examples are: Isaiah 1:1-2; Jeremiah 1:1-2; Hosea 1:1-2; Micah 1:1. An understanding of the character and times of the kings of Israel and Judah is necessary for an understanding of the nature of the Word of the Lord through the respective prophets of that period.

G.　Classification of Prophets

For the purposes of this section we will classify the prophets under two groupings: non-writing prophets and writing prophets.

1. **Non-writing Prophets**

   There are a number of prophets mentioned in Scripture who were not involved in the writing of Scripture. These ministered in the realms of guidance, forthtelling, foretelling, and words of wisdom and knowledge. God confirmed their ministries with signs and miracles. In the Old Testament there were men like Aaron, Nathan, Gad, Abijah, Elijah and Elisha. In the New Testament there were men such as John the Baptist, Agabus and Silas. John came at the "overlapping" of dispensations as the last of the Old Testament prophets.

2. **Writing Prophets**

   Out of the prophets God chose certain men to be inspired writers of Scripture (II Peter 1:20, 21). These prophets wrote Scripture in different styles: historical, prophetical and poetical.

   a. **Prophets who wrote Historical Books**

      Some prophets were primarily involved in writing history. Moses in writing the Pentateuch, and Samuel in writing the books of Judges, Ruth, I Samuel are two such men.

   b. **Prophets who wrote Poetical Books**

      Some prophets were inspired to write poetry. Two such men are David, who wrote many of the Psalms, and Jeremiah, who wrote Lamentations.

   c. **Prophets who wrote Prophetical Books**

      Many prophets were inspired to record their visions and prophecies. Daniel, Ezekiel and Zechariah, were especially prophets of vision. These they received and recorded under inspiration as infallible prophecy, foretelling the future and destiny of nations.

      The prophetical books of the Old Testament have been referred to as the Major and Minor Prophets. This distinction refers only to the volume of their contents.

      The Major Prophets are Isaiah, Jeremiah, Lamentations, Ezekiel and Daniel.

      The Minor Prophets are Hosea, Joel, Amos, Obadaiah, Jonah, Nahum, Habakkuk, Zephaniah, Haggai, Zechariah and Malachi. All of these books include both forthtelling and foretelling though greater emphasis in on the latter.

H. **Classification of Written Prophecy**

   In the writings of the prophets there can be found three major classifications of prophetic revelation. These are woven together throughout prophetic Scripture like a threefold cord, and are often so closely entwined that they are difficult to separate. The three are: Local Prophecy, National-Destiny Prophecy and the third one is Messianic Prophecy.

   1. **Local Prophecy**

      Local prophecy refers to those instances when the prophet spoke to his own generation about their spiritual condition and God's desire for them. This is viewed primarily as preaching in which the timeless principles and truths of God's character and being are revealed and applied to the life-situation of the prophet's own generation.

      Truth is eternal and remains the standard by which every generation is measured. This, truth is applicable to all generations and the truth applied to the prophet's day is also applicable today. However, before the interpreter can safely apply the prophet's message to present time he must be careful to study and accurately discern what the prophet was saying to his own generation. In order to do this the interpreter must thoroughly acquaint himself with the moral conditions of that day. Interpretation precedes application.

      Some examples of local prophecy are Isaiah 40:18-31; 55:6, 7; Jeremiah 26; and Micah

6:8. These prophecies obviously include timeless principles applicable to all generations.

2. **National-Destiny Prophecy**

National-destiny prophecy is when the prophet speaks concerning the future history of the nations. This is viewed primarily as prediction in which the prophet may use the nation's past history and its present condition as the stage upon which their future judgment and/or blessing is portrayed.

Though primarily concerned with the destiny of the chosen nation of Israel, the prophets also predicted the destiny of the Gentile nations.

Some examples of National-destiny prophecy concerning the nation of Israel are: Isaiah 11:11-16; 43:1-28; Jeremiah 30; Ezekiel 27 and Romans 9, 10, 11.

Some examples of National-destiny prophecy concerning the Gentile nations are: Isaiah 13-23; Jeremiah 46-51; Ezekiel 29-32; Daniel 2, 7; Amos 1, 2; Obadiah and Nahum.

In interpreting this area of prophecy, the interpreter must use the Hermeneutical Principle of Ethnic-Division so as not to confuse the destiny of the nations.

3. **Messianic Prophecy**

Messianic prophecy is when the prophet speaks concerning Christ and the Church. This is viewed primarily as prediction in which the prophet may use various elements of past history, the present local situation, and even the future national destiny to foretell the ultimate phase of God's purpose in the Messianic era. Messianic prophecy encompasses all that relates to Christ and the Church, from His first coming through to His second coming.

It was spoken of by Peter as ''the sufferings of Christ and the glory that should follow'' (I Peter 1:10-12). Messianic prophecy may be divided into three groupings, based on three stages of fulfilment:

a. **The First Coming of Christ**

These prophecies deal mainly with the birth, growth, ministry, sufferings and exaltation of the Lord Jesus Christ. Most of the Old Testament Messianic prophecies pertain to the first coming of Christ and its related events.

Some examples of these are: Genesis 3:15; Deuteronomy 18:15-18; Psalms 2, 8, 22 and 40; Isaiah 7:14; 9:6; 40:1-8; 52:14; 53:1-12; 61:1-4; Jeremiah 31:31; Micah 5:1-2; Zechariah 11:12-13; 13:9.

b. **The Church**

These prophecies deal mainly with that which was to be the fruit of Messiah's sufferings, even the glory of the Church (Ephesians 3:21). There are many Old Testament prophecies which deal with the coming of the Gentiles into the kingdom of the Messiah. The New Testament clearly shows that these prophecies were predicting the grafting in of the Gentiles into the olive tree so that both Jew and Gentile could become one Body in Christ (Psalms 18:49 with Romans 15:9; Deuteronomy 32:43 with Romans 15:10; Psalms 117:1 with Romans 15:11; Isaiah 11:10 with Romans 15:12; Romans 11:13-25; Ephesians 3:6; I Corinthians 12:13).

Some examples of Messianic prophecies concerning the Church are: Isaiah 9:6-9; 26:1-4; 35:1-10; 54:1-17; Jeremiah 31:33, 34; Joel 12:28-32; Zechariah 2:10, 11; Malachi 1:11.

c. **The Second Coming of Christ**

These prophecies deal primarily with Christ's return to consummate that which He initiated in His first coming. Though there were only a few specific prophecies in the Old Testament concerning Christ's second coming, there are many which deal with its related events. Many of these prophecies deal with ''the Day of the Lord'' and its climatic judgments. It should be noted that the burden of New Testament prophecy is the second coming of Christ.

Some examples of second coming prophecies are: Genesis 49:10; Isaiah 2:10-22; 13:6-16; 24:1-23; 30:26-33; 34:1-17; Daniel 2 and Daniel 7; Joel 3; Zechariah 14; Malachi 4:1-4; Matthew 24; Mark 13; Luke 21; I Corinthians 15; I Thessalonians 4:14-18; II Thessalonians 2; II Peter 3:1-13; Revelation 19.

I.   Christ, THE Prophet Like Unto Moses

Undoubtedly the greatest of all the Old Testament prophets was the prophet Moses. The Law was given by Moses (John 1:17). Moses was the foundation prophet of the Church in the Wilderness (Acts 7:38). All Old Testament prophets were tested, as to their authenticity, by what Moses had said. All who spoke were measured according to the revelation given to Moses.

Moses was the Mediator of the Old Covenant. He received direct revelation of the name of God, as the I AM. He was the architect, under God, of the Tabernacle of the Lord, the Aaronic Priesthood, the sacrificial system, and the Feasts of the Lord. The moral, civil and ceremonial law was delivered by the Lord God to and through him to Israel, the people of God (Exodus 20:18-21; Deuteronomy 4:10-40; Hebrews 12:18-21; Exodus 25-40; Leviticus 1-27; Numbers 1-32; Deuteronomy 1-34).

Under the inspiration of the Holy Spirit Moses wrote the Pentateuch, the foundational books of the Bible. All was done in the name of the Lord and as the Lord commanded. He was the faithful servant of Jehovah (Hebrews 3:1-6).

All true prophets of the Old Testament times were types of Christ, but Moses was the supreme type.

Moses prophesied of Christ (Deuteronomy 18:15-22), and warned of false prophets (John 5:39-47; 6:14; Acts 3:22-23).

There are particular phrases in the utterance of Moses concerning Christ which show Him to be THE Prophet of God, the Divine Spokesman for God.

1.   The Lord God would raise up to Israel a Prophet

As the Lord raised up true prophets, so He would raise up One who would be THE Prophet, THE Divine Spokesman. Whereas "the word of the Lord came" unto the other prophets, Christ would be THE WORD made flesh. The Word would not only come to Him. He would be THE WORD (John 1:1-3, 14-18). He was the Divine Word incarnate, God's mouthpiece. This sets Christ as a Prophet apart from, above and unique and distinct from all other prophets. All true prophets pointed to Christ. He was the fulfilment of their Messianic utterances and their office. Christ was raised up indeed to Israel (John 4:19; 7:40; 9:17; 1:21; 6:14).

2.   This Prophet would come from among the Brethren

This foretold the incarnation of Christ, the Word made flesh. The only way the Christ could come from the midst of His brethren after the flesh was by way of the virgin birth, taking upon Himself sinless humanity (Hebrews 2:10-14).

3.   This Prophet would be like Moses

As noted, Moses was one of the most remarkable types of Christ. There are many comparisons between Moses and Jesus. However, Christ the antitype was greater than Moses the type. Moses was the servant in the house while Christ was the Son over His own house (Hebrews 3:1-6).

We note some of the major comparisons:

a.   Both were born of the chosen nation Israel.

b.   Both were miraculously preserved from death as children and preserved in Egypt.

    c.   Both had the revelation of the Name of God, the I AM.

    d.   Both had signs and wonders in their ministry.

    e.   Both experienced rejection of their brethren.

    f.   Both were meek men.

    g.   Both came to exaltation in God's time.

    h.   Both had great intercessory ministry.

    i.   Both spoke the words of God.

    j.   Both built a house for the Lord to dwell in.

    k.   Both were mediators of Covenants.

    l.   Both were founders of a Church.

Many others could be given, but Jesus was indeed "like unto Moses", but excelled in glory (II Corinthians 3).

4. This Prophet would be a Mediator between God and Man

Israel did not want to hear God speak to them direct and asked that they might have a Mediator. God gave them Moses. Thus God spoke to Moses and Moses to Israel. So God has spoken to us in Christ and Christ speaks to His people as the New Covenant Mediator.

5. This Prophet would speak the words of God.

As God put the words in the mouth of Moses and Moses spoke them, so the Father put His words in the mouth of His Son who spoke them (Acts 3:32; John 17:8, 4:25; 8:28; 12:49, 50; 14:10, 24).

    a.   He forthtold (Matthew 5-6-7, etc.).

    b.   He foretold (Matthew 24; Mark 13; Luke 21).

6. This Prophet would speak in the Name of the Lord

Jesus not only spoke in His Father's Name, but also came in that Name, clothed in the nature, power and authority of the Father. Moses spoke in the Name of the Lord also, not in his own name (John 8:55-58; 5:43; 12:13).

7. Those who refuse this Prophet would be Judged

All who refused to hear Moses were judged by stoning. All who refuse to hear God the Father through His Son will be judged (John 12:48-50) in the day of judgment.

Christ is the only infallible Prophet for He was God THE WORD made flesh. He was God's mouthpiece (John 1:21, 25; 7:40; 6:14; 4:19; Matthew 21:11, 46; Mark 6:15; Luke 7:16; 24:19; John 9:17; Luke 9:8, 19; John 8:26; 14:10, 24; 17:8).

All prophets of Old Testament or New Testament times will be judged by Him and according to Him as to character, word and spirit.

J. Calling, Qualifications, Ministry and Recognition of New Testament Prophets

1. Calling

The Prophet, like the Apostle, or any other ministry must have a distinct calling from God, and know his calling. Old Testament prophets *knew* they were called of God. New Testament prophets should have this same inner conviction by the Holy Spirit. A prophet must know that God has "set" him in the Church (Ephesians 4:11; I Corinthians 12:28, 29). "The Word of the Lord" should come to him in clarity and truth.

2. Qualifications

The Prophet, as all of the fivefold ascension-gift ministries, should have the qualifications of an elder. The Prophet is also a ministry elder and must have character qualities in order to be all that God wants him to be. To be a prophet without qualifications leaves one open to deception because of the very nature of the prophetic ministry. To have charisma without character leaves one open and vulnerable to the enemy of the people of God.

3. **Ministry**

    A study of the prophets ministry mentioned in the New Testament, along with those in the Old Testament shows us what the ministry of the prophet is in the Church.

    a. Prophets have been *set* in the New Testament Church (I Corinthians 12:28, 29).

    b. Prophets are *second* in order in the Church (I Corinthians 12:29).

    c. Prophets are one of the fivefold ascension-gift ministries, an extension of Christ's own prophetic ministry and gift (Ephesians 4:11).

    d. Prophets have the spirit of prophecy upon them (Revelation 19:10).

    e. Prophets have the gift of prophecy (I Corinthians 14:3, 31; 12:8).

    f. Prophets are given for:

        1) The perfecting and maturing of the saints,

        2) The work of bringing the saints into their ministry,

        3) The edifying and building up of the Body of Christ (Ephesians 4:9-16; Ezekiel 37. Word and Spirit bring the body together).

    g. Prophets, undoubtedly, were used to confirm the separation of Paul and Barnabas to apostolic work from the Church at Antioch (Acts 13:1-4).

        Fasting, prayer, laying on of hands, and the Spirit speaking are the things seen in this matter here. Such here constituted a local presbytery of "prophets and teachers" involved in the ordination and sending out of other ministries (I Timothy 4:14; 1:18; II Timothy 1:14).

    h. Prophets, such as Judas and Silas, ministered in exhortation and confirmation in the Churches (Acts 15:22; also read Ezra 5:1; 6:14).

    i. Prophets, like Agabus, in warning predicted (foretold) by the Spirit the coming famine, which word came to pass (Acts 11:27-30). The disciples responded by sending relief to the saints.

        Agabus also foretold what would happen to Paul at Jerusalem, confirming what Paul already knew (Acts 21:8-14).

    j. Prophets had a distinctive ministry in the early Church, as seen in the Corinthians Epistle. The prophets spoke, two or three, giving complete testimony (I Corinthians 14:29-32).

        This chapter relative to prophecy includes:

        1) Exhortation — "to stir up"

        2) Edification — "to build up"

        3) Comfort — "to bind up"

        4) Conviction — "to open up" the heart and expose the secrets therein and cause people to fall down and worship God (I Corinthians 14:3, 24, 25 with I Samuel 11-12, Nathan and David's sin exposed by the prophetic word).

    k. Prophets are not infallible and their utterances must be judged by the infallible word of God (I Corinthians 14:29, 30; Galatians 2:9-14). A prophet should be humble enough to allow his word to be judged. If it is the mind of God there is nothing to fear. In the mouth of two or three witnesses shall every word be established (Deuteronomy 19:15; II Corinthians 13:1).

    l. Prophets must have their spirits under control and be subject to the Holy Spirit. The Holy Spirit will never cause prophets to act or speak contrary to His will or word (I

Corinthians 14:32, 33). The spirits of the prophets are subject to the prophets. Temperance or self-control is a fruit of the Spirit that should work with the gifts of the Spirit and the Lord (Galatians 5:22, 23).

m. Prophets may be given certain gifts of the Spirit, and signs of the prophetic office as the Lord wills. False prophets have counterfeit signs (Matthew 24:11, 24; Mark 13:22). Prophets may be given:

1) Visions — Numbers 12:6-8.

2) Dreams — Numbers 12:6-8.

3) Word of Wisdom — I Corinthians 12:6-9.

4) Word of Knowledge.

5) Miracles.

6) Healings

7) Gift of Faith.

8) Discerning of spirits.

9) Prophecy, exhortation, edification, comfort, conviction.

10) Peculiar signs, examples of which are seen in the following:

★   Jeremiah with a yoke on his neck — Jeremiah 27.

★   Hosea married a harlot — Hosea 1-3.

★   Isaiah walks uncovered and barefoot for three years — Isaiah 20:1-6.

★   Ezekiel in mock seige on a tile, on his side for many days, eating of cow dung, burning portion of his hair, prophesying to a boneyard, etc. — Ezekiel 4, 5, 37.

★   Ahijah tearing a new garment to 12 pieces — I Kings 11:30.

★   Jeremiah's signs — Jeremiah 13:1; 18:1; 19:1; 25:15.

★   Isaiah's sign children — Isaiah 8:1 (Hosea also, Hosea 1-2.)

★   Prophesying to mountains, digging through walls — Ezekiel 6:1-3; 12:1-6.

★   Agabus binding Paul with a girdle — Acts 21.

n. Prophets will be inspired (illuminated) preachers of the Word of God (Hebrews 1:1-2; II Peter 1:20, 21; I Peter 1:10-12).

Isaiah, Jonah, John the Baptist, Judas, Silas, Agabus, etc. All these prophets receive illumination on the revelation given by inspiration.

o. Prophets, with the Apostles, are foundational ministries in the Church (Ephesians 2:20-22; 3:5). They work together and lay the foundation which is Christ.

p. Prophets of God will always have to contend with false prophets. Elijah, Jeremiah, Micah, Amos, Paul and Silas, etc., all had such to contend with. The people will know the true prophets by having a love for the truth (II Thessalonians 2:1-12; Revelation 13; Matthew 24:11, 24).

q. Prophets will have Divine revelation given to them concerning the Church, along with the Apostles (Ephesians 3:1-5).

4. **Recognition**

It is important that God's people know how to recognize and accept the ministry of the prophet. In order for a prophet to be released in his ministry, he must be received, once he is recognized as a true prophet (Matthew 10:41, 42).

Often prophets are not received in their own country (Matthew 13:57; 23:29-37; Mark 6:4; Luke 4:24; James 5:10).

We are to believe the Lord's prophets and prosper and be established (II Chronicles 20:20).

We are not to touch the Lord's anointed prophets (Psalms 105:15).

John the Baptist was the greatest of all prophets because he came at the close of the Old Covenant Age and introduced Messiah of the New Covenant Age (Luke 1:76).

a.   **New Testament Prophets**

In the early church we have the following references to prophets, both named and unnamed.

1) Ananias was possibly a prophet to Saul (Acts 9:1-15; 22:10-15).

2) Judas and Silas were prophets (Acts 15:32).

3) Prophets and Teachers at Antioch (Acts 13:1-4).

4) Prophets sent from Jerusalem (Acts 11:27).

5) Prophets at Tyre (Acts 21:4).

6) Agabus was a proven prophet (Acts 11:28; 21:10-11).

7) Prophets at Corinth (I Corinthians 14:27, 29; 12:28, 29).

8) Prophets at Ephesus (Ephesians 4:9-11).

9) Prophets among the scattered Churches (II Peter 2:1-2; I John 4:1-3).

10) False Prophets at Crete (Titus 1:10-13).

As in all ministries and functions within the Body of Christ, so it is among the prophets of God. The "cluster of prophets", though all having the office of the prophet, will manifest great variety, according to the personality, the character, temperament, and gift of grace given them. This is evidenced in the variety of prophets spoken of as the Major and Minor Prophets in the Old Testament times. It is true in New Testament times also. It is according to "the measure of the gift of Christ."

Isaiah, Jeremiah and Ezekiel had the greater measure of the gift than did Micah, Joel, Amos and other of the lesser prophets; yet all were prophets of God.

There were prophets to the nations, Israel and Gentile nations.

There were prophets to the kings in the Old Testament.

There were prophets in and to the New Testament Churches.

Thus there is great variety of the gift and office of Christ's ministry as the Prophet. All are fragmentary extensions of His Prophetic office in His people.

b.   **Ministry of the Prophetesses**

God, at times, bestowed the prophetic ministry on women. In the last days, the Lord said he would pour out His Spirit on all flesh, including "sons and daughters, servants and handmaids" (Acts 2:17-22 with Joel 2:28-32). We note some of the Prophetesses mentioned in Scripture.

1) **Old Testament Prophetesses**

★   **Miriam,** Moses' sister, was a prophetess and led in the song of the Lord and the dancing women (Exodus 15:20).

★   **Deborah** was a prophetess, judge and mother in Israel and led in prophetic battle song with Barak (Judges 4:4).

★   **Huldah** was a prophetess who spoke and taught the Word of the Lord at Jerusalem (II Kings 22:12-20; II Chronicles 34:22).

★   **Noadiah** also was a false prophetess in times of restoration from the Babylonian Captivity (Nehemiah 6:14).

★ **Isaiah's wife** was a prophetess, along with her husband's ministry (Isaiah 8:3).

★ There were apparently false prophetesses in Ezekiel's time also along with false prophets (Ezekiel 13:17-23). Read the whole chapter for it deals with men and women in false utterances.

★ **Anna,** 84 years of age, of the tribe of Asher, served God with prayers and fastings in the temple as a prophetess and was accepted by the priests there (Luke 2:36-38).

2) **New Testament Prophetesses**

★ **Jezebel** is the only specific mention of a New Testament Church having a prophetess, who taught false doctrine as a prophetess and teacher (Revelation 2:20).

★ **Philip,** the Evangelist, had four daughters which did prophesy, but they were not called prophetesses. The Lord sent Agabus, a male prophet, to speak to Paul the apostle (Acts 21:7-9). However, it does show that the Spirit fell on "handmaidens" in the last days in prophecy.

The Holy Spirit is available for all flesh, men and women. If the Lord is pleased to pour out His Spirit on women as well as men, then we must be willing to recognize and accept any God-given in the Church, even as above. (The subject of *Women's Ministry* will be dealt with in a subsequent chapter).

K. **Distinction between Old Testament and New Testament Prophets**

It is essential to understand the particular difference between the Old Testament and New Testament Prophet for a proper recognition of the prophet's function in the New Testament Church. Christ did not choose any Prophet in His earthly ministry. He chose Twelve Apostles. THIS immediately shows a break with that which was in the Old Testament times in the powerful and dominant ministry of the Prophet. He chose no prophet before the Cross, but after His crucifixion, resurrection and ascension. He chose Apostles to be the foundation of the Church and the city of God (Revelation 21:14).

We note these further facts about the Old Testament prophets. They fall into two particular groupings, which help us to distinguish the New Testament prophets ministry from that of the Old Testament.

1. **Prophets of Guidance**

Moses, Aaron, Samuel, Elijah and Elisha, etc., were especially prophets used in the ministry of guidance. The word of wisdom, word of knowledge, forthtelling, foretelling, miracles, etc., confirmed to all that they were Prophets of Jehovah who revealed and declared the mind of God, and often times, His personal will to the people. They were God's spokesmen.

Guidance was given through Prophet, Priest, Urim and Thummin, Vision, Dream, Voice, Angelic visitation, etc., because the Holy Spirit was not available for "all flesh" under Old Covenant times. Man did not have direct approach to God through Christ, but through an earthly Mediator and Priest.

2. **Prophets of Vision and Scripture**

a. **Prophets of Vision**

Daniel and Zechariah were especially Prophets of Vision. They were Seers, in which God gave them visions, which they recorded under Divine inspiration as *infallible prophecy,* foretelling the future and destiny of the nations of earth. However, Daniel did not utter prophecy as a Prophet or Spokesman of God to the people, as far as we understand.

b. **Prophets of Scripture**

Ezekiel, Isaiah, Jeremiah, Joel, Hosea, Amos and all of the Writings Prophets, the Major and Minor Prophets, were particularly used in the realm of prophecy, the prophetic Scriptures. In the fullest sense of forthtelling and foretelling they spoke of the destiny of nations, both Israel and Gentile. God spoke and caused them to write *infallible Scripture,* yet He overruled the fallibility of these men, using their personalities through it all. In inspiration He overruled their infirmities and imperfections and caused infallible revelation to come through fallible men. Yet most of these Prophets were not used in the realm of the miraculous, as were the Prophets of Guidance, like Moses and Elijah and Elisha.

These Prophets of Scripture became God's voice for their present and the future generations.

3. **Distinctions between Old and New Testament Prophets**

The two essential differences between Old and New Testament Prophets are as follows:

a. Old Testament Prophets were especially used in guidance, direction, and enquiry of the mind and will of God, because the Spirit was not available for all flesh.

b. Old Testament Prophets were especially used to utter and write infallible Scriptures. (II Peter 1:20).

Thus although there will be variations of the Prophetic ministry in the New Testament Church, as there was variety in Old Testament Prophets as God willed to use them, yet these differences will always remain.

It is therefore important to note these facts and truths:

1) No New Testament Prophet was ever used in guidance and control of another person's life. They were used to *confirm* the already known and revealed will of God. But, for New Testament believers "as many as are led by the Spirit of God, they are the sons of God" (Romans 8:14). This is God's norm. To resort to a Prophet for direction, guidance or control, is to violate the ministry of New Covenant believers, of having access to God through Christ, by the Spirit, who is available for "all flesh" in this dispensation.

2) No New Testament Prophet was ever used in the utterance of infallible Scripture. All prophetic utterances were to be judged by the Word of Scripture (I Corinthians 14:29, 30, 32). Most of the New Testament was written by the Apostles!

Thus, for New Covenant believers:

★ Guidance and direction comes from the infallible Word of God, the Scriptures.

★ Guidance is also by the indwelling Holy Spirit, always leading in harmony with, never contrary to, the infallible Word He inspired (Romans 8:14).

★ Guidance may be confirmed through various ministries set in the Church, such as Prophets.

L. **Testing the Ministry of the Prophet**

There are some basic tests by which all Prophets, as well as other ministries, may be proven.

Both Old Testament and New Testament abound with evidences and warnings against false prophets. Undoubtedly this is because of its inspirational ministry and the emotional nature of the prophet that there is greater danger of deception. Many passages warn of *false prophets.* Wherever and whenever there are true prophets, Satan will stir up false prophets in order to deceive people.

Note — Matthew 24:11, 24; Jeremiah 5:30, 31; 26:15; 28:9; Ezekiel 13; Revelation 16:13; 19:20; 20:10; Jeremiah 23:18-22; Revelation 13; Matthew 7:15-23; Deuteronomy 18:22; I Timothy 4:1-2; II Thessalonians 2:1-12; I Kings 22; Revelation 2:2; I John 4:1-2; Luke 6:26; II Peter 2:1-2; II Timothy 3:13; I Corinthians 12:1-3; Isaiah 8:18-20; Micah 2:11; Mark 13:22; Acts 13:4-12). It seems as if there are more warnings against the false prophets than any other ministry, although the truth can be applied to all false ministries.

There are seven major tests of false prophets and these may be applied to any of the ministries for testing them.

1. **Test of the spirit** (I John 4:1-3)

    We have to discern and test the spirit of truth and the spirit of error.

    In I Kings 22 we see prophetic utterances by the prophets and the three spirits that can be at work in prophetic utterances.

    a. **The Holy Spirit** in the mouth of the *one true prophet* — verse 17.

       II Chronicles 15:1; 24:20; I Corinthians 14:29-33, 37; 12:28-29; Ephesians 3:5; 4:11; Revelation 18:20; Luke 2:36; Acts 13:1-2; 11:27; 15:32; 21:10. The Holy Spirit inspires true utterances of the word.

    b. **The Human spirit** — verse 15. Note also Ezekiel 13:1-6; Jeremiah 23:16, 17, 26-32. Here they spoke out of their own heart, their own spirit, and had seen nothing.

    c. **The Satanic spirit** — verses 22, 23. Here it was a lying spirit in the mouth of all the prophets of Baal. Read also Isaiah 8:19, 20; I John 4:1; II Peter 2:1-2; II Thessalonians 2:3-12; Revelation 13:11-18; 16:13, 14; 19:20; Matthew 8:29; Acts 16:17.

    Thus we have to "try", test or prove and examine the spirit behind the utterance.

2. **Test of Fulfilment of Prophetic Word** (Deuteronomy 18:22)

    Does the word come to pass or not? This is another test of prophecy. All knew that Samuel was established to be a prophet of the Lord for the Lord let none of his words fall to the ground (I Samuel 3:19-21).

3. **Test of Worship** (Deuteronomy 13:1-5)

    Though the prophet may give *a sign* or have dreams that come to pass, another test is whether his word leads one away from the worship of the true God to the worship of false gods (Revelation 13; Matthew 24:11, 24; II Thessalonians 2:1-12). It is the worship test. True prophets cause us to worship the true God.

4. **Test of Doctrine** (I John 4:1-6; I Timothy 4:1-3; Isaiah 8:18-20).

    All prophets have to be checked out doctrinally against the revelation of the Word of God. The major doctrines of redemption, the fundamental truths of salvation have to be checked out. If they speak not according to this Word it is because there is no light in them (Matthew 24:11, 24, 25; Mark 13:22; Matthew 7:15-23; Revelation 16:13, 14; Jeremiah 14:16; Ezekiel 14:10, 11).

5. **Test of Fruit** (Matthew 7:15-23; Revelation 2:20; Romans 6:16-22).

    False prophets may have gifts but lack holiness of living. What is the fruit of their ministry, their life? This is the test. By their "*fruits*" — NOT gifts — shall ye know them. Must not mistake charisma for character. Fruit is the outward evidence of the inner nature and character of the tree.

6. **Test of Covetousness** (Micah 3:11; II Peter 2:1-3)

    Covetousness is the root sin. You shall know false prophets and other ministries by their love of money. They make merchandise of the people of God.

Judas, Simon, Achan, Sapphira and Ananias all fell over money. The love of money is the root of all evil. It drowns men in destruction, perdition and numerous temptations (I Timothy 6).

7.   **Test of Ministry to the People** (Jeremiah 23:18-23)

Jeremiah's test of prophets was whether they turned people to God from their sinful lifestyle. Without holiness none shall see the Lord (Hebrews 12:7-14).

CHAPTER 21

THE MINISTRY OF THE APOSTLES AND PROPHETS

Introductory:

It is worthy to note that the apostle and prophet work closely together in the Body of Christ. Both act as "checks and balances" on the other, as these Scriptures show. Jesus sent the Twelve out two by two (Luke 9). He also sent out the seventy two by two (Luke 10). The two are stronger than the one. If the one falls, the other lifts him up. Two witnesses to each city was the order before Christ came to each city. So the apostle and prophet, as "two witnesses" work together.

They are like the two legs of the human body, foundational, and transport for the Body. They work together in unity.

Two is the number of witness, testimony, harmony, one with one.

A. Old Testament Type

One of the great Old Testament types is that seen in Moses and Aaron. Moses was the apostle and Aaron the prophet of the Church in the Wilderness (Exodus 1-7). They were foundational ministries. Acts 7:38.

B. New Testament Ministries

1. The Church is built on the foundation laid by the apostles and prophets (Ephesians 2:19-22). Other ministries build on this.

2. He gave some apostles and prophets until the Church is matured and perfected (Ephesians 4:9-11).

3. All are not apostles and prophets (I Corinthians 12:28, 29).

4. It is firstly apostles, secondarily prophets, in Divine order though all are co-equal as persons (I Corinthians 12:28, 29).

5. Babylonian systems hate the apostles and prophets who are against them (Revelation 18:20).

6. The revelation of the Church is given to the apostles and prophets (Ephesians 3:5).

7. In the wisdom of God, He will send apostles and prophets and teachers and some of them will be rejected and crucified (Luke 11:49).

8. Christ spoke of apostles, prophets and scribes coming (Matthew 23:34).

9. Paul and Silas, as apostle and prophet, worked together (Acts 15:22-40; 16:6, 7).

10. In Revelation 13 we see a false apostle (antichrist) and a false prophet working together in deception of the whole world in worship.

11. The Old Testament Prophets and New Testament Apostles work together in the sense that the Old Testament prophets prophesied while the New Testament apostles saw New Testament fulfilments (II Peter 3:1-2).

God must bring these ministries together, to work in unity of heart, mind, spirit and faith, for the body of Christ.

CHAPTER 22

THE MINISTRY OF THE EVANGELIST

Introductory:

"And He gave some . . . . *evangelists* . . ." (Ephesians 4:11).
"Philip the *evangelist*" (Acts 21:8-10).
"Do the work of an *evangelist*" (II Timothy 4:5).

We come now the ascension-gift ministry of the Evangelist. There is little problem or controversy over the ministry of the Evangelist compared to that which pertains to the Apostle and Prophet.

A. **Definition of Word**

There are three words relative to the ministry of the evangelist all coming from the same root word in the Greek. Our English word is derived from such.

There is the Hebrew thought pertaining to the Gospel which is also considered.

1. **Greek**

   a. **Euaggelizo** = "to announce good news or glad tidings." (SC 2097).
   It especially speaks of the *ministry* of the evangelist. Jesus Christ was THE Evangelist and His ministry evidenced that He was the announcer of good tidings (Matthew 11:5; Luke 1:19; 2:10; 8:1; 16:16; Acts 8:4, 12, 25, 35; 13:32; Ephesians 2:17). This word is used 11 times in the Gospel of Matthew and Luke. It is used about 45 times in the whole of the New Testament.

   b. **Euaggelion** = "the gospel or the good message" (SC 2098).
   It especially speaks of the *message* that the evangelist brings. It speaks of the saving gospel of the kingdom of our Lord Jesus Christ and all that pertains to it. It involves the death, burial and resurrection of Christ and salvation received by faith on that basis (Mark 1:1; Matthew 24:14; Acts 15:7; 20:24; 16:25; Galatians 2:2-7; Revelation 14:6; Ephesians 2:17).

   c. **Euanggelistes** = "a preacher or messenger of good news" (SC 2099).
   From EU = well, and ANGELOS = A messenger. It especially speaks of the *person* who is the evangelist, be it man or woman.

   This Greek word is specifically used only three times in the New Testament. It is used of Philip the Evangelist (Acts 21:8); of one of the fivefold ascension-gift ministries (Ephesians 4:11), and Paul exhorts Timothy to do the work of an Evangelist (II Timothy 4:5).

   In Summary, the Evangelist is a person with a distinctive ministry, and is a bearer of the message of good news in the saving Gospel of Christ.

   It may also be said that these related Greek words speak of the *ministry*, the *man*, and the *message* of the Evangelist.

2. **Hebrew**

   Although the New Testament holds the emphasis on the Gospel of Christ as being the good news for all mankind, there is a Hebrew word that carried with it the same thought.

   Basar = "To be fresh. i.e., full (rosy, fig., cheerful); to announce (glad news) (SC 13).

   It is translated:
   Messenger — I Samuel 14:17
   Preach — Psalms 40:9; Isaiah 61:1
   Publish — I Samuel 31:9; II Samuel 1:20

Shew forth (bear, bring, carry, preach, good, tell good) — I Chronicles 16:23; Psalms 96:2; I Kings 1:42; Isaiah 60:6

Tidings — Isaiah 61:1; II Samuel 18:19, 20; Jeremiah 20:15; I Chronicles 10:9; II Samuel 4:10; Psalms 68:11; Isaiah 40:9; 41:27; 52:7; Nahum 1:15.

It is mainly used of Christ and of those who bring good tidings (i.e., the coming Gospel). Isaiah 40:9; 41:27; 52:7; 61:1; Psalms 68:11; Proverbs 25:25.

In summary this Hebrew word speaks of a messenger who preaches, publishes and brings, bears and carries good tidings. It certainly pointed to the coming Gospel of Christ — The Evangel!

B. Christ THE Evangelist

Without doubt, Christ is THE Evangelist. He is the Messenger of God, the One who preached, published and brought good tidings. He is the "good news" personified. The Old Testament, especially Isaiah, the Prophet-Evangelist, wrote in his Scriptures of Christ as the One who would bring good tidings (Isaiah 41:27; 52:7; 40:9).

He *preached* righteousness in the great congregation (Psalms 40:9).

Luke's Gospel takes up the prophecy of Christ the Evangelist from Isaiah 61:1-2 in Luke 4:18, 19, and sets out in great sentences the ministry of Christ the Evangelist. We bring both prophecy and history together.

1. The Spirit of Jehovah is upon Me and He has anointed Me.
2. To preach good tidings or the Gospel to the meek.
3. To bind and heal the brokenhearted.
4. To proclaim and preach deliverance to the captives.
5. To recover sight to the blind.
6. To open the prison to them that are bound.
7. To set at liberty them that are bruised.
8. To preach and proclaim the acceptable year of the Lord (i.e., the year of release and the year of Jubilee. Cf. Leviticus 25).

Luke's Gospel uses the word *"euaggelizo"* about 10 times, especially in relation to Christ's ministry.

★ Gabriel announced "glad tidings" to Zacharias (Luke 1:19).

★ The Angel announced "glad tidings" to the Shepherds (Luke 2:10).

★ John the Baptist announced good tidings (Luke 3:18).

★ Christ preached the Gospel and glad tidings of the kingdom of God in His ministry (Luke 4:18, 43; 7:22; 8:1; 16:16; 20:1; Matthew 10:35, 36).

★ The Twelve announced the glad tidings also (Luke 9:6).

The above passage from Luke gives a good summary of the ministry of Christ as the Evangelist. This was His ministry and He abundantly fulfilled it. The Gospel story abounds with evidences of His evangelistic ministry. He is the pattern evangelist.

C. Calling, Qualifications, Ministry and Recognition of the Evangelist

1. Calling

As with every ministry, so the Evangelist must know that he has that distinctive calling in the body of Christ.

Christ must *give* this ministry gift of Evangelist to some (Ephesians 4:9-11).

It is simply an extension of His own evangelistic ministry in some members of the Body. It is Christ the Evangelist re-living His own life and operating His ministry through these members with that gift.

2. **Qualifications**

    As with each of the fivefold ascension-gift ministries, so it is with the evangelist. He should be a qualified Elder, as to character, doctrine, conduct, as well as charisma.

    Philip, the evangelist, as a qualified Deacon, was a man:

    a. Full of the Holy Spirit,

    b. Full of faith,

    c. Wisdom,

    d. Of good report among his local Church at Jerusalem,

    e. Had his home in order, four of his daughters having the gift of prophecy. Undoubtedly he had the other qualifications of Deacons and Elders also and rose to the ministry gift of the evangelist.

3. **Ministry**

    a. Evangelists are *set* in the Body of Christ by the risen Lord (Ephesians 4:9-11) until the Church comes to a perfect man.

    b. Evangelists are also given to the Body of Christ:

        1) For the perfecting of the saints, to mature them.

        2) For the work of bringing the saints into their ministry. That is, they are to stir the saints to personal evangelism, as well as equip and release others with the evangelistic gift.

        3) For the edifying of the Body of Christ.

    c. Evangelists especially are the messengers and bearers of glad tidings to a lost and dying world. They are called to evangelize.

    d. Evangelists should have a sound Gospel message and therefore need to be well grounded in the fundamental truths of redemption to present the Gospel rightly.

    e. Evangelists should have the gifts of the Spirit suitable to their ministry. They should have ''signs following'' their word (Mark 16:15-20).

    f. Evangelists have a passion for souls and a soul-saving ministry (Proverbs 14:25).

    g. Evangelists have great wisdom in winning souls (Proverbs 11:30). They are fishers of men, depending upon the Lord to move fish into the Gospel-net as they let down the right Gospel-bait.

    h. Evangelists have a compelling ministry to bring sinners to the Gospel feast (Luke 14:33).

4. **Recognition**

    The same basic principle of Matthew 10:41, 42 is applicable to the Evangelist also.

    The Body of Christ needs to recognize and receive the ministry of the Evangelist. To do so is to accept Christ in His members ministering both to the world and to the Church is this gift.

D. **Philip, A Pattern New Testament Evangelist**

    While there are a number of Apostles and several Prophets in the New Testament, Philip is the only person specifically evidencing and named in the ministry gift of Evangelist.

    A study of this man gives enough material to set him forth as a pattern of Christ's evangelistic ministry.

    We consider Philip in his evangelistic ministry in both Public and Personal evangelism.

1. **Philip-Public Evangelism** (Acts 8:1-25)

   a. **The Ministry**

   Philip is distinctly called an Evangelist (Acts 21:8).
   Christ gave this gift to him (Ephesians 4:9-11).
   Philip was one of the seven Deacons in the local Church at Jerusalem before he surfaced to his ascension-gift ministry as an evangelist (Acts 6:1-6).

   Thus Philip belonged to a local Church and proved himself as a servant (deacon) there first. He was approved there. Undoubtedly there is a good principle here implicit in this fact for potential ministries.

   b. **The Message**

   Philip's message is clear. He gave the evangel, the good tidings, the good news (Acts 8:1-25).

   1) He preached the WORD (vs 4).

   2) He preached Christ to the Samaritans (vs 5).

   3) He preached the Kingdom or the Rule and Reign of God (vs 12 with Matthew 24:14).

   4) He preached the Name of Jesus Christ (vs 12).

   He had signs following the preaching of the good news, signs of the evangel as promised by Christ (Mark 16:15-20).

   ★ Casting out of unclean spirits in possessed people.

   ★ Healing of palsied people.

   ★ Healing of the lame.

   ★ Miracles and signs (vs 7, 13).

   6) He baptized people in the Name of the Lord Jesus Christ (vs 12, 13, 16).

   7) He, however, did not discern the heart of Simon the sorcerer until the apostles, Peter and John, came down from Jerusalem and allowed him to expose himself under the right circumstances (vs 13-24).

   8) He brought great joy to the city of Samaria (vs 9, with John 4; Christ's own evangelistic ministry there).

   What a contrast to the sorcerer. He gave himself out to be some great one, and bewitched the people, doing counterfeit signs and wonders by the power of darkness, enslaving people in the Kingdom of Satan as an enchanter with drugs.

   Philip preached Christ, delivered people with signs and wonders of the Kingdom of Light, and brought joy to the city by the power of the Holy Spirit and the Gospel of Christ. Philip recognized the Apostolic ministry and did not "pastor" Samaria. This was the foundation of the local Church in Samaria.

2. **Philip-Personal Evangelism** (Acts 8:27-30)

   a. Philip was sensitive to the voice of the Lord and obeyed when he heard (vs 26).

   b. Philip did not fear to minister to the Eunuch, a man of authority (vs 27).

   c. Philip was willing to be led by the Spirit to this one soul in need (vs 29).

   d. Philip knew the Scriptures and was able to preach the Gospel to the Eunuch from the Old Testament in the light of Calvary (vs 30-34).

   e. Philip preached unto him CHRIST — a person, not merely a doctrine (vs 35).

   f. Philip preached saving faith to the Eunuch (vs 37).

   g. Philip saw that the new believer was immediately baptized in water (vs 38-39).

The wisdom and dependance upon the Spirit seen in Philip's personal evangelist is indeed a good example to follow in personal work.

E. **Woman Evangelists**

Because the Lord promised to pour out His Spirit on all flesh, ''servants and handmaids, sons and daughters'', there are times when the Lord used women in the evangel. This seemed to be in fulfilment to Psalm 68:11 (the same Psalm which speaks prophetically of the ascension-gift ministries; vs 18).

''The Lord gives the word (of power); *the women* who bear and publish (the news) are a great host.'' (Amplified Old Testament).

Paul mentioned ''women who laboured with him in the Gospel'' (Philippians 4:3).
(Refer to Chapter on ''*Ministry of Women*'' for fuller treatment of this subject).

F. **Areas of Evangelism**

There are various areas where evangelism can take place. The field is the world — the Gospel is for every creature, everywhere, wherever and by every opportunity that one can use.

1. Garden Park evangelism.
2. House to house evangelism — Acts 2:42, 47.
3. Beach evangelism.
4. Child evangelism — Matthew 19:14.
5. Rest Home evangelism — Psalms 71:9.
6. Hospital evangelism — Matthew 25:36, 43.
7. Prison evangelism — Matthew 26:36, 43.
8. Home Bible Class evangelism — Acts 20:18-21.
9. Secular employment evangelism — work mates.
10. Personal evangelism as the Spirit directs — Acts 8:27-40.
11. Public or mass evangelism — Acts 8:1-26.

CHAPTER 23

THE MINISTRY OF THE PASTOR

Introductory:

"And He gave some . . . *Pastors* . . ." (Ephesians 4:11).

The ministry of the Pastor is also one of the fivefold ascension-gift ministries of Christ given to and for the Body of Christ.

In contrast to the ministries of the Apostle and Prophet, which have generally been rejected by the Church, the pastoral ministry has been accepted over the centuries. However, there has been and still is much misunderstanding and confusion as a result, concerning the pastoral ministry.

Most of the textbooks dealing with the ministry of the Pastor lay upon one man a burden that is impossible to bear. This comes because there is not a recognition of the fivefold ministry, and a plurality of eldership in the local Church.

The "Pastor" is expected to be an all-round "one-man-ministry" and relate to every-one on every level, and every leader in every department of the Church.

The result is that numerous pastors, under such pressure break down, either mentally, emotionally, morally or spiritually. God never intended this to be.

The general denominational concept of the "pastor" is that he is responsible for the total flock under his care. Also, he may call in a teacher or an evangelist for any special occasions as the need arises. But the burden of the Church is on his shoulders.

But God's pattern is that the pastor is simply one of the fivefold ministries and has other co-equal elders working together and sharing the burden with him.

The word "pastor" may be used in a very broad sense and yet it may also be seen in its stricter sense as applicable to those gift ministries who distinctly have the ascension-gift ministry of a Pastor. Nothing can change the fact that Pastors are ministry gifts. It is one of the fivefold ascension-gift ministries given by Christ to the Church.

Christ is THE Apostle, Prophet, Evangelist, Pastor and Teacher! All offices and ministries are in Him. Yet He has but one heart pulsating in all — that is, *a shepherd's heart*!

Therefore, *all* ministries, regardless of calling and placement in the Body should have and should be motivated by the heart of a shepherd. In this sense we may say that all fivefold ministries are *"shepherding ministries"*. They together care for the flock of God.

However, Christ, when He ascended on high, gave gifts to men "and He gave some . . . *pastors.*"

All pastors are not apostles, prophets, evangelists or teachers. There are some persons who have a distinct pastoral call different from yet related to the other four of the fivefold ministries. This will be seen in the course of this chapter. Christ continues His pastoral ministry in some persons distinctly called pastors.

A. **Definition of Word**

We consider certain words from both Hebrew and Greek which help us to understand the ministry of the pastor.

1. **Old Testament Hebrew**

"*Ra'ah*" (SC 7462) = "to tend a flock; i.e., to pasture it; to graze (lit. or fig.); generally, to rule."

It is translated:

a. **Pastor** — peculiar to Jeremiah in King James Version (Jeremiah 2:8; 3:15; 10:21; 12:10; 17:16; 22:22; 23:1, 2).

    b. **Shepherd** — Genesis 46:32, 34; 47:3; 49:24; Exodus 2:17, 19; I Kings 22:17; Psalms 23:1; 80:1; Isaiah 44:28; Jeremiah 6:3; 23:4; Ezekiel 34:2-23; 37:24.

    c. **Herdsmen** — Genesis 13:7, 8; 26:20; I Samuel 21:7.

    d. **Keeper** — Genesis 4:2; 29:9; Exodus 3:1; I Samuel 16:11.

    e. **Feed** — I Samuel 17:15; I Chronicles 17:6; Psalms 68:71; Ezekiel 34:10; Zechariah 11:4, 7; Isaiah 40:11.

        Together then this Hebrew word means one who tends a flock, pastures, grazes, feed, keeps, herds, rules and shepherds sheep. This is the pastoral ministry.

  2. **New Testament Greek**

    "*Poimen*" (SC 4166) = "A shepherd" (lit. or fig.).

    It is translated "shepherd" 17 times, and "pastor" once.

    Matthew 9:36; 25:32; 26:31; Mark 6:34; 14:27; Luke 2:8, 15, 18, 20; I Peter 2:25; Hebrews 13:20; John 10:2, 11-16 and Ephesians 4:11.

    "*Poimaino*" (SC 4165) = "to tend as a shepherd, or shepherdize" (or fig. superviser).

    It is translated "feed, rule".

    Matthew 2:6; Luke 17:7; John 21:16; Acts 20:28; I Corinthians 9:7; I Peter 5:2; Jude 12; Revelation 2:27; 7:17; 12:5; 19:15.

    "*Poimne*" (SC 4167), contracted from SC 4165; = "a flock" (lit. or fig.).

    It is translated "flock, fold".

    Matthew 26:31; Luke 2:8; John 10:16; I Corinthians 9:7.

    "*Poimnion*" (SC 4168), derivative of SC 4167; = "a flock", i.e., (fig.) group of believers.

    It is translated "flock".

    Luke 12:32; Acts 20:28, 29; I Peter 5:2, 3.

    "*Bosko*" (SC 1006) = "to feed, pasture; to fodder, to graze".

    It is translated "feed, keep".

    Luke 15:15; Matthew 8:30, 33.

    Together these words show that a pastor is one who tends or herds flocks; feeding, guiding, and superintending them. A pastor excercises oversight of the flock of God, the believers. A pastor is a shepherd. The concept of shepherd is one of the oldest in the Bible. It is evidenced throughout the Scriptures, especially in Hebrew history. The shepherding ministry was "an abomination" to the Egyptians (Genesis 46:34). So is the pastoral ministry today to a godless world.

B. **Christ, THE Pastor**

  As with all ministries, Christ is indeed THE PASTOR; He is THE SHEPHERD of God's sheep. Many Scriptures attest to this fact as noted in the following list.

    1. The Lord God is our Shepherd (Isaiah 40:9-11; Psalms 23:1; 68:7; Zechariah 13:7). It reveals His Divinity.

    2. The MAN that is My Shepherd (Zechariah 13:7). This reveals the Humanity of Christ by virtue of the incarnation.

    3. The Shepherd of Israel dwelling between the Cherubims (Psalms 80:1; 99:1).

    4. The Shepherd-Stone of Israel (Genesis 49:24).

    5. The Shepherd (Isaiah 40:11; Jeremiah 31:10; Ezekiel 34:23).

    6. The One Shepherd (Ecclesiastes 12:11; Ezekiel 34:23).

7. The Good Shepherd (John 10:10).

8. The Great Shepherd (Hebrews 13:20).

9. The Chief Shepherd (I Peter 5:4).

10. The Shepherd and Bishop of our souls (I Peter 2:25).

> The Lord Jesus Christ is our Pastor, our Shepherd, our Feeder. He is Jehovah-Raah (Psalms 23:1). "The LORD is my Shepherd." He became the pattern shepherd to all who are called to this ministry. It is His redemptive ministry to and for the sheep of His pasture.

C. Christ, The Pattern Shepherd

In John 10 Christ is set forth as the pattern shepherd. The chapter may be outlined in this manner.

Verses 1-5. The Parable. Not as "parable, similitude" of Matthew 13 but (Greek), "*Paroimia*", or "Adage, Dark Saying" as of Psalms 78:1-2.

Verse 6. Lack of understanding.

Verse 7-18. The Dark Saying Interpreted to those who could hear.

The previous chapter revealed how Christ had healed a blind man in the Feast of Lights (John 9). Because of his testimony concerning Christ he had been excommunicated, cast out of the Judaistic "sheepfold" by false shepherds. Now Christ, the Good Shepherd, comes and cares for this sheep and brings Him into His fold. John 10 arises out this background.

1. **The Shepherd** vs 11, 14, 16; Ezekiel 37:24; Psalms 23:1.

   Jesus, Jehovah Raah incarnate is the Good Shepherd. He gives His life for the sheep. Moses, Joshua, the Priests and Prophets in the Old Testament were but "under-shepherds". They did not give their life in a sin-sacrifice for the sheep. They lived and died for them but could not redeem them from sin. But all pointed to THE Shepherd, Christ.

2. **The Father of the Shepherd** — vs 15, 17, 18, 29.

   God the Father is the owner of the sheep. He gave His sheep to His Shepherd, Christ (John 17:6, 9, 15).

3. **The Sheep**

   The true Israelites, the children of God are God's sheep. Not the seed after the flesh, but the seed after the Spirit (Romans 9:1-9; John 8). All other Israelites are but "goats", clean nations, yet not real "sheep" before God. There is a natural and a spiritual Israel (Psalms 79:13; 95:7; 100:3; Jeremiah 50:6, 17; John 10:26, 27; Matthew 10:6). Israel — the sheep of His pasture.

4. **The Other Sheep** — vs 16.

   The Gentiles would also come into the fold (Acts 28:28; Acts 10-11, 15; Romans 11). These would be the "other sheep" not of this fold, yet it would be onefold with Jew and Gentile.

5. **The Sheepfold** — vs 16.

   Greek = "*Poimne*", translated "one flock". John 17:11, 21-23; Ephesians 4:4-6. Thus one body, one Church, one flock, one fold. The unity of the sheepfold is revealed.

   The Eastern custom shows that there was but ONE Flock, many under-shepherds, each caring for part of the whole.

6. **The Door of the Sheepfold** — vs 7, 9.

   The Lord Jesus Himself is THE DOOR. It speaks of His own body and blood. He is the only entrance to the fold of God (John 14:1, 6; Hebrews 7:25-27).

   Noah's Ark had one door. There was the door of the Passover Lamb. There is the door of the sheepfold. It is one way, one door, one Saviour.

7. **The Porter** — vs 3.

    a. An Eastern custom refers to (Greek) "*Thuroros*", the door or gate-keeper. The door-keeper of the fold would open to true shepherds and allow them to get their flocks out to pasture in the morning, and then receive them into the fold at night. In this type, the Holy Spirit could be viewed as the Porter. He knows the true shepherds and opens to them.

        There were porters at the gates in the Temple of Solomon, the City of Jerusalem and the Tabernacle of David.

    b. Another custom is seen in this. Sometimes the folds were small enclosures to protect the flocks at night from wild animals; or a low building which opened into a courtyard. There was one entrance. The shepherd then would sit himself in that entrance, thus being both "the shepherd" and "the door". The sheep would have to get out over his body. Thus Jesus Himself said that He was both "the shepherd" and "the door" (verses 7, 9, 11, 14).

8. **Enemies of the Sheep**

    There are a number of enemies of the sheep which Jesus mentioned in this chapter.

    a. **The Stranger** — vs 5.

        The sheep hear the voice, but there is no witness within, but restlessness, caution, and eventually they wander away (Revelation 13:11).

        We are to know those that labour among us (I Thessalonians 5:12).

    b. **The Thief** — 1, 9, 10.

        The thief is one who steals by craftiness, by subtlety. His only purpose is to steal from the flock their wool.

    c. **The Robber** — vs 1, 9, 10.

        The robber is one who takes away violently, he takes by force. All who came before Jesus were thieves and robbers. That is, false Messiahs and religious leaders. NOT Moses, Joshua or true Old Testament ministries. True ministries recognized they were but "under-shepherds" and pointed to the shepherd, Messiah Jesus. They had a heart for the sheep. False ministries "fleeced" the sheep for what they could get out of them.

    d. **The Hireling** — vs 12, 13.

        A hireling is one who is paid to do a job. He has no real heart or call for the sheep. It is but a job to him; he gets paid for it. He will flee when the wolf comes. He will desert the sheep and the wolf will catch, scatter or devour them.

        This trio of false ministries are all characterized by their love of money (I Timothy 6) which drown men in destruction and perdition. You shall know them by their love of money.

    e. **The Wolf** — vs 12, 13.

        The wolf is applied to various ones who are the enemies of the flock of God. The Devil is a wolf; false prophets or other false ministries are wolves also. Matthew 7:15; Acts 20:29; II Peter 2:1; Jude 1-5; Revelation 13:11. The inner nature manifests itself even though they come in sheep's clothing.

D. **The Chief Shepherd and Undershepherds**

It is important to understand the concept of the "pastoral" ministry in the Scriptures for it illustrates what God intended to be manifest in the Church.

1. **Eastern Custom**

   In the East there was the custom of shepherds having large establishments, and there being over the total flock a Chief Shepherd. Then he would have under him many "under-shepherds". These would be given as many sheep as they could handle, thus being responsible for these sheep and accountable to the Chief Shepherd.

   These Scriptures speak of "the Principal of the flock" and "the Shepherds" (Jeremiah 25:34-36; Genesis 47:6).

   The New Testament speaks of "the Chief Shepherd" and then "the elders" who are "under-shepherds" of the flock of God (I Peter 5:1-5; 2:25).

   The truth of this may be applicable on a universal and local scale. Christ is THE CHIEF SHEPHERD. He is THE PRINCIPAL of the Flock of God. Then He has many, many "under-shepherds" throughout the world in His Church, both universally and locally. There is but ONE CHURCH, ONE FOLD, but many local "flocks" of sheep. The shepherds were watching over "their flocks" in the field at night (Luke 2:8, 9, 15-20).

   Christ gives as many sheep as we can handle. Thus around the world there are "flocks" of many thousands of people, to hundreds, to fifties, to tens. All ministries, in this sense, are but "under-shepherds", responsible for the flock of God and accountable to the Chief Shepherd. They are HIS sheep.

2. **Jethro Principle** — Exodus 18:13-26; Acts 7:38; Numbers 11:24, 25.

   The Jethro principle illustrates this truth. Moses was "the chief shepherd"; He was "the principal of God's flock, the nation of Israel". He could not care for them himself. The burden was too heavy. By a word of wisdom from Jethro Moses chose qualified men to share the burden with him.

   As already noted, we have Moses as "first among equals", and then other "elders" who shared the burden with him. They were given rule over thousands, hundreds, fifties, tens, etc. All were responsible and accountable to Moses for people.

3. **New Testament Church Application**

   So Christ is THE Chief Shepherd, THE Principal of the flock. They are His sheep. He entrusts His people to shepherding ministries. These in turn are responsible and accountable to Him for as many sheep as He gives them to handle (Hebrews 13:7, 17, 24).

E. **Old Testament and New Testament Shepherds**

1. **Old Testament Shepherds**

   Various men in the Old Testament were called shepherds. It will be noted that these men were saints, prophets, kings, princes and other rulers over people. For this reason we may speak of any of the ministries as "shepherding ministries" even though there is that distinctive "pastoral" ministry given to some.

   a. Abel was the first shepherd and first martyr (Genesis 4).

   b. Abraham, Isaac and Jacob were shepherds.

   c. Moses was a Shepherd-Prophet (Exodus 3:1), then a King and Mediator.

   d. Joshua was a Shepherd-Captain over God's people (Numbers 27:15-25).

   e. David was a Shepherd-King-Prophet in his ministry over the people of God.

   f. Jeremiah was a Pastor-Prophet of God's sheep (Jeremiah 17:16).

   g. Cyrus, a Gentile King was called "My Shepherd" because of what he would do for the flock of Judah (Isaiah 44:28; 45:1).

   h. Kings, Princes, Priests, Prophets and Elders in Israel were generally called "shepherds" in Old Testament times (Ezekiel 34:1-10; 22:23-31; Zechariah 11:3, 4, 8, 15-17; Nahum 3:18).

i.   There were also women who were "shepherdesses" and cared for their father's sheep.

Rachel was a shepherdess (Genesis 29:1-9).

The seven daughters of Midiam were shepherding also for their father (Exodus 2:16).

The Shulamite also was a shepherdess (Song 1:7, 8). She typifies the Church in shepherding ministry.

2.   **New Testament Shepherds**

As in Old Testament times leaders and rulers of God's people were "shepherds", so the thought carries over into the New Testament. As noted, all fivefold ministries should have the heart of a shepherd, yet there are those who do have that distinctive pastoral call. A study of the New Testament shows also an "over-lapping" of ministries as under the Old Testament.

a.   Jesus Christ is the Shepherd and Bishop of our souls, caring for sheep which have been led astray (I Peter 2:25).

b.   All New Testament Elders are Bishops and therefore responsible to shepherd the flock of God (Acts 20:17, 28; I Peter 5:1-5).

c.   It seems Peter was a Pastor-Apostle by the Lord's commission to him in John 21:15-19. The Lord told him to "feed" (i.e., pastor, shepherd, feed) His sheep and lambs. "Feed My sheep", 3 times. Yet we see Peter in apostolic travelling ministry (Acts 9:31, 32). His Epistles have a "pastoral" note in them.

c.   James seemed to become the Pastor-Apostle of Jerusalem after Peter had departed (Acts 21:18; Galatians 1:19; 2:9).

d.   Paul certainly evidenced Pastoral ministry and gave us, what are commonly called "The Pastoral Epistles" of I & II Timothy and Titus, yet he himself was more especially a Teacher-Apostle.

e.   Christ has set in the Church those who are Pastors as one of the fivefold ministries. It is a distinct ministry besides the Apostle, Prophet, Evangelist and Teacher (Ephesians 4:11).

The Pastor is also given FOR the perfecting and maturing of the saints, and FOR bringing the saints into the work of their ministry, and FOR the building up of the Body of Christ.

It is worthy to note that, as the ascension-gift ministry of apostles, prophets, evangelists, and teachers, so with the pastors — all are referred to in plural sense. There are many apostles, prophets, evangelists, teachers and there are many pastors also.

When it comes to the ministry of pastors there needs a point of clarification. "Pastors" designate those who "shepherd" the congregation of the Lord (Ephesians 4:11). Then in Acts 20:17, 28 and I Peter 5:1-5 Elders are told to perform the work of Pastors. Elders are carried over from the order of the Synagogue into the New Testament local Church.

Then Elders are also Bishops and have the oversight of the congregation. These Scriptures confirm this fact (Acts 20:17, 28; I Peter 5:1-5; Titus 1:5, 7).

Alex Rattray Hay, in *The New Testament Order For Church and Missionary* (pp. 233-235) quotes *Neanders Church History* (Vol. I, pp. 255-256) saying:

"The guidance of the communities was therefore most probably entrusted every-where to a council of *elders* . . . Besides the usual name, 'presbuteroi', given to the heads of the Church, there were also many others, denoting their appropriate share of action, as *shepherds (pastors)* . . . That the name 'episcopi' or *bishops* was altogether synonymous with that of presbyters, is clearly evident from those passages of Scripture where both titles are used interchangeably (Acts 20; Compare v. 17 with v. 28; Titus 1:5 with 1:7), and from those where the office of Deacon is named immediately after that of Bishop, so that between these two offices no third one could possibly intervene. This interchange of the two appellations shows that originally they were perfectly identical.''

And then again, from *''The Christian Ministry''* (p. 97) says:

''It is a fact now generally recognized by theologians of all shades of opinions that in the language of the New Testament the same officer is called indifferently '*bishop*' or '*elder*' or '*presbyter*' ''.

Thus there is general acknowledgement that in the Early Church the three titles, Presbyter (Elder), Pastor and Bishop, all referred to the ministry of one and the same person.

However, the three terms are not synonymous though referring to one and the same person.

As *Elder* or *Presbyter* it speaks of a man holding *office* in the Church.
As *Bishop* it refers to that person presiding and *overseeing* the congregation.
As *Pastor* it refers to the man *shepherding* the flock of God.
Or, as noted previously . . .

> The Elder refers to the person, the man.
> The Bishop refers to the office.
> The Pastor refers to the work, the function, shepherding.

Thus in a reasonably sized local Church there will be a group, a plurality of Elders. These Elders ''pastor'' or ''shepherd'' the flock of God.

Thus we have Apostle/Elders, Prophet/Elders, Teacher/Elders, Evangelist/Elders and Pastor/Elders, yet together they constitute a New Testament Eldership.

However, amongst this Eldership, these ''shepherds'', there must be a ''Chief Shepherd'' or ''Senior Elder'' as ''first among equals''.

E. Calling, Qualifications, Ministry and Recognition of the Pastor

1. Calling

As with all ministries, so with the Pastor. There must be the distinct call to shepherd God's people. All in Old Testament and New Testament times knew that deep call of the Lord to care for the flock of God. Without this inner conviction of the call of God no person could really handle the pastoral ministry.

a. The Pastor must be one who has entered into the sheepfold by THE Door, Jesus Christ (John 10:1, 9). The Pastor himself must come in by THE Way (John 14:6). If he has not lawfully entered the fold he is a false shepherd, a hireling or other.

b. The Pastor must have the heart of a shepherd. He is not self-called or self-employed. Moses (Numbers 27:15-17), Ezekiel (34:4, 5), Micah (I Kings 22:17; II Chronicles 18:16); Jeremiah (50:6) and Jesus (Matthew 9:36; Mark 6:34) all saw God's people as sheep without a shepherd and cared for them.

The Priests, Pharisees and Scribes were supposed to be ''the shepherds'' of the flock of God, but, as a whole, had no heart for the people.

c. The Pastor will be one to whom the Porter (i.e., The Holy Spirit) will open (John 10:3).

d. The Pastor will recognize that he is both shepherd and sheep (as Jesus was!)

e. The Pastor will know he is not called as a hireling and will not serve for filthy lucre (I Peter 5:2; I Timothy 3:3).

2. **Qualifications**

The Pastor is also a Bishop and Elder. As such he must have the qualifications of an elder as laid down in the Word of God. Without such he is disqualified from shepherding the people of God (I Timothy 3; Titus 1). He must have character, domestic and spiritual qualifications.

He must not neglect his own spiritual life and relationship with the Chief Shepherd, Jesus Christ, if he himself is to be a good shepherd (Jeremiah 2:8; Acts 6:2-4; 20:28; I Timothy 4:12-16).

3. **Ministry**

Most of the things mentioned here are applicable, in general, to all shepherding ministries, but they are especially characteristics of pastoral ministry.

a.   A Pastor will be one whose voice the sheep recognize. There will be that inner sense that he has the voice of the Spirit in him (John 10:3).

b.   A Pastor will be sensitive to the sheep. He will "sit where they sit" and identify with them (Ezekiel 3:15; Job 2:13).

c.   A Pastor will call his sheep by name. Personal contact is his delight (John 10:3).

d.   A Pastor will lead the sheep into fresh pastures of the Word which he is always searching out (John 10:3; Psalms 23).

e.   A Pastor will go before his sheep as a leader and the sheep are happy to follow him, knowing that he will not lead them astray (I Corinthians 11:1; John 10:4). He leads by his example in attitude, word and lifestyle (I Peter 5:3).

f.   A Pastor will have love and compassion for the sheep. He will love them and they will love him. Love will not be legislated but generated. It will be reciprocal (Matthew 9:36-38; Mark 6:34).

g.   A Pastor will be willing to lay down his life for the protection of the sheep (John 10:11, 15-18; I John 3:16; John 18:8).

h.   A Pastor will be willing to stay with the sheep when he sees the wolf coming. He will not flee and forsake them (John 10:12).

i.   A Pastor will constantly care for the sheep (John 10:13).

j.   A Pastor will always be on the alert for "other sheep" to bring them into God's fold (John 10:16).

k.   A Pastor will recognize the unity of the flock of God, and that there is only "one fold" and he has been entrusted with some of God's sheep (John 10:16).

l.   A Pastor will recognize that he is an under-shepherd, responsible and accountable to the Chief Shepherd, Jesus Christ. The sheep are not his but the Lord's. (John 10:16; I Peter 5:1-5; Hebrews 13:7, 17; Ezekiel 34:10).

m.   A Pastor will know his sheep and be able to distinguish between bleating and murmuring (John 10:27).

n.   A Pastor will feed the flock of God. He will supply fresh waters (I Peter 5:1-5; Ezekiel 34:1-3; Jeremiah 3:15; Acts 20:17, 28-32; Genesis 29:7; 30:38; Exodus 2:16; Psalms 23:2).

o.   A Pastor will minister healing to the flock. He will seek the lost, bring back that which is driven away, bind up the broken, heal the sick and strengthen the diseased. He will visit the flock (Ezekiel 34:4, 11-16; James 5:14; Luke 15:4; Jeremiah 23:1-5).

p.   A Pastor will not be lord over God's flock or rule them with force or cruel hand, but will rule with love (Ezekiel 34:4; Acts 20:17, 28-31; I Peter 5:3).

q.   A Pastor will excercise governmental ministry (Isaiah 40:10, 11; Matthew 2:6). He will oversee the flock of God, watching their needs (I Peter 5:2; Acts 20:28-31; Hebrews 13:7, 17; Luke 2:18).

r.   A Pastor will not drive the sheep or overdrive them. He will lead them. (Genesis 33:13).

s.   A Pastor will carry the lambs when needed (Isaiah 40:11, 29; John 16:12; Mark 4:33).

t.   A Pastor will be a porter also so that the sheep do not get over His body to be devoured of wolves or wild animals (John 10:3).

u.   A Pastor will use the measuring rod in love on his sheep (Leviticus 27:32; Jeremiah 33:13; Ezekiel 20:37; I Corinthians 4:21).

v.   A Pastor will seek God for fruitfulness and increase. Sheep beget sheep (Genesis 30:25-43; 31:1-16).

w.   A Pastor will watch against all forms of attack. The enemy will seek to smite the shepherd in order to scatter the sheep. He is a Watchman (Zechariah 13:7; Matthew 26:31).

x.   A Pastor will be the gatherer of God's people and not say, do or allow things that scatter the sheep (Isaiah 40:11; Luke 11:23; Matthew 12:30).

y.   A Pastor will protect the sheep from their enemies and will warn the sheep of such (Amos 3:12; I Samuel 17:34, 35; John 10:11-13; Isaiah 31:4; 56:11). He will not be a dumb shepherd.

z.   A Pastor will be well equipped with shepherd's equipment for the flock under his care.

C. W. Slemming in his book *"He Leadeth Me"* deals with the Eastern shepherd's equipment.

1)   Fleece sheepskin coat for warmth for himself and lambkins (Jeremiah 43:13).

2)   A wallet for carrying food (I Samuel 17:40).

3)   A sling and staff for beastly enemy attacks (Psalms 23:4).

4)   An oil bottle, protection against vipers, parasites on the sheep.

5)   A reed flute for music, song, that the sheep enjoy.

6)   A lamp for his feet in the darkness of the night.

4. Recognition

A Pastor will be recognized by having upon him a distinct "pastoral charisma". He is a feeder, a gatherer, a leader, a carrier of the lambs and a ruler (Isaiah 40:10, 11).

Great Churches are noted for the ministry or ministries that have that distinct "pastoral charisma" in them, besides the other of the fivefold ascension-gift ministries and plurality of eldership.

As with all ministries, so the Pastor must be received in order to release the reward of his ministry (Matthew 10:41, 42).

F. Judgment on the Shepherds

All ministries are accountable to the Lord. All have to come for judgment before Him. All have to appear before the Lord and give an account of the responsibilities laid upon them.

Just as there are true and false Apostles, Prophets, Evangelists and Teachers, so there are true and false Pastor/Shepherds.

Tremendous warnings of judgment are laid on such (Ezekiel 34).

1. False Shepherds

Characteristics of false or poor shepherds are seen in Ezekiel 34. The chapter may be sectionized as follows:

Verses 1-10. Judgments on the Under-shepherds.
Verses 11-16. The Lord, the Chief and True Shepherd.
Verses 17-31. Responsibilities and Judgments on the Sheep.

Ezekiel, as "the son of man" points to Messiah's Sonship. He is a Priest, Prophet, Watchman and Shepherd of God's people — vs 1.

a. The word is against (not for) the shepherds (vs 2, 10).

b. Woe is pronounced on them (vs 2).

c. They feed themselves and not the flock (vs 2, 3).

d. They eat the fat, take the wool, kill the sheep instead of feeding (vs 3).

e. They did not care for the sick, the diseased, broken, lost and driven away sheep (vs 4).

f. They ruled with force and cruelty as lords and dictators (vs 4).

g. The sheep were scattered as having no shepherd (vs 5).

h. The beasts devoured them (vs 5).

i. The sheep became wandering sheep and none sought for them (vs 6).

j. God will require His sheep at our hands (vs 10).

k. He will also cause some shepherds to cease from feeding His flock anymore. The flock will be taken out of their hands (vs 10).

l. The howling of the voice of shepherds is heard when this happens (Zechariah 11:3-9, 11-17; Jeremiah 25:34-38; 50:43, 44).

m. God's anger is kindled against these shepherds (Zechariah 10:3).
    He will judge them by the sword (Jeremiah 12:10-13; 50:6, 7, 43, 44; Zechariah 11:7, 8).

o. The Pastors transgressed against the Lord (Jeremiah 2:8).
    Note — Priests, Pastors, Prophets here.

    The Pastors become brutish and did not seek the Lord (Jeremiah 10:21). He would scatter their flocks.

    Many Pastors destroyed His vineyard (Jeremiah 12:10). Wind shall eat them up (Jeremiah 22:22).

    Woe to the Pastors for destroying and scattering God's flock (Jeremiah 23:1, 2). God is against them.

    Thus God says that they are HIS sheep and He will judge these shepherds by taking their flock from them and causing them to cease from being shepherds. Such has happened, and is happening today.

    Judgment will come upon all false shepherds. God loves His sheep very dearly.

2. **True Shepherds**

    God's purpose is clear. He will raise up true shepherd ministries. There are distinct prophecies where the Lord said He would raise up Pastors according to His own heart (Ezekiel 34:11-16). The Lord is THE Shepherd. Note the "I will's" in this section of Ezekiel.

    a. He will search and seek out His sheep as a shepherd his lost flock (vs 1, 2).

    b. He will deliver them in the cloudy and dark day.

    c. He will bring them to their own land, to feed and pasture them. They will lay down in a good fold.

    d. He will bring back the lost, heal the sick, restore the diseased, bind up the broken, and strengthen the sick.

e. He will also judge the fat and the strong sheep who hurt each other.

f. He will bring them into folds (i.e., Local Churches). Jeremiah 23:3, 4.

g. He will set up Pastors over them according to His own heart who will feed them with knowledge. The sheep will not be dismayed or fear. Jeremiah 3:15; 17:16; 6:2, 3; Ezekiel 34:23, 24.

There has always true and false shepherds and always conflict over the sheep.
Jeremiah had conflict with the Priests, Princes, Prophets and Rulers.
Ezekiel also had the same conflict with the same rulers of God's people.
Moses had to drive away the shepherds who over-powered the daughters of Midaim when they came to water their flocks (Exodus 3:16-19).

Jesus had to deal with the religious leaders in His day also; the Priests, Scribes, Pharisees and Elders of the nation.

Peter, Paul and the Apostles and the Early Church had the same conflict. All true shepherds will be opposed by false shepherds and the sheep will have to use their ears to discern that which is true and false.

G. The Marks and Responsibilities of God's Sheep

The sheep have their responsibility and accountability also under God and Christ the Chief Shepherd. They also will be judged by Him in that day (Ezekiel 34:17-21)

1. Must recognize that they are God's sheep (Isaiah 40:11; I Peter 5:2; 1:25; Isaiah 53).

2. Must recognize their need of a shepherd who is God-appointed and anointed (Zechariah 13:7; Numbers 27:16, 17).

3. Must realize that without a shepherd they will wander, go astray, as is the nature of sheep (Jeremiah 50:6; Isaiah 53:6). Dogs, cats, horses, can find their way back home but not sheep. Too stupid to return.

4. Must recognize that they are helpless and defenceless without a shepherd. Not like other animals.

5. Must realize they need cleansing by dipping as they cannot cleanse themselves.

6. Must realize they have to be led (Isaiah 40:11). Cannot lead themselves.

7. Must realize the shepherd puts a "sheep-dog" on to them to growl and bark at them to keep them in the flock, but not to hurt them. Independence not to be found in the sheep. Cannot go it alone. Gregarious nature. Safety in fold.

8. Must know their need of a sheep-fold. i.e., Local Church. There are different words translated "fold" in Scripture, each having a thought appropriate to the Local Church.

   a. Hebrew "Gedarah" = "Hedged or fenced place" (Numbers 32:16, 24, 36).

   b. Hebrew "Dober" = "Pasture land, or fold" (Micah 2:12).

   c. Hebrew "Naveh" = "Home, Cool place" (Jeremiah 23:3; Ezekiel 34:14).

   d. Hebrew "Miklan" = "Restrained Place, Fold" (Psalms 79:70).

   e. Greek "Aule" = "Court Yard" (John 10:16).

   The Local Church is all this to the flock of God. It is safety from the wolves and wild animals and the place of pasture and security.

9. Must recognize and come under the rod of the shepherd (Numbers 27:32; Ezekiel 20:27). Loving care and discipline for them.

10. Must learn to obey the shepherd's voice (John 10:26, 27). Learn to respond to it. Have ears to hear. Learn to discern "strange voices" and flee from those who are unproven and unknown ministries (John 10:5, 8). Lambs learn the voice of the shepherd if they stay with the sheep.

11. Must love and trust their shepherd who is the only friend of the sheep, otherwise they had better leave and go to someone they can love and trust.

12. Must be willing to follow their shepherd as the shepherd follows Christ (I Corinthians 11:1).

13. Must kneel to find rest with their padded knees (Ezekiel 34:15).

14. Must realize they need to give their wool while alive. No good after they are dead, "dead wool". Wool-blindness has to be removed or die otherwise.

15. Must recognize that part of the purpose of their existence is to reproduce themselves. Sheep beget sheep, not the shepherd.

16. Must learn to graize with the flock of God and move together as their shepherd leads them in green pastures and still waters.

17. Must stay with the shepherd and the fold to receive healing, binding up of wounds, restoration, etc., as needed (Ezekiel 34:4, 16; Psalms 23:3).

18. Must allow the shepherd to deal with "parasites" that cause problems in sheep, in their ears, eyes, heads, nasal and body parts.

19. Must realize that they, along with the shepherds, will be judged by THE LAMB of God and THE CHIEF SHEPHERD, Jesus Christ (Ezekiel 34:17-21).

    They must watch that they do not foul the sweet waters of God for other sheep who follow to drink after them.

Conclusion:

At the coming of Christ as Shepherd-King, all nations will be gathered before Him.

He will divide them as a shepherd does his sheep and goats.

The Goats = The religious, the unredeemed, the unsaved sinners and unGodly who are placed on His left hand for judgment.

The Sheep = The rightous in Christ, the redeemed sinners, the Godly, and these are placed on His right hand. They enter into the Kingdom as "One Fold" under "One Shepherd" and all under-shepherds and sheep are blessed together.

The Goats depart into everlasting fire and punishment.

All peoples in all nations are either "Goats" or "Sheep" according to their acceptance or rejection of Christ, the Chief Shepherd and Lamb of God who taketh away the sin of the world (John 1:29, 36). The most blessed local Churches are those who know the shepherd-sheep relationship between leaders and people (Ecclesiastes 12:11, Amp. O.T.).

CHAPTER 24

THE MINISTRY OF THE TEACHER

Introductory:

"And He gave some . . . *teachers*" (Ephesians 4:11).

"God hath set in the Church . . . Thirdly, *teachers* . . ." (I Corinthians 12:28, 29).

"He that *teacheth* . . ." (Romans 12:7).

The ministry of the Teacher is mentioned in all three of the lists of ministries and gifts and functions in the Body of Christ by the apostle Paul.

The Lord Jesus mentioned "apostles, prophets and scribes" also in Matthew 23:34 as ministries which He would send to His people.

There is certainly not the problem of understanding the ministry of the Teacher as there is with that of the Apostle and Prophet.

Evangelists, Pastors and Teachers have generally been accepted by the Church over the centuries.

However, it should be recognized that the Teacher is also a distinctive ministry among the fivefold ascension-gift ministries of Ephesians 4:11. It may be said that all fruit trees are trees but each brings forth a distinct kind of fruit for food. The apple, orange, fig, grape, plum, banana, and so forth are all TREES but each have their distinctive fruit. So with the ministries. All are ministries and ascension-gifts of Christ, but each bring forth THE WORD-ministry in their particular style to feed the Body of Christ. All of the five-fold ministries are *WORD MINISTRIES,* and each handle the Word in their unique manner by reason of their distinctive calling and gift. The Teacher handles the Word in a unique presentation which marks him out and sets him forth as a Teacher. The prophet Isaiah said "Thine eyes shall see thy teachers" (Isaiah 30:20).

A. **Definition of Word**
  1. **Old Testament Hebrew**
     a. **Yarah** (SC 3384) = "to flow as water (i.e., to rain); fig, to point out (as if by aiming the finger), to teach. Some of the ways this word is translated are:
        "direct, inform, instruct, lay, shoot, shew, teach through, rain".
        Exodus 4:12, 15; 18:20; 35:34; Deuteronomy 24:8; Psalms 45:4; II Kings 12:2; Genesis 46:28; Leviticus 10:11; Deuteronomy 17:10; Hosea 6:3; 10:11; Psalms 64:4; and Isaiah 30:20.
     b. **Lamad** (SC 3925) = "to goad, i.e., (by implic) to teach (the rod being an Oriental incentive). Some of the ways this word is translated are:
        "diligently instruct, learn, skilful, teach, teacher, teaching".
        Deuteronomy 5:1; 31:13; Psalms 119:7; Jeremiah 12:16; I Chronicles 5:18; Deuteronomy 11:19; II Chronicles 17:17; Ezra 7:10; Psalms 25:4, 5; 119:12, 26, 64, 66, 68, 108; 143:10; I Chronicles 25:7; Jeremiah 32:33.

        Together these words show that a Teacher is one who points out by the finger, directs, informs, instructs, shoots as an archer, and shows, by teaching the ways of the Lord. His teaching is to flow like water, and comes down like rain. He is the one who is skilful in instruction and causes others to learn. His teaching is like a goad, a rod, that causes the people of God to walk in the ways of the Lord (Deuteronomy 32:1-2; Isaiah 55:10-11; Hosea 6:2; 10:11; Ecclesiastes 12:11).

  2. **New Testament Greek**
     a. **Didasko** (SC 1321) = "to learn; to teach". Translated — teach.
     b. **Didaktikos** (SC 1317) = "instructive ('didactic')". Translated — apt to teach.

c. **Didaktos** (SC 1318) = "instructed or convicted by teaching". Translated — taught, which teacheth.

d. **Didaskalia** (SC 1319) = "instruction, the function or the information". Translated — Doctrine, learning, teaching.

e. **Didaskolos** (SC 1320) = "an instructor". Translated — Doctor, 14 times; Master, 47 times; and Teacher, 10 times; and Scribe 67 times, teacher of the Law.

f. **Didache** (SC 1322) = "instruction (the act or the matter)". Translated — Doctrine, hath been taught.

A teacher therefore is one who instructs, and by his teaching causes others to learn. It involves exposition, explanation and instruction of doctrine to others.

B. Christ THE Teacher

1. The Lord Jesus Christ is indeed THE Teacher, The Master Teacher, and Teacher of Teachers.

Nicodemus recognized Jesus as a Teacher come from God (John 3:2; 13:13).

Jesus spent much time in both "preaching and teaching" as well as healing the people (Matthew 4:25; 5:2; 9:35, 36; 11:1; 13:54; 21:23; 22:16; Mark 10:1; Luke 13:10; 20:21).

He fulfilled in measure the prophetic word of Isaiah "All thy children shall be taught of the LORD" (Isaiah 54:13 with I Thessalonians 4:9; John 6:45).

a. He taught everywhere He went, both in the Synagogues and the homes (Luke 13:26; 19:4; 21:37; Mark 14:49).

b. He taught everywhere (Mark 6:2; John 8:2).

c. He especially taught His disciples (John 13-14-15-16).

d. He balanced both preaching and teaching in His ministry (Matthew 4:25; 9:35, 36).

e. He taught with the anointing of the Spirit (Luke 4:18-19).

f. He taught with Divine authority, as a voice from God, not an echo like the Scribes and Pharisees (John 7:29; Matthew 7:28, 29; Mark 1:22).

g. He taught what His Father gave Him to teach (John 7:16; 8:28; 12:48-50).

h. His final commission to the Church involved "teaching (discipling)" all nations by "teaching them to observe all things" which He commanded (Matthew 28:18-20). Matthew's Gospel is especially the "Didactic Gospel" — The Teacher of Divine Law. Christ becomes the pattern teacher to follow, even as He is for all other ministries and believers to follow. We need to note the basic laws of Christ's teaching.

C. Old Testament Teaching Ministry

Teaching has been one of the major ministries right from Old Testament times to today. Most people spend a number of years under teachers and instructors, whether receiving Secular or Religious Education. It is this that basically shapes peoples lives, builds good or bad character and affects all a person thinks, all a person says, all a person does, and all a person is! Thinking, saying, doing and being are primarily the result of teaching given, believed, received and obeyed. In Old Testament times the instruction of people fell under two major areas.

1. **Teaching in the Home**

   a. **Patriarchal**

   It seems clear that the Patriarchs, Adam, Noah, Abraham, Isaac and Jacob taught their families the ways of the Lord (Genesis 18:18, 19; Hebrews 11:10-16). All were men of faith in God, and instructed in the ways of the Lord in this Godly line. Patriarchal priesthood was the order of that day (Job 1). These men were men of faith, and acted as priests in their homes.

b. **Parental**

Also the word of the Lord to Israel was that the parents instruct their children in the Law of the Lord (Deuteronomy 6:7). They were to talk of them in their home, whether walking, sitting or standing. The words of the Lord were to be everywhere as frontlets between their eyes.

The Books of Proverbs and Ecclesiastes are the instructions of the father and the mother to a son, and applicable to sons and daughters of the family. The father and the mother are first responsible to their children and accountable to the Lord for teaching their own children. This is a top priority; parental instruction in the Word of God.

2. **Teaching in the Nation of Israel**

a. **Levitical**

The Levitical Priesthood was especially given the ministry of teaching the tribes of Israel the Law of the Lord (Deuteronomy 33:8-11; Malachi 1:1-9; II Chronicles 35:1-6; Deuteronomy 24:8; Ezekiel 44:23; 22:26; Romans 2:20).

There was a time in Israel when they had been a long time without a *teaching priest* (II Chronicles 15:3).

b. **Ministerial**

Princes, Priests and Prophets were also supposed to instruct people in the Laws of the Lord (Ezekiel 22:23-31).

The Prophets were inspired preachers and teachers and interpreters of the Law of Moses (Isaiah 43:27; 42:19; Hosea 12:10).

At times there were *teaching seminars* by the Priests and Princes also in the cities of Judah (II Chronicles 17:7-9). Ezra was a Scribe and Hermeneutician in Law (Ezra 7:25).

c. **Synagogical**

Scribes and Elders generally taught the Scriptures in the local Synagogues. The Scribes were the official interpreters of the Law, but sad to say, they became some of the worst opposers of Christ's teaching because of wrong hermeneutics combined with the sins of pride and unbelief (Matthew 5:20; 7:29; 12:38; 15:1; 16:21; 23:1-34; 26:3, 57; Luke 11:44, 53; Acts 4:5).

They were called "Doctors" in Luke 2:46; "Masters" in John 3:10, and "Teachers" also in Messiah's times.

The Scribes took away "the key of knowledge" from the people and brought woes on themselves (Luke 11:46-49).

One of the main methods of instruction in Jewry was "Catechism" classes. The word "instructed" in Luke 1:4; Acts 18:25; Romans 2:18 means "orally instructed. The Greek word "*katecheo*" means "to instruct by asking questions and correcting answers." It is the word from which we derive Catechism. It is about the best method of instruction. By this method they set forth in order a declaration of the things which were most surely believed among them and set them forth in order, following the instruction through.

D. **New Testament Ministry of The Teacher**

The teaching ministry continues in the New Testament. It is the ministry of Christ THE Teacher continued in and through members of His Body, the Church (Acts 1:1-2).

When He ascended up on high, He gave gifts to men, and He gave some, *Teachers* (Ephesians 4:11).

God hath set in the Church, thirdly *Teachers* (I Corinthians 12:28, 29).

There were certain Prophets and *Teachers* at the Church in Antioch (Acts 13:1-4; 15:35).

The *Teacher* is to wait on his teaching (Romans 12:7).

The Great Commission of Christ involves teaching ministries (Matthew 28:18-20).

The Teacher is to teach faithful men who can teach others (II Timothy 2:2).

The Teacher comes under greater judgment if he does not teach rightly (James 3:1).

He that is taught in the word must minister to the Teacher (Galatians 6:6).

Paul was a Teacher-Apostle (Acts 18:1; I Timothy 2:7; II Timothy 1:11; Colossians 1:28).

Apollos also was a great teacher of the word (Acts 18:24).

There are some who combine in themselves the ministries of Pastor-Teacher.

The teaching ministry is one of the continuing important ministries in the Body and touches all ages groupings.

It should be remembered that, as with all ministries, so in the teaching ministry, there is "the cluster" of teaching abilities. These would range from teaching of women, teaching of children, teaching of youth, teaching of Bible classes for all age groups in the Church to the distinctive ministry of the five-fold ascension-gift Teacher to the Body. God has set such a cluster of variety of this teaching ministry in the Church.

E. **Calling, Qualifications, Ministry and Recognition of the Teacher**

1. **Calling**

    As with each ministry, so it is for the Teacher. He must know that this is his distinctive calling and that this is his place in the Body. This call should be confirmed by the Spirit in his own heart and confirmed in the Church by the God-given ability of a teacher.

2. **Qualifications**

    Because the Teacher is also an Elder in the Body the qualifications of Eldership are laid on him as with the other fivefold ascension-gift ministries.

3. **Ministry**

    a. A Teacher should have anointing (unction) on his teaching. It is the anointing which teaches (I John 2:20, 27). The Church has often rejected or neglected the teacher's ministry because teachers have been dull, dry and uninteresting in their material, approach and presentation.

    b. A Teacher should learn to depend on THE INNER TEACHER, the Holy Spirit, as well as THE TEACHER, the Lord Jesus above (John 14:26).

    c. A Teacher should remember that the Letter kills but it is the Spirit that gives life (II Corinthians 3).

    d. A Teacher should be able to speak with authority, knowing from whom he received his words (Matthew 7:28, 29; John 7:46; Mark 1:22). He must be a voice and not an echo as the Scribes and Pharisees were in their teaching.

    e. A Teacher should follow the Laws of Communication and bridge the gap between himself and his hearers.

        (Note — There are a number of good books published on "*The Laws of Teaching*" to help any Teacher who desires to be a good communicator of the Divine truth).

    f. A Teacher should be a sound theologian, and be able to give wholesome doctrine (I Timothy 6:3; Acts 2:42).

    g. A Teacher should be a sound hermeneutician and know both the science and the art of rightly dividing the Word of Truth and interpreting the Scriptures. Without such he cannot be a sound exegete of the Word of God.

        (Note — There are excellent textbooks available on "*Principles of Hermeneutics*" for any Teacher who wants to excel in this area).

h.   A Teacher should be able to take the Divine seeds of truth given to the Apostles and Prophets and the writers of both Old and New Testament Scriptures and water them by the Spirit and bring forth fruit upon which God's people can feast. He should receive illumination on the revelation that was given by inspiration.

Because a Teacher appeals more to the *logic* of people, he needs to depend more on the Holy Spirit's unction and illumination (Ephesians 1:17, 18).

Of the fivefold ministries, it seems that they may be grouped (without being limited to such) into two groupings:

Inspirational	**Logical**
Quickening	Illumination
Appeal more to emotional than logical	Appeal more to intellectual than the emotional
Preaching	Teaching
Apostles	
Evangelists	Pastors
Prophets	Teachers

At times these ministries may involve preaching and teaching and overlap into both areas, both inspirational and logical. Therefore, this must not be used to limit the ministries. But there is, without doubt, the inspirational and the logical ministries in the fivefold ministries.

However, the Teacher does, by reason of the very nature of his ministry, appeal more to the understanding, reason, intelligence and logic than to the emotions. He is especially systematic, following the rules of logic. Therefore, the Teacher needs the unction of the Holy Spirit to make the teaching a channel for the impartation of *life* as well as *knowledge*!

His will be a ministry of the *Spirit* and the *Word* (I John 5:7, 8).
He will compare "spiritual things with spiritual" (I Corinthians 2:6-14).
He will depend upon the Holy Spirit to take the Word he teaches and witness within the heart of the listeners (Luke 12:12; John 14:26; I John 2:20, 27).
At times he will "teach/preach" to balance his word (Acts 13:1; I Corinthians 4:17; Acts 15:35; 18:11; II Timothy 1:11; Acts 15:22; II Timothy 4; 2, 3; 2:2; I Timothy 3:2; Titus 1:9; Acts 20:28).

i.   A Teacher should be a diligent student of the Word of God. He should have a Divine passion for the Word (I Timothy 4:13; Job 23:12; Psalms 119:47; Jeremiah 15:16; Ezekiel 13:1-3; Matthew 4:4; Revelation 10:8-10).

j.   A Teacher should be a man given to much meditation in the Word (Psalms 1:2; Joshua 1:8; Psalms 119:48, 78, 148). Meditation brings spiritual illumination.

k.   A Teacher should be creative in his teaching, not just for creativity's sake, but to maintain interest and communicate well. Consider how Jesus used the "created" things about Him often in teaching (Matthew 13).

l.   A Teacher should always be teachable. How can he teach others if he himself is not teachable? How can he expect others to learn from him if he does not or cannot learn from others? (Romans 2:21; I Corinthians 2:13).

Apollos was a great teacher, yet humble and teachable to learn from others (Acts 18:24-27; 20:19; I Peter 5:5; I Corinthians 16:12; 3:6-10; Proverbs 16:23; James 1:21).

m.   A Teacher should be able to reproduce other teaching ministries (II Timothy 2:2). He should teach others, who can teach others.

n. A Teacher should be a living example of what he teaches others. People learn more by example than by precept. A Teacher therefore must teach:

   1) By Precept — what he says (II Timothy 3:10),

   2) By Example — what he is (II Timothy 3:10),

   3) By Conduct — what he does (John 13:12-15; Matthew 5:19; Acts 1:1; Isaiah 2:1-4).

   The danger of Phariseeism is "they say and do not" (Matthew 23:1-3).
   Jesus practiced what He preached. He will teach us His ways, he will walk in His paths, Doctrinal is followed by Practical!

   A Teacher's ultimate aim in teaching is *application* of the Word to the life-style, and not just *information* of the Word. It is to bring about obedience to the Word (Deuteronomy 4:5, 14; 31:12, 13; II John 4; III John 3, 4; Isaiah 2:1-5). Teaching His ways is to be followed by walking in His paths.

o. A Teacher should be well equipped with the principles of homiletics in order to get the message through to the hearers.

p. A Teacher should be characterized by the Spirit of knowledge, understanding and wisdom.

   1) Knowledge — the possession of facts of truth.

   2) Understanding — the interpretation of truth.

   3) Wisdom — the application of truth.

   Proverbs 1:1-6; Ecclesiastes 1:18; I Corinthians 2:13; Colossians 2:3.
   This means he has to be intellectually honest when handling the Word. Otherwise he can make the Word say whatever he wants it to say. This leads to deceptive teaching (Luke 8:15; II Corinthians 4:2; II Peter 3:15, 16).
   A Teacher needs wisdom to be able to handle knowledge!

   Moses as an Apostle, Aaron as the Prophet and Bezaleel and Aholiab as Teachers were filled with the "spirit of wisdom, knowledge and understanding" to teach others in the building of the Tabernacle of the Lord (Exodus 35:34).

q. A Teacher should aim at balance in his teaching to avoid his hearers taking any areas of his teaching to extreme, turning to the right hand or the left hand (Isaiah 30:20, 21).

r. A Teacher should be a well instructed Scribe in the things pertaining to the Kingdom of God and be able to bring forth out of his treasure things both new and old (i.e., New and Old Testaments). (Matthew 13:52; Leviticus 26:10.)

s. A Teacher should wait or attend to his teaching service (Romans 12:7).

t. A Teacher should beware of pride of intellect, for "knowledge puffs up" (I Corinthians 8:1).

u. A Teacher, as all ministers, should beware of "flattering titles" (Matthew 23:8-10; Job 32:21, 22).

v. A Teacher is also given for the perfecting of the saints, to bring them into the work of their ministry, and for the building up of the Body of Christ (Ephesians 4:9-16). Read also Psalms 144:1.

w. A Teacher will speak as the oracle of God according to the ability which God gives to him (I Peter 4:10, 11).

x. A Teacher must be judged by the infallible Word of God in all matters of faith and practice (I Timothy 6:3).

y. A Teacher must remember that the greater judgment is on him than on his hearers

(James 3:1). This means that he will seek to guard his tongue in all that he teaches. The Tongue Chapter is especially related to Teachers (James 3:1-12).

z. A Teacher must possess a sound mind and sound judgment (II Timothy 1:7). A sound mind has several distinct qualities:

1) Well-balanced
    a) Not highly fanciful
    b) Not hasty in judgment
    c) Not given to extremes or vain and foolish notions

2) Quick and clear in perception

3) Acute in intellect

4) Good judgment and reasoning ability

5) Able to communicate clearly

6) Always studies the Word from whole to part and part to whole.

A Teacher must build on that foundation laid by the Apostles and Prophets and learn to work with other ministries in the Body. He will not be an isolationist but check his teachings with other ministries in the Body of Christ for his own "checks and balances" and safeguard.

4. **Recognition**

As all ministries in the Body so believers need to receive the Teacher in order to receive the reward of his labours in the Word (Matthew 10:41, 42). As noted we have "the cluster" of variety of teaching ministries in the Church.

a. **The Teacher** (Ephesians 4:11; I Corinthians 12:28, 29).
    This is the Teacher of the fivefold ascension-gift type.

b. **The Elder**

    All elders must also have a measure of ability to teach. "Apt to teach" means they are able to teach (I Timothy 3:2; I Peter 5:2).

c. **Levels of Teachers**

    Believers are not always to be babes but to grow up and be able to teach others (Hebrews 5:12). Thus there are many levels and varying measures of the teaching abilities in the Body of Christ besides the Teacher of the ascension-gift type of ministry.

    1) Parents teach their children.

    2) Older women teach younger women (Titus 2:1-5).

    3) Saints can teach and admonish one another in Psalms, Hymns, Spiritual Songs (Colossians 3:16; Ephesians 5:18).

    4) Bible Class teachers for youth, adults, children, all ages.

    5) Teaching one another on personal approach (Hebrews 8:11).

        Everyone learns to do something by doing it. i.e., Learn to play by playing, sing by singing, teach by teaching, etc.

        All should be able to take what the Teacher gives and break it down to the varying levels and needs of believers in the Church.

F. **Warnings and Judgments on False Teachers**

Just as there are false apostles (II Corinthians 11; 13); false prophets (Matthew 24:11); false evangelists and false shepherds, so there are false teachers. The Scriptures warn us to beware of such (II Peter 2:1; II Timothy 4:3; Revelation 2:20; Jude 3, 4; Titus 1:11; I John 4:1).

To whom much is given shall the more be required. Because of the power of the teaching ministry, used by false cults, humanistic philosophies, religions of the world, greater judgment comes upon such when it is false (James 3:1-2).

The following are certain teachers which God's people need to watch against:

1. **Teachers of the Law-Legalizers**

    Acts 13:27; John 18:28; 5:39, 40; Galatians 3:1-2; 4:1-21; Acts 15:1-29; I Timothy 1:3-7. The Priests, Scribes, Pharisees became legalizers. They were the Judaizers who by letterism and legalism corrupted the Gospel of Christ. Paul resisted them and their teaching because of the bondage it brought on the Churches. The same is true today of certain religions.

2. **Teachers of the Traditions of Men-Traditionalists**

    Mark 7:1-13. The Pharisees and Scribes taught the traditions of men and made the Word of God of none effect through their traditions. Jesus resisted these. So the Church needs to do the same today. Anything that nullifies the Word of God is not of God but traditions of men.

3. **Teachers of False Doctrine-Heretics**

    There were teachers who handled the Word of God deceitfully (II Corinthians 4:2), and twisted the Word in their trickery of error (Ephesians 4:14. Amplified New Testament). There were those who also wrested, misconstrued, distorted and misinterpreted the Word of God (II Peter 3:16). They brought destruction on themselves and others.

    Jezebel was a woman Teacher/Prophetess who taught false doctrine in the Church at Thyatira (Revelation 2:20), usurping authority over the apostles doctrine (Acts 2:42; I Timothy 2:12).

    Examples of false doctrines are seen in:

    a. Those who denied the bodily resurrection (II Timothy 2:16-18).

    b. Those who turned the grace of God into lasciviousness (Jude 3, 4; Revelation 2; 20).

    c. Those who caused division contrary to sound doctrine (Romans 16:17).

    d. Those who taught material prosperity for gain (I Timothy 6:6-19; II Peter 2:3; Titus 1:10, 11).

    e. Those who taught the Doctrine of Balaam (Revelation 2:14).

    f. Those who taught the Doctrine of the Nicolaitans (Revelation 2:6, 15).

    g. Those who teach fables as truth (II Timothy 4:3).

    h. Those who teach Doctrines of Devils, as forbidding marriage and eating of meats (I Timothy 4:1-5).

Whatever teaching or philosophy a person receives and believes determines their character (what they are), lifestyle (what they do) and destiny (where they go). The true Teacher must ground people in the pure Word of God so that they are not carried about by every wind of doctrine and trickery of men (Ephesians 4:9-16).

CHAPTER 25

CHALLENGE TO CHANGE THE TRADITIONAL SYSTEM

With all that has been written in the previous chapters relative to Church Government, Eldership, Deacons and the Fivefold Ascension-Gift Ministries, the writer believes this chapter needs to be written.

This chapter is written as a challenge to the true church, as a whole, and more especially to those in leadership ministry.

It has to do with titles and offices as well as the content of previous chapters on the subjects mentioned above.

One of the great areas which needs to be addressed is in the matter of giving men "flattering titles" instead of recognizing and accepting men in their functioning office and ministry.

Therefore, it is at the risk of being charged with having a fixation or being too technical over semantics that the writer dares to write on such a subject as our chapter title suggests.

Various responses may be expected, especially from those in ministry, on this chapter. Some will discard it as being too technical over semantics. Some may reject it as false teaching. Some may be totally indifferent to its content, believing that, after all, it really does not matter. Some who are strong on titular authority may even oppose it.

However, there will be those who will respond to the challenge of the Spirit of God, who have ears to hear what the Spirit is saying, and will do something about it, no matter how difficult change may be. Change is always difficult and needs grace and wisdom, for human nature resists change. It is for the latter group of leaders that this chapter is written.

Jesus said to the religious leaders of His day that "the traditions of men made of none effect the word of God" (Mark 7:1-13).

Traditions of men which are contrary to the word of God, need — in principle — the ministry of Jeremiah; that is, they have to be "rooted up, pulled down, plucked up, torn down and destroyed" before one can "build and plant" what we believe is Divine truth (Jeremiah 1:10). Tradition generally dies fighting for survival.

A. Statement of the Problems

The reader will bear the repetition of some things noted in previous chapters as we seek to consider the major areas that need to be addressed.

There are several major things that strike any honest believer in an unbiased reading of the New Testament, especially in relation to the Book of Acts and the church Epistles. This is particularly seen in relation to church ministry and leadership.

We list them out for our consideration.

★   The Absence of the Monarchial or One-Man Pastoral System.

★   The Plurality of Eldership in the Church.

★   The Local Government of the Church.

★   The Fivefold Ascension-Gift Ministries.

★   The Absence of Titular Authority.

We consider these in their respective order.

1. The Absence of the Monarchial or One-Man Pastoral System

It was quite an astounding revelation to the author in his study of the New Testament church and churches to discover the following facts.

★   There is not one New Testament church among 48 churches (house-churches or other) seen that had the traditional "pastor" or one man over it.

★ There is not one person in the New Testament ever called "pastor" or addressed by that title in any church. No-one was ever called "the pastor".

★ No-where can it be shown from the New Testament that "a pastor" has to be the head of the local church. Scripture does not say that "God has set in the church, firstly . . . pastors . . ." (1 Corinthians 12:27-29).

★ The Greek word for "pastor" ("poimeen") is only translated ONCE in the whole of the New Testament in that way. It should have been translated, by consistency, as the other 17 usages of the same Greek word were, that is, "shepherd", (or else consistently "pastor").

For the benefit of the reader we list from New Englishman's Greek Concordance the related Greek words pertaining to shepherding, feeding or pastoral ministry. As will be seen "pastor" is only translated as such once while the other times it is translated "shepherd".

4165   11 690/831   6:485   4166

ποιμαίνω, poimaino.

Mat. 2: 6. shall rule (lit. shall tend) my people Israel.
Lu. 17: 7. a servant plowing or feeding cattle,
Joh. 21:16. He saith unto him, Feed my sheep.
Acts 20:28. to feed the church of God,
1Co. 9: 7. who feedeth a flock, and eateth not
1Pet. 5: 2. Feed the flock of God which is
Jude 12. feeding themselves without fear:
Rev. 2:27. he shall rule them with a rod of iron;
       7:17. midst of the throne shall feed them,
      12· 5. who was to rule all nations with
      19:15. he shall rule them with a rod of iron:

4166   18 690/831   6:485

ποιμήν, poimeen.

Mat. 9:36. as sheep having no shepherd.
      25:32. as a shepherd divideth (his) sheep
      26:31. I will smite the shepherd,
Mar 6:34. as sheep not having a shepherd:
      14:27. I will smite the shepherd,
Lu. 2: 8. shepherds abiding in the field,
      15. the shepherds said one to another,
      18. told them by the shepherds.
      20. And the shepherds returned,
Joh. 10: 2. is the shepherd of the sheep.
      11. I am the good shepherd: the good shepherd
          giveth his life
      12. and not the shepherd,
      14. I am the good shepherd,
      16. one fold, (and) one shepherd.
Eph. 4:11. and some, pastors and teachers ;
Heb 13:20. that great Shepherd of the sheep,
1Pet. 2:25. returned unto the Shepherd and Bishop of
          your souls.

4167   5 691/831   6:485   4165

ποίμνη, poimnee.

Mat. 26:31. and the sheep of the flock shall
Lu. 2: 8. over their flock by night.
Joh. 10:16. one fold, (and) one shepherd.
1Co. 9: 7. who feedeth a flock, and eateth not of the
          milk of the flock ?

4168   5 691/831   6:485   4167

ποίμνιον, poimnion.

Lu. 12:32. Fear not, little flock;
Acts 20:28. and to all the flock,
      29. not sparing the flock.
1Pet. 5: 2. Feed the flock of God which
      3. being ensamples to the flock.

As seen by these references, the Greek word *"poimeen"* is translated *"shepherd"* 17 times and only one time as *"pastor"*.

We ask why. Why did the translators not translate the 18 references as "pastor", or else "shepherd" and maintain consistency?

If Ephesians 4:11 had been translated, ". . . He gave some apostles, some prophets, some evangelists, some *shepherds* and teachers . . .", would leadership have taken "shepherd" to be the titular power for use?

Why not call leaders "shepherd, shepherd, shepherd . . ." (so forth), instead of untold thousands being called "pastor, pastor, pastor . . . ?"

To add to the enigma, the church today hesitates to call people "apostles" or "prophets". "Evangelists" and "teachers" are a little more recognized and accepted. But, untold thousands of ministers, be they apostles, prophets, evangelists or teachers take this one title of the fivefold ascension-gift ministries and are called "pastor, pastor, pastor . . .".

We ask, why choose this one out of the five offices and call almost every ministry by this title whether they be evangelists, prophets, teachers or apostles? Such is inconsistency indeed! Would they be content to be called "shepherd?"

Do we not believe in the other ministries and offices in the church? Do we fear to use these other designations? Do we fail to recognize and receive the other ministries for various reasons, such as failures of men, hurts, unbelief and traditions?

Many men in the present pastoral system have been forced, for various reasons, to become a one-man ministry. Many ministers feel they have to be a "pastor" to be able to function, or else there is no place for them.

The one-man ministry and most of the present pastoral system becomes, either wittingly or unwittingly, *"the cork in the bottle"* and all other ministries are suppressed, under the cloak of submission and cannot get by or around him. The sad result often manifests itself in division in order for these other ministries to surface.

In Revelation chapters 2 and 3 the leader of the church is called *"the angelos"* (i.e., the angel, literally, the messenger). If "the angelos" is a pastoral ministry, then he can become *"the capstone"* on the pyramid of the local church. It means that apostles, prophets, evangelists and teachers generally struggle to find identity and expression and fulfilment.

This ought not to be and is certainly not New Testament order.

As has been mentioned, there is not one church in the New Testament that had a one-man ministry over it. There was no "pastor" over any one church. With all the churches mentioned in the Acts or the Epistles there is not one person specifically called "pastor".

It is worthy to note that most textbooks on pastoral ministry seem to indicate that the "pastor" is to be everything to anyone and everyone in every department of the local church.

From the Table of Contents of *"Pastoring the Smaller Church"*, by John C. Thiessen we note the following emphasis on "the pastor". This places such a burden on the one man. It places a unscriptural burden on the shoulders of the one-man pastor/shepherd.

This is typical of most of the textbooks on pastoral theology. As noted, this places such a burden of responsibility on the one man. No wonder there is such a break-down in the ministry today, morally, mentally, emotionally, physically and in other ways.

God never intended one man to shoulder such a burden in any church and bear it alone.

Only Christ, who is the CHIEF SHEPHERD (pastor) can handle the universal flock of God because of who He is, the God-Man and because of His moral and essential attributes. Christ is the chief shepherd, or, literally, the origin-shepherd (1 Peter 5:4. Concordant Literal).

We believe in the shepherding ministry. However, it seems that the title "pastor" that is used by so many today has become one of the greatest hindrances to the recognition and acceptance of the other four ascension gift ministries.

Where did the concept in the modern day church of the pastoral system come from? What gave rise to this one-man ministry? History shows it was the rise of the MONARCHIAL BISHOP over and above the other elders that precipitated the rise of this system. This monarchial bishop became "the pastor", the controlling, and often times the suppressing head of the church.

R. M. Riggs in *"The Spirit-Filled Pastor's Guide"*, (p.139), after recognizing that there was plurality of eldership in the early church, has this to say concerning the pastor of a church.

> " It seems that these considerations abundantly justify and render God-appointed the practice of the present-day church of having one pastor only, dispensing with a plurality of elders. Our conclusion therefore would be that, although there were many elders in the early church, it is not God's will that there be a board of elders in our present-day church."

With this statement we have to disagree! We not believe it is justified or that it is God's will that only one man be "the pastor" of a church and bear the burden alone.

The New Testament always shows plurality of leadership in the affairs of the church, although there was evidence of a presiding elder. This truth is confirmed in both Old and New Testaments. However, he does not have to be THE PASTOR. It seems that he could be any one of the gifted ministries, according as God has graced him with leadership abilities.

This presiding minister becomes "the set man" of Numbers 27:15-27 along with other elders.

He is also "the angelos" of the church according to Revelation 1:20. But he was not alone. He was not a one-man ministry.

There are indeed numerous leaders who are true shepherds of the flock and are not governed by titular authority. However, there are those who are like Diotrephes (2 John 9,10), who love to have the pre-eminence and will manifest the characteristics of the monarchial bishop, enforcing his own authority by the power of a title as "the pastor!" The writer has heard this over the years. "I am THE PASTOR, everybody must submit or . . . ."
It is this titular power that has generally suppressed the other ministries.

With all that has been said here, this is not to say there is no "set man" or "first among equals". This has been spelt out clearly in Chapter 15 on "*Church Government*".
This section is simply to note that the traditional one-man pastoral system is not to be found in the New Testament.
There are men named as apostles, and men named as prophets, and Philip named as an evangelist, and others named as teachers.

In Acts we see apostles, prophets, an evangelist and teachers, but no mention of "pastor" or "pastors". However, we do see that elders are told to "feed", as a shepherd, the flock of God.

The following chart of the major New Testament churches confirm the above statement.

MINISTRY/GIFTS IN NEW TESTAMENT CHURCHES

Jerusalem	Samaria	Antioch	Ephesus	Philippi	Crete	Corinth	Rome	Asia Minor	Dispersion
The twelve Apostles	Evangelist	Prophets	Apostles	Apostles	Bishops	Apostles	Prophecy	"Angel"	Apostles
Deacons	Apostles	Teachers	Prophets	Bishops		Prophets	Serving	Messenger	Fellow-
Elders		Apostles	Evangelists	Deacons		Teachers	Teaching		Elders
			Pastors	Saints		Governing	Exhorting		
			Teachers			Wisdom	Giving		
			Elders			Knowledge	Ruling		
			Deacons			Faith	Mercy		
						Healing			
						Miracles			
						Prophecy			
						Discerning			
						Tongues			
						Inter- pretation			
						Helps			

In all of the above mentioned churches, not one person is ever called "the pastor" of the church. This is in stark contrast to our system today!

Without doubt, changing the one-man pastoral system will be one of the hardest things to do. The present day concept of "the pastor" is so entrenched universally, it will be a challenge to change this order and return to New Testament order.

2. The Plurality of Eldership in the New Testament Churches

The next problem we need to address is the matter of plurality of eldership as seen in the New Testament local churches.

We do not need to amplify this sub-heading too much, for details of this matter of plurality of eldership in the New Testament churches have been covered in Chapter 15, "*Church Government*".

However, because this sub-heading arises out of the previous section, as an answer to the monarchial or one-man pastoral system, some comments need to be made.

★ The churches in the Acts and the Epistles had the ministry of elders. There was never ever one elder over any church or churches. Every New Testament church basically had elders over it. It was "church" (singular), and "elders (plural) when speaking of any particular locality.

★ These elders together shepherded (pastored) the flock of God. They were the shepherding or feeding elders according to Acts 20:17,32-37 and 1 Peter 5:1-5. These *elders* were called to be *overseers* (bishops) of the flock of God and were charged to *feed* (Grk. "poimaino", tend, rule and feed) the church, the flock of God.

★ These elders worked closely and in conjunction with the apostles (Acts 15:1-35; note vs 2,4,6,22,23), in solving doctrinal issues and practical church problems.

a) **In Jerusalem**, in the beginning, it was the apostle Peter along with the other apostles (Acts 2).

b) **In Jerusalem**, later on, it was the apostle James and the elders (Acts 21:18).

c) **In Ephesus**, the apostle Paul spoke to and charged the elders to oversee the flock of God and feed them as a shepherd feeds his flock (Acts 20:17-37).

d) **In Philippi**, the apostles, Paul and Timothy, wrote to the elders (bishops), deacons and saints (Philippians 1:1).

e) **In Ephesus**, later on, Paul wrote to Timothy, who seemed to be an apostle yet doing the work of an evangelist, and gave instruction concerning the qualifications and ordination of elders and appointment of deacons. These things are in what are known as "The Pastoral Epistles" (1 & 2 Timothy).

f) **In Crete**, the apostle Paul wrote to Titus concerning the ordaining of elders in every city (Titus).

g) **In Asia**, the apostle John wrote to "*the angel*" (Greek "angelos", or "the messenger") of the churches of Ephesus, Symrna, Pergamos, Thyatira, Sardis, Philadelphia and Laodicea.

It seems that the New Testament points more to apostolic or other ascension-gift ministries over the flock of God, along with elders, caring for the church.

This is seen to be true, especially with the post-ascension apostles, such as Paul and Barnabas, and others, more than under the 12 apostles of the Lamb in the church's beginning.

The point of the matter is clearly seen that no New Testament church was ever governed by any one man ministry or "pastor", but by apostles in conjunction with a plurality of elders or a presbytery.

Each local church had Scripturally qualified elders, qualified by character and gift and feeding ability. These elders had to learn to flow together in a spirit of recognition, not competition, according to the measure of the gift of Christ in them.

Without doubt, the principle is applicable to the fivefold ascension-gift ministries of apostles, prophets, evangelists, shepherds and teachers, along with the local elders. It should be remembered that "the eldership" will include the ascension-gift ministries. As a general statement it may be seen that all ascension-gift ministries are elders, but not all elders are ascension-gift ministries. Even though there is difference of opinion on this statement, the matter involves plurality of leadership in the local church, never the one-man leader.

What a challenge to churches today which lack this kind of ministering leadership and plurality of elders supporting the "set man".

3. **The Government of the Church**

   Another thing which strikes one in a study of New Testament order is the total absence of the type of church government we have in many places today.

Again, not much needs to be said in this section as it has been dealt with previously. However, some comments need to be addressed in the challenge to change the traditional system.

★   There was no ''one-man'' form of church government. Autocrats were not God's will.

★   There was no ''deacon-board'' form of church government. The ministry was not ''hired and fired'' by any deacon-board control.

★   There was no ''democratic'' form of church government in any New Testament church. The church, or the congregation, did not vote the ministry in or out of office, as is often the case today.

   Can any one imagine the church at Corinth, or Philippi, or Jerusalem having a deacon-board meeting, or a congregational meeting, to vote for or against the apostle Paul, or Peter, or Timothy, Titus and others?

   Can any one imagine the church in the Old Testament (Acts 7:38) calling a democratic meeting to vote for or against Moses, or Joshua, or Samuel, and others of the ministry that God called? The answer is evident.

★   There was no central headquarters which controlled the local churches either.

Undoubtedly one of the most difficult things to be done in any denomination is the changing of the form of church government.

Who is willing to change the deacon-board control, or the democratic processes of ''hiring and firing'' the set minister? History alone proves the heartache and disaster, both to ministry and congregations, in church after church where the deacon-board or democratic voting operates. Congregations or boards can vote ministry in and out any time they like for a variety of reasons. The ministry is *''on the block''* for hire every several years. How unscriptural!

Of course, this deacon-board control and/or congregational process arose out of abuses from the one-man authority and the lack of ''checks and balances'' on him. The problems of autocracy, bureaucracy and democracy have been evidenced in church history. The delicate balance of this ''threefold cord'' has to be seen.

However, the fact is that in neither Old Testament nor New Testament was there such board-control or congregational-control or voting over the ministry. No one could vote Moses in or out of office. Can one imagine Israel doing this? No one could vote Joshua in or out of his leadership. No one could vote Peter, John, James or Philip, Paul, Silas, Barnabas, Agabus, Timothy, Titus or a host of others in or out of ministry by deacon-board or democratic processes. The whole idea is foreign and preposterous to the whole Bible. It is the way of the world to do this.

The basic step in this is for leadership to teach the word of God and discover God's form of church government. Then all must be willing to dissolve unscriptural practices and do the will and word of God.

The reader is referred again to Chapter 15 on ''*Church Government*''.

4.   The Ascension-Gift Ministries

Another part of the challenge to change the traditional system pertains to the ascension-gift ministries.

In Ephesians 4:9-11; 2:20; 3:5; Luke 11:49-52 and 1 Corinthians 12 we see the fivefold ascension-gift ministries Christ has set in the church. These ministries, or gifts, were given by Christ to the church AFTER His ascension, exaltation and glorification and the subsequent outpouring of the Spirit.

These ascension-gift ministries have been covered fully in previous chapters. They are apostles, prophets, evangelists, shepherds and teachers. They are given for the equipping and adjusting of the saints, to bring the saints into the work of their ministry and for the building up of the body of Christ unto a mature man.

The time of their function is clear. They are given UNTIL we all come into the unity of the faith, unto the knowledge of the Son of God, unto a perfect and mature man (Ephesians 4:13).

Where are these ministries today? Why are they not all recognized? Why do we not see them functioning harmoniously in the body of Christ as they generally seemed to in the New Testament church? These are the issues addressed in this present section.

It is basically traditional unbelief, and/or fear that causes difficulty in recognizing and accepting the total fivefold ascension-gift ministries of Ephesians 4:9-11.

Though generally accepting, at least in measure, evangelists, shepherds and teachers, unbelief rejects the ministry gifts of apostles and prophets. Fear often causes lack of acceptance of any who claim to be apostles and prophets. Bad experiences of self-styled apostles and prophets have done their evil work also. However, such experiences or traditional unbelief have not caused people, generally speaking, to reject evangelists, shepherds and teachers.

Also, there is often a false concept of apostles and prophets, as if they are inhuman and "saint-ified" to an unnatural level, almost de-humanized. A study of the New Testament shows they were as human as evangelists, shepherds and teachers as any other member of the body of Christ.

Faith in the Scriptures and God's purpose for the church must destroy the traditional unbelief and ultra-dispensationalism that teaches "apostles and prophets are not for today, only for the establishment of the early church in the period of transition".

Faith must also overcome fear of false apostles and false prophets, as well as the other generally accepted ministries, who have brought hurt, often times, to the people of God. There are also false evangelists, false shepherds (pastors), and false teachers. But we do not reject all evangelists, shepherds and teachers because of this.

The Scriptures clearly warn of false ministries in these last days. There has always been false ministries along with the true, the counterfeit along with the genuine. Because of this, God's people have to exercise their senses to discern between good and evil (Matthew 7:15-23; 24:4,5,24; 1 Corinthians 11:13-15; 2 Peter 2:1-3; Revelation 2:2,13; Ezekiel 34).

The challenge comes here to change the traditional, denominational church system and recognize and accept the fivefold ascension-gift ministries of the risen Lord so the church can be all that the Lord intends it to be.

5. The Authority of Titles

The fifth area of challenge to change the traditional system is in the matter of titles.

It is evident in the early church that there was an absence of titular authority or the authority of titles. Though recognizing and receiving ministries in their offices and function, there was not the evidence of title-power as used so much in the modern church.

It is important in this section to realize that the ascension-gift ministries are not merely titular but functional. There is recognition of the office and function, not merely titles.

This is one of the most difficult things to handle, because of man's fallen nature and human tradition in the matter of titles, or what we call, titular authority.

Jesus warned His disciples about the dangers of titular authority or title power. Many novices in the faith have been destroyed by pride and fallen under title power given to them too soon. Paul warns against such pride and condemnation of the devil in his qualifications for elders and deacons (1 Timothy 3:6,7).

We consider the dangers of titular authority.

★ Worldly Titular Authority

The reader should carefully read Mark 10:42-45; Matthew 20:25-28 along with Luke 22:24-27, as they are too full to be quoted here.

There was strife among the disciples as to who would be the greatest. Jesus plainly told them. He said that the Gentiles rule and exercise *lordship* over the people, and their great ones *exercise authority* upon them, but it was not be so among them. The chiefest of all was to be the servant of all. The Son of Man, who is LORD, and THE apostle and THE prophet, THE evangelist, THE shepherd and THE teacher, came to serve and to give His life a ransom for all. Jesus said, I am among you as one that serves.

All ministers should have the servant spirit and attitude. Jesus is the greatest, holding all the titles in the universe, with the Father, and all authority is given to Him, but He serves people. His authority is not a titular authority, but servant power.

Peter warns the elders against being "lords over God's heritage" (1 Peter 5:1-5). We are to be under-shepherds, but not under-lords! We are to be examples to the flock of God.

In the world system, title-power is counted much for recognition of the powers that be ordained of God. People are recognized as kings, queens, presidents, prime-ministers, doctors and others in their professions and positons of authority.

Here the Gentiles rule and exercise *lordship and authority* over their subjects.

However, Jesus said this was not to be done among His people in the church. All from the least to the greatest are to have a servant spirit, servant power, not title-power!

★ Flattering Titles

Job said, "Let me not, I pray you accept any man's person (i.e., be a respecter of persons), neither let me give *flattering titles* unto man. For I know not to give *flattering titles;* in so doing my maker would take me away" (Job 32:21-22).

Jesus said, in speaking of title-power, to the multitudes and His disciples, what His standard was. It must have been humiliating and devastating, to say the least, to the religious leaders of His day who enjoyed titular authority and recognition by titles. He condemned those who loved the uppermost rooms at the feasts, and the chief seats in the synagogues, and greetings in the market place and being called by flattering titles. Note what He said to them.

"But be ye not called *Rabbi,* for One is your *Master,* even Christ; and all ye are *brethren.*

And call no man your *father* on earth; for one is your *Father,* which is in heaven." (Matthew 23:6-10).

"Neither be ye called *masters*; for one is your *Master,* even Christ.

The greatest among you shall be your servant. Whosoever shall exalt himself shall be abased; and he that humbles himself shall be exalted."

Some of the "*flattering titles*" used by various denominations are noted here. Each denomination sets their own titles.

a) Roman Catholic Titles

The Pope, Holy Father, His Holiness, His Excellency, The Vicar of Christ, Mother Superior, Cardinals, Arch-Bishops, Priests, Father, Saint John the Divine, etc., etc.

(Note — Paul was "a father in the Lord", but he was not called "Father" (1 Corinthians 4:14-15). One could not hear Paul being called "Father Paul". Deborah was "a mother in Israel", but she was not called "Mother Superior" (Judges 5:7).

Numerous titles are used in the Roman Church, indeed, "flattering titles" and generally speaking, unscriptural and contrary to the words of Christ.

b) **Protestant Titles**

In the Protestant world, while rejecting, and generally speaking, repulsed by Roman titles, Protestants draw on other titles, some of these indeed being "flattering titles".

One of the most prominent titles is "Reverend". However, the Scriptures say "Holy and reverend (to be revered) is HIS name" (Psalm 111:9), not our name! To speak of the "Right Honourable Reverend, Very Reverend", etc., is certainly contrary to Scripture. It takes the title from God and assumes it for man.

The Salvation Army uses army titles for their various ranks of officers, such as "General, Colonel, Brigadier, Major, Captain, Lieutenant, Sergeant-Major, Corporal, etc.

Most Baptists, Pentecostals (and some other denominations) call their ministers "Pastor". Some are called "Doctor," or "Reverend".

What then is the difference, in principle, or in spirit, are Roman and Protestant titles?

Titular power belongs to the spirit of the world. How foreign and far removed from the Bible and the New Testament church. We are not to love the praise of men by receiving title power (John 5:44; 12:43).

Often it is argued that ministers must have titles in order to be recognized by the Gentile world and to have the respect of people. However, it is possible to have numerous titles and still not have the respect of people. The reverse is true also.

One of the sad things is that flattering titles which distinguish ministry has produced a "clergy/laity" system, which again is contrary to Scripture.

We have noted then the five areas that need to be challenged to change relative to the traditional system. We consider now solutions to these problems which we believe are Biblical solutions.

B. Summary of the Solutions

In our summary of the solutions, we address the problems in the order we have covered them.

1. The Set Man

With all that has been written concerning the one-man pastoral system or the monarchial bishop, the following "checks and balances" need to be remembered. This is done so here.

Although there was no person ever called "pastor/shepherd" in the New Testament, and there are no Scriptural grounds for a autocratic ministry or monarchial bishop, there is Scriptural ground for "the set man".

Moses, when about to pass from the scene of his shepherding ministry over Israel, the flock of God, and the church in the wilderness (Acts 7:38), asked the Lord to "*SET A MAN over the congregation*" that the people be not as sheep without a shepherd (Numbers 27:16).

The thought of the "set man" is one who is to oversee, to muster, to charge, and Joshua who was Moses successor, chosen by the Lord — not the people — was charged before Eleazar the high priest to care for Israel (Numbers 27:19,22).

Therefore it is recognized that each local congregation must have "a set man". However, he does not necessarily have to be the traditional "pastor". Of course, he must, as must all of the ascension-gift ministries, have the heart of a shepherd. He must "*have the smell of sheep on him*" and care for the flock of God.

It seems that "the set man" could be any one of the fivefold ministry if the Lord gives him the necessary grace and ability to be such.

The set man must have vision and direction. Otherwise the other ministries, the elders and the congregation live under frustration and suppression under the guise of submission.

It does not appear in either Old or New Testament that any one elder or group of elders entirely governed the church. It does appear that any government was always in conjunction with a "first among equals" ministry.

The Book of Revelation indicates that this "set man" was "*the angelos*" or simply "*the messenger*" of the local church (Revelation 1:20; 2:1, etc.).

The thing that determines who "the angelos" should be is the calling, gifting, anointing, vision and direction in leadership evidenced in that man's life.

The measure of the gift, grace and ability determines the measure of responsibility, authority and accountability. The Lord confirms this to all the eldership and the congregation in clear ways.

To show that "the set man" or "the angelos" could be any one of the ascension-gift ministries we list out the following men and their ministry. In the Old Testament there were tribal elders but there was always the chief among the elders. Not all elders were gifted, anointed and appointed as some of these men of Divine distinction. This is true in both Old and New Testament churches.

THE OLD TESTAMENT

The Man	The Ministry
* Aaron	— Prophet, Priest, Intercessor, Mediator
* Moses	— Prophet, Priest, King, Judge, Shepherd
* Joshua	— Captain, Commander, Shepherd
* Samuel	— Priest, Prophet, Seer, Shepherd
* David	— King, Prophet, Worshipper, Shepherd
* Isaiah	— Prophet, Statesman
* Ezekiel	— Prophet, Seer, Visionary, Watchman, Priest, Shepherd
* Nehemiah	— Governor, Builder, Leader
* Ezra	— Scribe, Teacher, Interpreter, Priest
* Jeremiah	— Priest, Prophet, Shepherd
* Cyrus	— King, Shepherd

THE NEW TESTAMENT

The Man	The Ministry
* Peter	— Apostle, Evangelist (fish), Shepherd (sheep)
* James	— Apostle, Shepherd
* John	— Apostle, Shepherd, Seer, Visionary, Prophetic
* Paul	— Apostle, Teacher, Preacher
* Timothy	— Apostle, Evangelist, Shepherd
* Titus	— Apostle, Shepherd
* Barnabas	— Teacher, Apostle

In both Old and New Testament, ministers "shepherded" the people of God, but, as evident above, each had their respective ministry and calling of God, not title-power, but functional ministries.

So we are saying that "the set man", or "the angelos" of the local church could possibly be any of the fivefold ascension-gift ministries IF THE LORD has graced and equipped him with all that is necessary for direction and leadership in the church, along with the eldership. But he does not have to be the traditional "pastor", for *ALL* ascension-gift ministries are "shepherding ministries" along with the local elders who are feeding God's flock.

In the Old Testament, prophets, priests and kings and princes, as leaders of Israel were collectively called "shepherds" by reason of their responsibility to the people of God (Ezekiel 22:6,25-28; Ezekiel 34). The same principle is true in New Testament ministries, while recognizing their distinctiveness as apostles, prophets, evangelists, shepherds and teachers along with the elders.

In summary we say that there must be "the set man" or "the angelos" of the church, or the "first among equals", but he does not have to be the traditional "pastor". He could be any of the ministries if gifted for that place, but all should have the heart and spirit of a shepherd.

2. The Presbytery

The presbytery is simply the group of local elders, although at times it could involve elders/ministries from outside the local church. However, we are considering the local church and its need of plurality of leadership.

Enough has been written on this matter in Chapter 16 on *"The Office of the Elder"*, so brief comments only are needed here.

While recognizing the need of a set man, yet he is not to be alone and become a dictator, an autocrat or a Diotrephes. There must be the working together of the team of elders with him.

Joshua, while placed and charged as the set man, the shepherd over Israel, worked with the elders. It is *"Joshua and the elders"* in a number of places (Joshua 7:6; 8:10,33; 23:2; 24:1,31; Judges 2:7).

Other examples have been listed in Chapter 16 to which the student is referred once again.

So in any local church it should be "the set man and the elders". These are his "checks and balances" as all seek to flow together in harmony and unity for the building of the body of Christ and the care of the flock of God.

3. Local Church Government

Brief comments only are needed here. The writer believes that the set man and the eldership constitute New Testament form of church government. It is not the government of one man. It is not the government by the people. It is not the government of a bureaucracy or a deacon-board or eldership. It is the united government of the set man with the eldership under Christ's headship as they seek His will and mind on all things pertaining to His people.

Together this provides "the checks and balances" for proper government in the house of the Lord.

The reader is referred again to Chapter 15 on *"Church Government"*.

4. Recognizing and Receiving the Ministries

Enough has been written concerning the governmental ministries of apostles, prophets, evangelists, pastor/shepherds and teachers. However, some comments are needed here.
If we do not seek for titular authority, how then can the ascension-gift ministries minister in the body of Christ, both in the church local and the church universal? What do we call them? How will people respect them if there are no titles given them?

Jesus gave us a principle in Matthew 10:40-42 when He spoke the following words to His disciples.

"He that *receiveth* a prophet in the name of a prophet shall *receive* a prophet's reward; and he that *receiveth* a righteous man in the name of a righteous man shall *receive* a righteous man's reward.

And whosoever shall give to drink unto one of these little ones a cup of water only in the name of a disciple, verily I say unto you, he shall in no wise lose his reward."

The key word is "receive". We can only receive when we recognize. The principle is laid out clearly by our Lord.

If we recognize and receive a prophet, or an apostle, a shepherd, a teacher or evangelist, we receive the reward of their labours, of their ministry. If we do not recognize and receive them, we bind them so that they cannot minister and we cannot receive.

This principle is true of all ministries in the body of Christ, as also of all members of the body of Christ.

Paul often spoke of his call to be an apostle, not by the will of man but by the will of God. His epistles generally commence with "Paul, *an* apostle of Jesus Christ . . .", never "THE apostle Paul . . ."

He began his Epistles on a first-name basis, then stated his calling, his work, his function in the church.

Apostles, prophets, evangelists, shepherds and teachers are more designations of spiritual tradesmanship than titular.

In society there are some who are bakers, butchers, plumbers, electricians, carpenters, technicians, etc., but these are designations of their trade, not merely titles.

In summary then, we believe it is right and proper to recognize and receive ministries in their office and function as apostles, prophets, evangelists, shepherds, teachers, elders, deacons, etc., but call or address them as appropriate and suitable by their first name or "Brother . . ."

The writer endeavours to follow this by recognizing publicly a man's ministry gift and asking the congregation to receive them in that ministry and then introducing them as "Brother . . ."

Paul, Peter, James, John and others were apostles. Philip was an evangelist. Barnabas was a teacher. Agabus and Silas were prophets. Others were elders or deacons.

All were recognized and received in their respective ministries, but none were called by titles. All were "*brothers*" and in the brotherhood of the church.

But this brings us to our final section concerning the matter of flattering titles and what we call each other, more especially ministries amongst us.

5.   **Love the Brotherhood**

If we are to avoid "flattering titles", what then should ministry be called? What is the Biblical answer? What do we call "the angelos" (the messenger) of the church, or "the set man"?

The Biblical answer is simple and clear. It comes, first of all, from the lips of the Lord Jesus Himself. For those who love titles and hold to titular authority, the answer may be humbling, but it is the answer of our Lord and of His apostles. Let us see it in His words.

"The scribes and the Pharisees sit in Moses seat . . . (of authority. Amp. N.T.) And love the uppermost rooms of feasts, and the chief seats in the synagogues, and greetings in the markets, and to be called of men, *Rabbi, Rabbi*. But be ye not called *Rabbi*: for one is your Master, even Christ; and all ye are *brethren*.

And call no man (in the church, Amp. N.T.) your *father* upon the earth: for one is your *Father*, which is in heaven.

Neither be ye called *masters*: for one is your *Master*, even Christ. But he that is greatest among you shall be your servant. And whosoever shall exalt himself (with haughtiness and empty pride. Amp. N.T.) shall be abased (humbled, brought low. Amp. N.T.), and he that shall humble himself (who has a modest opinion of himself and behaves accordingly. Amp. N.T.) shall be exalted (shall be raised to honour. Amp. N.T.)'' (Matthew 23:2,6-12).

★ We are Brothers

Jesus is so simple, clear and specific. We are not to be as the scribes (the theologians and hermeneuticians of His day), or the Pharisees (the fundamentalists of His day). We are not to seek for flattering titles. We are not looking to be called *''rabbi''*, or *''father''* or *''master''*.

Could we add, we are not to be called *''Reverend''*, *''Father''*, *''Holy Father''*, *''Doctor''*, *''Master''*, *''Pastor''*, *''Right Honourable''*, ad infinitum.

Jesus said, ''. . . we are *brothers* . . .''

The other is the way of the Gentile world. It is the way, so often, of the scribes and Pharisees. It is not the way of Christ. It is not the way of the early apostles or the early church.

To return to our question then, we ask, What should ministry or members be called? Our Biblical answer is twofold. We are related brothers.

One of the pictures of the church is the likeness to the family of God, a family of sons and daughters of God, a family of brothers and sisters (Ephesians 3:14-15).

The Lord says, ''I will be to you a Father and you shall be my *sons* and *daughters*, says the Lord Almighty'' (2 Corinthians 6:18).

Christ is the firstborn among ''a vast family of *brothers*'' (Romans 8:29).

''He is not ashamed to call them *brethren*, saying, I will declare thy name unto My *brethren*, in the midst of the church will I sing praise to thee (Hebrews 2:11-12; Psalm 22:22).''

On the resurrection day, Jesus said to the women . . . ''go to My *brethren* . . .'' (John 20:17).

Peter says, ''Honour all men. Love the *brotherhood*. Fear God. Honour the king'' (1 Peter 2:17).

Again Peter speaks of ''unfeigned love of the *brethren*'' (1 Peter 1:22).

The writer to the Hebrews exhorts the believers to ''let *brotherly* love continue'' (Hebrews 13:1).

The apostle Peter referred to the apostle Paul as ''our beloved *brother* Paul . . .'' (2 Peter 3:15).

Ananias, as a result of a vision from the Lord, went and laid his hands on Saul (Paul), saying ''. . . *brother* Saul . . .'' (Acts 9:17). No flattering titles, just ''brother!''.

All are brothers and sisters in the family of God. Paul exhorts Timothy, as far as the church family is concerned, to treat the older men as *fathers* (not call them ''father''); and elder women as *mothers* (not call them ''mother superior''); the younger men as *brothers* and the younger women as *sisters*.''

Read also James 2:1; 3:1; Galatians 1:2; Romans 12:12.

The New Testament believers, while recognizing ministries in their Divinely appointed offices predominantly received one another as ''brethren'' or related brothers.

They speak of each other and often addressed each other as ''brother'' — not with the flattering titles we have today in our religious systems. This is what Jesus told His disciples, for He said, ''. . . and all you are brethren . . .'' (Matthew 23:8).

★ **Personal Name Basis**

Another significant thing in Bible days is that believers especially are known on a personal name basis.

Our Western world speaks of a person's "Christian name". More correctly it is a person's given or personal name. However, all Bible saints, be they prophets, kings, apostles, teachers, shepherds, evangelists, judges or other are known by their personal names. Whatever office or ministry was held by these saints, all are known on a personal name basis.

We think of Moses, Jeremiah, Joshua, Isaiah, Elijah and Elisha, Daniel, Amos, Joel, Micah, Malachi, Zechariah, Peter, Paul, James, John, Matthew, Mark, Abraham, Enoch, Samuel, David, Luke, Timothy, Titus and numerous others. They are never ever called "Reverend", "Holy Father", "The Right Honourable", "Archbishop", "His Highness", "Doctor", "Prophet", "Pastor", ad infinitum.

They did not look for titular power. Titles were not to them as to many today, "security blankets". They were not title conscious. They were in the brotherhood, in the great family of God. They did not insist on titles. They were recognized and received in their ministries but not by titles.

It is a blessing today to know of many great men of God. Ministries in the body of Christ, who are content to be known on a first name basis and not insist on titles or titular authority, but are recognized in their respective ministries.

★ **Ministers of the Gospel**

One final thought may be helpful regarding the relationship of a minister to the world system. How is one to be known in the world system?

The writer believes that the simplest designation is that of "Minister . . ."

Paul recognized the powers that be as ordained of God and called them the "ministers of God" (Romans 13:4,6) several times in these verses.

So the ascension-gifts of the risen Lord are ministers of the gospel of Jesus Christ.
Judas fell from "this ministry" (Acts 1:17).
Matthias took part in "this ministry" (Acts 1:25).
The apostles fulfilled their ministry (Acts 12:25).
All are to take heed to the ministry received in the Lord and fulfil it (Colossians 4:17).
Paul told Timothy to make full proof of his ministry (2 Timothy 4:5).
Paul said Mark was profitable to him for the ministry (2 Timothy 4:11).
The Lord put Paul into the ministry (1 Timothy 1:12).
The believer has been given the ministry of reconciliation (2 Corinthians 5:18-21).
We are ministers of the New Covenant (2 Corinthians 3:6).
We must be honest, giving no offence, so that the ministry be not blamed (2 Corinthians 6:3).

In the government of this world, there are those who are known as Minister of Finance, Minister of Education, Minister of Social Services, and a host of other areas in which society is served.
So Christ has gifted men who are "*ministers* of the Gospel", as far as the world is concerned, but they are "*brothers*" in the church regardless of gifting.

In the government of this world, there are those who are known as Minister of Finance, Minister of Education, Minister of Social Services, and a host of other areas in which society is served.
So Christ has gifted men who are "*ministers* of the Gospel", as far as the world is concerned, but they are "*brothers*" in the church regardless of gifting.

SUMMARY:

We conclude our chapter on "*Challenge to Change the Traditional System*" with five summary points.

1. The church needs to recognize that the one-man rule of a pastor is not New Testament order. Also the church needs to recognize that any one of the fivefold ascension-gift ministries may be "the angel" or "the set man" of the local church in conjunction with the elders and deacons, if the Lord has so graced and gifted him with that ability.

2. The church needs to recognize that God has ordained plurality of eldership in the local church, or, a presbytery and these work with the ascension-gifted ministry or ministries.

3. The church needs to recognize that a one-man, or deacon-board or democratic form of church government is unScriptural and dissolve such returning governmental responsibility to the eldership, which includes the ascension-gift ministries and local eldership.

4. The church needs to believe in, recognize and accept the fivefold ascension-gift ministries of apostles, prophets, evangelists, pastors/shepherds and teachers along with elders and deacons in their respective function. These are set there for the governing, ministering and serving of the members of the body of Christ.

5. The church needs to recognize the God-given offices and ministeries in their midst, but not hold such by titular authority. All ministries are brothers in the church family, and ministers of God both in the church and in the society.

CHAPTER 26

CONGREGATIONAL MINISTRIES AND FUNCTIONS

Introductory:

As already seen in Chapter 14, one of the greatest revelations of the Church is in the fact that the Church is the Body of Christ in the earth.

In I Corinthians 12:1-31, Paul uses the human and natural body as a figure of the Church, the spiritual Body of Christ. This is distinctly a Pauline revelation (Ephesians 5:23-33; 1:22-23; 3:6; 4:4-16; Colossians 1:18).

There are numerous comparisons and lessons which may be seen, learnt and applied to both the natural body and the spiritual body, which is the Church.

The Church is a spiritual body, made up of spiritual members, having spiritual gifts and ministries and talents to be used for the spiritual building of this body. Everything in the Body is from the Head to the Body, in the Body, for the Body and for the Head, even Christ.

We note some of the most important lessons to be learnt from the natural body as being applicable to Christ's spiritual Body.

★ Every member in the natural body must have *life* conveyed by *blood* and *breath*.
So every member in the spiritual Body must have life by the blood of Jesus and the Spirit and Breath of God (I John 1:7, 8; John 3:1-5; Revelation 5:9; I Corinthians 12:13).

★ Every member in the natural body has its own God-ordained and set place, as it pleased the Creator in the formation of that body (Psalms 139:13-16).
So every member in the spiritual Body has their God-ordained and set place as it pleases Him (I Corinthians 12:12-28).

★ Every member in the natural body is a living, functioning member; otherwise there is death. There are no inactive members (Matthew 25:15; Mark 13:34; Luke 19:13; Romans 12:3).
So every member in the spiritual Body is to be a living, functioning member or else there is death (James 2:26).

★ Members have various gifts given to them to make them a functioning member. i.e. the ear is a *member* of the body, and has the *gift* of hearing, otherwise it is deaf. The eye is a *member* of the body, having the *gift* of sight, otherwise it is blind. So for the tongue with speech, the nose with smell, etc. It is the gift in the member that makes it a functioning member!
So it is in the Body of Christ. Every member of the Body has some gift to make them a functioning member. This needs to be discovered.

★ No member has another members place or gift. i.e., the eye has its place and gift. The ear does not see, nor the eye smell, nor the nose see, etc. Each has the gift suitable to it as a member, as the Lord wills. We cannot separate members and gifts, otherwise it is a many-membered body without gifts to function. So many Churches are like this, having members but no gifts in them to function.

★ Every member works in harmony with every member, without jealousy or competitive spirit. It is the same life blood and breath in all, though varying in place, gift and function. Unity and harmony in the body is the key. It is recognition and not competition. This must be so in the Body of Christ.

A. **Diversity in the body** 1 Corinthians 12:1-7.

In this chapter Paul shows how the Godhead is involved in relation to the various gifts and functions in the Body of Christ. These verses reveal the great diversity in the Body of Christ, and ''the cluster'' of these diversities because of the many members in the Body.

1. **The Holy Spirit**

   There are *diversities of gifts,* but the *same Spirit* (vs 4).
   i.e. Spiritual gifts given by the Holy Spirit as in verses 8-10, 7, 11.

2. **The Son**

   There are *differences of administrations* (ministries), but the *same Lord* (vs 5).
   i.e., Spiritual ministries given by the Lord Jesus, the Son (Ephesians 4:9-16; Romans 12:1-8).

3. **The Father**

   There are *diversities of operations,* but it is the *same God* which worketh all in all (vs 6).
   i.e., Spiritual power and abilities given by the Father God.

Thus Father, Son and Holy Spirit work in the many-membered Body. The Son gives the various Ministries. The Holy Spirit gives the needed Gifts for these Ministries. The Father God gives the power and enablement for both Ministry and Gift to function.

The Spiritual Gifts are given by the Holy Spirit. The Ministry Gifts are given by the Son. The Father God works all and in all.

B. **Measure and Fulness of Grace and Gift**

One of the most important things to recognize in relation to all ministries, gifts and functions in the Body of Christ is the truth pertaining to the *measure* and *fulness* of grace and gifts in this Body.

1. **The Fulness in Christ**

   In Christ Jesus, as the Head of the Church, His Body, is all the Divine fulness.
   It pleased God that in His Son should all fulness dwell (Colossians 1:9).
   In Him dwells all the fulness of the Godhead in bodily form (Colossians 2:9).
   He received the Holy Spirit without measure (John 3:33, 34).
   He was THE WORD made flesh, full of grace and truth (John 1:14, 16. Amp. N.T.)
   He is the fulness of Him who fills all in all (Ephesians 1:23).
   The Lord wants the Body to come to that fulness (Ephesians 4:13).
   The Greek word "Pleroma" denotes fulness, that of which a thing is full.
   In Christ are all the ministries, gifts and grace of God. This fulness is to be let down into the Body and flow through the many members of the Body in the earth. Jesus is the fulness personified.

2. **The Measure in the Church**

   No one member has the Divine fulness of Christ, but each receive and partake in measure of that fulness. So the fulness is not in one member of the Body but in the total Body, each member sharing of that fulness.

   Of His fulness have all we received and grace for grace (John 1:16).
   We receive the measure of faith, not fulness of faith (Romans 12:1-8).
   We prophesy according to the proportion of faith given, not going beyond. Paul speaks of the measure of the gift of grace (Ephesians 4:7). This measure works in every part to bring us to the measure of the stature of Christ (Ephesians 4:13, 16).

   The word "Metron" is used for measuring, a measure. It is used (a) Of a vessel fig., Matthew 23:32; Luke 6:38; John 3:34; (b) Of a rule or rod for measuring (Matthew 7:2; Revelation 21:15), and of (c) A portion measured off (Romans 12:3; II Corinthians 10:13; Ephesians 4:7).

   Thus the gifts of grace are measured off and given according to the will of Christ to the various believers, as it pleases Him.

   The measure is to bring the Church in time to the fulness of God, to the fulness of Christ.

Read Colossians 1:19; 2:9; Ephesians 3:7; 1:23; 3:19; 4:13; Acts 6:3-8; 7:55; Romans 15:29; Joel 2:29.

The Greek words for grace/gifts are related.

"Charis" = Grace, Divine favour, and also includes the thought of Divine enabling.

"Dorea" = gift, spiritual or supernatural gift (Acts 2:38; Ephesians 4:17; 3:7; Gift/grace).

"Charisma" = gift, a gift of grace (I Corinthians 1:7; 12:4, 9, 28, 30, 31; I Timothy 4:14; II Timothy 1:6; I Peter 4:10; Romans 1:11).

The gifts are "grace-gifts" or "gifts of grace" given to the members of the Body of Christ for the building up of the Body.

C. Congregational Ministries, Gifts, Talents, Functions

It should be remembered that within each and all of the following list there is "the cluster" of variety according to the place in the Body, as well as the varied personalities of the members. None can be stereotyped. No snow flake is alike, all differ, yet each has perfect design. No blade of grass is alike, yet all is grass, each blade having its design. So it is with the members of the Body of Christ.

We list the following, though, undoubtedly there are numerous other functions in the Body that are not specified but are there nonetheless.

1. In Christ The Head

Because the fulness is in Christ, every ministry, gift and grace is seen in Him also. We note some of these things "in Christ".

★ Christ the Apostle and High Priest (Hebrews 3:1).

★ Christ the Prophet (John 4:19). The Seer.

★ Christ the Teacher (John 3:2).

★ Christ the Pastor and Shepherd (John 10:11).

★ Christ the Evangelist (Isaiah 61:1). The Gospels.

★ Christ the Ruler, Bishop and Elder (Romans 8:29; Daniel 7:22; I Peter 2:25).

★ Christ the Servant and Deacon (Luke 22:27).

★ Christ the Overseer and Bishop of our souls (I Peter 2:25).

★ Christ the Governor, Governments (Matthew 2:6; Isaiah 9:6).

★ Christ the Intercessor (Hebrews 7:25).

★ Christ the Giver (Galatians 2:20).

★ Christ the Tabernacle and Temple of God (John 1:14; 2:21).

★ Christ the Wisdom of God (I Corinthians 1:30).

★ Christ the Knowledge of God (Colossians 2:3).

★ Christ the Faith of God (Galatians 3:23).

★ Christ the Helper (Hebrews 13:6). Ministry of helps.

★ Christ the Shewer of Mercy (Hebrews 2:17; Romans 12:6-8).

★ Christ the Power of God (I Corinthians 1:24).

★ Christ the Love of God (John 17:26).

★ Christ THE WORD of God (John 1:3, 14).

★ Christ the Fulness of God (Colossians 1:19).

★ Christ the Head of the Body (Ephesians 1:22).

★ Christ the Exhorter (John 3).

★ Christ the All and in All (Colossians 3:11).

The list could continue. But enough is given to show that all is Christ and Christ is to be all and in all. His fulness is to be taken and distributed in the many members of the body according to God's will. All are extensions of Christ's ministry in the Body.

2.   In the Members of the Church

★   Apostles — Greek, "apostolos" = One sent as a messenger, the bearer of a commission, Church planter, spiritual father of Churches (Ephesians 4:11; I Corinthians 12:28).

★   Prophets — Greek "prophetes" = A spokesman for another, an interpreter for God, a seer, a divinely commissioned and inspired person, a foreteller of the future gifted for the exposition of the truth (Acts 15).

★   Evangelists — Greek "evangelistes" = One who announces glad tidings, one who enlarges and extends the kingdom of God, one who shares in edifying and building the Church (Ephesians 4:11; Acts 21:8; II Timothy 4:5).

★   Pastors — Greek "poimen" = one who tends the sheep, a shepherd, one who cares for the sheep. One who leads, feeds, waters and guards the sheep, guardian (John 10:16; 21:16; I Peter 5:2, 3).

★   Teachers — Greek "didaskalos" = One who instructs, the occupation of teaching, someone qualified to instruct others, someone who imparts Bible truth to others (I Timothy 3:2; II Timothy 2:2, 4; I Corinthians 12:28; Romans 12:6).

★   Elder — Greek "presbuteros" = a senior man, seasoned in years and spiritual growth, presbyter of the Church (Acts 11:30; 14:23; 20:17; I Timothy 4:14, 5:17-19).
Bishops — Greek "episkopos" = an overseer, a watcher or guardian of the Church (I Peter 2:25; Acts 20:28; Philippians 1:1; I Timothy 3:1-8; Titus 1:7).

★   Preacher — Greek "keerux" = herald, public messenger, proclaimer, publisher (as evangelist) (I Timothy 2:7; II Timothy 1:11; II Peter 2:5).

★   Deacons — Greek "diakonos" = One who renders service to another, an attendant, one who executes a commission, a servant of the Church in natural and spiritual areas (Philippians 1:1; Romans 16:1; I Timothy 3:8, 12; Acts 6:1-6).
Ministry — Greek "diakonia" = he who ministers, service ministry, the act of rendering relief and aid to another (Acts 6:1; 11:29; II Corinthians 8:4).
Deacons and Deaconesses = function in office in the Church (Romans 12:7; I Corinthians 12:5; Colossians 4:17; II Timothy 4:5).

★   Word of Wisdom — Greek "sophia" = The quality of being wise by the Holy Spirit, a flash revelation given by the Spirit (I Corinthians 12:8).

★   Word of Knowledge — Greek "gnosis" = The fact or state of knowing by the Holy Spirit. A revelation of facts not known by natural understanding as given by the Spirit (I Corinthians 12:8).

★   Discerning of spirits — Greek "diakrisis" = To recognize clearly what is the Spirit of God, spirit of error or the human spirit at work. Perception of error or truth.

★   Gift of Faith — Greek "pistis" = Special and supernatural faith given by the Spirit for the miraculous (I Corinthians 12:9).

★   Gifts of Healings — Greek "charismata iama" = Those who have various gifts or a gift of healing by the Spirit, restoring health (Acts 4:22, 30; I Corinthians 12:9, 28, 30; Hebrews 12:13).

★   Worker of Miracles — Greek "dunamis" = Works of power, those who do or perform miracles (I Corinthians 12:28; I Thessalonians 1:5; I Corinthians 4:19, 20; 2:4; II Timothy 1:7; Romans 1:16).

★   Prophecy — Greek "propheetia" = He who prophesies, a gifted faculty of setting forth inspired utterance in known language (Romans 12:6; I Corinthians 12:10; 13:2; I Timothy 1:18).

★ Diversities of Tongues — Greek "glossallia" A speaker in kinds of tongues, those who speak languages they have never learned, by the Spirit (I Corinthians 13:1; Mark 16:17; Acts 2:4).

★ Interpreter of Tongues — Greek "diermeanutees" = To interpret tongues or languages by the power of the Spirit (I Corinthians 14:5, 13, 27; 12:30).

★ Helps — Greek "antilepsis" = Those who help others, helpers, one who aids, assists, helps or supports the weak, do others service (I Corinthians 12:28; Luke 1:54; Acts 20:35; I Timothy 6:2).

★ Directors — Greek "kubernesis", Governments, Pilotage = To control the course of a ship, to steer or direct the Church (Acts 27:11; Revelation 18:17; I Corinthians 12:28).

★ Exhorter — Greek "paraklesis" = To warn, to admonish, to be cheered or comforted, to entreat, to urge, persuasion or excitement (I Thessalonians 5:14; Titus 1:9; Corinthians 14:3; Hebrews 3:13; 10:25; II Corinthians 1:4, 6; Acts 20:12).

★ He that Giveth — Greek "didomi" = He that imparts, to share, to bestow, a distributor of alms, to give a part of what we have (Luke 3:11; Romans 1:11; 12:8; I Thessalonians 2:8; Ephesians 4:28).

★ He that Ruleth — Greek "prosteemi" = He that takes the lead, to set before, appoint with authority, to preside, govern, superintend (I Thessalonians 5:12; I Timothy 3:4, 5, 12; 5:17; Titus 3:8, 14; Romans 16:2).

★ He that Sheweth Mercy — Greek "elebs" = Have compassion, to show gracious favour, saving mercy towards (I Timothy 1:13, 16; Romans 9:15, 16, 18; Jude 23; Matthew 5:7; 6:2-4; 9:27; 15:22; Hebrews 2:17).

★ Hospitality — Romans 12:6-8; Hebrews 13:1-2.

★ Ministry of Intercessory Prayer — Hebrews 7:25.

★ Ministry of Singers and Singing — The Choir. Tabernacle of David (I Chronicles 15).

★ Ministry of Musicians/Directors (I Chronicles 25).

★ Ministry of Comfort (John 14:26; 15:26).

★ Ministry of Counselling (Isaiah 9:6-9).

★ Gleaner in the fields (Ruth 2-3).

★ Ministry of Scribe/writer.

★ Personal Evangelism (John 4; Acts 8).

★ Ministry to Children.

★ Ministry to Youth.

★ Administration and Organization.

★ Ministry to the Widows (Acts 6:1-6).

★ Ministry to younger Women of the Church (Titus 2).

★ Ministry of Home Meetings.

★ Skilled Tradesmen.

★ Secretarial work.

★ Stewardship, Treasurer, Business, Finance.

★ Mothers in Israel (Judges 5).

★ Door Greeter/Porters in House of the Lord.

★ Instructors in natural and spiritual areas.

★ Fathers in the Lord (I Corinthians 4:19-20).

There are many avenues of service in the body of Christ. God gives to all various gifts, graces, talents, ministries and functions in both natural and spiritual areas to minister to the Body of Christ.

It is every one's responsibility to find their grace-gift and minister accordingly.

The Student should study many of the above functions in the Scriptures for fuller insight into these grace-gifts, talents and ministries.

D. **Christ in You** (Colossians 1:27-29).

Every ministry and gift of grace is really Christ functioning in the members of His Body by the Spirit. It is really the revelation of "Christ in you" the hope of glory. It is Christ re-living His life, revealing His nature, manifesting His grace and gift in the members. It is Christ the apostle, Christ the intercessor, Christ the shower of mercy, Christ the comforter, etc., working in the members of His own Body, the Church.

This is Pauline revelation (I Corinthians 11:19; Galatians 4:19; I Corinthians 8:12, 13; Acts 9:1-18; Matthew 25:31-46; Galatians 1:12-16, 24; 2:20).

When we discern the Body of Christ we discern Christ in His members, accepting and receiving their grace and gift and the Lord in them.

Every member with whatever grace-gift is given them should seek to follow Christ and allow Him to express Himself through their redeemed personality.

The Head of the Church wants to continue His ministry in the earth. He can only do this through His Body, the Church (Acts 1:1).

There will be infinite variety in all these operations because of the infinite variety of personalities in the Body of Christ.

Members should seek to find their place in the Body, accept the privileges and the responsibility along with such and know that they are accountable to the Lord in that day for their spiritual stewardship (Luke 16; Matthew 25:31-46).

CHAPTER 27

DWELLING TOGETHER IN UNITY

Introductory:

The Psalmist said it was good and pleasant for brethren to dwell together in unity. This unity was likened to the anointing upon Aaron's head flowing down over his body to the very skirts of his garments. It was also likened to the refreshing dew of Hermon (Psalms 133).

The Psalm certainly can be applied to Christ, our Great High Priest, and to His priestly Body, the Church. The key is UNITY.

The same anointing flows from the Head to the members of the Body. And where there is UNITY there is blessing, there is life.

Although the principle of this Psalm is applicable to the whole Body of Christ, the Church universally and locally, in this chapter it is applied more especially to the ministries in the local Church. For, if the ministries, the elders and deacons, do not flow together in UNITY, then the people will find it difficult to do so.

As a local Church grows, then the plurality of leadership will emerge. It is imperative that all work together as a team, brethren dwelling together in unity. Otherwise plurality can never work as God intended it to. The Bible shows the working together of ministries and principles that make the team work. Whether we speak of "the staff" or "eldership" or "ministry", all together they constitute a team; the brethren dwelling together in unity.

Some of these principles were listed in Chapter 15, but they are developed more fully in this chapter on TEAM WORK and principles of the leadership in the local Church working together.

A. Definition

Webster's Dictionary defines a team or teamwork as:

1. To harness or yoke together as a team.

2. To join in a co-operative activity.

3. Joint action by a group of people, in which each person subordinates his individual interests and opinions to the unity and efficiency of the group.

4. Co-ordinated effort, as of an athletic team.

The word was especially used of a team of horses, harnessed to the same vehicle or plow and pulling their weight together.

So we may say that "team ministry" is when two or more ministers minister together. It is a co-ordinated joint effort in which individual ministries blend together in submission, to each other to reach a common spiritual goal. It is being "yoked together" (Matthew 11:28-30).

Ministers become "fellow-workers" together (Colossians 4:11).;
"fellow-soldiers" (Philippians 2:25; Philemon 2);
"fellow-servants" (Matthew 18:29, 33; Colossians 1:7; Revelation 19:10);
"fellow-labourers" (I Thessalonians 3:2; Philemon 1, 24; Philippians 4:3);
"fellow-helpers" (III John 8; II Corinthians 8:23);
"fellow-disciples" (John 11:16);
"fellow-citizens" (Ephesians 2:19);
"fellow-heirs" (Ephesians 3:6);
and in fellowship with each other (Galatians 2:9; I John 1:3-7; Acts 2:42; Philippians 4:3; Romans 16:27; II Corinthians 4:1, 7, 10).

A team therefore is a group of persons joined together in the *same mind,* speaking the same thing and going in the *same direction* (I Corinthians 1:10).

David was able to weld the men in distress, who came to him, into a great team, a great army of soldiers (I Samuel 22:1-3).

B. **The Necessity of a Team**

In the beginning of a work, many times a ministry has to be an all-round person, because of the lack of personnel. However, as a local Church grows and increases, it is absolutely impossible for any one-man to meet everyone's needs. Hence the need for developing a team.

Rev. Frank Damazio in ''Leadership'' notes lists ten problems of the one-man-ministry which accentuates the need for plurality and team-work.

1. One man cannot shepherd successfully a large flock of God.
2. One man is limited in his ministry and gifts.
3. One man may fail in wisdom, knowledge and judgment.
4. One man will have difficulty in finding the mind of God for everything.
5. One man limits the potential growth.
6. One man has no one to adjust or correct him.
7. One man has no ''checks and balances''.
8. One man may break physically, mentally, emotionally and morally under pressure.
9. One man may become an autocrat or dictator.
10. One man ministry is contrary to the revealed will of God in the Scriptures which teaches plurality of leadership as well as someone who is ''first among equals''.

C. **Team Ministries**

The Bible not only provides us with the standard of Christian character and lifestyle but it also provides us with examples of ministries working together as a team, yoked together in the Gospel of Christ.

1. **In the Godhead**

    The very nature, character and function of a team is seen and demonstrated in the Godhead as Father, Son and Holy Spirit.

    God never asks men to do anything that He has not demonstrated in His own eternal Being (Matthew 28:18-20; John 17). The Father, Son and Holy Spirit as three persons, each with distinctive ministry and function, are one in mind, will and judgment, one in purpose.

    In the Godhead there is plurality, co-equality, distinctive ministry and function, submission, order and unity. Thus in the Godhead we see this unity in plurality.

2. **In Israel — The Jethro Principle** (Exodus 18:13-26; Deuteronomy 1:9, 10)

    This point was referred to briefly in Chapter 15 but is developed more fully here.

    Moses was the Pastor-Shepherd, Educator, Official Representative and Administrator of the Church in the Wilderness (Acts 7:38).

    The burden upon one man was too great (vs 14, 18). Jethro gave Moses a word of wisdom by suggesting that he bring in team-work of qualified men (vs 18, 19, 23).

    a. **Qualifications**

        1) Men who were *able* men (Matthew 25:14-30; I Peter 4:10, 11). God gives various abilities to men which need to be discerned and recognized.
        2) Men who *fear* God (Proverbs 3:7; 9:10; 24:21). Not fear men or devils. Fear = a constant awareness that God is watching me in all I think, do, say and am.
        3) Men of *truth* (Psalms 51:6; Zechariah 8:16; Ephesians 4:15). Honest, transparent, men of integrity. No hypocrisy, deception.

4) Men hating *covetousness* (Proverbs 28:16; Romans 7:7; Ephesians 3:3-5; Ezekiel 33:31; I Timothy 6:9-12). Covetousness is the root sin. Can covet position, power, glory, money, etc. Not to be bribed.

5) Men of *wisdom and knowledge and understanding* (Proverbs 1:1-6; I Kings 3; Ephesians 1:17, 18).

★ Knowledge — the possession of facts.

★ Understanding — the interpretation of facts.

★ Wisdom — the application of facts.

6) Men known among the tribes (I Timothy 3; 6; I Thessalonians 5:12-13). Not novices, but knowing those who labour among us.

b. **Responsibility of Rulers**

1) Men placed to be *rulers* over the people.

★ Rule their own spirit (Proverbs 16:32; 25:28).

★ Rule over own house (I Timothy 3:4).

★ Rule over the house of God (I Timothy 3:4, 5).

Placed as heads to rule over the thousands, hundreds, fifties and tens, as they can handle.

(Note — Some have rejected the Jethro Principle because it was given by Moses' father-in-law, and that, if advice taken literally, there would have been 78,600 judges in all over the nation of Israel. However, subsequent Scriptures confirm the principle set forth here in Elders and Judges over the people. Moses could not be the one man ministry forever. He did have Aaron with him, then the Elders of Israel, then these judges. Jethro said "If God . . ." and God did not rebuke Moses for it).

2) Men able to *judge* the people at all times. Discern needs. Give good counsel, and answers to the problems, insight, decisions based on principles of God's laws, not poor judgment.

★ Judge with justice (Isaiah 1:17).

★ Judge with mercy (Psalms 101:1).

★ Judge without partiality or favouritism (Proverbs 24:23; Deuteronomy 1:17).

★ Judge beyond natural senses (Isaiah 11:1-5).

★ Judge with knowledge, understanding and wisdom (II Chronicles 1:7-12).

3) Men to bear the *burden with thee* (Numbers 11:11-17; Exodus 18:14-18, 22).

4) Men having the *same spirit* upon them (Numbers 11:16, 17; I Corinthians 1:10; Psalms 133).

c. **Responsibility of Moses**

1) Relationship to God — Godward (vs 19).

2) Relationship to Leaders — Manward (vs 20)

★ Teach them ordinances and laws — theory (Philippians 4:9).

★ Shew them the way to walk, the work to do (Isaiah 2:1-5; II Timothy 3:2).

Thus the measure of *ability* is the measure of *responsibility,* which becomes the measure of *authority* and the measure of one's *accountability.* One only has authority where they have responsibility.

The Jethro Principle illustrates the "team ministry" under Moses. It is worthy to note that the qualifications of these judges are similar in some respects to that of the New Testament Elders.

3. **The Priestly Tribe of Levi** (Numbers 1-2-3, 18; Exodus 28, 29).

    The principle of working together as a team in unity is seen also in the tribe of Levi.

    Under this order God was ruler, then Moses, then Aaron and his sons, and then the tribe of Levi was given to be the servant tribe to the High Priestly household as well as to the 12 tribes of Israel. The Levites were given as a gift and to be joined to Aaron and his sons for the work of the ministry in the Tabernacle.

    Incorporated into this was the Jethro Principle, as seen in Deuteronomy 17:8-12; 19:17-18. Thus we have Judges (Exodus 18), and Priests, Levites AND Judges (Deuteronomy 17:8-12), and the Priests and Judges (Deuteronomy 19:17-18) together here. Note that Judge/Eldership was common in Israel.

    a. In Patriarchal times the heads of families and Elders were Judges (Genesis 38:24).

    b. In Moses time, in pre-Canaan days there were Judges (Exodus 18:13-27; Deuteronomy 1; 9-17).

    c. In the order of Israel there was Moses, Aaron the High Priest and the Levites (Numbers 1, 2, 3, 18 chapters).

    d. In the period of the Judges there were Judges and Elders over the tribes (Judges 4:5).

    e. In David's time he consulted with the heads of the thousands and hundreds of Israel also (I Chronicles 13:1).

    f. In Ezra's times there was Ezra the Scribe-Priest and Teacher and Judges too.

    g. In Messiah's times there was the High Priest, the Sanhedrin and the Elders of Synagogues and Deacons.

    h. In the Early Churches there were the chief shepherds and eldership together caring for the flock of God.

    All of this demanded ''team-work'' and brethren working together in unity. There the Lord could command the blessing, even life for ever more.

    Thus the Jethro Principle is confirmed in Israel's history as well as New Testament principle in the local Church.

4. **Team Ministries in the New Testament Church**

    The same truth continues in the New Testament concerning God making ''team ministries'' as seen in the Old Testament.

    a. Jesus and the Twelve Apostles (Matthew 10). Jesus sent them out two by two into every city.

    b. Jesus sent out the 70 two by two into every city (Luke 10:1-2).

    c. Peter and John worked together (Acts 3).

    d. Philip, then Peter and John at Samaria (Acts 8).

    e. Peter and six other brethren (Acts 10-11).

    f. Paul and Barnabas worked together (Acts 13:13, 14). Paul and his company mentioned.

    g. Judas and Silas join Paul and Barnabas in Acts 15.

    h. Barnabas and John Mark travel together (Acts 15).

    i. Paul and Silas team together (Acts 15).

    j. Timothy joins Paul and Silas (Acts 16).

    k. Paul takes Priscilla and Aquilla with him in the work (Acts 18).

    l. Timothy and Erastus sent to Macedonia by Paul (Acts 19).

    m. Apostolic company into Asia was Sopater, Aristarchus, Secundus, Gaius, Timothy,

Tychicus, Trophimus along with Paul (Acts 20).

n. Bishops and Deacons worked together in Philippi (Philippians 1:1).

o. Apostles, elders and brethren in council (Acts 15:1-2; 21:17-18).

p. Elders at Crete with Titus (Titus 1:5).

q. Elders at Ephesus with Timothy (Acts 20:17).

r. Prophets and Teachers at Antioch (Acts 13:1-4).

Thus we have a number of references to show that ministries worked together in the early Church. There must have been good team spirit and principles there to be what the Lord intended the Church to be, even though there was, at times, some dissension and disputation.

D. Practical Principles of Team-Work

The basic theory of plurality of leadership has been covered in the Chapter on Eldership and Church Government (Chapter 15). We consider some practical principles of working together as a team. For, it is not only the "mechanics" or "letter" of it that counts, but the "spirit" and "life" of it, otherwise there is death. It can be organization without organism, structure without life!

1. The Head or Leader of the Team

Whatever the Head of the team is, so will be the team. Whether he be called the Senior Elder or Minister, or whatever title he carries, he is one of the keys to successful team-work. Hence the importance of the leader working according to Biblical principles.

a. He must be an *example* the team can follow (I Corinthians 11:1; Ephesians 5:2; Philippians 4:9). Paul said that the believers had learned, heard, received and seen in him the things they were to do. A leader must be an example spiritually, morally, ethically, socially, doctrinally and in his family. He must conform to the standard of the Word at all times (Romans 12:1-2).

1) Lead by Principle — What you believe.

2) Lead by Precept — What you say (Psalms 119:4, 168). Rule of moral conduct.

3) Lead by Practice — What you do (Matthew 23:1-3). Not hypocrite.

4) Lead by Personal Example — What you are (Philippians 3:17; I Peter 5:3). A specimen, a pattern for others to follow (Philippians 4:9; II Timothy 3:10).

b. Must not have a dictatorial spirit (Luke 22:24-27; Mark 10:42-45; II Corinthians 1:24; Daniel 5:19). Not like running for USA Presidency or Political Office. Not lordship, domineering, authoritarianism, etc.

Someone has listed out the difference between A Boss and A Leader.

1) A boss drives men — a leader coaches them.

2) A boss depends on authority — a leader depends on good will.

3) A boss inspires fear — a leader inspires enthusiasm.

4) A boss assigns the task — a leader sets the pace.

5) A boss gives orders — a leader makes suggestions.

6) A boss fixes the blame for the breakdown — a leader fixes the breakdown.

7) A boss pushes people — a leader persuades people.

8) A boss gets complaints — a leader gets co-operation.

9) A boss says "Get going" — a leader says "Let's go".

10) A boss builds machines — a leader builds men.

The world needs leaders — nobody wants a boss!!!!! (Selected. Author unknown).

c. He must have a *servant spirit* (Mark 10:45; I Kings 12:7, 8).
   If one rules as a king with a servant spirit, people will serve you.

d. He must be a person who can have others work with him and not just for him. Many ministers cannot have people work with them as they become insecure in their position and then get rid of them. (John 13:3; I Timothy 1:12).

e. He must allow for mistakes in the development of the team. i.e., Jesus did with the Twelve apostles.

f. He must have confidence in the team and not question their integrity or motives.

g. He must be willing to delegate responsibilities and the corresponding authority (Mark 13:34), yet require accountability.

h. He must respect his own chain of command given to team members.

i. He must be willing to share his honour and not be jealous of others when they succeed (Numbers 27:20; 11:14-17).

j. He must seek to release the ministry of the team and not suppress them.

k. He must be willing to admonish, confront and counsel team members and not pass the spade to others to do it. Deal with problems while small.

l. He must keep the lines of communication clear and open always. Communication breakdown is one of the greatest causes of trouble in team-work. Need to speak freely without taking offence, or being on the defensive.

m. He must recognize three major problems to watch for in team ministry:
   1) Misuse — unqualified persons, not trained, failure to train others for responsibility.
   2) Disuse — uninvolved; feeling you can do it better yourself and not involve others.
   3) Abuse — overload and overwork the most talented and gifted ones.

n. He must build all members of the team into a team by concept, precept and practice. Organization.

o. He must seek to maintain unity of speech, mind, judgment and vision (Psalms 133).

p. He must build relationships with the team members. Relationships do not just happen. They have to be built. Relationships cannot be legislated; cannot relate the unrelatable.
   1) Relationships begin with God first (I John 1:7-9).
   2) Relationships built with others (I John 1:5, 6). Vertical, then horizontal.
   3) Relationships precede commitment to each other.
   4) Relationships have to be maintained. The same things that bring relationship are the things which maintain it.

      In a building one stone can only relate to six other stones and this is so throughout the whole building.
   5) Relationship is in the spirit; one in spirit; commitment ``for better, for worse, till death do us part''.

q. He must be loyal to the team even if they make errors. He rebukes privately. He will support his fellow elder and not allow attack on them, even as he would not allow children to attack parents.

r. He should surround himself with strong men who can strengthen his weaknesses and vice versa; not have a group of "yes men" (Proverbs 15:22). In the multitude of counsellors there is safety.

s.   He must maintain clear vision (Proverbs 29:18), for his own personal life and ministry; for the Church as a whole; for the leadership and for the Body of Christ as a whole. There must be purpose, vision, goals, direction.

t.   He must make time for the team getting together; fellowship, teaching.

u.   He must have Divine love for them (I Corinthians 13).

v.   He must always attack problems, never personalities.

w.   He must give encouragement (not flattery) for work well done.

x.   He must be a man of principles which are Word based.

y.   He must be a man of courage himself to encourage others.

z.   He must have Godly character.

aa. He must be a gracious man.

ab. He must be humble.

ac. He must have his priorities in order.

ad. He must be able to make decisions based on sound judgment.

ae. He must be sensitive to people, but not over-sensitive, touchy.

af. He must be impartial in his dealings with others; unprejudiced.

ag. He must have pure motivation.

ah. He must not be a hypocrite, a stage-actor, a man of many masks (Matthew 23).

ai. He must be a faithful man; his word is as good as himself. (Luke 16:10-12).

2. **Choosing Leadership**

There are certain things to watch for in the choosing of potential leadership to be developed into a team, some of which we list here.

a.   Watch for the ambitious spirit, political manouvers. Promotion comes from the Lord (Psalms 75).

b.   Leadership position must not be "bought".

c.   Watch for faithfulness in little things. Well done, thou good and faithful servant. One can be good (i.e., pianist) but not faithful (Proverbs 25:19; I Corinthians 4:1, 2; Luke 19:17; Matthew 25:14-36).

d.   Watch for men of character qualities (I Timothy 3; Titus 1).

e.   Watch for self-will. Test the will to watch responses or reactions (Titus 1:7; II Peter 2:10; Isaiah 14:12-14; Daniel 11:36).

f.   Watch for a teachable spirit (Psalms 27:11; 86:11). Need meek spirit.

g.   Watch that one is flexible, available, adjustable, dispensable; can receive discipline, rebuke (James 4:7; Hebrews 13:17; Ecclesiastes 10:4).

h.   Watch that he has love for the sheep more than love for his ministry (I Peter 4:7; Romans 12:10).

i.   Watch for the servant spirit; love slave (Mark 10:43-45).

j.   Watch that he relates to people and people to him. Do people desire to follow him? Does he relate or turn people away?
Is he acceptable to his brethren (Deuteronomy 33:24).

k.   Watch for zeal and diligence. Is he slothful? Zeal without knowledge? (II Peter 1:5; Romans 10:1-2).

l.   Place in period of probation (I Thessalonians 5:21; I Timothy 3). Prove in small areas first where they cannot hurt themselves or people. It takes time to prove.

m.   Do not allow charisma to blind to character. Character alone can handle charisma.

n.   Watch that he is an ethical person; of good behaviour, good conduct.

o.   Watch that he is a good communicator.

p.   Watch for a co-operative spirit and good attitudes (I Peter 2:17; Romans 12:17). Develop the ''lamb'' spirit before the ''lion'' boldness.

q.   Make evaluation checks periodically. Deal with positives and adjust the negatives.

r.   Watch for tests of loyalty; to senior minister, leadership, family, the Church and vision of the Church.

s.   Watch for a submissive spirit (I Peter 5:1-5), however, not overdependent.

t.   Watch for a spirit of humility. Beware of pride or arrogance.

u.   Watch for his spiritual life; prayer, word, worship, good relationship with the Lord.

v.   Watch for pure and strong motivation. Or does he have to be always motivated?

w.   Watch for self-centredness.

x.   Watch for discouragement, despondency, moodiness, murmurings or rejoicing spirit.

3.   **Successful Functioning of the Team**

The following are some principles and practical guidelines for the proper functioning of team ministry.

a.   There can only be one head of a team, as seen in the role of ''first among equals''. The principle of leadership must be recognized in Team Ministry. Though no one is more important than another, for the sake of order and efficiency there must be someone who takes the leadership and has the final responsibility. Failing to recognize this is to head for disaster.

b.   The Team must be brought together by the Lord (Mark 16:20). If the Lord is not in it, then the team will fail. Each member must seek the Lord that this is His will that they work together. cf. The Twelve and Seventy sent out by Jesus two by two (Luke 9-10).

The Law forbids the ox and the ass plowing together (Deuteronomy 22:10).

c.   The Team must be men whose hearts God has touched (I Samuel 10:26). Internal joining of the heart to the leader. If only external, it will not last. Must have one heart to keep rank together (I Chronicles 12).

d.   The Team must have the same spirit upon them as their leader (Numbers 11:14-17).

e.   The Team must have and maintain loyalty to each other.

f.   The Team must keep the lines of communication open at all times. Avoid impartial information, or inadequate information.

g.   The Team must have clear job description. Write out and define areas of responsibility. This is their ''charge''.

h.   The Team must be accountable for areas of responsibility.

i.   The Team must have individual and corporate devotional life. Ministry to the Lord determines ministry to the people. The team that prays together stays together.

1)   Pray together — spiritual times.

2)   Share together — friendship, fellowship.

3)   Being with each other (Mark 3:14).

4)   Discussion and dialogue together. Retreats, etc., maintain team spirit.

5)   Business and staff meetings together.

By doing this the team will come to speak the same thing, be joined together in the same mind and the same judgment (I Corinthians 1:10).

j.   The Team must recognize that safety is only in the team. There is strength, security, checks and balances in the team. No one person has it all. Each have strengths and weaknesses, but together there is the many-sided wisdom of the Lord. Use each others strengths to balance weaknesses.

k.   The Team must know the principle of submission (Ephesians 5:21). Submission will be tested from time to time.

l.   The Team must know the strength of commitment. Each member should be committed to the other and to the vision of the team.

m.   The Team must surrender personal rights and do all to support the vision the Lord has given the team.

n.   The Team must endeavour to maintain the unity of the Spirit at all costs. Unity is a ''must'' in love and in truth. Beware of anything that would bring division, schism or splits into the team.

We list some of the things that destroy team-work:

1) A competitive or comparative spirit (Matthew 18:1-4).

2) A dictatorial spirit, or lordship (I Peter 5:1-5; Matthew 23:11).

3) A proud, self-exalting spirit (Luke 22:24) that brings strife. Pride brings contention (Proverbs 13:10).

4) Party spirit (I Corinthians 1:10).

5) A Diotrephes spirit loving the pre-eminence (III John 9, 10). The fruit of such is evil deeds, malicious spirit, rejection of others, forbidding fellowship and excommunicating others.

6) Lack of communication.

7) Lack of transparency, dishonesty with each other cf. (Ephesians 5:8-14.) Light.

8) Lack of Divine love.

9) Lack of tolerance. cf. The Twelve apostles.

10) Lack of forgiving spirit (Ephesians 4:32; Matthew 18:21, 22).

11) Lack of spiritual maturity; carnality manifested (I Corinthians 3:1-4).

12) Lack of true humility (Matthew 18:1-4; Mark 9:33-37).

13) Lack of wisdom, doing a thing the right way, time, place, words.

14) Lack of submissive, servant spirit (I Peter 5:3; Mark 10:42-45; I Kings 12:7-11).

15) Lack of confidence in each other (Philippians 4:13).

16) Lack of consecration or wrong priorities (Matthew 6:33).

17) Lack of organization in the team; misdirected efforts.

18) Lack of spiritual concern for others (Matthew 23).

19) Lack of knowledge (Hosea 4:6; Proverbs 3).

20) Lack of mutual respect for each other (Ephesians 5:29, 30).

21) Lack of co-operative effort.

22) Lack of appreciation for one another; taking one another for granted.

23) Lack of maintaining vision (Proverbs 29:18).

24) Lack of involvement in the work (Haggai 1:4).

25) Lack of pure motives. Beware of Judas or Simony spirit (I Timothy 6).

26) Lack of a teachable spirit; leaning to own understanding.

E. **Purpose and Blessings of Team Ministry**

The blessing is to be found in the cluster of grapes, not in one grape alone (Isaiah 65:8).

Rev. Ken Malmin in Leadership notes gives the following points on team ministry.

1. A Team Ministry provides a living demonstration of Body ministry (I Corinthians 12).

2. Team Ministry makes it better in speaking ''present truth'' for there is more than one voice speaking the same thing (Deuteronomy 17:6; Matthew 18:16; II Corinthians 13:1).

3. Team Ministry makes it easier to find the mind of the Lord and His will in things (Matthew 18:19, 20; Daniel 2-4. Daniel and his friends).

4. Team Ministry is more effective and produces greater results (Ecclesiastes 4:9-12).

5. Team Ministry provides for greater safety and checks and balances (Proverbs 11:14).

6. Team Ministry helps to guard against the immoral or other snares set by the enemy which have ensnared so many lone ministries.

7. Team Ministry provides strength and encouragement for the ministries themselves (Exodus 17:12). Hands may be upheld giving inspiration and spiritual strength in the fellowship of team-work.

8. Team Ministry provides an opportunity for the development of disciples in the Lord and releasing their ministries. i.e., Timothy, Titus, Joshua, Elisha, all were trained under other ministries.

When brethren dwell together in UNITY, then the Lord commands the blessing, even life for evermore. This unity must be demonstrated in the leadership of the local Church in order to be manifested in the congregation (Psalms 133).

Conclusion:

In concluding this chapter we may illustrate the RELATIONSHIP that should exist between the leader and the team.

Various pictures could be used to show this, God has given numerous types of Christ and the Church, and the same principle follows through to the leadership and the congregation.

★   There is one head, but many members in the Body of Christ. Christ is the Head. All believers are equal as members, but all have their particular place and function.

★   There is one hub in a wheel but many spokes. All spokes are equal, all are related to each other by the rim and the hub, yet each have their proper location.

★   There was one true Israel of God, yet 12 tribes. All tribes were equal before God, yet all have their Divinely appointed place in the camp of God.

★   There was but one Moses, yet many Judges and Elders counselled together with him on behalf of the thousands of the nation of Israel under the Jethro principle.

★   There was one Tabernacle of the Lord, yet many parts, and various furnishings, yet all together were related to the Ark of God and His glory.

★   There was one High Priest, namely, Aaron, yet many priests in the Levitical tribe, and these constituted the priesthood to the nation of Israel.

★   There was only one Temple of the Lord, yet many stones and other materials. All stones were equal, yet all had their proper placement in the house of the Lord.

★   There is one Pyramid, yet many stones that make up a Pyramid. The Pyramid has but one Capstone, and one Cornerstone. All other stones relate to each other in their placement.

★ There is one King over the Kingdom of God but numerous citizens having equal rights under the laws of the Kingdom, yet there is Divine order.

★ There is one Throne of God and the Lamb, but myriads of angels and saints who gather in a circle around the Throne in their midst. All have their place and their relationship to each other and to that throne.

★ There is one Chief Shepherd but numerous under-shepherds and myriads of sheep in the one fold, the flock of God.

There is no conflict as to which of these illustrations is used for all point to the same truth, Christ and the Church, or the Leader and the Team.

Christ is the Head of the many-membered Body.

Christ is the Hub of the many-spoked Wheel.

Christ is the King of the tribes of spiritual Israel.

Christ is the great High Priest in the Melchisedekian Order of King-Priests.

Christ is the Ark of God in the midst of His Tabernacle, His Temple — The Church.

Christ is the Capstone and the Cornerstone, the Beginning and the End, the First and the Last, in the Pyramid of many stones.

Christ is the Lamb of God in the throne of God, and all angels and saints worship around that throne.

Christ is the Chief Shepherd in the flock of God, over the one fold.

In the earthly and practical expression of Team Ministry, the principle of the above can also be applied. The leader of the team and the team relate to each other as Christ relates to His people. Whether the structure of the Church or the Team be as a Body, a Wheel, a Nation, a Temple, a Pyramid, a Kingdom, a Flock or other, *it is the spirit and attitude that makes any of these structures good or evil, not necessarily the structure itself.*

All in the team are equal as persons, but each have the measure of the gift of Christ. This measure determines their function and place in the team. All in the team relate to each other and the team leader who also relates to the team members. This is the truth illustrated in each of these pictures here.

It is possible to have structure without life, and life without structure. God's ideal is to have UNITY in the structure, and LIFE therein. It is here the Lord commands the blessing, even life for ever more.

Any of the above types could be used here but we use the following Pyramidal diagrams to illustrate the principle that has been noted here.

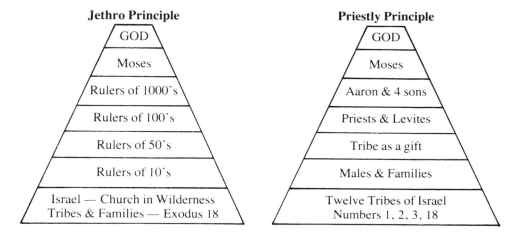

Jethro Principle

GOD
Moses
Rulers of 1000's
Rulers of 100's
Rulers of 50's
Rulers of 10's
Israel — Church in Wilderness
Tribes & Families — Exodus 18

Priestly Principle

GOD
Moses
Aaron & 4 sons
Priests & Levites
Tribe as a gift
Males & Families
Twelve Tribes of Israel
Numbers 1, 2, 3, 18

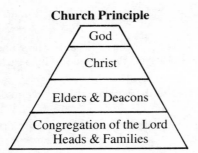

Church Principle

God

Christ

Elders & Deacons

Congregation of the Lord
Heads & Families

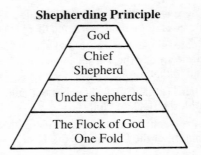

Shepherding Principle

God

Chief
Shepherd

Under shepherds

The Flock of God
One Fold

CHAPTER 28

THE MINISTRY OF WOMEN

Introductory:

The subject of this chapter is one of great controversy. It has been so throughout Church history and undoubtedly will continue until Christ comes.

Some Churches allow total equality of the woman with the man when it comes to ministry. Others permit no ministry at all by women. Some endeavour to take a middle of the road approach, endeavouring to avoid extremes.

Most times, the subject is dealt with in such a negative way, in traditional bigotry, instead of searching the Scriptures fully and dealing with the positive things pertaining to the place of women in the Church. Many Churches have far more women believers than men. Salvation is for both men and women.

In these days of "Equal Rights", and "Women's Liberation Movements" and various militant Feminist Movements and groups arising, the Church needs to re-evaluate this subject and take a deeper look into Scripture on this matter. This is a generation when there is such reversal of roles as pertaining to men and women. If ever women should find their place and find fulfilment, surely it should be in the redemptive and covenant community, the Church.

Oftentimes men react to dominant mothers or passive fathers. World Wars bring women into working positions and men's jobs, emptying the home. Women become independent of the man's salary, doing their own job. Thus women are no longer satisfied with being a mother and wife, a homemaker, with a family to raise for God.

The "liberation" humanistic philosophy brings dissatisfaction to the woman and the woman tries to be something she was not created to be. She tries to be a man, and failing to be such becomes frustrated that she does not even fulfil her womanhood. The prophecy of Isaiah is applicable today in the rise of ungodly women's movements when he says "Children are their oppressors and *women* rule over them" (Isaiah 3:12). Such was an inditement on the men who failed to take their leadership under God. Many cultures degrade womanhood. The woman is the slave of the man. This is seen in nations like India, Africa, Muslim countries, etc. Only where the Judeo-Christian Ethic has touched has there been any standard set for the protection of womanhood.

The major Principle of Interpreting Scripture is "*The Context Principle*". Therefore one must take the total Biblical revelation concerning women and not base the rejection of women's ministry upon one or two verses of Paul's writings, which have been misinterpreted to suppress woman's role.

Each local Church should come to some conviction based on the Word of God and act accordingly.

The final court of appeal for all matters of faith and practice is the Word of God and not the standards of a society or lack of them.

This chapter endeavours to present a balanced view on this vital subject. At the conclusion of this chapter the "problem Scriptures" will be dealt with.

A. **Order in Creation**

Genesis 1:26-28; 2; I Corinthians 11:8. In these passages we have the account of the creation of man and woman. There are some important things to notice as to Divine order as established in creation of man and woman before the entrance of sin.

When God created the man and woman, His Divine order was first the MAN, then the WOMAN (I Timothy 2:13).

This was before the Fall or entrance of sin. This was Divine order.

The man and the woman were created *equal* as persons, to rule and reign together over all creation as king and queen. God blessed *them* and gave *them* dominion. There was joint-relationship. He called ''their name Adam'' (Genesis 1:26-28; 5:1-2).

This order of the man and the woman did not mean superiority of the man. It did not mean inferiority of the woman. It did not mean inequality as persons. It simply was the Divine order in the family as God intended the family to be. It was an order demonstrated in the Divine persons in the Godhead as Father, Son and Holy Spirit, That is:

1. Equality as persons
2. Plurality of persons,
3. Unity of persons,
4. Priority of persons,
5. Order,
6. Submission,
7. Harmony,
8. Perfect love.

Adam was first formed, then Eve. Priority in creation sets the order of man first, not the woman. The man was created first by God. Eve was not created to direct or control Adam. In this order in creation, the woman did not have the authority over the man. The man was her covering, authority, headship and protection. They were heirs together of the grace of life. Order in this original home was thus established by God.

The original woman was created to be a ''help meet'' (Genesis 2:18) for the first man. It means ''a helper suitable'' (NAS); ''suitable, adapted, completing'' (Amp. OT); ''counterpart'' (Berry in Interlinear OT); or ''a completing partner''.

It was not a term describing the woman as a subordinate. They were to rule together as mutual rulers over creation.

Thus they were partakers of the one name ''Adam'' (Genesis 3:20; 5:1-2).

The woman was complementary, yet distinctive. It is worthy to note that the first woman, the original female was called:

a. ADAM or MAN. The ''MAN'' in the image of God was (Hebrew) ''*Ish*'' and ''*Ishshah*'' (Genesis 1:27; 2:23; 5:2). Thus we have the masculine part of the man, and the feminine part of the man made in God's image.

b. WOMAN (Genesis 2:23). Literally meaning ''man-ess''. It is more a generic term than a name. It is associated with her relationship to Adam which she was created to fill. That is, to be his counterpart, his wife.

   Woman is the womb-man, or man with the womb (Genesis 2:7, 8, 18-25). Therefore we have MAN and WOMB-MAN (Wo-Man).

c. EVE (Genesis 3:20). Eve means ''Life, life-giver, mother of all living, mother of the living one.'' It was a prophetic name. Adam gave his wife this name after the Fall. Previously they together were ''Adam'', but now it is ''Adam and Eve''.

   The woman was created to be the help-meet of man. That is, she was to be his aid, help, to surround, protect and succour the man. Each were to complete the other. The woman was created to be the mother of his children (Psalms 128:3).

   She was to be virtuous, prudent and the builder of the family household (Proverbs 12:4; 14:1; 19:14; 31:10-31). When Adam found his wife he found a good thing (Proverbs 18:22).

   The woman is not without the man, neither the man without the woman in the Lord. The woman is the glory of the man and man is the glory of God. The woman was made for the man (I Corinthians 11:1-16).

   The man and the woman were co-equal when both were without sin. Each had their distinctive function as persons. One was the man, to be the husband and the father. The other was the woman, to be the wife and the mother. Together they would raise the family for God. They would be fruitful and multiply and thus reproduce themselves (Genesis 1:26-31).

Thus before the Fall we have Divine order and the male headship. This is seen by the very fact that the order of creation was first the man, then the woman. It was not superiority of the man nor inferiority of the woman. It was Divine order in creation (I Timothy 2:11-13; I Corinthians 11:3, 7-9).

B. **Order in the Fall** (Genesis 3; I Timothy 2:14; II Corinthians 11:1-3).

In Genesis 3 we have the account of the Fall of the Man and Woman, and the entrance of sin into the human race.

Paul says that Adam was not deceived, but the woman being deceived was in the transgression. In the Fall, therefore, we see a reversal of the order of creation.

The woman, apparently away from her husband, from her headship and covering in Adam, was deceived into violating the commandment of the Lord. (Note — it is hard to think that Adam was just standing there listening to a serpent talk to his wife without him saying anything!!)

The Scripture account records that Eve herself said, "The serpent *beguiled me and I did eat."* *This is her own confession of how she was led into sin. No doubt God had given the original commandment to Adam, so the woman was responsible to her husband in this matter of obedience to the commandment of the Lord.*

Thus we see in the Fall, the woman took the leadership over the man, over her husband and headship. She ate first and gave to her husband. Creation's order was reversed. The woman, not the man, was the *first* to sin, the *first* and *original sinner*! Man sinned by taking from the woman. Adam confessed "The woman gave me and I did eat."

Thus the man who was the first in order now takes orders from the woman. The order of creation was reversed in the order of the Fall. The woman was *first* deceived. Adam and Eve both violated their positions and there was a reversal of roles.

Eve was deceived by "the doctrine of devils" (cf. I Timothy 4:1-2). She needed to have a covering on her head because of the angels (i.e., The fallen angel, Satan, who deceived her). She was away from headship. She was out from under covering. As noted, it is hard to perceive why the Devil came to the woman and not to Adam. It is hard to conceive that Adam stood silently by while the serpent carried on this deceptive conversation with his wife without him saying a word against it when he had been specifically given the word of commandment (Genesis 2:16, 17).

The woman was more easily led astray than the man. The woman thus usurped authority over the man. Man subordinated himself to this out of love, obeyed her and ate of the forbidden fruit. Sin corrupted the loving headship of the man and the submission of the woman. Both became guilty rebels before God (Romans 5:12-21).

C. **Order in Divine Judgment** (Genesis 3)

We note the order of Divine judgment after the Fall and the entrance of sin. This order pertains to God's redemptive plan. These things have a definite bearing on God's order as it pertains to man and woman, the husband and the wife. The whole purpose in redemption from sin is to bring man and woman back to God's order in creation before sin.

1. **Judgment on the Serpent** (Genesis 3:14, 15; Isaiah 65:25).

   a. The serpent cursed with an irrevocable curse.

   b. The seed of the woman would crush the serpent's head in due time, and it would be a MAN-CHILD that would do this, born of a virgin woman.

2. **Judgment on the Woman** (Genesis 3:16; I Corinthians 11:2; Ephesians 5:22).

    a.   Multiplied sorrow on the woman.

    b.   Multiplied conception. Sorrow in birth and motherhood (I Timothy 2:15).

    c.   Headship of the man over the woman. She would be subject to her husband and know the rule of man over her. ''Thy desire shall be subject to thy husband, and he shall rule over thee.''

    It seems evident that Eve had disobeyed the command of the Lord through Adam's lips, for he had been given that word (I Timothy 2:12-14). She usurped authority over her husband.

    Some expositors suggest ''You shall desire to have your husband's place of authority. You shall want his place of leadership over you, but it shall not be. He shall be your authority. The woman would desire to take his rule away from over her, to assert herself.''

    Before they ruled co-jointly together. Now the man would rule over her.

    It is evident that there was more judgment on the woman because of her initiative in the Fall. It is evident also that there was a subjection of the woman to the man. Instead of *joint-rulership,* rulership was left to the man while *subjection* is placed on the woman (Genesis 3:16. Amp. OT). ''Your desire and craving shall be for your husband, and he shall rule over you.'' Strong's concordance says: ''*To rule*'', i.e., have dominion, govern, reign, have power (SC 4910).

    Before sin, both ruled together. Since sin came by the woman (though charged to the man. Romans 5:12-21), the woman is ruled over by the man.

    So the woman would seek to rule her husband and not be subject to him. This thought is confirmed in Ephesians 5 where Paul tells wives to be subject to their own husbands in the Lord.

3. **Judgment on the Man** (Genesis 3:17-19; 2:17).

    a.   To eat of a cursed earth in sorrow all the days of his life.

    b.   Work to be sweat and toil, hard labour.

    c.   Death would return them to the dust of the earth from whence he was taken (Ecclesiastes 2:23; 3:20; Job 21:26).

    d.   Death would pass upon all of Adam's race for sin entered his seed (Romans 5:12; I Corinthians 15:22).

    Thus order in Divine Judgment is first on the Serpent Satan, then on the Woman, then the Man and finally the Earth.

D. **Order in Redemption**

In the midst of these judgments God promised that redemption would come through ''the seed of the woman'' (Genesis 3:15).

Thus, even though sin and death entered by the woman, yet God would bring redemption by the seed of the woman.

However, this seed would be A MAN born of A WOMAN to redeem both the MAN and the WOMAN and restore man back to the image of God from whence he had fallen. In I Timothy 3:15, according to the best authorities, the woman (as also the man), will experience salvation by the bearing of the Christ-child (Matthew 1:18-21; Luke 3:30-33; Isaiah 7:14; 9:6-9; Galatians 4:4; I Timothy 2:15, Amp. NT).

God would use A WOMAN for the bringing forth of His only begotten SON, the Saviour of the world. He would not use the seed of A MAN, though the Saviour would be A MAN!

Thus we have the seed of the woman, then through the seed of Abraham, Isaac, Jacob, Judah, David and then the virgin Mary, of whom Christ, after the flesh, was born. Paul, softening the seeming severity of the reasons given in I Timothy 2:13, 14 brings in the first prophecy of redemption from Genesis 3:15. Blessing is secured through Christ's birth of a human mother, a woman. There is salvation for the woman though subject to man's authority.

There is a Satanic hatred and enmity against women manifest throughout human history. Undoubtedly this is because Eve exposed the fact that the serpent, Satan, was a deceiver, and also because of the promise of the Lord that "the seed of the woman" would in due time crush the serpent's head (Genesis 3:15).

Thus in I Timothy 2:13 was the Order in Creation; Man first, then the Woman (Genesis 1-2); and in verse 14, is the Order of the Fall; Woman first, then the Man (Genesis 3:1-6); and in verse 15 we see Order in Redemption; Woman brings forth the Man Christ (Genesis 3:15).

Jesus Christ will bring us back to God's original order which will be Man (Christ) first, then the Woman (The Church), which is NEW CREATION ORDER! (Ephesians 5:23-33). Even though Christ has made redemption possible by the word of Calvary, and both man and woman will be ultimately restored to that from which they fell, yet there will still be Divine order.

Though there is equality as persons, yet, the man is first, then the woman. Even in the spiritual plane, Christ the Man is first, then the Woman, the Church is next in place and in order. This will be so throughout eternity. Christ is the HEAD of the Church, which is His Body. This is Divine order.

Redemption brings back *order in the home* between husband and wife.
Redemption brings *order in the Church* between man and woman.
Both the natural and spiritual relationships between husband and wife and Christ and His Church are woven together in Ephesians 5:23-33. Paul blends them into each other by Divine revelation.

E. **Order in the Christian Home** (Ephesians 5:23-33; I Corinthians 7; 11; I Timothy 2:13-15).

Redemption's work is to bring back the man and the woman into Divine order. The Christian home should be a place of order. Husband and wife relationships should exemplify and typify the relationship of Christ and His Bride, the Church.

Paul's writings are very clear as to the order in the home. The husband is the head, the covering, the protecting lover and the provider for the home. The wife is to be submitted to love and honour and reverence her husband's headship. She is to be under his love and covering. Though co-equal as persons, yet there is Divine order. Nothing alters this fact (I Corinthians 11:3, 7; Ephesians 5:22, 25, 28, 33).

The husband is to love his wife AS Christ loves the Church. The wife is to submit herself to her husband and reverence him. Read I Peter 3:18 also.

The basic calling of God on the woman is to become a daughter, a wife, a mother and a home-maker. The basic calling of God on the man is to be a son, then a husband, a father and a home-builder and provider.

Together the husband and wife make the team. These Scriptures should be studied in connection with these comments. Genesis 2:18-25; I Corinthians 11:1-10; Ephesians 5:23-33; I Peter 3:1-8; Proverbs 31:10-31; Titus 2:4, 5; I Timothy 5:14; Proverbs 12:4; 14:1.

Humanist Philosophy takes the woman out of her home, makes her feel she is a slave by being a home-maker, and thus seeks to destroy the first God-ordained basic unity, that is, the family.

Blessed is the man who has a prudent wife, who can guide the house, love her husband, love her children and be the glory of her husband (Proverbs 19:14; 18:22).

In the home we have the natural house. Here the wife is subject to the husband as the husband is subject to Christ. Here the woman exercises authority because she is under authority. She does not usurp authority. The man is the covering, the protection, the head of the house because he himself is under the covering, protection and headship of Christ. He exercises authority because he himself is under authority.

The Christian home should demonstrate Divine order. For, how can a man or a woman exercise ministry in the house of the Lord, the Church, if their own house is out of Divine order? For, beyond the natural house and home order, God may place a spiritual calling on either the man or the woman relative to the Church, the house of God. But as it is in the natural, so it is in the spiritual. There must be Divine order of the man and the woman.

Many good textbooks are available dealing with relationships of the husband and wife in the home.

F. Order in the Church — The Old Testament

We come now to the major purpose of this chapter and that is concerning God's order in the New Covenant community of believers — the Church. Whether we speak of the Old Testament Church in the Wilderness (Acts 7:38), or the New Testament Church, there must be Divine order.

In this section we consider the order of men and women under the Old Testament times. Then, we consider subsequently Divine order for men and women under New Covenant times. The Apostle Paul deals with such in the New Testament Epistles.

The point to be remembered is that men and women are *redemptively equal but functionally different,* whether in Old or New Covenant times.

In redemption, Christ is THE MAN, representing rulership, headship, covering and loving care and protection. Christ represents that which is masculine, and objective truth.

The Church is THE WOMAN, representing submission, that which is feminine and subjective truth. The figure of the Church as "the woman" is used of both men and women who are "in Christ" (Ephesians 5:23-33; Revelation 7:1-4; 14:1-4; 12:1).

In the natural house, as the wife is subject to her husband, so in the spiritual house, the Church is subject to Christ. Paul speaks of both the natural and the spiritual house in I Timothy 2:9-15 and I Timothy 3:1-16.

1. Ministry of Women in the Old Testament

We consider the ministry of women in the Old Covenant times as to Godliness and any calling of God they fulfilled under Divine order and headship.

There are many women mentioned in the Scriptures, both Godly and Ungodly, even as it is written of men.

Godly women are noted such as Eve, Rahab, Naomi, Miriam, Esther, Sarah, Rebekah and so forth. These were women of faith and of Godly character qualities.

Ungodly woman also are seen in people like Jezebel, Michael, Lot's wife, Vashti and women harlots who destroyed the lives of men as well as their own.

(Herbert Lockyer deals with these in his excellent book "*All the Women of the Bible*).

Godly women fulfilled the virtuous woman of Proverbs 31:21-31 while wicked women are likened to the evil woman of Proverbs 4. However, we especially look at the list of women who were gifted of the Lord in spiritual giftings and ministry.

a. Women Prophetesses

There were a number of women whom God called to be His mouthpiece and prophetesses with the prophetic word and the word of the Lord in their mouth.

★ **Miriam** was a prophetess (Hebrew "Nebiah", a female preacher; SC 5031, feminine of SC 5030; a prophetess, or generally, inspired woman; by implication, a poetess; by association, a prophet's wife). She prophesied before the hosts of Israel (Exodus 15:20). She sang the song of the Lord and led the women with timbrels and dancing before all Israel (Psalms 68:25; Numbers 12:1-10). God classes Miriam with Moses and Aaron and declared through the prophet Micah (Micah 6:4), ''For I brought you up out of the land of Egypt, and redeemed you out of the house of bondage; and I sent before you Moses, Aaron and Miriam.''

★ **Deborah** was a Judge, a Prophetess and a Mother in Israel for a period of 40 years (Judges 4:4; 5:7-15). She had the authority of a prophetess, a revealer of God's will to Israel, and was acknowledged and submitted to as in the cases of the male Judges who succeeded her. She was also the military head of 10,000 men because Barak refused to go to battle without her. She was a married woman, the wife of Lapidoth. Her heart was towards the Governors of Israel that offered themselves willingly among the people. A curse came on some of the inhabitants because they failed to come to the help of the Lord under her leadership. Blessing came also on another woman, Jael, who was used to smite the head of Sisera, the enemy of the people of God. Deborah also sang the song of the Lord, the second recorded song in Scripture. No other of the Judges was called a Prophet until Samuel came, who was the last of the Judges and first of the Prophets.

★ **Huldah** was a prophetess. In II Kings 22:12-20 and II Chronicles 34:22 we have the account of the king sending the high priest, the scribe and others to Huldah, the prophetess, and wife of Shallum, who dwelt at Jerusalem, at the college, to enquire at her mouth the will of God with reference to the book of the law found in the temple of God. Here leading men recognized the word of the Lord in the mouth of this women and accepted her ''Thus saith the Lord.''

★ **Isaiah's wife** was a prophetess also, sharing in her husband's ministry somehow (Isaiah 8:1-3).

★ **Noadiah** was a false prophetess in the time of Nehemiah (Nehemiah 6:14). There were true prophets at that time also, these being Zechariah and Haggai.

★ **False prophetesses and prophets** are also dealt with in Ezekiel chapter 13.

★ **Anna** was a prophetess. She was a widow of 84 years of age, serving God in the temple.

And she (Anna) was a widow of about 84 years, which departed not from the temple but served God with fastings and prayers night and day. She coming in at that instant, gave thanks likewise unto the Lord, and spake of Him to all that looked for redemption in Israel (Luke 2:37, 38).

Simeon had just prophesied before hand of the Christ-child. Now Anna, a prophetess follows likewise. It was during the same service. It was public, before men and women. The Jews accepted her as a prophetess. She was the first woman to publicly proclaim Jesus at His circumcision and naming in the temple.

b. Women were also used in the making of the Tabernacle of the Lord (Exodus 38:8; I Samuel 2:22). The word ''assembled'' means ''to be in the host or to serve it.''

c. The Law of the Nazarites was for women as well as men. Nazarites were consecrated and separated to the Lord for sacred purposes (Numbers 6:1-27).

d. A wise woman saved a city from destruction (II Samuel 20:16-22).

e. A little girl witnessed to Captain Naaman about the true God of Israel who could heal leprosy (II Kings 5).

f. The woman Abigail gave David the king a word of wisdom. David was humble enough to receive it and save himself from bloodshed that he would regret in the time he came to his throne (I Samuel 25).

g. The five daughters of Zelophehad came before Moses, Eliezer the high priest, and the princes of the congregation and received their inheritances by the law of the Lord. Daughters were then entitled to receive inheritances if there were no male inheritors (Numbers 27:1-7; Joshua 15:6-19; 17:3, 4; Job 42:14).

h. Esther the Queen saved her own nation from death under the counsel of Mordecai and her request to her husband (Esther 1-11).

i. Ruth the Moabitess came into the faith of Israel and her name is in the genealogy of the Messiah (Ruth 1-4; Matthew 1).

j. Athaliah was a wicked queen who usurped the authority of the throne by slaying the royal seed (II Kings 8:26; II Chronicles 22:1-12).

k. Rahab, the harlot, was saved by faith. She also has her name in Messiah's seed-line (Joshua 2; Hebrews 11:31; Matthew 1).

l. Women had faith for the resurrection of their children (Hebrews 11:35; II Kings 4:18-37).

m. Women were involved in the restoration of the walls of Jerusalem after the Babylonian Captivity (Nehemiah 3:12).

n. Heman, the singer, had daughters, as well as sons, who sang the songs of the Lord (I Chronicles 25:5, 6).

o. In the restoration from Babylon there were "singing men and singing women" also. The temple chambers were set aside for singers (Nehemiah 7:67; Ezekiel 40:44).

p. God used widows to minister hospitality to the prophets, Elijah and Elisha (I Kings 17; II Kings 4).

    Widows were honoured of God (Exodus 22:22; Deuteronomy 14:28; 16:11; 24:17; Jeremiah 49:11).

q. Hannah was a godly woman, married to Elkanah. She was a woman of much prayer, and when Samuel was born, she gave forth a prophetic song of the Lord and was the first person to speak of "The Anointed", or "The Messiah" under Old Covenant times (I Samuel 1-2).

r. God speaks of His nation Israel as a "Woman", thus including both men and women under this figure (Jeremiah 3:1-20).

Thus, we have a variety of things in which women were involved under Old Testament times besides their responsibilities as wives and mothers in the home.

The highest calling that God ever gave to women in the Old Testament was on those He placed the prophetic mantle. To be His mouthpiece and His voice to the people of God was indeed the highest calling. Prophets and Prophetesses were the channels of bringing the word of the Lord to His people.

2. **Old Testament Prophetics**

While there were many more male prophets that female prophetesses, the Old Testament prophets foretold of a coming day when the Spirit would be poured out on ALL flesh and the prophetic Spirit would be available for all men and women.

a. In the last days the Lord would pour out His Spirit on all flesh and "the sons and daughters, and servants and handmaidens" would prophesy. There is no mistake about the fulfilment of this prophecy, for, Peter, the Apostle on the Day of Pentecost quotes from Joel 2 and told the astounded Jews that this was the fulfilment of this utterance. Men and women spake in tongues the wonderful works of God.

b. In Psalms 68:11 we also have a prophetic word. It is a prophetic Psalm which the Apostle Paul takes up in Ephesians 4 and speaks of the gifts of the ascended Christ which He gave unto men.

"The Lord gave the word, and great was the company of those that published it" (Psalms 68:11). The Hebrew thought is "Great was the company of women publishers, of women evangelists."

Matthew Henry says on this verse: "God gave them His word (the word of the Lord came unto them), and then great was the company of the preachers — prophets and *prophetesses,* for the word is feminine. When God has messages to send He will not lack messengers. Or perhaps it may allude to the women's joining in triumph when the victory was obtained, as was usual (Exodus 15:20; I Samuel 18:7)."

"The Lord gives the word of power; the women who bear and publish the news are a great host" (Psalms 68:11, Amplified Old Testament).

The good news or good tidings would be the proclaiming of the Gospel of Christ (Isaiah 52:7; 40:9).

Certain expositors say that the literal rendering of Isaiah 40:9 is "O woman, that bearest good tidings . . ." This may refer to the women who preached the Gospel, or it may refer to the Church, as the Woman, the wife of Christ, bearing the good tidings to all nations. These things find fulfilment in the New Testament where women laboured in the Gospel along with Christ and the Apostles.

Some also suggest that "the great company of women" who published and sang the song of the Lord refers to the women under Miriam who sang the victory song when Israel crossed the Red Sea (Exodus 15). However, the women are involved in publishing the good tidings!

It should be noted that while women were in the shadows in other nations, Israel, as God's nation, had tremendous laws of protection for their women. This was in such contrast to heathen nations. This honour of women is continued in the Judeo-Christian ethic unto this day.

The laws of God in Israel were designed to protect the woman's weakness, safeguard her rights, and preserve her freedom. Vows could not be made by a woman without the protection of the father or the husband (Numbers 30). Note also (Deuteronomy 21:10-14; 22:13, 28; Numbers 5:11-31).

Under Divine law her liberties were greater, her tasks more varied and important, and her social standing more respectful and commanding than that of heathen women.

Godly women had great influence in the nation. Ungodly women seemed to lead the way in idolatry and immorality (Jeremiah 7:8; Ezekiel 8:14; Exodus 22:18).

However, it is when we come to the New Testament that we see the Lord Jesus and Christianity lifting the life standard of the woman to its highest plane in our fallen state.

Women were used by the Holy Spirit under Old Covenant times in a limited way. Under New Covenant times the Spirit is available for all, men and women. The New Covenant is no less than the Old Covenant. To say that God would use women under the Old Covenant and not under the New Covenant is to belittle the work of Calvary. Living under the dispensation of the Holy Spirit is vastly different to living under the dispensation of the Law.

As we note the women in the Gospels, the Acts and the Epistles, we will see how the Holy Spirit equipped women in a greater way and greater numbers. This was because of the prophetic word that the Spirit would be poured out on "all flesh" regardless of nation, social distinctions, or sex (Joel 2:28-32).

G. Christianity and Women

Under the New Covenant women find a position "in Christ" that is far beyond that under the

Old Covenant.

Christianity brings the greatest honour and respect to the woman above all other nations and cultures.

★   The Muslim world degrades the women. A Muslim can verbally divorce his wife. She is left to prostitution or starvation.

★   The Hindu religion degrades women also. They are taught to worship the male organs, a total perversion in this system of Satan.

★   In Africa the women are to bear children and be the slaves of men.

★   Even the Jews in the time of Christ put women down. This was contrary to the Divine laws. When Jesus came the Jews had great prejudices against women.

   John A. Anderson, M.D., in *"Woman's Warfare & Ministry"* (p.13), lists some of the Oral Laws from The Talmud concerning women. We quote but several of them.

   "A woman should not read in the Torah for the honour of the synagogue."

   "The testimony of 100 women is not equal to that of one man."

   "It is a shame for a woman to let her voice be heard among men."

The Talmud records that Rabbi Eliezer reproved a lady asking a question about the law in the synagogue. In the synagogue a woman was denied recognition. A woman could not be counted along with nine men to form a congregation. Ten men only would form a congregation.

A Jewish prayer "thanked God that he was not born a woman, a dog or a Gentile". It was the Babylonian Talmudic traditions that Christ and His Apostles had to overthrow, and especially the Jewish attitude to women, not to be found in the Old Testament Scriptures. Even the Apostles had to be delivered from these traditions. It is worthy to note that in the life of our Lord there is not a single instance of a women's voice being raised against Him.

★   In the Western world, influenced by the Judeo-Christian ethic, women have had the greatest honour, as a whole, in society. However, with the cultural explosion, and the rise of Humanist Philosophy, Feminist's Movements and Women's Liberation, the great blessings of the family, marriage and the home are being undermined. Male and female Humanists spread their philosophies that work like leaven in the educational systems, and all this under the guise of "liberty".

Only the laws of God revealed under the Judeo-Christian ethic can really protect the total family and the institution of marriage and the honour and dignity of man and woman.

We consider Women in the Gospels, Women in the Acts and Women in the Epistles, and see how the New Covenant brings Divine order in the redemptive community.

1.   **Women in the Gospels**

   The coming of Jesus Christ into the world brought a whole new revelation of the place of women in the redemptive community. As already seen, the Jews were bound by many of the Oral Laws in the Talmud in their attitude to women. Jesus cut right across these things. He exalted womanhood.

   ★   Gabriel, the archangel, came to two women, Elizabeth and Mary, and announced the miracle births of John and Jesus (Luke 1-2).

      Both of these women sang prophetic songs. The spirit of prophecy was upon them both at the glorious announcements of John the Baptist's birth, Messiah's forerunner and then of Messiah's birth of the virgin Mary.

   ★   Jesus was born of the virgin Mary in fulfilment of the prophetic word concerning the seed of the woman (Genesis 3:15). What exaltation of womanhood is seen here that the Son of God Himself was born of a virgin woman (Matthew 1).

   ★   Four women are named along with their husbands in the Genealogy of Messiah in

Matthew 1. This was a great honour especially seeing that several were Gentile women.

★ Jesus allowed women to touch Him (Mark 5:34). He cleansed them.

★ Jesus ate with harlots and sinners and forgave them their sins while the Pharisees would not even associate (Luke 7:36-50).

★ Jesus taught women the Word of God, as well as men. The Rabbis refused to teach women as they counted them incapable of grasping Divine truths. Mary and Martha heard His word (Luke 11:38-42).

★ Jesus touched women and healed them. The Jews would not for fear of defilement (Matthew 9:20-22).

★ Mary anointed Jesus with ointment for His burial (John 12:1-8)

★ Jesus commended the widow in the Court of the Women for the giving of her mite (Luke 21:1-4).

★ Jesus allowed women to minister to Him and the apostles of their substance (Luke 8:1-3).

★ Jesus ministered salvation to the woman of Samaria at the well. She witnessed to the men in the city opening the way for Christ (John 4). The disciples were surprised at His speaking to a woman who was a notorious sinner.

★ Jesus ministered to both men and women together. Though the temple courts separated men and women, and the Jews would only count a congregation of ten men, even if a hundred women were present, Jesus ministered to a mixed congregation.

★ Anna, the prophetess, spake of redemption to those in Jerusalem at the temple. The temple priests recognized her prophetic words over the Christ-child (Luke 2:36-38).

★ Luke's Gospel has special emphasis on the ministry of Christ to women. There are more references in this Gospel concerning women than the other Gospels.

★ Jesus honoured marriage. He confirmed that marriage was to be indissoluble in nature, that marriage of one wife and one husband was God's original pattern (Matthew 19:3-11). Jesus did not endorse polygamy even though it was permitted under the law of Moses. Jesus condemned divorce "for every cause" but one (Deuteronomy 24:1-3; Matthew 19:3-11).

Jesus condemned fornication and adultery, as did the Law, to protect the sanctity of marriage and the woman (John 8:1-10; Matthew 5:27-32).

★ Pilate's wife sought to have Jesus released after her Godgiven dream. The daughters of Jerusalem wept for Christ. Women were last at the cross and first at the tomb. If Pilate had heard his wife he may have been saved from the eternal injustice in crucifying the Christ of God (Matthew 27:19; Luke 23:27-29; John 19).

★ On the morning of the resurrection, the FIRST announcement of Christ's resurrection was given to two women. They were told to go and tell the brethren, and this by Christ Himself (Matthew 28:9, 10). The Apostles failed to believe them and counted their word as idle tales (Luke 24:10, 11, 24). Perhaps because it was a woman who sinned first in the Garden of Eden that Christ gave the resurrection word to two women at the Garden Tomb. A new era had dawned for both men and women now that Calvary's redemption was accomplished.

There is not one record of a woman ever speaking against Jesus in the Gospels. Christ came to emancipate women from the traditions and bondages of the Talmudic Law and bring them into the liberty of the Gospel of Christ.

Judaism was predominantly a man's religion. Jesus made the way open to God and brought access to both men and women. Every believer, regardless of sex, is now a priest unto God under the New Covenant. This is in contrast to the Old Covenant where only the Levitical tribe were priests. The Old Covenant only allowed men to be priests, and these being of the tribe of Levi, along with Aaron the High Priest. There were no women priestesses in the Old Testament. The New Covenant grants all believers, male or female, to be members of the priestly body, Christ Himself being the great High Priest. The veil has been rent. Men and women may enter within the veil (Matthew 27:50-52).

2. **Women in the Acts**

★ There were men and women in the Upper Room prayer meeting preceding Pentecost (Acts 1:13-15). These women had been touched by the Lord Jesus and waited for the outpouring of the Spirit along with the men.

This was a departure from Jewish custom of those days. The temple had the Court of the Women and another court for the men. The men and the women did not pray together. Even today men and women are separated at the Jerusalem wailing wall. But now, since Jesus came, a new day was dawning. Men and women prayed together, and together they waited for the Holy Spirit to be outpoured and make them witnesses of the risen Christ! (Joel 2:28-32 with Acts 2).

★ On the Day of Pentecost, the Holy Spirit sat on the men as well as the women. Women and men were waiting together for Pentecost. Both men and women were filled with the Holy Spirit, and together became living stones in the New Covenant temple. Both men and women spoke in tongues as the Spirit gave them utterance. Peter, filled with the Spirit, had no hesitation in saying that this was the fulfilment of Joel's prophecy concerning the last days outpouring of the Spirit on "all flesh". In the last days the Spirit would be poured on "sons and daughters, servants and handmaidens" — that is, both male and female believers (Acts 2:16-18 with Joel 2:28-32). It was a new day!

★ Dorcas, a woman of good works, experienced resurrection life under Peter's apostolic ministry (Acts 9:36-43). God saw fit to raise a woman from death whose ministry was making garments for the needy.

★ Lydia was a woman whose heart God opened. She was the first convert in Europe and she opened her house to the Gospel (Acts 16:14, 15).

★ Leading Greek women in Thessalonica heard and received the Gospel through the Apostle Paul (Acts 17:4).

★ Prominent women in Berea also believed the Gospel (Acts 17:12).

★ In Athens a woman named Damaris believed (Acts 17:34).

★ Priscilla and Aquilla were husband and wife team and together taught the word of the Lord as teachers (Acts 18:24-26).

★ Men and women were hailed to prison for being Christians (Acts 8:1-4).

★ Philip, the evangelist, had four daughters, virgins, which did prophesy (Acts 21:9). Eusebius, the ancient ecclesiastical historian, says that Philip's four daughters lived to a good old age, always abounding in the work of the Lord. "Mighty luminaries," he writes, "have fallen asleep in Asia. Philip, and two of his virgin daughters, sleep at Hierapolis; the other, and the beloved disciple, John, rest at Ephesus.

Thus the Book of Acts shows no conflict concerning women receiving the Gospel or functioning in the gifts of the Spirit as they were endowed.

3. **Women in the Epistles**

The Epistles also confirm the fact that women were involved in the Gospel in various ways.

★ Phebe was a servant of the Church at Cenchrea and Paul asked that the Church at Rome assist her in whatever business she had need of them (Romans 16:1, 2).

The word "servant" is the Greek word "Diakonas", translated "Deacon" three times, "Minister" twenty times, and "Servant" seven times.

That means, Phebe was a minister, a servant, a deaconess of the Church. Paul says that she had been a succourer of many as well as himself.

★ In Romans 16 Paul mentions about ten women's names who were fellow-workers in the Gospel in some way or another. Note verses 3, 7, 12. These are mentioned as ''helpers'', or co-labourers, companions in labour, work-fellows in Christ. Paul was not a male chauvenist as there are many references to women in his Epistles.

He claims that he and Barnabas have as much right as other Apostles to take with them a sister, or a wife to help them (I Corinthians 9:5).

★ Paul says that men and women may pray and prophesy in public meetings of the Church (I Corinthians 11:5; I Timothy 2:12).

★ Paul also says that ''in Christ there is neither male nor female'' (Galatians 3:28). This is the only doctrinal statement in the New Testament concerning male and female position as to spiritual and redemptive equality. Physically there is male and female. Paul, the same writer, speaks clearly in his Epistles of the roles of husband, wife and children in the home.

★ Paul also spoke of Euodias and Syntyche as fellow-workers in the Gospel (Philippians 4:2, 3).

★ Paul exhorts that older women teach younger women (Titus 2:4,5; I Timothy 5:2).

★ John the beloved Apostle wrote to the Elect Lady in his Epistle (II John).

★ Christ reproved the Church at Thyatira for allowing the ministry of Jezebel, a false teacher and prophetess in the Church, who taught idolatry and immorality (Revelation 2:18-29).

★ There was an accepted ministry of widows in hospitality in the Early Church as seen in I Timothy 5:1-16; James 1:27.

★ Timothy had a Godly grandmother and mother who taught him the Word of God from a child (II Timothy 1:5). Their names were Eunice and Lois.

★ In Hebrews 11 the writer mentions WOMEN of faith as well as MEN of faith. Sarah, Rahab, the widows of Zarepheth and the Shunamite who received their dead raised to life (Hebrews 11:35 with II Kings 4:18-27; Hebrews 11:1-40).

★ Elders and Deacons were not to be polygamists but the husband of one wife in order to hold office in the Church (I Timothy 3; Titus 1).

★ The woman was given promise of safety in childbirth as she continued in the faith in sobriety and holiness, Paul said (I Timothy 2:13-15; Galatians 3:13; Genesis 3:14-16).

★ Children were to honour their parents, to obey their father and mother (Exodus 20:12; Ephesians 6:1-3; Psalms 127:4, 5).

Note also Peter's words to husbands and wives in I Peter 3:1-8.

The New Testament Epistles, and especially Paul's writings, give women a place of honour and dignity. Paul, in no way, was a male chauvenist, as is attributed to him because of two ''problem Scriptures'' which will be dealt with in time.

The student should take every reference in Paul's writings concerning women and then interpret these ''problem Scriptures'' in the light of such, as well as the historical and cultural setting of his time.

There is plenty of scope in the New Testament Church for the ministry of a Godly woman without violating Divine order.

4. **Historical Evidences of the Early Church**

There are evidences that women were involved in teaching and preaching during the first several centuries of Church History, as they were gifted of the Lord and by the Holy Spirit.

a. ''Justin Martyr, who lived until about A.D.150, says, in his Dialogue with Trypho the Jew that 'both men and women were seen among them who had extraordinary gifts of the Spirit of God, according as the prophet Joel had foretold,' and Dodwell in His Dissertions of Irenaeus, says that 'the gift of the Spirit of prophecy was given to others besides the Apostles: and that not only in the First, and Second but in the Third Century — even to the time of Constantine — men had these gifts; yea, and women too' '' — Mrs Catherine Booth.

b.   ''Tertullian, one of the earliest Latin Fathers, notes that women appear in every early reference to ecclesiastical orders. Four titles, he writes, are applied to the women clergy, of all which occur in the New Testament, 'Widow', 'Deaconess', 'Presbyter', 'Virgin'. The two former, he adds, are Apostolic orders.

c.   Marcella preached Christianity publicly in Rome, and Jerome (born about 340 A.D., and the translator of the Latin Vulgate Bible), writes of her: ''all that I learn with great study . . . the blessed Marcella learnt also but with great facility.'' He also celebrates her immense influence for good in Rome.

d.   In the Catacombs are found representations of women clergy, and they are shown presiding at the Lord's Supper . . .

e.   Mabillion, a French writer on ecclesiastical biography and antiquities, records that the evangelization of Europe was due in great part to the Nuns of St. Benedict many of whom publicly preached the Gospel.

f.   Among the Montanists, who were the evangelicals of the Third Century, Priscilla and Maximilla, ladies of rank, served as evangelists over a wide extent of country. Women were elected by the Montanists as Deacons, Pastors, President-Presbyters or Bishops. Opinions vary as to when the recognized order of women clergy died out. All agree it lingered longer in the East than in the West . . . It seems as if the decay of women's ministry took place with the decay of Christianity, the rise of the Roman Apostacy, and the proud pretensions of an exclusive priesthood.

(Letters a-f quoted from THE INDIAN STANDARD, the early official organ of the Presbyterian Church in India from the subject of ''Women Preachers'')

g.   Eusebius of the 4th Century speaks of Potamania Ammias, a prophetess, in Philadelphia, and others, ''who were equally distinguished for their love and zeal in the cause of Christ.''

H.   The Ministry of Women Under New Covenant Times

Assuming that the New Covenant is greater than the Old Covenant days, we bring together the total Biblical revelation on the function of women as to ministry, and spiritual standing before God, through Christ.

1.   Women's Place and Ministry in Christ

a.   Women may be born again of the Holy Spirit and become new creatures in Christ, even as men (John 3:1-5).

b.   Women may receive the Holy Spirit baptism and anointing as well as men (Acts 2:1-11). This is in fulfilment of Old Testament prophecy of Joel (Joel 2:28-32 with Acts 2:14-21). God said He would pour out His Spirit on the sons and daughters, servants and handmaidens.

c.   Men and women may speak in tongues as the Spirit gives them utterance (Acts 2:1-4). Both men and women were baptized into the one body of Christ, which is the Church, at Pentecost (I Corinthians 12:13).

d.   Men and women are together priests in the New Covenant Church. It is no longer a Levitical priesthood available only for one tribe of a chosen nation, and for men only (I Peter 2:5-9; Revelation 1:5, 6; 5:9-10).

e.   Women may prophesy as well as men (Acts 2:17-21 with Joel 2: 28-32). This may include:

1)   Preaching and exhortation. Old Testament prophesying as also New Testament prophesying includes such.

2)   The Gift of Prophecy, as a gift of the Spirit (I Corinthians 12:1-8; 11:5; Acts 21:9).

3)   The Ministry of a Prophetess, as seen in:
(i)   Miriam (Exodus 15:20),
(ii) Deborah (Judges 4:4),
(iii) Huldah (II Kings 22:14; II Chronicles 34:22),
(iv) Isaiah's wife (Isaiah 8:3),
(v)   Anna (Luke 2:36-38).

There were true and false prophetesses as well as prophets in Bible times. Note Nehemiah 6:14; Ezekiel 13; Revelation 2:20.

Is there anything higher than to be a mouthpiece of the Lord in speaking the prophetic word? Both men and women under this dispensation may prophesy. The Spirit is available for all regardless of nation, social distinction, or sex.

4)   Prophecy includes edification, exhortation and comfort, according to Paul (I Corinthians 14:3).
Edify = "to instruct and improve; to profit morally or spiritually"
Exhort = "to incite by words or advice; to advise or warn earnestly"
Comfort = "to impart strength and hope to; to console".

f.   Women may have faith for the miraculous (Hebrews 11:35; II Timothy 1:5).

g.   Women may witness of Christ's resurrection, even to men (Matthew 28:8-10).

h.   Women may evangelize and bring the Gospel to men, even as the woman of Samaria did, bringing men to Christ (John 4). Eternity alone will evidence the thousands of souls brought to Christ under the ministry of women.
"Great was the company of women that published the good news" (Psalms 68:11; Isaiah 40:9).

i.   Women may have a ministry of prayer and intercession. This can include:

1)   Prayer with their husbands (I Peter 3:1-8),

2)   Prayer for the sick (Mark 16:15-20),

3)   Prayer in the public meeting in the Church (I Corinthians 11:5; I Timothy 2:8-10; Acts 16:13; I Samuel 1:27).

4)   Prayer with other women (Acts 16:13).

5)   Prayer of mourning (Jeremiah 9:17-21; Isaiah 32:9-15).

6)   Prayer with men of the Church (Acts 1:13-15).

j.   Women may teach. This may include:

1)   Teaching with their husbands, as Priscilla and Aquila (Acts 18:18, 24-28; Romans 16:3; II Timothy 4:19).

2)   Teaching younger women to be sober, love their husbands, love their children, discretion, chastity, being good home-makers and obedient to their husbands (Titus 2:4, 5).

3)   Teaching the children and youth the ways of the Lord (II Timothy 1:5. Eunice and Lois taught Timothy the Scriptures).

4)   Teaching under authority of the man, not usurping authority (I Timothy 2:9-15).

5)   Teaching Christian Education in the Church in various age-groups according to ability God gives.

k.   Women laboured with Paul and others in the Gospel of Christ (Philippians 4:3; Romans 16:3, 6, 12; Acts 18:26). This surely included more than cooking food and mending clothes!

l.   John wrote to the Elect Lady who seemed to have care for the children of the Lord (II John 1:1).

m.   Women may operate the gifts of the Spirit as He wills. This includes word of wisdom, word of knowledge, faith, healings, miracles, prophecy, discerning of spirits, tongues and the interpretation of tongues (I Corinthians 12:1-13).

n.   There was an evident ministry of widows in the Early Church who ministered hospitality, good works, cared for children, washed the feet of saints, relieved the afflicted (I Timothy 5:1-16; James 1:27).

o.   Women may be Deaconesses, Phoebe was a "servant", a "minister" or a "deaconess" of the Church at Cenchrea and Paul asked the saints at Rome to assist her in any business she had need of. She was a succourer of Paul as well as many others. She is often referred to as the beginning of the Order of Deaconesses (Romans 16:1, 2).

Mrs Catherine Booth quotes "Theodoret as saying 'The fame of Phebe was spoken of throughout the world. She was known not only to the Greeks and Romans, but also to the Barbarians,' which implies that she had travelled much, and propagated the Gospel in foreign countries."

p.   Women may lead in the song of the Lord with dancing (Exodus 15; Judges 4-5).

Note the "singing men and singing women" in the restoration from Babylon and in the Order of David's Tabernacle (I Chronicles 25:5, 6; Nehemiah 7:67).

Read the Songs of the Lord of Elizabeth, Mary and Hannah (Luke 1-2; I Samuel 1-2).

q.   Women may minister to women in counselling (Titus 2:4, 5).

r.   Women may play musical instruments before the Lord and His people (I Chronicles 15, 16; 25:5, 6).

s.   Women may attend to children, the young of the flock, in nursery work.

t.   Women may minister hospitality to the saints (Proverbs 31:20).

u.   Women may be "Mothers in Israel", as Deborah also was (Judges 5).

v.   Women, as well as men, are called to be witnesses for Christ (Acts 1:5-8).

w.   Women can visit hospitals, especially to sick women, far better than men can in certain cases.

x.   Women can help in water baptismal services and help other women far better than men can also.

y.   Women may also have the ministry of helps (Romans 12:6-8). There are many other areas, though not designated specifically in Scripture, which can come under the ministry of "helps".

1) Writing	— Books, Tracts, Bulletins, Curriculum for Bible Classes, Bible Stories, etc Such have blessed thousands.
2) Music	— Choir, Orchestra, Soloist, Worship Leader, Song of the Lord, Prophetic Songs, Group Singing, etc.
3) Office	— Secretary, Typist, Bookkeeper, Graphics, Phones, Receptionist, Filing, etc.
4) Weddings	— Arrangements for receptions, Floral arrangements, and

numerous other details for blessed weddings.

5) Publications	— Tape Ministry, Printing Department, Librarian, Tract Distributions, etc.
6) Children	— Nursery, Baby Showers, Dedication arrangements, Baby-sitting, Child care, Organizing Games, etc.
7) Youth	— Camping, Retreats, Spiritual and Recreational activities, etc.
8) Church Property	— Janitorial, Kitchen Staff, Flowers, Plants, Decorations, etc.
9) Hosting	— Hospitality for visiting Ministries, Church visitors, Refreshments, etc.
10) Visitation	— Visiting the sick and needy at home or in the hospital, showing mercy, etc.
11) Distribution	— Clothes to needy, sewing and mending clothes, ministry of giving, etc.

These things are indeed great "helps" and ministry in the Body of Christ. Each local Church has other areas of need that can be filled.

Undoubtedly there is within these things a great variety of functions that can involve many of the women in serving the Lord and the members of His body.

Multitudes of men and women were saved in Acts 5:14, and thus added to the Church. Multitudes were water baptized. Whereas only men were circumcised in Old Covenant times, water baptism (New Testament circumcision) is for men and women. All are new creatures in Christ.

In Christ there is neither male nor female (Galatians 3:28). This spiritual status and the natural must be kept in proper balance before the Lord.

If it pleases the Lord to anoint and equip women for any of the functions above, then Godly men and women will rejoice and accept the blessings of the Lord that flow through them.

2. **Women and Male Headship**

A study of the complete Scriptures on the matter of women's ministry clearly points to Divine order of the man and the woman, whether in the natural house, or the spiritual house of the Lord which is the Church.

It is important, therefore, to understand Biblical headship. It is here that the **key** to Divine order in the function of men and women lays. Women may function under male headship in Divine order and in this there is safety of the Lord. Headship therefore must be understood.

Headship does not mean superiority or dictatorship of the man or inferiority of the woman or her suppression under the guise of submission.

The order of Headship is demonstrated in the Godhead, in the relationship existing between the Father, Son and Holy Spirit.
God is the Head of Christ.
Christ is the Head of the man.

Man is the Head of the woman, or, the husband is the head of the wife and home (I Corinthians 11:1-3).

Man and woman are together under the Headship of Christ.
Christ is THE MAN, the husband and head of the Church. The Church is THE WOMAN, the wife and mother (Ephesians 5:23-32; Colossians 1:18; 2:9).

Headship means authority, order, loving care, discipline, covering, protection, provision, responsibility and security. If we want to understand Biblical Headship is, then we see it is perfectly manifested in the Godhead and the headship of Christ over the Church. This illustrates the order of the home, that loving order between husband and wife, the man and the woman.

It also illustrates the order that should be in the Church, the house of the Lord. One exemplifies the other. Headship should not be looked upon negatively because of its misinterpretation and abuse as in many places today.

It is first the natural, then the spiritual. If the woman is not to have headship in the natural home, then it would be contradictory to have it in the house of the Lord. It would be violation of the Divine principle.

Women, therefore, can minister in many realms except where it involves taking authority over men. Women can minister in the gifts of God as given to her subject to oversight and male headship. This is the pattern of the Word of God.

In the light of these comments we note those women gifted of God who *ministered and excercised spiritual authority as they acted under authority*. They did not usurp authority but acted under it.

Examples of women who fulfilled their function under authority are seen in the following:

★　The husband is the head of the house, the head of the wife. Woman is subject to male headship (I Corinthians 11:3). The wife is under the husband's rule (Genesis 3:16; I Peter 3:1). She submits voluntarily to his leadership.

　　This typifies the Church, the wife of the Lamb, who is subject to the headship of Christ, the husband. The Church is under the rule of Christ (Ephesians 5:23-32).

★　Miriam, the prophetess, acted under the authority of Moses and Aaron, but was judged when she criticized him (Exodus 15:20; Numbers 12).

★　Deborah, the Judge, Prophetess, and Mother in Israel, was a married woman, her husband's name being Lapidoth. She acted with authority with Barak, when he failed to go to battle without her, and the victory became hers (Judges 4-5). She counselled with Israel's Governors.

★　Queen Esther, married to King Ahasuerus, acted under Mordecai's words and brought deliverance to her whole nation from the sword of death (Esther 1-11).

★　Huldah, the prophetess, was a married woman, her husband's name Shallum. Yet she also had responsible men about her. Godly king Josiah, the High Priest and the Princes of Israel were her council. Yet they also recognized the mantle of the word of the Lord in her mouth, even though they were men (II Kings 22; II Chronicles 34).

★　Isaiah's wife was a prophetess, yet her husband Isaiah was over her in the Lord (Isaiah 8:3). There was male leadership.

★　The four women named in Matthew 1 were all married women and their husband's are mentioned along with them (Matthew 1).

★　Philip's four daughters were under their father's authority when they prophesied (Acts 21:9).

★　Any woman who made a vow must do it under the authority of her father or her husband, or they could nullify that vow (Numbers 30).

★　Priscilla taught under her husband, Aquila's authority (Acts 18). In every reference, but one, Priscilla, the woman, is mentioned first.

★　Phebe, the Deconess of the Church of Cenchrea, acted under Paul's authority in her service at the Church of Rome (Romans 16:1, 2).

★　Anna, the prophetess, was under temple authorities, as she lived in the temple chambers where also the priests of the Lord lived (Luke 2:36-38).

★　Athaliah usurped authority over the throne of Judah and murdered all the royal seed to do so. She recognized no male leadership (II Kings 11; II Chronicles 22).

★　Wicked Queen Jezebel usurped authority over her husband Ahab and brought about idolatry and the death of Naboth to gain his vineyard for her husband's inheritance (I Kings 21; Revelation 2:20).

★   The woman Jezebel usurped authority in the Church at Thyatira and taught idolatry and immorality and was judged accordingly (Revelation 2:20).

Note the warnings in Proverbs against contentious and strange women (Proverbs 9:13; 21:9, 19; 23:27; 25:24; 27:15; 30:21-23). The woman is responsible *to* a man, and the man is responsible *for* a woman.

The Divine pattern is seen throughout this chapter.
The Order in Creation is first the man, then the woman.
The Order in the Fall is first the woman, then the man.
The Order in Divine Judgment is first the woman, then the man.
The Order in Redemption is to restore the man and the woman.
The Order in the Christian Home is first the man, then the woman.
The Order in the Church is the man, then the woman.

In this manner, both male and female fulfill together their roles under Divine order, even as the Church (the woman), is subject to Christ (the man) and fulfills her role and ministry accordingly.

In concluding this chapter we may say that any woman who functions in the Church in any gift or capacity should:

a.   Have the home in Divine order, for how can they minister in the house of the Lord when their own home is out of order?

b.   Be Scripturally qualified as a Godly woman with character qualities.

c.   Be Scripturally gifted and anointed of the Lord.

d.   Be under male leadership, either her husband's, and/or Church leadership, so that she is acting under authority and not usurping authority.

e.   Recognize and accept God's order, first the man, then the woman, as noted in Order in Creation, the Fall, Redemption, the Home and the Church.

f.   Beware of Humanistic Philosophy that teaches "Women's Liberation", "Feminist Movements" and rebellion against male leadership in the home or the Church or society.

g.   Be an example of a Godly woman in word and deed and character to all other women in the house of the Lord and the home. The woman should beware of having a "masculine" spirit, even as the man must beware of having a "feminine" spirit. Many women today are "mannish" while men are "womanish" because of much reversal of roles and the "uni-sex" mentality.

I.   Problem Scriptures in Paul's Writings

We come now to the two major passages of Scripture from Paul's writings which have been used and are used to silence the ministry of women in any shape or form.

The two main texts used to discredit women's ministry and limit such are found in I Timothy 2:11, 12 and I Corinthians 14:34, 35. Expositors need to be honest in dealing with these Scriptures and such should be done in the light of the context of the whole Bible, as well as Paul's other writings.

It is in the light of all that has been covered in this chapter on the ministry of women that we now consider Paul's writings.

1.   Paul's Epistle to Timothy — I Timothy 2:11, 12

"Let the woman learn in silence with all subjection. But I suffer not a woman to teach, nor to usurp authority over the man, but to be in silence."

The verse should not be taken out of its surrounding context. The context should be read and studied for this verse is but a part of it. We break open this verse in order to help us to understand it more clearly as to what it is really saying.

a.   **Silence** — Verse 11, 12

"Let the woman learn in silence . . . but to be in silence." The Greek word for "silence" (used twice here) is *"Hesuchia"*, meaning "stillness, quietness". It means to be still or peaceable, by implication, to keep one's seat or be undisturbing.

Strong's Concordance says it means "stillness, i.e., desistance from bustle or language."

It does not mean absolute silence as used in Acts 21:40; I Corinthians 14:28, 34 and Revelation 8:1. The Greek word used in these verses is *"Sige"* meaning "to hiss or hush, silence."

Timothy, as Paul's companion and son in the faith, knew of women who travelled with him. He knew of Paul's writings concerning men and women praying and prophesying (I Corinthians 11:4). He knew that Paul was at Philip's house where four daughters prophesied (Acts 21:9). He also knew of Paul's love for Priscilla and Aquila as teachers together (Acts 18:24-26; Romans 16:3). Also he certainly knew of Phebe the Deaconess of Cenchrea (Romans 16:1, 2). Timothy would know Paul's word to Titus about older women teaching younger women (Titus 2:3-5). Paul would not contradict himself. Timothy would understand that Paul is not bringing women to absolute silence.

No Church today, generally speaking, takes this literally. Otherwise women could not sing or pray even in a mixed congregation of men and women, let alone in women's meetings only. Nor could they teach Sunday School classes, and so forth.

Paul is saying that "the women are to learn in *quietness*". She is to be peaceful, restful, tranquil. He is not calling for muteness, dumbness or absolutely no communication. The same word is used in verse 2 of this chapter. It speaks of stillness of spirit, undisturbed by strife or discord. So a woman must be quiet, peaceful, restful and not strive.

b.   **Subjection** — Verse 11

The Greek word *"Hupotasso"* = "hupo", under, and "tasso", to arrange.

In the context it speaks of the marriage relationship (Colossians 3:8; Titus 2:5). It means that the woman is to learn in quietness and submissiveness. It means she shall not assert her rights but yield to the preference of others, especially her husband's, as the context is here.

c.   **The Man** — Verse 12.

The Greek word *"aner"* speaks of "a man". Some expositors say that it is more expressly speaking of "the husband". The Pauline Epistles use this word 59 times, 34 of which King James Version translates "husband". Of the remaining 25 occurrences, 18 are cases where the text is clearly speaking of a husband. Therefore it makes a justifiable translation in this case. That means, the woman is not to usurp authority over the man, her husband.

The context in verses 13-15 speak of Adam and Eve, the first husband and wife and points to how Eve usurped authority over her husband in the Fall. This has already been noted. Therefore, the woman, a wife, must not usurp authority over her husband but be in subjection to him. This is the word of the Lord through Paul in his Epistles (Ephesians 5:22-33).

d.   **Usurp Authority** — Verse 12

The Greek word *"Authenteo"*, only used once means "to seize and hold in possession by force or without right." Various translations translate this as follows:
"excercise authority" (NAS)
"to have authority" (Rotherham)

"to rule over" (Alford)
"to claim authority" (Conybeare)
"to domineer over" (Berkley)
"to dictate to" (Moffatt)
"issue commands" (Knox)
"lord it over" (Living Bible)

Jack Hayford in his comments says "In this spirit, the woman is not to 'usurp authority', i.e., *not to be domineering* (authentew). This verb occurs this one time in the entire New Testament. The intent of instruction here is against an overbearing, demeaning control of her spouse. If the idea intended had to do with authority in the Divine structure of the Church, other terms more consistent with New Testament usage would have been employed."

Williams Translation confirms this: "I do not permit a married woman to practice teaching or domineering over a husband."

Earnest Gentile says "It appears, therefore, that our paragraph under consideration is basically talking of the proper husband-wife relationship and their respective testimony to the world. The men are unashamedly to take the leadership in prayer and the women are to dress moderately and maintain a demeanour that is modest and serious. Women have the need and right to learn (at that time women were not given educational and vocational opportunities like men), and they will do so if they maintain a contented, peaceable spirit, free of strife and discord, as they listen to the instructions and explanations of their husbands. Paul forbids the wives to dominate their husbands."

The whole issue is the word "usurping authority". Webster defines "usurp" as "to take possession by force, to seize and hold in possession."

The Greek thought is "one who acts upon the basis of his own authority, one who does a thing himself." It is an "autocrat" or one self-governed.

It is an artificial authority, an authority that is taken or grasped by one from nowhere (not having a source), and exercised in a despotic manner. Paul speaks very plainly that a woman is not to, on the basis of her own authority (an artificial authority, not a delegated authority), rise up and begin to teach the congregation, and thereby not recognize the headship and leadership already established in the husband or the man in the Church.

This was the situation in the pagan temples where sometimes the *women* conducted the whole religious ceremony from the worship to the teaching.

Ephesus had the great Temple of Diana, a goddess, and Timothy was at Ephesus when he received this injunction. The authority in the Church must not be self-styled and authoritarian but under authority. Godly women must not be like that goddess, Diana!

Queen Athaliah usurped authority over the man and seized the throne of Judah after killing all the royal seed (II Kings 11).

Queen Jezebel usurped authority over her husband, king Ahab, and had Naboth killed to gain his vineyard (I Kings 21).

The woman Jezebel of the Church at Thyatira usurped authority over the Church (some expositors say "the angel" was her husband) and taught idolatry and immorality (Revelation 2:20).

Understanding the setting of the times for this injunction is necessary to understand this passage more clearly.

Vine's Expository Dictionary adds the fact that this word meant "not to have dominion over a man''. It involved the word for "playing the master, a self-doer, a master, an autocrat."

Paul is not forbidding women to teach as he has already told Titus that older women may teach younger women (Titus 2:3-5). He is saying that a wife must not usurp authority over her husband and try and teach him. Of course, this must be understood to be a believing husband. Many unbelieving husbands have been saved by a believing wife having to teach him the way of salvation!

Paul is not demanding absolute silence of the woman for he also says the woman can "pray and prophesy" as well as "teach other women".

The whole issue is that women must not seize the authority over the man, be it her own husband or male leadership. But she can act under authority, not usurp authority!

The Holy Spirit would not anoint women to contradict the Word He inspired if women were to keep absolute silence. The Spirit and the Word agree.

2. **Paul's Epistle to Corinthians** — I Corinthians 14:34, 35

The next passage of Scripture that is used against women's ministry and to silence women in the Church is this passage in Corinthians.

"Let your women keep silence in the churches: for it is not permitted unto them to speak; but they are commanded to be under obedience, as also saith the Law. And if they will learn anything, let them as their husbands at home: for it is a shame for women to speak in the church."

The Corinthian Epistle is dealing with order in the Church, in the public gatherings.

In Chapter 7 Paul deals with marriage problems.
In Chapter 8 he deals with the problem of meats offered to idols.
In Chapter 9 he deals with the support of the ministry.
In Chapter 10 he deals with temptations like Israel of old had.
In Chapter 11 he covers grooming codes for men and women and also order at the Lord's table.
Chapters 12, 13 and 14 deal with the operations of the gifts of the Spirit. At the close of chapter 14:34, 35 he deals with talkative wives who disrupt the services by asking their husbands questions in the services.

Again, it should be remembered that Paul has already said in I Corinthians 11:5 that men and women may pray and prophesy in the Church. He does not contradict himself. The verses in chapter 14 must be interpreted in the light of custom and also of Paul's whole teaching concerning women. He is speaking to the same Church. We break open the verses as follows to help us understand what he is saying more clearly.

a. **"Let your women keep silence in the churches"** — Verse 34

Compared with verse 35 it is referring to wives, as they are to ask their husbands at home. The R.V., says "let the women", not "your women". It is not a general statement to silence ALL women for saying anything in the churches. Women may pray and prophecy at least.

b. **"Keep silence in the churches"** — Verse 35

The Greek words for "silence" are "*Sigao*" from "*Sige*" (SC 4601/2) and mean "to be silent", "to hiss, or hush, silence." The words are used in Acts 15:12, 13; 21:40; 12:17; Romans 16:25; I Corinthians 14:28, 30, 34; Revelation 8:1; Luke 9:36; 20:26.

If a person speaks in tongues and there is no interpreter then they are to be silent (I Corinthians 14:28). If the prophets have something revealed to them, then the first is to be silent and let the other speak (I Corinthians 14:30). And if a woman wants to ask questions of her husband, she must do it at home and be silent in the church (I Corinthians 14:34).

It is not a mandate to silence the woman in church any more than to silence the speaker in tongues or a prophet.

c. **"For it is not permitted unto them to speak . . . For it is a shame for women to speak in the church.** " — Verses 34, 35

The Greeks used several different words to express speech, each of which are translated by the same English word "speak".

"Legein" — "to deliver an ordered discourse"
"Eipien" — "to speak in ordinary conversation"
"Lalein" — "to chatter, babble, prattle, gabble or talk in an undertone".

It is the word *"Laleo"*, meaning "to talk, utter words," that is used here.

In *Liddel & Scott's Lexicon*, the following meanings are given: "to chatter, babble; of birds, to twitter, chirp; strictly, to make an inarticulate sound, opposed to articulate speech; but also generally, to talk, say."

Paul is correcting Corinth for disorder in the services, and says "Let the wives be quiet, they are not permitted to gabble, talk in an undertone in the Church, for they are disturbing both speaker and hearers."

The women had lately been converted from heathenism. They were hungry for the Gospel and thus disturbed the meetings as they had little or no education.

In those days, and still in some places today, it was customary for men and women to sit either side of the building. The women disrupted the meeting by calling out to their husbands various questions when they did not understand what was said. Generally the women were not educated and so their questions disturbed the gatherings. Paul told them to be quiet and ask their husbands at home.

He is not talking about women praying or prophesying, singing or speaking. Of course they would have to have believing husbands to fulfil this injunction of Paul.

Halley's Bible Handbook (pp. 596, 597) says "It was customary in Greek and Eastern cities for women to cover their heads in public, except of immoral character. Corinth was full of temple prostitutes. Some of the Christian women, taking advantage of their new-found liberty in Christ, were making bold to lay aside their veils in Church meetings, which thus horrified those of more modest type. They are here told not to defy public opinion as to what was considered proper in feminine decorum."

Denominations that enforce "silence" in their Churches permit their women to sing with the congregation, in solos, pray in prayer meetings, teach Sunday School classes, and even be Missionaries to heathen nations. What a contradition this is to their stand and interpretation of Paul's writings in both Timothy and Corinthians!

Paul is simply saying that the wives must not disturb the gatherings by inconvenient asking of questions, ignorant talking and chattering among themselves. He is not enforcing absolute silence on women in Churches.

d. **"But they are commanded to be under obedience, as also saith the Law"** — Verse 34.

It does not say the Law commands *silence*, but to be under *obedience*. There is not one verse from Genesis to Malachi where "the law of Moses" said that women were to be silent.

This present phrase has been the cause of much controversy. There are two views presented here concerning the interpretation of this verse.

1) Some expositors believe that Paul is quoting back to them their own questions, that he is quoting some of the words of the Judaizers from the Oral Law in the Talmud.

John A. Anderson had a friend who wrote to the Chief Rabbi of England some years ago asking if these two verses were taken from the Jewish Talmud. The Rabbi replied that the passages are not literally reproduced from the Talmud but that they are close parallels.

The Oral Law taught that it was "a shame for a woman to let her voice be heard among men" — almost the very words used in the language quoted by the Apostle.

It is possible that Paul is quoting what the Judaizers, who were trying to silence women, in the Corinthian Church were saying.

If this is so, he reproves them by saying that the word of God came UNTO them, and not FROM them, and that he himself was giving the commandments of the Lord (I Corinthians 14:36-40).

2) Some expositors follow this second view and this does not violate the whole context of Scripture concerning the role of women in the home or the Church.

Women, and as here, it is referring to married women, are to be under obedience to their own husbands. Paul's Epistles tell the wife to obey her husband in the Lord (Ephesians 5:23-32; Colossians 3:18-20 with I Peter 3:1-8).

Some authorities refer to Genesis 3:16 concerning Adam's rule over his wife as "the law" referred to here.

In the light of the Corinthian problem, it is Scripturally correct to say that wives who were disturbing the services by asking questions, or chattering, needed to be under obedience to their husbands indeed, and ask their questions at home.

Jews and Gentiles did not worship together until they saw that the cross had broken down the dividing wall. They did not worship together as one until they saw they were "in Christ" neither male nor female (Ephesians 2:12-19; Galatians 3:26-29). The Judaizers tried to bring the Gentiles under the bondage of the Law as well as Talmudic Laws. Paul opposed such legalisms continually.

In the Jewish Synagogue, the pulpit was in the middle and the men gathered around while the women were in the balcony. While the word was being ministered, it was permissible for a man to stop and ask him a question. But Paul here is telling the women not to yell down at their husbands but wait until they got home as they were creating so much noise and confusion in the services.

The ones that are learning are to keep quiet, not the ones that are teaching. So it is dealing with *wives,* not women's ministry!

Under obedience as wives to husbands, as also saith the Law. Talkative wives embarrass their husbands and it is poor behaviour in public Church gatherings. A good place to show proper husband-wife relationship is in public gatherings indeed. Therefore, talkative wives should not disrupt public meetings and embarrass their husbands, or the Church!

Jim Beall states in "*The Female of the Species*" (p.33). "In those days, custom dictated that men and women be separated in public services. This was true in the Jewish Synagogues and Greek gatherings as well. Women were usually confined to a side room or a screened-off balcony where they could scarcely hear what was being said. Consequently, attention would soon lag and they were on their way talking and chattering. In some buildings, the men and women were separated by an aisle."

In India today, some places still separate the men and women.

In Cairo, Egypt, the writer was in a Church where men and women were separated by a wooden stained wall built up to the middle of the pulpit!

In China, a Missionary told of the separation in the Church meetings of men and women and the like disturbance that Paul spoke of having to be handled. Women should not be domineering whether at home or in the Church. This is Divine order!

The argument that false religions have been founded by women is the same argument that may be used of numerous men. Christian Science (Mary Baker Eddy); Spiritualism (The Fox Sisters), Women Witches (I Samuel 28), and the mixture in Seventh Day Adventist (Allen G. White) prove nothing more than many false and mixed religions have been founded also by men.

No failure of any women cannot be applied to men. Both are failures apart from the grace of God in Christ.

e. **"And if they will learn anything, let them ask their husbands at home"** — Verse 35.

Of course, this would imply believing husbands. Otherwise believing wives with unbelieving husbands would have to ask other believing men or women in order to learn what was meant. Some women would be sent back to heathenism or to Judaism, for spiritual help, or, in some cases no help at all, since many women may be without husbands.

Peter exhorts believing wives to be Godly women that their unbelieving husbands may be won to the Lord without them preaching the word at them but by their lifestyle (I Peter 3:1-8).

In conclusion then, it is not being honest to use I Timothy 2 or I Corinthians 14 to silence all women's ministry in the Church, only by faulty interpretations, and this in the light of the total Biblical revelation of women's role under God, and under headship.

CHAPTER 29

DISCERNING THE BODY OF CHRIST

Introductory:

In I Corinthians 11:23-34 Paul speaks of the revelation given to him concerning the table of the Lord. He showed the Corinthian believers that many of them were weak and sickly and many died prematurely because they failed to *discern the Lord's body*. It is absolutely important in both the Church universal and the local that there be proper discernment of the body of Christ.

We find that there are two aspects of "Discerning the Lord's Body" as taught by Paul. To discern means "to perceive, recognize, apprehend, to see and understand, to have insight into". These two aspects of discerning the Lord's body are:
★ Discerning the Natural Body of Christ, the literal and physical.
★ Discerning the Spiritual Body of Christ, the spiritual and mystical in the Church. I Corinthians 10:15-21; 11:23-34; 12:1-29 all deal with these two aspects of the Body of Christ. Both the literal and the spiritual aspects of the Body are seen here.

A. Discerning the Physical Body of Christ

"The Bread which we break, is it not the communion of the body of Christ?"
"The Cup which we bless, is it not the communion of the blood of Christ?"
I Corinthians 10:15-21; Matthew 26:17-30; Luke 22:7-20; John 6. Jesus instituted the Lord's supper at the time of the Passover supper. He took the bread, gave thanks, blessed it and break it, saying "This is My body, broken for you."

He then took the cup, gave thanks, blessed it and gave it to His disciples, saying "This is My blood, drink ye all of it". This was the establishment of New Testament communion. It speaks of the body and blood of the Lord Jesus Christ, the atonement, the table of the Lord, the Lord's supper.

1. Discerning the Bread

We discern the Lord's body in the bread we break. That is, we recognize, perceive and have insight into the truth that the BODY OF JESUS was a perfect, sinless, human but incorruptible body. His body was prepared of God in the virgin Mary by the power of the Holy Spirit (Hebrews 10:5; Luke 1:33-35).

We discern that this body took our sicknesses, diseases and sins on the cross (I Peter 2:21-25; Isaiah 53; Matthew 8:16-17). We discern that this body bore 39 stripes according to the broken Law for our healing, and with His stripes we are healed. We discern that healing is in the atonement for our physical bodies, through His broken body (Psalms 103:1-5). We discern that healing and Divine health are available to us through His broken body.

These truths we discern, perceive and have insight into as we partake of His broken body in the bread.

This is truly discerning the Lord's body. That is, His literal, natural and physical body at Calvary which was broken for us and which we remember each time we partake of the Lord's supper. How many of God's people fail to discern this in the communion today? For this cause, many are weak, sickly, and many sleep, for not "discerning the Lord's body". This body is the children's bread as seen in Matthew 14, and Exodus 15:26.

2. Discerning the Cup

We discern also the blood of Jesus in the cup. That is, we recognize, perceive and have insight and understanding of the truth that the BLOOD OF JESUS was perfect, sinless, Divine and therefore incorruptible (Acts 20:28). It was the blood of God. It was not Jewish blood nor Gentile blood, but the blood of God. It came from the Father God, in the Divine Seed of THE WORD.

His blood was shed for the remission of our sins (I Peter 1:18, 19; Hebrews 9:22).

His blood was given as an atonement for the soul (Leviticus 17:11-14).

His blood is the blood of the NEW Covenant and has brought a cessation to all Old Testament animal sacrifices and oblations (Hebrews 10:1-2; Daniel 9:27; Matthew 26:26). His blood brings us near to God, cleanses us from all sins as the fountain opened for sin and uncleanness and is the ground of our perfection.

There is victory in the blood (Revelation 12:11; I John 1:6). There is life (John 6). All the benefits of the atonement are made available through Christ's blood. These truths we discern when we partake of the cup in the Lord's supper. This is truly discerning the cup and His blood.

His literal physical body and blood are incorruptible and become the source of our redemption. Both are in heaven for us now, and are symbolized in earth in the bread and the fruit of the vine.

How many discern this in the communion?

3. **Do in Remembrance of Me** — I Corinthians 11:23-34.

It is to be in remembrance of Him and His sacrifice on Calvary. It shows forth His first coming, His death, the purpose of His first advent. It shows forth His second coming, "until He come". We examine ourselves before Him so as not to partake unworthily of His body and blood. To fail to discern is to bring chastisement on ourselves. For this cause many are weak, sickly, and many die for not discerning the Lord's body. The opposite should be true if we do discern. We should have strength, health and life through it.

4. **The Lord in Heaven**

The Lord's table with the bread and cup are the symbols of the Church of the New Covenant. It is *spiritual meat and spiritual drink* to us (I Corinthians 10:1-4; John 6:53-67). His words are spirit and they are life. The literal is in the spiritual and the spiritual is in the literal. There was literal Manna, literal Waters from a literal rock, yet there was spiritual meat and the drink therein. The literal bread and literal cup minister to us spiritual meat and drink. The literal body and blood of Jesus are both in heaven for us now. The body of Jesus, crucified, risen, ascended and glorified is there (Acts 1:9; 7:55, 56). The blood of Jesus, sinless and incorruptible, is also in heaven for us (Hebrews 9; 12:22-24). We discern this in the table of the Lord.

Paul received this by revelation. That which was given externally to the Twelve Apostles of the Lamb is now given to Paul by the Lord. He received the inner, mystical truth of the table.

Thus this discerning pertains to the physical body and blood of the Lord in the table.

B. **Discerning the Spiritual Body of Christ**

Paul also tells us in these Scriptures that the believers are members of the Body of Christ (I Corinthians 10:15-21; 11:23-34; I Corinthians 12). That is, the Church is Christ's Body, the spiritual Body of Christ.

I Corinthians 12:12. "For as the (natural) body is one, and has many members, and all the members of that one body, being many, are one body, *so also is Christ*".

I Corinthians 12:27. "*Ye* are the Body of Christ and members in particular."

I Corinthians 11:17. "*We* being many are one bread and one body."

Hence the dual aspects of the Lord's Body are seen. His literal and physical body, and then the spiritual body, which is the Church are the two aspects. The spiritual Body of Christ must also be discerned. It is necessary to perceive, to have insight into, to recognize, understand and apprehend the members of the Church, the Body of Christ.

1. **Discerning the Bread**

    We discern the Lord's *spiritual body* as we partake of the bread (I Corinthians 11:17). "We being many are one bread."

    The bread speaks first of Christ, but here it speaks of the believers, the members of Christ's spiritual Body. The bread, therefore, is the symbol of Christ's physical body and also of His spiritual Body, the Church. The dual truth is in the one bread. We discern the physical and spiritual truths of the Body of Christ in the bread. That is, we recognize and perceive believers worldwide as members of the Body of Christ.

    In this is healing, health and life for the members of the Body. For this lack of discernment, many members are weak, sickly and many die prematurely. Sectarianism, schisms, divisions, heresies, jealousies, envies, strifes, carnality — all these things reveal the lack of discerning the unity of the Body. Such things bring weakness, sickness and death.

    Therefore as we partake of the bread, we must discern the truth of the ONENESS of the body of Christ, the one bread, the one Church. This is true discernment of the Lord's spiritual body.

2. **Discerning the Cup**

    As the bread has a dual meaning in discerning, so does the cup of the Lord (I Corinthians 11:15, 16). The cup which we bless, is it not the communion of the blood of Christ? The one cup, blessed by believers in communion and fellowship speaks of the one blood by which every member of the Body of Christ is united and by which He lives. God has made all nations of *one blood* (Acts 17:26). That is, of Adam's blood. There is union of the race through original blood from Adam. So God has made all believers, redeemed out of every kindred, tongue, tribe and nation, of one blood, which is the BLOOD of Jesus Christ!

    In the natural and physical body, every cell and member has the same life, the same blood flowing through them, thus uniting all to each other and to the head. So in the spiritual Body of Christ. Every cell, every member, has the same life, the same blood, the life of Jesus, flowing to and through them. The blood of Jesus unites every member to the other, and to the risen Head, Christ. Blood relationship of every member in Christ is seen. Each are cleansed by the same blood, each live by the same blood (John 6:53-67).

    As we discern the cup, we discern that we are united to every member by the blood of Jesus Christ, and the same life unites us to the living Head. This is the cup of blessig indeed.

3. **For this Cause**

    Paul says "For this cause many are weak, sickly, and many die, for not discerning the Lord's body." I Corinthians 11:29.
    Proverbs 26:2. "The *curse* shall not come without a *cause*."

    Sometimes we endeavour to get rid of the *curse* without getting rid of the *cause*! For not discerning the Lord's body, both physically and/or spiritually is the cause for much weakness, sickness and death in the Church. The same table becomes blessing of life or judgment of death accordingly.

4. **Discerning the Body**

    Following we note a number of points involved in a proper discerning of the body of Christ. We are to discern:—

    ★   That there is one body, not many bodies (I Corinthians 12:12). Unity of the body.
    ★   That it is one body with many members, not one member (I Corinthians 12:14, 17, 19).
    ★   That it is the one body of Christ in His members (I Corinthians 12:12; II Corinthians 5:16, 17).

★ That the Holy Spirit baptized all members into one body, all have the same Spirit (I Corinthians 12:13; Ephesians 4:4).

★ That every member has a place, function and operation in the body.

★ That not all have the same gift, office or function (Romans 12:1-6; I Corinthians 12).

★ That God has set a variety of ministries in the body (I Corinthians 12:17).

★ That there is unity in diversity in operations of the same Spirit, yet there is harmony, unity, co-ordination.

★ That every member needs the other members (I Corinthians 12:12, 21).

★ That we recognize all spiritual gifts in the body. It is recognition, not competition (I Corinthians 12:1-12).

★ That God hath tempered the body together as it pleased Him (I Corinthians 12:24).

★ That there be no schism in the body (I Corinthians 12:25; Romans 16:17).

★ That all members have the same love and care for each other (I Corinthians 12:25).

★ That all members suffer and rejoice together (I Corinthians 12:26; Romans 12:15; Colossians 1:24).

★ That the communion is the fellowship of the body (I Corinthians 10:16-18).

★ That there is no independence in the body, but all are inter-dependent on the other and Christ.

★ That each member is responsible to function in his place in the body (Romans 12:1-7).

★ That individually and corporately we hold the Headship of Christ (Colossians 1:19; 2:9).

★ That we are bone of His bone, flesh of His flesh (Ephesians 5:23-33).

★ That ministries are set in the body for the perfecting of the saints (Ephesians 4:11-16).

★ That there are different administrations but the same Lord (I Corinthians 12:4-6).

★ That all members are united through the blood of Christ.

★ That no one member is complete in himself, but needs the total body to find fulfilment (Romans 12:3, 6-8).

★ That only in the whole body is the completeness of Christ. No one member has the fulness (John 1:16; 3:33, 34; Ephesians 3:19; Romans 12:1-6).

★ That there must be submission in the body not rebellion in the cells and members.

★ That unity is an absolute to maintain the health of the body. There must be recognition, co-ordination and co-operation for the members to be in good health and be what God intended it to be.

The Church is THE BODY OF CHRIST in the earth and He desires to continue His life and minitry through this body, that the will of God might be done in the earth (Hebrews 10:5; Romans 12:1-2).

CHAPTER 30

CHURCH DISCIPLINE

Introductory:

Wherever there is a group of people, there must be order, there must be rules of ethics. If one is alone, then there is no need of laws governing interpersonal relationships. Laws are needed to preserve order and happiness and good relations between persons. If there are laws, then there needs to be submission to these laws for harmony to be maintained. If people violate these laws, then there comes the need for disciplines (Romans 13:2; Matthew 5:25, 26). These laws should not just be obeyed externally but internally, to have a clear conscience before God (Romans 13:5). Therefore there is the need for the ''I will'' of every person to be submitted to the supreme will, the will of God. The will of God is expressed in the laws of God. Scripture shows His will is law, and His law is His will. God's law is king. Because of the sinfulness of man and the imperfection of believers, oftentimes there is need of Divine discipline in the Church.

This discipline may be executed under *Divine sovereignty,* directly by God Himself, or by *human responsibility,* acting in accordance with the principles of Scripture. Without discipline in a natural family, there would be disorder and chaos. The same is true in the Church, the family of God.

The second reference of the Lord concerning the Church, as mentioned in Matthew's Gospel, involves the need and the procedure for Church discipline. Read Matthew 16:15-20 with 18:15-20.

Church discipline is one of the hardest and the most delicate areas in Church life. This comes because of misunderstanding concerning the nature and purpose of discipline or because of human sympathies which stand against the spiritual administration of the same. However, Church discipline is absolutely necessary to maintain a strong, healthy and holy Church.

A. **Definition of the word**

The word discipline means:

1. Teaching, learning, to disciple.

2. Training that corrects, molds, or perfects the mental faculties or morals.

2. Punishment, to inflict pain or a penalty.

4. A rule or system of rules which govern conduct or activity.

B. **The Meaning of Discipline**

Without question, the New Testament teaches discipline. Discipleship is impossible without it. It ranges from self-discipline to Church discipline; from exhortation to excommunication. What is implied by the fact that the Scriptures teach the responsibility of the Church to discipline its members when necessary?

1. It means that I am my brother's keeper. ''If any man be overtaken in a fault, ye which are spiritual, restore such an one. Bear ye one another's burdens'' (Galatians 6:1, 2).

2. It demonstrates that ''none of us liveth unto himself'' (Romans 14:8). Some times someone will tell you to mind your own business and not meddle in theirs, but the fact is that your brother is your business as being members of God's family.

3. It plainly says that God is holy and sin is not an insignificant thing. The early Church had purity and power while the Church today lacks much of this.

4. It teaches that sin is contagious. Discipline is not to divide between the good and the bad, but it is to quarantine contagious sin in order to keep others from ''catching it'', for we are sufficiently alike to make us all susceptible to the same evils. It is restorative rather than punitive.

5. It manifests the fact that a Christian life is a corporate life. We are all baptized into one body, and when one member suffers we all suffer. Individualism is the sin of division (I Corinthians 12:13, 23).

6. It shows the mind of spiritual membership that existed in the New Testament. People became a part of the New Testament Church, or they could never have been put out of it (Matthew 18:17). People who are merely "members-at-large" of the mystical, invisible, universal Church can never fulfill the pattern found in Scripture. This does not refer to "having a card", rather to "membership", as a hand is a member of the body.

7. It proves the sovereignty of the local Church. Disciplined people in Matthew 18:17, 18 find in the local Church a supreme court on earth. There is no superstructure of ecclesiasticism, district leaders, superintendents, bishop, or popes to which they might appeal. The local Church has its Head in heaven.

C. The Necessity of Discipline

As in the natural family, so in the spiritual family. Discipline is needed for the following reasons:

1. Discipline is basically designed to make order and happiness possible. Without it there would be lawlessness and anarchy (Judges 18:1; 19:1; 21:25).

2. Discipline introduces the principle of submission; my will submitted to or crossing the will of God.

3. Selfishness and selfwill bring destruction and misery in any home (Isaiah 14:12-14).

4. Discipline excercised in love gives individuals and a congregation a sense of security; saves a backslider from hell, and prevents worse problems.

5. Discipline is needed to uphold the moral standard of God's word, maintaining the holiness of God in the Church.

6. Discipline guides the immature, stabilizes the weak, and causes people to come to maturity in the Lord.

D. The Twofold Purpose of Discipline

There are two main aspects of discipline seen in Scripture, these being as follows.

1. Discipline unto *restoration* (Galatians 6:1; Revelation 3:19; Hebrews 12:5-11).
   This is correction to bring about repentance unto restoration. It is correction of the error, not rejection of the person. There is acceptance of the person with the view to restore them. One cannot restore unless one accepts the person being restored. Unconditional love and total acceptance of the person is necessary but not the evil behaviour.

   It is worthy to note that "restore" in Galatians 6:1 means "to set, mend as a dislocated bone, to completely and thoroughly mend." It is a wound to be healed. Even in the Corinthian case, excommunication led to repentance and restoration (II Corinthians 2:6-8; James 5:19-20; I John 5:16; Proverbs 10:12; Psalms 51:12; Jeremiah 3:22; 20:16, 17; Hosea 14:4; Micah 7:18, 19). God desires us to save a soul from death and give him life. This is through Scriptural disciplines.

2. Discipline unto *condemnation* (I Corinthians 11:29-32; II Corinthians 2:6-8, 11).
   The Corinthian case is a point in view. He was excommunicated from the Church but still with the view to restoration by repentance.

God will judge, punish and chastise in order to bring a restoration of fellowship with Himself and believers. If men refuse to accept God's judgment of sin at Calvary, then God judges them with eternal judgment (John 5:24-29; 3:36; I Peter 4:17; I Corinthians 5:1-5, 12-13; 6:1-11; Isaiah 4:4).

E.   **Examples of Discipline**

1.   **Old Testament Disciplines**

There are many examples of Divine discipline under the Old Testament times. We list a number of these cases.

a.   Adam and Eve received Divine discipline and judgment for sin (Genesis 3). They were dismissed from Eden, placed under the penalty of death for sin. The wages of sin is death (Romans 3:23).

b.   Abraham was reproved by Pharoah for his "situational ethics" (Genesis 20).

c.   Cain was judged by the Lord for rejecting the lamb and for the sin of murder (Genesis 4).

d.   Aaron was rebuked for the sin of golden calf idolatry (Exodus 32:20, 21).

e.   Miriam was smitten with leprosy for sin of criticism of leadership (Numbers 12). Then she was restored after 7 days.

f.   Korah, Dathan and Abiram were judged by death for their rebellion against God and His leadership (Numbers 16).

g.   Achan was judged by death on his family for sins of deceit (Joshua 7).

h.   Saul was rebuked publicly and judged for his sins (I Samuel 13:13; 15:14).

i.   A stubborn and rebellious son was stoned to death by the elders (Deuteronomy 21:18-21).

j.   Hophni and Phinehas were judged by death for immorality and presumption (I Samuel 2:25).

k.   Ahab the king was rebuked by the prophet Elijah for his evils (I Kings 18:18).

l.   King Uzziah was smitten with leprosy for pride and presumption until his death (II Chronicles 26).

m.   Ezra reproved those with strange wives (Ezra 10:18-23).

n.   Nehemiah contended with the rulers and nobles because of Sabbath violation and forsaking God's house (Nehemiah 13:11, 17).

o.   Daniel reproved the king for his pride and presumption (Daniel 5:22, 23).

p.   The days of Noah were days of judgment (Genesis 6-8; Luke 17:26, 27).

q.   The days of Sodom and Gomorrah were days of judgment (Genesis 18, 19; Jude 7; Matthew 11:20-24). Remember Lot's wife.

r.   The Nation of Egypt was judged by God (Genesis 15:14; Exodus 5-14).

s.   The Tower of Babel was Divine judgment (Genesis 10-11).

t.   The Nations of Israel and Judah were judged even though they were God's people (Exodus 31-33; Deuteronomy 27-28).

Some of the Divine disciplines in Israel involved *excommunication* and sometimes the *death penalty*. All these were types and ensamples to us upon whom the ends of the age have come (I Corinthians 10:6, 11).

Excommunication:

Under the following Old Testament examples we see the Divine reasons given when persons had to be excommunicated from the camp of Israel, or "cut off from his people" as it was commonly referred to. Some of these reasons were:

★   Failure to accept the covenant seal of circumcision (Genesis 17:4).

★   Eating leavened bread during the Feast of Unleavened Bread (Exodus 12:15).

★   Counterfeiting the holy anointing oil or incense (Exodus 30:33, 37).

★ Eating blood (Leviticus 7:27).

★ Offering burnt offerings away from the Door of the Tabernacle (Leviticus 17:8, 9).

★ Partaking of the Peace Offering on the third day after it was sacrificed (Leviticus 19:7).

★ Carnal relationships with a women in her natural uncleanness (Leviticus 20:18).

★ Coming to the holy things in an unclean state (Leviticus 22:3).

★ Failure to keep the Feast of Passover (Numbers 9:13).

★ Having a plague of leprosy in the person (Numbers 5:2-4).

★ Sinning presumptuously (Numbers 15:31).

★ Failure to purify oneself from death's defilement (Numbers 19:13).

Death Penalty

Some serious violations of the law of God were punishable with the death penalty, under two or three witnesses. Some of these are listed here:

★ Idolatry (Deuteronomy 17:2-6).

★ Contempt and rebellion against Priestly judgments in certain matters (Deuteronomy 17:8-13).

★ False witness (Deuteronomy 19:18).

★ Stubborn and rebellious sons (Deuteronomy 21:18).

★ Discovery of violated virginity by a husband (Deuteronomy 22:13-21).

★ Adultery (Deuteronomy 22:22).

★ Immoral behaviour to one betrothed (Deuteronomy 22:23, 24).

★ Homosexuality (Leviticus 18:22; 20:13) and beastiality (Leviticus 18:23-30; 20:15, 16).

New Testament Disciplines

The New Testament shows various things also that have to come under Divine discipline in the Church. Unless leadership deals with those in error, then the whole congregation can be defiled. The Corinthian Church exemplifies this truth. We note a list of things which were and need to be disciplined in a Church.

No Church can prosper if it allows sin to go unjudged. The Lord will withdraw His blessing (Revelation 1-2-3).

Sin is contagious. The spiritual health of the Body is at stake. Sin in a member is like "leaven" (I Corinthians 5:6, 7). Sin can affect the whole Body (Joshua 7, Achan; I Corinthians 5, Fornicator; and Revelation 2:14-16, 20-23; Idolatry, Immorality and False Doctrines).
What offences require Church discipline?

Doctrinal Offences

★ Paul dealt with Hymenaeus and Alexander over the doctrine of the resurrection (I Timothy 1:20; II Timothy 2:17-26). Also Hymenaeus and Philetus.

★ Doctrines not according to godliness were dealt with (I Timothy 6:3-5).

★ Doctrines of idolatry and immorality were dealt with (Revelation 2:12-17).

★ Doctrines which bring division contrary to apostles doctrines dealt with (Romans 16:17, 18).

★ Heresy and doctrines of devils (I Timothy 4:1-3; Titus 3:9, 11; I John 4:1; Matthew 7:15; Galatians 1:7-10; II Peter 2:1-4; Jude 4).

Such must be "shunned" (II Timothy 2:16); "purged" (II Timothy 2:23); "avoid discussion" (II Timothy 2:25); "withdrawn from" (I Timothy 6:3, 5); "delivered to Satan" (I Timothy 1:20); "not received into house, or bless" (II John 10); and "charged not to teach other doctrine" (I Timothy 1:7).

These must be "reproved, rebuked and exhorted" to continue in the sound doctrine (II

Timothy 4:1-2; Titus 1:11; II Peters 1-3).

Read also (Matthew 5:19; John 15:9; Matthew 24:11-13; Romans 16:17-18; Titus 3:10; Galatians 1:7-9).

False doctrine causes people to "put away faith" and "shipwreck" (I Timothy 1:19). In Church discipline God's protection is withdrawn from these, and they are delivered to Satan from whom they received their false doctrines.

Behavioural Offences

Offences against the members of the Body of Christ have to be dealt with also. As members one of another, none of us live to ourselves (Matthew 25:40; I Corinthians 8:2; Matthew 10:40; 18:5; Luke 10:16; Acts 9:4).

This has to do with a brother or sister's perpetual lifestyle, not just single incidents or mistakes. It is dealing with "brothers and sisters" in the family of God — NOT outsiders. God judges them — not the Church (I Corinthians 5:12-13).

★   **Fornicator** — I Corinthians 5:1.

Generally speaking it is immorality of the unmarried. In Matthew 19:5; 5:32 it here includes adultery (immorality of marrieds). It deals with moral impurity. In totality this can include Sodomites and Sodomitesses (Homosexuality, Lesbianism, Moral Perversions). In I Corinthians 5:1-5 it involved incest; a man with his own mother.

In broadest terms it includes all illicit sexual relationships. This works as leaven in the Church unless dealt with (Read I Corinthians 5 with II Corinthians 12:20-21). Not to eat or company with immoral persons. Immoral persons hide under the cover of the Church. When excommunicated by the Church God can deal with him.

★   **Covetous** — I Corinthians 5:11.

One who is inordinately desirous, greedy. Unlawful lustfulness.
Cf. Ananias and Sapphira (Acts 5:1-11).
Cf. Gehazi (II Kings 5:20-27). Covetousness evidenced.
Cf. Simon the sorcerer (Acts 8:18-23).
Cf. Balaam the soothsayer prophet (Numbers 22; Jude 11).

Covetousness can include many things, but it is evidenced in the love of money in numerous cases (I Peter 5:2). Covetousness is idolatry (Ephesians 5:3). Read also Philippians 3:15-19; Luke 12:15, 34; John 6:26, 27; Romans 1:29; 13:9; Colossians 3:2-6; I Thessalonians 2:5; I Timothy 3:3; 6:5-17; II Timothy 3:2; Hebrews 13:5; James 4:2; II Peter 2:3; I John 2:15. Remember Judas!

★   **Idolater** — I Corinthians 5:11.

Inordinately fond of a person or thing. Anything that comes between God and the believer is idolatry.

1)   **Literal Idols** — I Corinthians 6:9; 10:14, 20; Revelation 21:8. Thus pictures, statues, worship of saints, Buddha, etc., and material, physical or spiritual objects, and selfism — all equal idolatry. We are to have no other gods before or beside God.

2)   **Spiritual Idols** — Ephesians 5:5; Colossians 3:5. Covetousness is idolatry. Romans 1:23. Anything between God and a believer becomes an idol.

★   **Railer** — I Corinthians 5:11; I Peter 3:9; Proverbs 26:4.

"A verbal brawler, evil speaker, contentious, extremely argumentative." It speaks of abusive language, scornful, one who is against everything, speaks evil and blasphemously of leaders and brothers. One impossible to get along with.

I Timothy 6:4; Colossians 3:8; Ephesians 4:31. Evil speaking is condemned. Some are not afraid to speak evil of dignitaries (II Peter 2:10). John would deal with Diotrephes for his arrogance (II John 9, 10).

★ **Drunkard** — I Corinthians 5:11.

One who habitually drinks, and is perpetually under the influence of alcohol or strong drink. Habitual intoxication is a moral weakness.
Galatians 5:19. Drunkenness is a work of the flesh.
Ephesians 5:18. We are not to be drunk with wine.

Read also Romans 13:13; I Thessalonians 5:7; Proverbs 20:1; 23:20-21; 23:29-35; Isaiah 5:11; Deuteronomy 21:20, 21.

★ **Extortioner** — I Corinthians 5:11.

"To obtain from a person by oppression, or abuse of authority." It is deep desire for advantage and speaks of one who seizes upon them and takes them by force, or one who gets money (or whatever he wants) by threat, force, fraud, or illegal use of authority. It is akin to covetousness.

It is the crime of one using ones official position to obtain money or other things of value unlawfully (i.e., False cheques written, etc.).

A thief . . . extortioner (I Corinthians 6:10). Read also Psalms 109:11; Isaiah 16:4; Ezekiel 22:12; Micah 3:2, 3; Matthew 23:25; Luke 18:11.

★ **Disorderly Conduct** — II Thessalonians 3:6-15.

"Not keeping order", as a military team marching, and one who gets out of step. One who is insubordinate and obstinate in attitude; one who violates regularly the principle of labour and support. Idle busybodies! From this person one is to "withdraw" (II Thessalonians 3:6, 14), but not treat him as an enemy but a brother under discipline (II Thessalonians 3:5). Thus this is not a case of excommunication as in Matthew 18:17.

An *unruly* person needs to be quiet, and work and eat his own bread (I Thessalonians 5:14, 11-12; II Thessalonians 3:11). No food = no rations if he does not work.

Disorderliness = "slothfulness, laziness, sluggard, busybody". It involves irresponsibility (Luke 16:11; I Timothy 5:8, 13; II Thessalonians 3:7-9; Proverbs 6:6-11; 18:9; 19:15; Matthew 25:26; Romans 12:11).

He should be encouraged to get work and not become a "parasite" on the hospitality of saints in the Church. Then he can meet his own needs and help others.

★ **Divisionaries** — Romans 16:16-18.

Those who bring divisions contrary to sound doctrine need to be disciplined. They are to be marked and avoided. Deliberately not seek their company. Even leadership may draw disciples after themselves and divide the Church (Acts 20:28-32).

Doctrines especially contrary to the redemptive truths of the Bible are to be avoided.

★ **Sectarianism** — I Corinthians 3:1-3; Ephesians 5:12; II Corinthians 7:11, 12.

Sectarianism is evidence of carnality and needs to be disciplined also. Paul's Epistle was corrective and disciplinary to deal with such.

★ **Unforgiving attitude** — Matthew 5:25; 18:15-35; Luke 12:58.

This person brings themselves under Divine discipline for failing to forgive.

★ **Not discerning the Body** — I Corinthians 11:23-32.

This has been dealt with previously. But, weakness, sickness and premature death are all part of Divine discipline. If we would judge ourselves we would not be judged, but the Lord chastens us with these things so that we will not be condemned with the world.

★ The Sorcerer was judged for resisting the Gospel of Christ (Acts 13:6-12).

★ One refusing to be reconciled to his brother and refusing to hear the witnesses and the whole Church is to be excommunicated (Matthew 18:15-20; 5:21-26).

★   Lying to the Holy Spirit brought Divine judgment (Acts 5:1-11).

These things can work like leaven or leprosy and spread through the Body if not dealt with. The Church is God's house, His covering for His people. While under this covering, they often escape discipline. God will get them out sometimes to deal with them (I Samuel 2:25).

Sins of ignorance were dealt with in the Church in the Wilderness (Leviticus 4; Numbers 15:24-31), as well as sins of presumption. Leprosy in the person, the garment or the house must be cleansed (Leviticus 13, 14).

F.   Who Administers Discipline?

Who is the one or who are the ones who should administer discipline, especially when it comes to the local Church.

1.   Sovereign Discipline

Sometimes God in His own sovereignty administers discipline. He chastens His own people (Hebrews 12:5; Proverbs 3:11; 12; I Corinthians 11:29-32; James 5:14, 15; I John 5:16, 17). Sometimes there "is a sin unto (physical) death".

2.   Spiritual Members (Galatians 6:1).

"Ye which are *spiritual* restore such an one in the spirit of meekness." Carnal handling of problems only makes matters worse (I Corinthians 6:4). Only the spiritually mature should discipline and this should be done in the Eldership. Parents generally discipline their children and not the children the parents. So the spiritual parents in the Church should do the same. Paul, as a father in the Lord, asked the Corinthians whether he should come with a rod of correction or not (I Corinthians 4:15-21).

3.   The Whole Church

Sometimes the whole Church attests to the discipline of a person. This is confirmed by a study of Matthew 18:15-20.

"Tell it to the Church . . . if he neglect to hear the Church . . . ."

"When ye are come together . . . deliver such an one over to Satan for the destruction of the flesh, so the spirit can be saved." (I Corinthians 5:4).

"Which was inflicted of many . . ." (II Corinthians 2:6).

Thus the man was disfellowshiped or excommunicated. This was to be respected by the whole Church. The only contact was to see him come to repentance and restoration; otherwise they were not to eat with him at all.

G.   Principles of Disciplinary Judgment

Certain principles should be evidenced in any area of Church discipline. It should be remembered that the whole purpose of discipline is restorative.
Discipline should be administered:

1.   By and according to the Word (John 12:47, 48; II Corinthians 11:3; Revelation 2:2; Matthew 24:11; II Peter 2:1).

2.   Balanced with the mercy of God (James 2:12, 13; Luke 17:2-4; Leviticus 19:17).

3.   In truth and righteousness (Zechariah 7:9-10; Ezekiel 44:17-24; Isaiah 32:1, 16; 16:5; Psalms 122:5; 101:1). Mercy and truth should meet together; righteousness and peace kiss each other, in Divine balance.

4.   In Divine love (I Corinthians 13; Revelation 3:19).

5.   In a spirit of meekness and humility, realizing ones own humanity (II Timothy 2:25; Galatians 6:1; Ephesians 6:4).

Discipline without love and meekness creates rebellion. Discipline without punishment generally is ineffective, producing little or no results.

H. Scriptural Procedures in Discipline

Leadership cannot act rashly in Church discipline and expect God to back it up as His discipline.

1. Private Discipline

Most discipline should be done on a private level. Nobody generally airs their "dirty linen" to the neighbours. If the transgression or fault is private, then it should be dealt with privately.

How much trouble would be averted in the Church amongst members if the first basic principle of Matthew 18:15-20 was followed through. "Go to your brother . . ." Note the emphasis on "Go to him . . ." in these Scriptures (Matthew 5:24; 18:15; Luke 17:3, 4; Leviticus 19:17).

2. Public Discipline

Matthew 18:15-20 lays out the clearest order for reconciliation between members of the Church and excommunication if they stubbornly and willfully refuse to be reconciled and hear the Church. Note the steps laid out by Jesus for this.

a. First Step and Admonition

If there is any offence between brothers (or sisters) "Go to him *alone* . . ."
This involves:

★ A right attitude and manner of approach;

★ The right words said in the right spirit;

★ A genuine desire for reconciliation with the brother;

★ Acceptance of the person you want reconciliation with.

(Matthew 18:15; Galatians 6:1; Proverbs 25:9; 16:28; Matthew 5:24; Luke 17:3-5). You are to go to him ALONE! This is the FIRST and foundational step for reconciliation according to Christ, the Head of the Church, His Body.

b. Second Step and Admonition

After genuinely and honestly and meekly before God and taking the initiative to go to your brother, and he refuses reconciliation, then the Scripture says to take two or three others (Matthew 18:16).
This would involve:

★ Perhaps some of the persons close friends;

★ People he or she has confidence in and trusts;

★ Spiritually mature persons;

★ Persons who have discernment;

★ Persons who also desire to see reconciliation come about.

Read again (Galatians 6:1; Romans 15:14; I Corinthians 4:14; Colossians 3:16).
These two or three witnesses can hear and weigh the whole case, excercising loving discernment, meekness and judgment, with a view to affect reconciliation.

This second admonition is designed to shake the offender and help them see the seriousness of their error and the need to correct it. It is to bring the influence of spiritual members and their admonitions to bear so that the offender will break down his resistance to reconciliation. It also involves showing the offender the next step before going to the Church should he fail to respond to these two steps (Proberbs 25:9-12; 27:5, 6; 16:28).

c. Final Step and Admonition

Matthew 18:17; I Timothy 5:20; I Corinthians 5:13; John 20:23. The final step and admonition is to bring the person who refuses to be reconciled before THE CHURCH! It seems as if the whole local Church should rise up, or various ones, representing the congregation and plead with the person to be reconciled. After hearing the offended alone, hearing the two or three witnesses, and then being brought before the Church, surely he will hear the Church!

This no doubt would involve the ministry of the Church, along with the two or three witnesses, presenting the situation to the congregation. The step here even is to effect a reconciliation. The purpose is not to judge or condemn him, as a trial in court, but to win him. It is not to humiliate him but to reconcile him. How hard the heart must be to refuse these three steps of reconciliation!

"If he neglect to hear . . ." — This is the final sin, not necessarily the one fault originally to be dealt with. It is his REFUSAL TO HEAR his brother, the two or three others, and then his refusal to hear THE CHURCH!

There is no other alternative but the fourth step.

d.   Fourth Step — Excommunication

This step is indeed the last resort, when all else has failed. He has been rebuked before all (cf. I Timothy 5:19-21).

Excommunication now takes place. He is cut off from the local congregation, even as Old Testament people were "cut off" (Exodus 12:15-19; Leviticus 17:4-9; Numbers 19:20).

Even as others were put out of the Synagogue, so this person is put out of the Church (Luke 6:22; John 9:22; 12:42; 16:2). A Jew was excommunicated from the local Synagogue and from the community at large. It was banishment, anathemetized (cursed). The Jews anathemetized Jesus (I Corinthians 12:3). All who love not the Lord Jesus will be anathemetized at Christ's coming (I Corinthians 16:22).

The person here is cast out of the Church, becoming as a heathen, publican and sinner. It is by the authority of the whole Church. God backs it up. Read I Corinthians 5:4; II Corinthians 2:6; I Samuel 2:25.

Here the Church puts away from them that wicked person. There must be unity in the Church. All members are concerned and all must consent to this act. If some do not believe, then division of opinion comes, sympathies arise against the Word of God (I Corinthians 1:10).

This is "binding and loosing" spoken of in the matter of Church discipline. The person is "bound" and cannot be "loosed" until he comes to repentance.

e.   Fifth Step — Repentance/Reconciliation

If the desired discipline works, then the person should come to genuine repentance, confession, reconciliation with the offended person, and public confession and reconciliation in the Church. He is then "loosed" and restored to favour as before.

I.   Biblical Effects of Discipline

Having covered rather fully the area of discipline we note some of the things that happen in discipline.

1.   Unrepentant persons are excommunicated from the Church and treated as heathen, or publican or sinner. They are bound until loosed by the Church (Matthew 18:15-20).

2.   The fornicator was turned over to Satan for the destruction of the flesh (I Corinthians 5:3-5).

3.   Ananias and Sapphire died for lying to the Holy Spirit, Peter only declaring it (Acts 5:1-11).

4.   The sorcerer was smitten with blindness for a season for opposing the Gospel of Christ through Paul (Acts 13:6-13).

5. Divisionaries were marked and avoided (Romans 16:16-18).
6. Brothers who are of the number in I Corinthians 5:1-13 were disfellowshiped by the saints.
7. Brothers were walked disorderly were to be withdrawn from, but not treated as enemies (II Thessalonians 3:6-15).
8. Sins are retained against persons until they repent and are reconciled (Mark 2:7; John 20:23; Matthew 18:18; II Corinthians 5:19).

J. **Discipline of Ministry**

The Scripture shows that even the Ministry have to come under discipline. Unless those in leadership who are in error, are dealt with, then those under their charge will be affected by following their leadership.

If there is public knowledge of the Elder's faults, then they should be dealt with and settled in the congregation.

It is important for any congregation to realize that it is GOD who disciplines leadership ministries — NOT the people!

If the people take it into their hands to do it, then God judges the people even though the ministry needs discipline. He says "Touch not the Lord's anointed and do His prophets no harm" (Psalms 105:15).

David would not touch king Saul, as the Lord's anointed, even though Saul was in the wrong (I Samuel 26:9). David respected the office, even though Saul had forfeited the anointing and the Spirit of the Lord. Though David was urged by his men to slay Saul, God used these occasions to test out the heart of David.

Revelation 1-2-3 show that the "angels" are in His hand, upheld, supported by and disciplined by Christ, the Head of the Church.

1. **Touch not the Lord's Anointed**
    a. The stars are in His hand to be disciplined (Revelation 1:20).
    b. The leadership is His anointed to be disciplined by Him (I Chronicles 16:22).
    c. Miriam and Aaron were judged when they touched Moses (Numbers 12).
    d. Korah and his company were judged when they touched Moses and Aaron (Numbers 16). Read also Jude 11.
    e. Nadab and Abihu were judged in death by God as ministry (Leviticus 10:1-3).
    f. God judged Saul in time, not David (I Samuel 26:9-11).
    g. Against eldership receive no accusations without two or three witnesses (I Timothy 5:1, 19-21).
    h. God will judge the shepherds of His people (Jeremiah 23:1-3; Ezekiel 34:1-10).

2. **Divine Sovereignty**

    Sometimes God, in His own sovereignty, deals discipline to His leaders. It was not left to the people to do it.
    a. Nadab and Abihu, sons of Aaron, were Divinely judged (Leviticus 10:1-3).
    b. Miriam was smitten with leprosy, Aaron rebuked by the Lord (Numbers 12).
    c. God allowed Saul to be killed in battle, confirming Samuel's word (I Samuel 28).
    d. Korah and his rebellious company knew Divine discipline (Numbers 16).
    e. God sent the plague on thousands who touched Aaron's priesthood (Numbers 16-17).
    f. Moses and Aaron both missed the promised land, as leadership, under Divine discipline (Numbers 20:12; Psalms 106:30-33).
    g. Ananias and Sapphire were Divinely judged (Acts 5:1-11).

3. **Human Responsibility**

Sometimes God used ministries to deal with ministries; but again, never the people.

a. Nathan reproved David for his sin (II Samuel 12:7). A prophet reproved a king.

b. Samuel, a prophet reproved Saul, a king, for his sin (I Samuel 13:13).

c. The Man of God reproved Eli, the priest (I Samuel 12:27-29).

d. Paul reproved Peter, the apostle (Galatians 2:11-14).

e. Peter, the apostle, speaks to the Eldership (I Peter 5:1-5).

f. Moses reproved Korah and company (Numbers 16).

g. The apostles and elders discussed the doctrinal matters of Jew and Gentile (Acts 15).

h. Prophets were sent to reprove and rebuke kings for their evils in the Old Testament times.

i. John the apostle dealt with Diotrephes (II John 9, 10).

j. Undoubtedly the Eldership tested out the false apostles (Revelation 2:2).

k. Elders are to deal with others when they fail and need rebuke (I Timothy 5:19-21). Eldership comes under great attack, criticism, complaints, etc. But if there is a violation of qualifications of I Timothy 3 and Titus 1, then there should be proper investigation by the authority and it should be dealt with. Otherwise there is loss of respect and authority in the Church. An elder should be rebuked before elders. If it is public, then it should be clarified in the Church. Military leaders experience the great and terrible shame of being "defrocked" in front of their regiment. Elders are to be respected, loved and obeyed, for they are responsible and accountable for the flock of God (Hebrews 13:7, 17, 24).

4. **Ministry and Morals**

Perhaps one of the most devastating areas of breakdown in the ministry is that which pertains to morals. Immorality affects a person, and more especially the ministry, in the following areas of life and should be dealt with according to Scriptural principles; otherwise redemptive restoration cannot be properly effected.

We note some of the important things pertaining to discipline of ministry in the matter of morals.

a. **Morally** — A minister disqualifies himself where there is a breakdown especially in the area of morals. A wife can also disqualify her husband from the ministry by immoral conduct.

b. **Domestically** — If an elder (minister) does not have his own house in order, he cannot rule the house of God. This order and rule involves husband/wife relationships and his children. The husband/wife relationship has to be rebuilt and restored.

c. **Mentally and Emotionally** — Moral breakdowns affect one mentally and emotionally also. The great damage done and the torment of guilt has to be dealt with God's way. This is done by genuine repentance, confession, cleansing and renewal. Rationalizations for the sin cannot be justified or tolerated; otherwise one opens themselves to great deception.

d. **Ethically** — Any minister who fails morally, if he governed by any Scriptural ethics should step down from public ministry for a period of time.

e. **Spiritually** — Moral breakdowns seem to have the most damaging and devastating affect especially in the ministry, as being so much in the public view and held up for an example of a Godly lifestyle. Therefore there needs to be spiritual restoration first of all.

f. **Ecclesiastically** — Because the minister in function is before the Ekklesia, his area of influence is great. Because none of us live to ourselves, but we all affect others there needs to be proper and Scriptural discipline. Otherwise the Church suffers, and we set precedents for all or any other moral breakdowns. The elder that sins should be rebuked before all so that others may fear. These things generally become Church, or public knowledge and therefore should be dealt with Scripturally. This can then cause gossiping and imaginations to cease because sin has been dealt with in a Scriptural manner.

g. **Practically** — General and practical guidelines for restoration would be as follows:

1) Genuine repentance and confession on the part of the guilty, depending on the person(s) involved, and depending whether public or private knowledge.

2) Forgiveness of God and the party(ies) or others involved in the Church, as to the sin and reproach brought on the Name of the Lord, the husband and wife, the family, the leadership and the Church.

3) Disciplinary measures taken by stepping down from public ministry.

4) A period of probation to be determined, giving time for "rebuilding the walls" broken down through immorality, in the various areas above. Clearing away the damage and rebuilding the marriage relationship takes time, but is top priority. God's order is forgiveness, *probation,* then restoration as the plan of redemption through the whole Bible shows.

5) Counselling in an on-going manner through relationship with someone who can minister redemption in a restorative manner.

6) Restoration after suitable probationary period to ministry.

This must not be done in any legalistic or Pharisaical "holier-than-thou" attitude or spirit. It should be done to restore one in a spirit of meekness, considering thyself lest thou also be tempted in the same area.

These guidelines are based on the Qualifications of Eldership as set forth in the Pastoral Epistles (I Timothy 3:1-7; Titus 1:5-9 with I Timothy 5:17-25).

K. Eternal Judgment

There are many things which escape Church discipline and judgment. These will be judged at the Judgment Seat of Christ, or the Great White Throne Judgment.
Note (I Timothy 5:24, 25. Amplified New Testament).

1. The Word of God teaches a future judgment (II Corinthians 5:10-11; I John 4:17; Romans 14:10-12; John 12:47-48; Revelation 11:18).

2. There are two judgments in the Word of God as to eternal judgment.

a. **Judgment for Believers**

This is according to a believers works (I Corinthians 3:11-15; II Corinthians 5:10; I John 4:17; Romans 14:10-12; John 12:47-48).

1) **Threefold aspect of judgment for the believer**

★ Judgment Past — As a sinner at the Cross.

★ Judgment Present — As a son at the table of the Lord (I Corinthians 11:23-34).

★ Judgment Future — As a servant at the Bema Seat of Christ.

2) **Five Crowns as Rewards for believers**

★ Crown of Life (James 1:12; Revelation 2:10).

★ Crown of Righteousness (II Timothy 4:8).

★ Crown of Glory (I Peter 5:2-4).

★ Crown of Rejoicing (I Thessalonians 2:19-20).

★ Crown of Incorruption (I Corinthians 9:25-27; I John 2:28).

b. **Judgment for Unbelievers**

This is also for works. It is judgment at the Great White Throne — Eternal Judgment.

1) God is the perfect Judge. He is incapable of making any errors of judgement because He has all the facts before Him by reason of His essential attributes (Genesis 18:25; Hebrews 12:23; Psalms 89:14; 19:7-8; 94:2; 96:13; 98:9; Jeremiah 11:20; I Peter 1:17).

2) Wicked angels will be judged (II Peter 2:1-3; 3:7; II Peter 2:4-9; Jude 6).

3) Satan will be eternally judged in the Lake of Fire (Revelation 20:1-15).

4) All ungodly will be judged, all who have rejected the Word of God and Christ Jesus. They will be judged by the Word (Psalms 149:1-9; 1:5; 9:7, 16; Revelation 14:7; I Timothy 5:24; Hebrews 9:27; 10:27; Romans 2:5).

This will be eternal judgment — eternal discipline. If men refuse to accept God's discipline unto restoration in Christ, then there is no alternative but to know God's discipline unto damnation for all eternity!

CHAPTER 31

CHURCH STEWARDSHIP AND FINANCE

Introductory:

Both Old and New Testaments teach the believer that God is the Owner, Possessor and Giver of all things to man, and believers, in particular are Receivers and therefore Stewards of all they have. They are responsible and accountable to God for everything (Luke 16:1-13).

The Subject of Stewardship

Stewardship has been defined as "Stewardship is the practice of systematic and proportionate giving of time, abilities, and material possessions, based on the conviction that these are a trust from God to be used in His service for the benefit of His Kingdom. It is a Divine-human partnership, with God the senior partner. It is a way of living; the recognition of God's ownership of one's person, one's powers, and one's possessions and the faithful use of these for the advancement of Christ's Kingdom in this world."

There are five major areas of life that all believers are responsible and accountable for unto God. God desires to develop the Owner-Steward relationship between Himself and His people.

These five areas are:

1. Life — What you have received.)
2. Time — What you have been allotted.) These have been given.
3. Talents — What you have been given to use.) They are not owned.
4. Possessions — What has been entrusted to you.)
5. Finance — What you have laboured for.)

GOD is the Giver, the Possessor, and the Owner, and the Rewarder.

MAN is the Receiver, Steward, responsible and accountable to God. He may use, abuse and lose what he has been entrusted with. The faithful will be rewarded. Man is A TRUSTEE!

The Parable of the Unjust Steward (in Luke 16:1-13), given by Christ to His disciples is a challenge to faithful stewardship. This especially has to do in the area of finance. We note some of the important lessons from the Parable.

A. The word "steward" comes from the Greek word "*oikonomon*" ("*Oikos*" = House; "*Nemo*" to distribute or dispense). It means "one charged with the administration of the affairs of the true owner." A Steward is a Manager. The believer is a steward, managing what God has given into his care.

B. The Steward in the Parable was accused of wasting His master's goods, squandering his master's possessions. As the pay-master he assigned to each member of the household their duties, giving to them out of the household store (verse 1).

C. The Steward was called to give an account of what he was doing with his master's goods (verse 2). All believers will be called to the Day of Accountability in due time.

D. This Steward forfeited his position (verse 3). Believers can forfeit their position both now and in eternal glory.

E. The displaced Steward went to his Lord's debtors and reduced all their debts (verses 5, 6). He reduced the oil and wheat and unjustly altered their figures.

F. The Lord, however, commended the unjust Steward (verse 8). This was NOT because of his action, which was unjust, but because of his *wisdom,* his shrewdness, concerning money matters.

The Lord's comment was that "the children of this age are *wiser* than the children of light." This should not be so. The Steward did this wise but unjust act when he forfeited his position. By this act he gained friends who received him into their habitations after he had lost his position.

So the believer should make wise and just use of the unrighteous mammon (i.e., money, riches, and temporal possessions of this life [Chaldee word]). If he cannot do this, how can he be trusted with the true riches; those eternal, spiritual and incorruptible riches?

How then can a believer make to himself "friends of the unrighteous mammon?" (verse 9). Only by a wise and just use of the finance (or possessions) that God entrusts to him.

The key word is FAITHFULNESS (verses 9-13). A Steward must be FAITHFUL (I Corinthians 4:1, 2). The application of the Parable may be summarized as follows:

Rich Man & Steward	**— God & The Believer**
Earthly lord and land-owner	— Heavenly Lord, Master, Owner of all
Steward, unbeliever, child of world	— Steward, believer, child of light
Wasting his master's goods	— Waste or use wisely God's goods?
Shrewd, wise, altered debts	— Unrighteous mammon (finance)
Unrighteous mammon, unjust handling	— Faithful and wise use of mammon
Failed in position	— Fail in death
Made friends by wise, wrong action	— Souls benefited by money used for the Gospel
Received him into earthly habitations	— Received into heavens habitations

Thus stewardship is "one charged with the administration of the affairs of the true owner." It is a Divine trust, a Divine-human partnership and sharing. We are stewards rather than owners.

Therefore it is important to recognize the difference between:

★ OWNERSHIP — God is the Owner of all things (Genesis 14:19, 22; Psalms 24:1; 50:1-12; 68:19; 89:11; Haggai 2:8).

Without heaven's blessing, earth would perish. Rain, sunshine, dew, seasons of blessing all depend on His hand (Genesis 1:11; Job 5:10; Matthew 5:45; Acts 17:28; I Chronicles 29:14). When we give to God we are but giving back what comes from Him. Of thine own have we given Thee.

★ STEWARDSHIP — We are but Stewards, not Owners. As such we have responsibility, and accountability to God for all we are given, all we have and what we do with it (Matthew 25:14-30; Luke 19:11-26).

A. Warnings Against Covetousness

There are some interesting facts in the Scriptures concerning money. Money is a very sensitive area. What is there about the subject of money that often causes people to react. The answer is found in I Timothy 6:7-10. The LOVE of money is the root of all evils. It can drown men in destruction and perdition.

Money in itself is not evil. But the LOVE of it is. Judas Iscariot, the son of perdition, coveted after money and perished. He never lived to spend the money he sold out Christ for.

Note the following:

1. The Gospels contain more warnings against money and its misuse than any other subject.

2. One verse in every four verses in Matthew, Mark and Luke deals with money.

3. One verse in every six in the New Testament as a whole deals with or has reference to money is one way or another.

4. Almost half of the Parables of Jesus have reference to money in one way or another; generally warnings against covetousness.

5. The first sin in Israel which brought defeat to the whole camp concerned a Babylonish garment, a wedge of silver and gold, the symbol of world finance (Joshua 7:20, 21).

6. The first apostle to fall was Judas. It was over the love of money. He sold Christ for money that he never lived to spend (John 12:4-8; 13:27-29; Acts 1:25; Matthew 26:14-16; 27:3-10).

7. The first sin in the early Church concerned the giving of money to the Lord. Note how Satan entered the scene of glory in the early Church over money, where the spirit of giving was upon the people (Acts 5:1-10).

8. The sin of "Simony" concerns money and seeking to buy the gifts of God with it (Acts 8:14-24).

9. It is worthy to note that two New Testament words whose numerical value equal 666 are Wealth and Tradition. This is the number of the world system. The power to buy or sell is finally connected with it (Revelation 13:16-18).

The Money Microbe

Walter David Cavert in "*Remember Now . . .*" provided an interesting article called the "Money Microbe". It read as follows:

"Two scientists made a series of bacteriological experiments on paper money after it had been in circulation a short time. Nineteen hundred germs of various kinds were found on the average bank note, and one microbe was discovered which was peculiar to paper money in that it had never been found anywhere else. It seemed to thrive and multiply only on the kind of paper out of which money is made.

So it might be said, by way of a parable, that there is a money microbe. Whatever may be true of real microbes, there is a germ called covetousness, which often goes with money and is a deadly peril to the soul. "Thou shalt not covet" was the tenth commandment of Moses, and Jesus emphasized it by saying, "Take heed, and beware of covetousness." The person who is envious of the riches of others or allows his thoughts to be dominated by the desire for gain has been infected by the money microbe and is in danger of becoming sick with a deadly disease.

God never asks us to do what He Himself does not do. God Himself is the great Giver though He is Lord and Owner of all things, He gives Himself and all things to bless His creations. God the Father gave His Son (John 3:16). The Son loved and He gave Himself (Ephesians 5:23-27). The Spirit loves and gives gifts (I Corinthians 12:1-9).

God is Love and LOVE GIVES!

God is the great BLESSER. Upon obedience, God blesses man with all good things. (Deuteronomy 16:10-17; 28:1-14; Matthew 6:33; Malachi 1:8-12; Philippians 4:19).

B. Old Testament Financial Order

The Old Testament, especially as it relates to Israel, "The Church in the Wilderness" (Acts 7:38), sets forth many patterns and shadows of the New Testament Church.

★ The pattern of *worship* is seen in the Tabernacle of Moses, and David and the Temple of Solomon order.

★ The pattern of *Priesthood* is set out in the Aaronic and Levitical Priesthood order.

★ The pattern of *redemptive truth* is set forth in the Feasts of the Lord.

★ The pattern of *Covenantal relationship* is set out in the Covenants.

And so it is when it comes to financial matters and the support of the Lord's ministry and the house of the Lord. It is a matter that very few believers and Churches have studied. It is the only financial system that God ordained and blessed, and yet many have failed to see it and the Divine principles therein.

★ The pattern of *Church finance* therefore is seen in the Old Testament Scriptures, especially amplified in Israel. Then the basic principles are carried over into the New Testament Church, which arose out of the Old Testament Church.

In studying God's order in Israel we find that their giving was covered in two areas called "Tithes and Offerings" (Malachi 3:8).

We consider these two areas as in Israel and see how the principle of such overflows into the New Testament Church.

1. **Tithes**

    The word "tithe" simply means "tenth". Tithing is actually a teacher to give. One hundred percent belongs to the Lord. He gives us 9/10ths to use, but the first tenth He says is His. "The tithe is HOLY to the Lord" (Leviticus 27:30-33). The tithe is really not ours to give. It is already God's. He has claimed it as the firstfruits of our increase. So in tithing we are giving to God what is already His.

    a.   **Abraham — A Tither**

         The first account we have of tithing is in Genesis 14:17-20. Abraham tithed to Melchisedek in connection with receiving the bread and wine. We note some of the outstanding thoughts connected with this scene.

         1)   Abraham is the Father of all who believe (Romans 4).

         2)   Abraham gave tithes to Melchisedek, Priest of the Most High God; Tithes of all.

         3)   Abraham gave tithes before the Law Covenant existed. This was in connection with the Abrahamic Covenant. It was a specific amount.

         4)   Melchisedek gave Abraham communion of bread and wine.

         5)   Melchisedek is King of Righteousness and King of Peace (Hebrews 7).

         6)   Melchisedek blessed Abraham of the Most High God, the Possessor of heaven and earth.

         Thus the first mention we have of tithing in the Scriptures is with Abraham and Melchisedek.

         The Books of Romans and Hebrews together show that believers are the seed of Abraham and that we are under the Order of Melchisedek Priesthood, as kings and priests with Christ Jesus. Also the Gospels show Jesus Christ, our King Priest establishing the Communion of bread and wine at the New Covenant table. Thus we share in the bread and wine and give our tithes to Melchisedek, Jesus Christ, who lives in the power of an endless life.

         Tithing was *before* the Law, not of the Law. His Priesthood abides forever. Can we claim to be children of Abraham and claim the communion and the Priesthood of Jesus and still neglect to give tithes in this covenantal relationship?

    b.   **Jacob — a Tither**

         The Lord says "I am the God of Abraham, Isaac and Jacob." The next account we have of tithe giving is in Jacob. This was in connection with Bethel, the House of God. We note some of the salient points (Genesis 28:10-22).

         1)   Jacob has a God-given dream of a ladder reaching from heaven to earth.

         2)   The angels of God ascend and descend on the ladder.

         3)   The God of Covenant confirms the Abrahamic promises to Jacob.

         4)   Jacob anoints the Bethel Stone, calling it the House of God.

         5)   Jacob makes a vow to give tithes of all he receives from the Lord.

         6)   Jesus interprets the Ladder to be Himself, "the Son of Man" (John 1:51).

         Thus Jacob has a visitation from God and undoubtedly kept his *vow of tithes*. We see how God blessed him in all his life.

         We note also that this vow of tithing was before the giving of the Law. Those who accept the God of Jacob, as the God of Abraham, will also keep their vow of tithes and give back to the Lord a tenth of all He gives them. This is done at Bethel, the House of God. Angels, as ministering spirits, minister to the heirs of salvation, even as they did to Jacob (Hebrews 1:13, 14).

c. **Israel — Tithers**

The fullest revelation of the tithing order is found in the nation of Israel. The tithing here, though not of the Law, was confirmed under the Law. But it should be remembered that tithing did not originate under the Law. Tithing was *before the Law,* but *confirmed under the Law!*

Under the tithing system in Israel then we see the following:

1) **The First or Lord's Tithe** — Leviticus 27:30-33; Numbers 18:21; Nehemiah 10:37.

   The 12 tribes tithed to the Lord and this tithe of the people's income was given to the Priestly Tribe of the Levites.

   Numbers 18:24-32 needs to be studied carefully for this. The Levites had no inheritance in the land but were kept by the tithes of the people. Twelve tribes tithed to the one tribe.

   This was called the Lord's Tithe (Leviticus 27:30-33).

   It went to the Levites, the ministers of the congregation (Numbers 18:21-24).

   The person in Israel had no control over it, received none of it back except in the services of the priests, who used it for their livelihood.

   In the restoration of the Temple after Babylon, the tithes were again given to the Levites (Nehemiah 10:37).

   Israel was to tithe *all the increase* each year (Deuteronomy 14:22).

   If any used their tithes then they were to pay 20% or 1/5th interest to the Lord for using His money (Leviticus 27:30).

2) **The Tithe of the Tithe** — Numbers 18:25-32.

   Not only did the 12 tribes tithe to the Levitical or Priestly tribe, this tribe in turn paid a "tithe of the tithe". It taught that the ministry were as obligated to tithe as were the people. How can ministers teach others to tithe and give if they themselves do not tithe or give?

   Thus Aaron and his sons received tithes (type of the fivefold ministry of Ephesians 4:9-11).

   In times of restoration from Babylon the tithe of the tithes was given to sons of Aaron also (Nehemiah 10:38, 39). Tithes were put in chambers.

   The principle is that tithe of the tithes from local Churches may be kept aside for visiting ministries (Cf. I Corinthians 9:7-14 with I Timothy 5:17-19; Nehemiah 13:10).

3) **The Second Tithe** — Deuteronomy 12:5-14, 17; 14:22-26.

   This second tithe was like a budgeting system. This tithe was for the individual himself and for his household to cover expenses at the national times of Feasts. This was for his own and his family's spiritual development. It consisted of the tenth of their seed in the field; corn, wine and oil, and herds and flocks (Deuteronomy 14:22, 23).

   It was to be brought to the place of God's choice, to His house and not to be consumed in their own homes (Deuteronomy 12:5, 17).

   The whole purpose was so that they could attend the Feasts of the Lord, not empty handed, but be able to *rejoice* and *worship* God with these tithes. They ate of these tithes with great joy (Deuteronomy 12:7, 12, 18; 14:26). The principles of giving, worship, rejoicing and fear of the Lord are seen here (Deuteronomy 14:23).

This second year tithe could also involve ministering to the Levites again, as well as family needs at festival occasions.

4) **The Third Tithe** — Deuteronomy 14:28, 29; 26:12-14.

Every third year a tenth of the person's increase during that time was to be given to the Levite, the stranger, the fatherless, and the widow. It was stored away and at the end of every three years it was brought out and distributed to these above. It was "hallowed" because it was devoted to this purpose (Deuteronomy 26:13). The reason for this tithe was so they would not forget the ones in need. God blessed their obedience (Deuteronomy 14:29).

It was like a "saints relief fund" set aside for those out of work, sick, widows, orphans, etc. (I Timothy 5:10; Acts 11:29; II Corinthians 9; Romans 15:26). Read also Acts 4:31-37; 6:1; 2:44-47; Galatians 2:10; Dueteronomy 15:7-11; I Timothy 5:3-16; Amos 4:4, 5; Proverbs 3:9-10.

5) **The Government Tithe** — I Samuel 18:10-22.

When Israel chose to have a king over them, they imposed upon themselves another tithe. It was a self-imposed tax-tithe for the upkeep of the kingdom, and the support of his revenue (II Kings 23:35). Taxation was exacted by the king. It was a self-inflicted tithe above other tithes in their desire to have a king like the other nations about them.

6) **The Tithe of the People** — Nehemiah 11:1-2.

In the times of restoration from Babylon they took a tithe of the people to be used in the Lord's work at Jerusalem.

This is a good principle for any local Church to have.

In times of religious decline, the people neglected to pay tithes and robbed God in tithes and offerings. In times of restoration, the tithes and offerings were always restored and God blessed the people accordingly.

Hezekiah encouraged the restoration of tithes and offerings (II Chronicles 31:4-12; Nehemiah 10:37; 12:44; 13:5, 11; Acts 3:19-21; Malachi 3:7-12). Tithing dropped off always in spiritual declension but always rose in spiritual awakenings.

God blessed His people so much in the six years of labour in the land that it was enough to carry them over the seventh, the eighth and into the ninth year (Leviticus 25:21, 22).

2. **Offerings**

Not only did the Israelites tithe, they also gave offerings to the Lord, which were above and beyond their tithes. The secret of it all was THE BLESSING of the Lord. If a person does not give or pay tithes he is robbing God, for the tithe is not ours to give. It is already the Lord's. But if a person gives tithes and no offerings he is not giving anything to God at all. God says "Prove Me now . . ." As Israel obeyed God there was abundant blessing.

We could divide Israel's giving into seven groupings as follows:

a. Burnt Offerings (Leviticus 1:1-3; Mark 10:21; Luke 19:8). Symbol of sacrifice of oneself.

b. Sacrifices of Thanksgiving (II Samuel 24:24; Luke 2:24; 17:16; I Peter 2:5-9; Romans 12:1-2; Hebrews 13:13-16).

c. Heave Offerings (Numbers 18:8-29). Tithe of the tithes.

d. Vows — Conditional promise (Deuteronomy 12:6, 11; Psalms 22:25; I Samuel 1:11; Acts 18:18; Ecclesiastes 5:4, 5).
Read also Leviticus 22:18-20; Psalms 50:14; 116:14, 18.

e. Gifts (Leviticus 23:38).

f. Firstfruits (Exodus 34:22, 26; Nehemiah 10:37; Proverbs 3:9, 10; Romans 8:23; I Corinthians 15:20, 23).

g. Freewill offerings (Leviticus 23:38; Deuteronomy 16:10; Exodus 36:1-7; I Chronicles 29:9-19; Malachi 3:8-12).

Note — It is worthy to note that tithes were not used for the building of material Sanctuaries. The Tabernacle of Moses, and Temple of Solomon were built from the freewill offerings of the people.

★ Tabernacle of Moses (Exodus 25:2; 35:5, 21-29; 36:6).

★ Temple of Solomon (I Chronicles 29).

★ Restored Temple (Ezra 1:6; 2:68; 7:15).

These offerings were given to the Lord, to the poor, the widows, orphans, the Levites, the Priests, as well as the material needs of the Sanctuary of the Lord.

Such was the spirit of giving in the building of the Tabernacle of Moses the people had to be restrained from giving.

There is a ministry of giving (Romans 12:8; I Corinthians 13:3; Acts 10:2, 4, 31; Proverbs 19:17; Matthew 6:1-4; Proverbs 28:27; Luke 6:30-38). Israel was to give of their substance to the poor. God said the poor would always be there amongst them. This would be a test of both the rich and the poor in the matter of giving and receiving. (Proverbs 11:24; Deuteronomy 15; 26:12-15; 16:10-12; Luke 12:13-21).

C. Old Testament Support of the Ministry

We answer the question concerning what happened to the tithes in the Old Testament. Who received them? This has already been noted so we summarize the matter here.

1. Melchisedek, the King Priest received tithes of Abraham (Genesis 14:18-20). Christ is our Melchisedek, so tithes are given to Him (John 8:52, 59; Hebrews 6:20; 7). Abraham was blessed of Melchisedek in tithing.

2. The Priestly Tribe of Levi received tithes of the 12 tribes and ministered in their priestly duties at the tabernacle and to the people accordingly. They were told not to forsake the Levite (Numbers 18:25-32; Nehemiah 10:38, 39).

   Note that the writer of Hebrews says that although Levi *received tithes,* they also *paid tithes* in Abraham to Melchisedek for he was yet in the loins of his father Abraham when Melchisedek met him (Hebrews 7).

3. The Levitical Tribe also paid a tithe of the tithes to Aaronic Priesthood, or the High Priestly household (Numbers 18:21-24; Hebrews 7:5).

Thus the tithes were strictly for the ministry — no one and nothing else! This was God's principle in the Old Testament, under Mosaic and Abrahamic Covenants. Is it any less under the New Covenant? The answer is no, for the New Covenant was in the Abrahamic Covenant and typified also under the Old or Mosaic Covenant.

The Levites took tithes of their own brethren according to the Law.

The Levites had no inheritance in the land (Numbers 18:20, 24; Deuteronomy 10:8, 9).

They were set aside over the Tabernacle and for the ministry of the 12 tribes (Numbers 1-2-3; Deuteronomy 18:1-8; II Chronicles 15:3).

They were to teach the Law of the Lord (Deuteronomy 33:8, 10; Nehemiah 10:37; 12:44; 13:5-14).

The Levites were given cities and houses to dwell in. These were not sold or rented to them but given to them (Numbers 35:1-8; Luke 10:1-9; Mark 10:28-30).

This was the Levitical principle of support. God originally took the nation to be a kingdom of priests, but then used the tribe of Levi to be the priestly tribe (Exodus 19:1-6; Numbers 1-2-3). All believers are priests, but God chooses some to be ministries to the priestly Body, the Church, which supports them as possible.

D. **The Storehouse**

The Lord through Malachi told the people to bring the tithes into "the storehouse" (Malachi 3:8-10). We ask: What and where is the storehouse? Where did this originate? It certainly was not at Mt Sinai. Tithes were brought to the Tabernacle and to the priesthood.

We note the Lord's command concerning the tithes.

1. **Brought to the Place where His Name was recorded** — Deuteronomy 12.

    God told Israel to bring their tithes, offerings, freewill offerings, sacrifices and firstfruits, etc., to the place where His Name would be recorded. This was at the Tabernacle of the Lord.

    God's tabernacle and temple now is Christ. It is in Him where God's name is recorded. We bring our tithes to Him (John 1:14-18; 2:20-21).

    Then again, the Church is now God's Temple, so we bring our tithes to the Church where His Name dwells (Matthew 18:18-20; I Corinthians 6:16; Deuteronomy 12:5-14).

2. **The Storehouse**

    It was under King Hezekiah that the storehouse originated. This storehouse was the temple of the Lord. Read II Chronicles 31.

    Under Hezekiah there was an awakening in Israel and a return to the giving of tithes and offerings for the ministry.

    Note how this was done in order to distribute to the ministry everywhere, not just the ones ministering about the temple.

    a. The Levites themselves had to minister and disburse the tithes (verses 12-19). The ones who brought them did not control the tithes or dispensing of them.

    b. The tithes were not rationed or percentaged out (verse 10). All had plenty at the temple to meet their needs. The temple was used as a storehouse for surplus tithes (cf. Deuteronomy 24:4; I Corinthians 9:9, 10).

    c. The whole purpose was that the Levites might have food to eat and be encouraged to minister the Law of the Lord (verses 2, 4). This would provide "meat in My house" (Malachi 3:8-10). Tithes were used, not locked in treasury or account but for the Levites.

    d. Note the number of ruling Levites over the tithes and the number over the freewill offerings (verses 12-15). Compare with the Book of Acts and early Church history.

    Thus the Temple, the house of the Lord, where the priests and Levites ministered the Word of the Lord was the storehouse where people brought their tithes and offerings unto.

    The fulfilment is seen in the New Testament by bringing our tithes and offerings to the place where we are spiritually fed, so that the ministry may study the Word of the Lord to feed us therewith.

    In the temple there were chambers of stores for the tithes and offerings from which the priests and Levites could draw.

    The restored temple likewise had chambers for the tithes (Nehemiah 13:10-14; 12:44).

E. **Blessing or Cursing** — Malachi 3:8-10.

Blessing or cursing automatically follows tithing and offering to the Lord. It is what God says that counts, not our opinions of it. Those who say they cannot afford to tithe really cannot afford NOT to tithe. Man cannot afford not to pay income tax, otherwise there is greater debt to be paid. God follows the same principle. It is not for Himself, but His laws for your blessing that are at stake. God can make the $9 go further than the $10 if we do not rob Him of His tithe. In Haggai's time they put "money into a bag with holes in it" (Haggai 1). With what measure we meet, it will be measured to us. Give and it shall be given, is a Divine principle (Luke 6:38).

The curse does not come without a cause (Proverbs 26:2). The cause for the curse often is lack of paying tithes, the sin of robbing God.

★ The Lord says He changes not. Some seek to change God and teach that tithing is no longer for today. The Lord does not change. This is placed relative to the Scripture on tithing.

   Christ Jesus has an unchanging priesthood, and is the same yesterday, today, forever (Hebrews 13:8).

★ Israel was accused of robbing God, in tithes and offerings. No thieves can inherit the kingdom of God (I Corinthians 6:10).

★ Ignorance was no excuse. Wherein have we robbed Thee? Pled ignorance.

★ They were cursed with a curse, even the whole nation. The cause was robbing God.

★ Tithes to be brought to God's storehouse. Not sent to the poor, overseas, etc. Offerings were for that need. The storehouse is the place where I am spiritually fed and cared for by the ministry.

★ There would be meat in God's house. i.e. Spiritual food. The ministers could tread out the corn to feed the people.

★ God says to prove Him as to His rewards and blessings for tithers and givers.

★ The blessings would be on the land. The devourer (Satan) would be rebuked if they would give to God what is His.

   Tithing honours God (Proverbs 3:9, 10). Honour the Lord with the firstfruits of thy substance, so shall thy barns be filled with plenty and presses with new wine.

F. New Testament Financial Order

It should be remembered that the early believers were mostly converts from the Old Covenant Church. They already knew the principles of tithes and offerings, so these things did not have to be re-taught. They continued the same principles. The principle of tithes and offerings was not "nailed to the cross". They continued to do as they had under the Mosaic Covenant in principle. For, tithes and offerings were *before* the Mosaic Covenant, but amplified more so under it. The New Covenant continues the Abrahamic Covenant in Christ.

The Lord prophesied of the New Covenant (Jeremiah 31:31-34; Hebrews 8; II Corinthians 3:3-14). Now if tithing had originated under the Old Covenant, and the Old Covenant was abolished, done away, cancelled, then we could truly say that tithing was abolished. But tithing was under Abraham and the only priesthood he knew about, which was Melchisedek.

The believer is under the New Covenant, and the Melchisedek Priesthood and is the seed of Abraham through Christ, thus tithing continues in the New Covenant community. We note then what Jesus and Paul taught about tithes and offerings.

1. Jesus Taught Tithing

Jesus commended the Pharisees for tithing of all they did tithe, but condemned them for their omissions of weightier matters of mercy, judgment and faith (Matthew 23:23).

Jesus said these things we ought to have done and not to leave the other undone (Luke 11:42; 18:12). The Pharisee paid tithes of all. He was not condemned for this but for his hypocritical attitude. Our righteousness should EXCEED the righteousness of the Pharisees (Matthew 5:20; Luke 18:12). That is, exceed tithing as well as other things they did. It must be of the heart.

We are to render to Caesar what belongs to him and render to God what belongs to Him.

The tithe is already God's. Tax belongs to Caesar (Luke 20:25).

It is possible that the "alms for the poor" was an alllusion to the third tithe (Matthew 6:1-4).

2. **Jesus Taught Giving**

Jesus told us to lay up treasure in heaven (Matthew 6:19-21).

Jesus commended the widow for she gave all her living in these two mites (Luke 21:1-4). The rich still had much left and never missed what or how much they gave. The widow had nothing left, she gave all she had. Jesus still sits over against the treasury today in spirit. He sees who gives, how people give, what they give and why they give (Mark 12:38-44).

He said give and it shall be given to you, according to the measure you give (Luke 6:38). Mary gave of her ointment and it sent forth a swell-smelling savour (Mark 14:1-11). Jesus taught that it was more blessed to give than to receive (Acts 20:25). The Lord told the rich young ruler to sell all he had, give it to the poor and to follow him. Perhaps this is an allusion to the third year tithe again where the poor and the orphans, the widows, the strangers, and needy had their needs met (Matthew 19:6).

The Law was a schoolmaster to bring us to Christ. The tithe is a teacher that all we have is the Lord's. The tithe is a teacher to be a giver (Galatians 3:24).

3. **Hebrews Taught Tithing**

Assuming that Paul wrote Hebrews, tithing is confirmed again in this Epistle. In Hebrews 7 we have the matter of tithing brought in. It is in connection with Abraham, Melchisedek, the Levites receiving and paying tithes, and then the fact that Christ lives in the power of an endless life and receives tithes.

From there Hebrews 7 deals, as Hebrews 6, with the Abrahamic and the New Covenants. Tithes cannot be separated from Covenantal relationship. This is seen in the Abrahamic, Mosaic and New Covenants and their respective Priesthoods.

Paul emphasizes the fact that the Melchisedek Priesthood is ETERNAL and must be supported by the children of Abraham (Hebrews 6:20; 7:1-11, 17, 21).

The Levitical Priesthood (which was under the Law) was commanded to take tithes of their brethren, though they came out of the loins of Abraham (verse 5). It proves that, though we come out of the loins of Abraham, we also are obligated to give tithes (Romans 4:16). Melchisedek had commandment to take tithes of Abraham. If Abraham gave tithes, then his natural and spiritual seed should continue to give tithes to this Priesthood since it is now replacing the Aaronic Priesthood (verses 9-12).

Would God require tithing under this priesthood at the first, then discontinue it now when Christ is after that same order of Melchisedek? Being under grace does not lessen man's obligations, but increases it.

Jesus as Melchisedek:

★   Ministers the Bread and Wine (Communion).

★   Blesses and reveals His Name and Priesthood.

★   Receives tithes as a priest forever.

In Christ we have communion eternally in remembrance of His redemptive work (Matthew 26:26-28; Luke 22:30). We will eternally be giving to God of all He ever gives to us. Abraham is our father and we follow in his steps of faith and obedience.

4. **Paul Taught Tithing**

Paul also confirmed the tithing principle in I Corinthians 9:1-14. He shows that even under the Old Covenant the ones who served at the altar ministered and were supported by the things of altar. He uses the Law to establish the truth that the ministers should also, as the Levites, live of the Gospel that they minister. He fully supported the fact that the Levites were supported by the tithes of the Israelites who brought sacrifices to the altar and says that the Old Testament principle is applicable to the New Testament Church also.

He says of the offerings of the Philippians that they were like a sweet-smelling savour and well pleasing to God (Philippians 4:10-19).

5. **Paul Taught Giving**

I Corinthians 16:1-4. Concerning the collection for the relief of the saints Paul also taught that these should be on the first day of the week, as God had prospered them. This may have been an allusion to the third tithe for the poor. Paul taught giving weekly, systematically, proportionately, cheerfully.

In II Corinthians 8-9 we have the most outstanding teaching of Paul in the matter of giving. The Macedonian Church out of deep poverty had given joyfully beyond their ability. They first gave themselves to the Lord, then of their substance. Note Luke 8:1-3.

G. Giving in the Early Church

It should be remembered that the early converts were mainly from Jewish Synagogues and from the Temple order of the Mosaic Covenant. They knew the truth of tithes and offerings and the principles of such continued into the New Covenant. This was because it was really of the Abrahamic Covenant.

★ They laid the money at the apostles feet and this was distributed as was needed (Acts 4:32-37).

★ First sin and judgment was over money withheld in deceptive giving (Acts 5:1-11).

★ Saints relief was sent according to ability (Acts 11:27-30). These were gifts for the poor (Romans 15:25-29; Galatians 2:10; Acts 20:33-35).

★ The widows had been neglected in the daily ministrations (Acts 6:1). These had been possibly taken care of in Temple services previously.

★ The widows of certain qualifications were supported by the Church (I Timothy 5:1-16; I Kings 17:8-16).

★ We must communicate to the saints of our goods (Hebrews 13:15, 16; II Corinthians 8:11).

★ They had all things in common (Acts 4:34; Matthew 25:40; 10:40-42).

★ Some have a ministry of giving in the Body (Romans 12:8; Luke 6:34-38; I Timothy 6:6-11).

H. New Testament Support of the Ministry

Some believe that the ministry should work as every one else does and not be in any way supported by the Church, either by tithes or freewill offerings. The New Testament confirms the fact that, if possible, the ministry should be supported so that they minister freely the Gospel without unnecessary load on them.

All things in the Old Testament were written for types and ensamples and our learning and admonition (Romans 15:4; I Corinthians 11:6, 11).

As the Old Testament Priests and Kings were supported by the tithes and offerings of the people, so it shadows forth also the principle of New Testament of the ministry. Such was not abrogated or nailed to the cross (Colossians 2:14-17).

1. Jesus told the Twelve to trust God for their care and that they were worthy of their support (Matthew 10:7-14; Luke 9:3; 10:1-7; 12:33; Acts 3:6). Note Luke 22:35. They were not to supply their own funds, nor go from house to house.

2. The labourer is worthy of his hire and reward, especially elders labouring in the word and doctrine (I Timothy 5:17-19).

3. The oxen who treads out the corn should not be muzzled. So the minister who treads out the corn of the word should not be muzzled. God does not say this for the oxen's sake but ours (I Corinthians 9:9, 10). The principle of the law is double honour.

4. The one who ministers spiritual things should partake of carnal things (I Corinthians 9:11; Galatians 6:6).

5. Those that minister of the temple live of the things of the altar (I Corinthians 9:13-14).

6. Not to forsake the Levite (Deuteronomy 18:1-2; 10:8, 9; 14:27), but to communicate (Hebrews 13:15, 16; Galatians 6:6).

7. Paul laboured with his hands in tent-making because some in the Church were lazy and busybodies. So he set them an example in ministry, even though he could live of the Gospel (II Thessalonians 3:6-15).

9. Paul received offerings from Philippi as a sweet savour well pleasing to God (Philippians 4:15-19). He took "wages" off other Churches so as not to be chargeable to Corinth (II Corinthians 11:8-9; I Corinthians 4:2; Acts 18:3; 24:17).

    ★ He worked to be an example to others; no work, no food.

    ★ He worked to support the weak (Acts 20:32-35).

    ★ He worked so as to present the Gospel without charge (I Corinthians 9:18).

    ★ He worked to stop the mouths of false ministers and their charges (II Corinthians 11:7-13; 12:12-18. Moffatt's).

In the Old Testament there was such trust that no account was even made of the money because the priests dealt FAITHFULLY with it (II Chronicles 34:9-17; II Kings 22:1-17).
The money was placed in a chest with a hole in it.

The people brought an offering to the courts of the Lord (Psalms 96:8).

Thus if the Old Testament Levitical principle was for the support of the ministry from the 12 tribes, then the same principle is applicable today to the ministry and the Body of Christ..

I. **Principles of Giving**

The principles of giving are seen in these references:

1. Give ourselves to the Lord first (II Corinthians 8:5).

2. Give willingly (II Corinthians 8:3, 12). Also Exodus 25:2; I Chronicles 29:9.

3. Give hilariously, cheerfully (II Corinthians 9:7).

4. Give generously, liberally (II Corinthians 8:2; 9:13). Also James 1:5.

5. Give proportionately (II Corinthians 9:6; 8:14-15).

6. Give regularly (I Corinthians 16:1-2).

7. Give systematically (II Corinthians 9:7).

8. Give lovingly (II Corinthians 8:24).

9. Give thankfully (II Corinthians 8:24).

10. Give as a ministry to the Lord and His saints (II Corinthians 9:11, 12, 13).

11. Give according to ability (Deuteronomy 16:17; Ezra 2:69; Acts 11:29; II Corinthians 8:12).

12. Give as sowing the seed of faith (Galatians 6:7; Proverbs 11:24; Jeremiah 48:10).

13. Give with simplicity (Romans 12:8).

14. Give freely, as you have received (Matthew 10:8).

15. Give as unto the Lord, not unto man (Matthew 6:3, 33).

A LEGAL giver gives because he has to. A LOVING giver because he loves to!
We should not give with impure motives. We should not give:

★ Out of compulsion.

★ Out of obligation.

★ Out of hope of gain.

All giving should be out of love to God for all He is and all He has done for us. We cannot bribe God with anything. Our motive should not be to get from God. Tithing is an acknowledgement that God is the owner of all we have, and we are covenant partners with God.

J. Basic Rules for Church Stewardship

H. A. Kent in ''The Pastor and His Work'' suggests 12 basic rules for Church finance which we adapt here in concluding this chapter.

1. Preach and Teach the Biblical Method of supporting God's work. Do not apologize for it. Worldly methods are taxation, assessments, pew rentals, socials, bazzars, etc. Teach the principle of giving.

2. Encourage regular weekly giving (I Corinthians 16:2). Breaking of bread is on the first day of the week, giving also. Teach people to be systematic givers. For USA keep Tax records. Avoid ''racket schemes'' and wrong motivations in trying to get people to give, such as tax deductions, etc.

3. Have a Budget.

   The Government and business set a budget for spending. So the Church, as God's business can (Luke 14:28).

   a. A budget provides a goal for the Church.

   b. A budget encourages weekly systematic giving to meet it.

   c. A budget eliminates wrong methods of raising finance.

   d. A budget helps the Church plan systematically for the year's program.

   e. A budget helps secure balanced Church programmes.

4. Teach everyone to give, or ''every-member-support'' (I Corinthians 16:2).

5. Teach giving as an act of worship. Worship and offerings are associated (Matthew 2:11).

6. Literature on Biblical principles of finance should be available.

7. Tithing should be the basis of all giving. Old and New Testament confirm this, not as a legal thing. Believers cannot give less than this. Tithing acts as a specific amount, specified by the Lord. It acts as a gauge.

8. Church accounts should be paid promptly. Churches generally ''poor risks'' in the world. This is a bad witness. They will not hear you spiritually if you are not right financially.

9. Beware of excessive indebtedness. Do not overdrive people on finance (Romans 13:8).

10. Should have wise persons to handle the funds of the Lord. i.e., Secretary, with another witness to handle intake of funds; Treasurer, and double signer for checks to handle outflow of funds. Books and accounts should be audited. Church Business meetings yearly also. Precautions and protection in finance so that all suspicion is lifted from anyone handling the Lord's finance.

11. Designated funds in a Church should not be used for other purposes without the consent of the people. People lose confidence otherwise, and this is dishonest.

12. A minister should be an example of a tither and giver. Learn to handle own personal finance or never be able to handle Church finance (II Corinthians 8:5). A minister should not live above his means. He should budget his finance, avoiding great debts. He should be prompt in payment of accounts. He should avoid all shadiness in business. He should not downgrade or jest about giving to God. To do such is to beget a bad mentality in the mind of people.

The local Church is now God's Temple, the Place where His Name is recorded, and God's Treasury (Deuteronomy 12:1-21; 16:1-17; II Chronicles 31; Malachi 3:8-10; Proverbs 3:9, 10; Luke 10:3-11).

Practically then in our times the tithes and offerings may be used in this manner:

★   The local ministry, chief shepherd and elders may be supported by the Lord's tithe as the membership allows.

★   The visiting ministry may be supported by "tithe of the tithe", and not necessarily take up "love-offerings" unless prompted by the Spirit.

★   Overseas ministry (missionary) can be supported out of tithes also.

★   Subsidize by love offerings if needed.

★   Budget tithe can be used for Festivals, Seminars, Camp Meetings for people themselves.

★   Church support by relief fund for widows, orphans, alms. Third year tithe.

★   Freewill offerings for building funds, general expenses.

H. A. Kent says of the building of the Tabernacle of Moses in Exodus 35-39 that all was built by the freewill offerings of the people.

★   It was an offering from the Lord's people, not from the Gentiles about them. The Lord's people, the saints, not the sinners, gave (Exodus 35:5).

★   It was a voluntary offering (Exodus 35:5). They were willing givers.

★   It was an offering according to ability (Exodus 35:5). Not all could bring the same amount of offering; some brought more, some less.

★   It was an offering prompted by zeal, from those whose heart stirred them (Exodus 35:21, 26).

★   It was an offering to the Lord (Exodus 35). Ten times "offering to the Lord" — not Moses.

★   It was a sufficient offering for every need. The people had to be restrained from giving (Exodus 36:5-7).

If such happened under the Old Testament Church in the Wilderness, what should and could happen under the New Covenant Church?

In Conclusion:

Tithing	Tithing	Tithing
Before the Law	Under the Law	Under Grace
Abrahamic Covenant	Mosaic Covenant	New Covenant
Melchisedek Priest Abraham — Gen. 14 Jacob — Gen. 28	Aaronic/Levitical Priest Twelve Trives Levite Tribe Aaron & Sons 1. First or Lord's Tithe 2. Tithe of tithe 3. Second or Festival tithe 4. Third year tithe 5. Tithe — Tax 6. Tithe of people Blessing of Lord Lapse — Devour, Curse Revival — Hezekiah Restoration — Nehemiah 7. Freewill offerings Tabernacle/Temple	Christ our Priest Spiritual Israel Ministry Fivefold Ministry Matthew 23:23 Hebrews 7:5-9 I Corinthians 8-9 Luke 18:12; Matthew 5:17, 18; 11:13 Give all — Matthew 25:23-40 Give weekly — I Corinthians 16:1, 2 The Church, God's House

The secret was THE BLESSING of the Lord (Genesis 41:47-49; Leviticus 25:18-22).

CHAPTER 32

ORDINANCES OF THE CHURCH

Introductory:

The word "ordinance", according to Webster's Dictionary means:

1. A direction or command of an authoritative nature.
2. A custom or practice established by usage or authority.
3. An established religious rite.

Biblically "ordinance" means:

1. Hebrew (SC 2706,2708):
   An enactment, an appointment.
   Thus the Passover and other things were ordinances God ordained in Israel (Exodus 12:14, 17, 24; 13:10; Numbers 18:8; 19:2; Psalms 99:7; Malachi 3:7).
2. Greek (SC 3862, "Paradosis") = precept (I Corinthians 11:2), translated; tradition, ordinances.
   Or, (SC 1378-79, "Dogma") = to prescribe by statute, a law, civil, ceremonial or ecclesiastical. Translated Decree, ordinances (Ephesians 2:15; Colossians 2:14, 15).

There were ordinances of the Law Covenant that were fulfilled and abolished (Hebrews 9:1, 10), nailed to the Cross (Ephesians 2:15; Colossians 2:14, 20), but there are other ordinances that Paul gave to the Churches to keep (I Corinthians 16:2).

Thus we speak of ordinances that are Scriptural and carry on through the cross into the New Covenant Church. Certain traditions that nullify the Word of God are bad (Mark 7:1-13; Colossians 2:8; Galatians 1:14), but there are certain traditions that are good and Scriptural (II Thessalonians 2:15).

The Lord has ordained two major ordinances in His Church, these being Water Baptism and Communion.

Others have been suggested such as Footwashing, Confirmation, Marriage, Dedication of Children and Anointing with Oil. However, these are covered more particularly under "*Pastoral Ministry*."

The importance of Water Baptism and Communion should be manifest in any New Testament Church. For Christ, the Head of the Church, we see Baptism for Himself, at His *inauguration* to ministry (Matthew 3), and then at His *ascension* for the Church's ministry (Matthew 28:19-20).

Then we see *Communion* established just prior to His *crucifixion*, and then after His *resurrection* (Matthew 26:26-28; I Corinthians 11:23-34; John 13:17). Although these things may not be essential to eternal salvation, they are essential to full and complete obedience. Therefore the need of instruction of believers in these ordinances in the Church. Many believers fail to keep these things either through ignorance, lack of teaching and understanding, or plain disobedience feeling that such are not really essential.

Christ, The Head	Ministry 3½ years	The Church, His Body
Baptism Begins Ministry	Communion Crucifixion Close of Ministry	Resurrection

A. Water Baptism

Water Baptism is a very important step in experiencing the First Principles of the Doctrine of Christ (Hebrews 6:1-2). Water Baptism is not merely a form or a meaningless ceremony, but a definite experience in the life of a New Testament Christian, as recorded for us, not only in the Gospels but also in the Acts of the Apostles and the Epistles (Acts 2:38-47).

1. What is the Meaning of the word "Baptize?"

Baptism or baptize means "to dip, to plunge, to immerse" (Mark 1:5; John 3:33; Acts 8:36-39). By definition and usage the word means "to put into or under water so as to entirely immerse or submerge."

2. Why have the Ordinance of Water Baptism?

a. Jesus commanded it (Mark 16:16; Matthew 28:16-20).

b. Jesus Himself was baptized (Matthew 3:13-17).

c. The Apostles commanded it (Acts 2:37-47; 10:44-48).

d. If we love Him, we will keep and obey His commandments (John 14:15).

e. We validate our faith by our obedience to His Word (James 2:17-18).

3. Who is this Ordinance for?

In every Scripture listed below it will be seen that people heard, believed and received the Word, and then they were baptized. Repentance and faith always preceded water baptism. Therefore it is a "believer's baptism."

a. "He that believeth and is baptized . . ." (Mark 16:16).

b. The Samaritans believed and were baptized (Acts 8:12-15).

c. The enuch believed and was baptized (Acts 8:35-38).

d. Peter commanded that the believing Gentiles be baptized (Acts 10:47-48).

e. The Ephesian disciples believed and were baptized (Acts 19:4, 5).
Also read Acts 9:17-18; 16:30-34; 18:8. Water baptism is an essential part of obedience; it is not an optional. To refuse water baptism is to live in disobedience to the revealed Word and will of God. The Word enlightens a believer as to any sin of ignorance if he will be instructed.

4. What are the requirements for Baptism?

a. Hearing and heeding the Word (Acts 2:41; 16:14, 15; 19:5).

b. Conviction (Acts 2:37).

c. Repentance (Acts 2:38).

d. Faith (Mark 16:16; Acts 8:12, 37; 16:31, 33).

e. Obedience (Acts 9:6; 22:16).

f. Confession of Christ's Lordship (Romans 10:9-10). Water baptism involved a confession of faith in the Lordship of Christ (Acts 8:36-39). The pre-requisites for baptism are repentance, faith and confession. (This clearly excludes infant baptism).

g. A clear conscience (Romans 9:1; I Peter 3:18-20).

5. When were people Baptized in New Testament Times?

a. The same day (Acts 2:41; 8:36-38).

b. When they believed (Acts 8:12, 37, 38).

c. The same hour (Acts 16:33).

6. What is the meaning of this Ordinance?

Christian baptism is an outward act of obedience by which the believer fulfills or complete the inward righteousness received through faith in the death and resurrection of Christ.

It is a symbolic yet real spiritual experience. It is baptism into the death, burial and resurrection of the Lord Jesus Christ. By baptism in His death, we are "cut off" from the former life. By immersion into the water we bury the "old man" or the "old life" and by rising up out of the water we experience resurrection to walk in newness of life.
Thus baptism is into His:

1) Death (Romans 6:3, 4, 5, 11).

2) Burial (Colossians 2:12).

3) Resurrection (Colossians 3:1; Romans 6:4, 5).

Baptism is identification with Christ. In salvation we accept Christ's death, burial and resurrection. In water baptism we are identified with this triune act.

1) By baptism we stand as "dead" to the old life and world.

2) By immersion we bury the "dead".

3) By raising up out of the water, we rise to walk in newness of life.

Baptism is an act of obedience, attesting to our repentance and faith (Acts 2:38, 41; 8:37, 38).

Baptism involves the remission of sins and attests to this fact (Acts 2:38; Hebrews 9:22; Acts 10:43; Luke 24:47).

Baptism is symbolic of cleansing from sin (Acts 22:16; Revelation 1:5). Thus we have the witness of the blood and the water.

Baptism has to do with circumcision of the heart (Colossians 2:11, 12; Galatians 6:15; Deuteronomy 10:16; Jeremiah 4:4; Romans 2:28, 29). Circumcision was the sign and seal of the Abrahamic Covenant (Genesis 17:10-12; 21:3). Water baptism is the New Testament circumcision "made without hands" and it is performed by Christ.

Old Testament Circumcision	New Testament Circumcision
1) Circumcision of flesh & blood	Body & blood of Christ in death
2) The rite on the eighth day	Resurrection on the eighth day
3) Invocation of the name	Exalted Name of Lord Jesus Christ

So the believer experiences identification with Christ in His death, then resurrection and the invocation of the Godhead Name on the new nature. Water baptism in its three related parts fulfills the Old Testament rite of circumcision. It is spiritual circumcision, not physical.

7. **Into what Name are we Baptized?**

   a. We are baptized into the Name of the Eternal Godhead; the Name of the Father, Son and Holy Spirit (Matthew 28:18-20).

   b. This finds its fulfilment in the triune Name of the Lord Jesus Christ which is interpreted to be the triune Name of the Godhead (Acts 2:34-36; 4:12; John 5:43; 14:26; Colossians 1:15, 19; 2:9; II Corinthians 5:19; Galatians 3:27; Acts 19:1-6; 10:44-48; I Corinthians 10:1, 2, 6. Amplified New Testament).

8. **Old Testament Types of Water Baptism**

   There are a number of Old Testament pictures which illustrate the truths of water baptism, of which we note a few.

   a. The Spirit moved on the face of the waters in creation and restoration (Genesis 1:1-5; II Corinthians 4:3-6).

   b. The Flood in the Days of Noah showed the whole world baptized in judgment on ungodly flesh and the rising of Noah and family (8) to a newness of life (Genesis 6-7-8).

   c.   Israel was baptized unto Moses in the Cloud and the Red Sea after experiencing deliverance from Egypt world by the power of the blood of the Passover (Exodus 12-13-14; I Corinthians 10:1, 2).

   d.   Israel crossed the baptismal waters of Jordan into the land of promise (Joshua 3, 4 chapters).

   e.   Elijah and Elisha passed through the waters of Jordan to double portion ministry (II Kings 2).

   f.   Naaman, the leper, experienced complete baptism and healing as a Gentile in obedience to the command of Elisha (II Kings 5).

   g.   The axe-head experienced burial and resurrection out of the waters of Jordan (II Kings 6:1-7).

   h.   Jonah also experienced three days and three nights of death, burial and then resurrection to preach to the Gentiles. This became the sign of the Lord (Jonah 1, 2 with Matthew 12:39, 40).

   i   John's baptism of repentance unto faith and the remission of sins pointed to Messiah's baptism and Christian baptism also (Matthew 3:5-12; Mark 1:4, 5; Acts 13:23, 24; 19:1-6).

As there were three steps in the life of the Son of God, so there are for the believer. These steps involved His Birth, His Baptism in Water, His Baptism in the Holy Spirit. So the believer experiences New Birth, Water Baptism and Holy Spirit Baptism. In this we are washed in the *blood*, baptized in *water* and receive the *Spirit,* thus receiving the *three witnesses* — a complete Divine testimony of salvation (I John 5:5-8).

In Summary:

Some practical points for a water baptismal service are appropriate as we summarize the Ordinance of Baptism.

a. **Preparation**

   1)   Spiritual truth and instruction from the Word needed. Symbolic truth.

   2)   Physically

      a)   For believers only. Not "baptismal regeneration" or "mystics powers" but need Genesis 1:1-5 in principle.

      b)   Suitable, appropriate and modest garments for men and women and suitable change rooms with men and women respectively in charge. Deacons/Deaconess suitable for such.

      c)   Watch water, depth, temperature for old or young, etc.

      d)   Suitable time for Church to witness and rejoice with candidates.

      e)   Place, not totally important. Could be ocean, tank, river.

b. **Procedures for Service**

   1)   Appropriate exhortation on ordinance.

   2)   Hymn or suitable songs during baptisms.

   3)   Candidates testify (Acts 8:35-38).

   4)   Upon confession . . . Baptismal words by quickening of the Spirit.

   5)   Immersion with propriety, yet rejoicing. Instruction to candidate on breathing, folded arms, position, surrender to one baptizing. Need to allay any fears.

   6)   Avoid any electrical contacts with microphones, etc.

   7)   Baptismal Certificate appropriate to be given to candidate.

Communion — The Lord's Table

The next major ordinance the Lord has set in the Church is Communion, or the Lord's Table. It was generally associated with Water Baptism in Early Church history. We note again in outline form the significance of this ordinance in the Church. The more believers understand the table of the Lord, the more benefit they will receive from it. In numerous places the Communion has become a mere form and a meaningless ceremony, or a memorial service. It is observed sometimes once a year, every six or three months, or a special occasion. Lack of insight into the significance of the table is evidenced by so many ministers, and so, because of this it is celebrated so little. Between the extremes of the Roman Church and the Protestant Church the Communion has been robbed of its significance to the people of God (I Corinthians 11:23-34; 10:16-17; Matthew 26:26-29; Mark 14:22-26; Luke 22:15-20).

1. **What are some of the titles given to this Ordinance?**

    a. It is called the Lord's Supper (I Corinthians 11:20).

    b. It is called the Lord's Table (I Corinthians 10:21).

    c. It is called the Communion (I Corinthians 10:16).

    d. It is referred to as "the Eucharist" which means "Thanksgiving" and "The Sacrament".

2. **Who Instituted the Communion?**

    a. The Lord Jesus Christ instituted this service at the Feast of Passover. He commanded the disciples to "Do this in remembrance of Me" (Matthew 26:26-29; Mark 14:22-26; Luke 22:15-20; I Corinthians 11:25). This is the first reason we have it.

    b. The Lord Jesus saw fit to give to Paul distinctive revelation and insight into this ordinance (I Corinthians 11:23). Paul received of the Lord Himself the revelation of the Table of the Lord. This he gave to the Gentile Church at Corinth. Thus Jesus gave and instituted Communion. Paul received revelation and taught Communion. Christ gave the seed of truth during His preparation for His death. Paul gave the revelation of that truth after Christ's resurrection.

3. **What are the Symbols used in the Communion?**

    a. The Table (I Corinthians 10:21; Luke 22:30).

    b. The Bread (I Corinthians 10:16; Luke 22:19).

    c. The Wine [fruit of the vine] (I Corinthians 10:16; Luke 22:17-20).

4. **What is the Significance of the Symbols?**

    a. **The Table**

    This is a place of love and fellowship, sharing and communion. It is the "family table", a love feast, a meal (Leviticus 24:5-9; Psalms 23:5; Revelation 3:20). It is the New Testament "Table of Shewbread".

    b. **The Bread**

    This represents His broken body (Matthew 26:26). It fulfills the body of the Passover Lamb, and all other sacrificial bodies of animals under the Old Testament times and Covenants (John 6:48-56).

    It also symbolizes the Church, the Body of Christ (I Corinthians 10:16, 17; 12:12, 27; 11:29).

    c. **The Wine**

    This represents His blood which was significant of the New Covenant (Matthew 26:27; Mark 14:24; Luke 22:20; I Corinthians 11:25). His blood was for remission of sins.

    Fruit of the vine is the lifeblood of the grape. (Note — Alcoholic wine is certainly not a fitting symbol of His incorruptible blood!)

5. **What are some Old Testament Shadows of the Communion?**

There are many shadows in the Old Testament of the New Testament Communion. However, it should be remembered that these things were not just "types or shadows" to those that experienced them.

a.   Melchisedek ministered Bread and Wine to Abraham at the receiving of tithes (Genesis 14:18). This is the first specific account of "communion" in Scripture and it is significant that it with the father of all believers and the pristhood of Melchisedek (Hebrews 7). It was covenant time.

b.   The Table of Shewbread with its Drink Offering of outpoured wine pointed to the Lord's Table (Exodus 25:20; Leviticus 24:5-9). Shewbread actually means "The Bread of His Face, or Bread of His Presence." It was "presence bread". The priests set it in order every weekly Sabbath day. Only the priests could eat it in the Holy Place of the Tabernacle. His presence kept the bread fresh and free from corruption.

All believers are priests to God in New Covenant times and should partake (Numbers 28:7; Exodus 25:23-30).

c.   The Manna-Bread from heaven in the wilderness for 40 years, and the waters from the smitten Rock also pointed to communion, that spiritual meat and that spiritual drink (I Corinthians 10:1-6 with Exodus 16-17).

d.   The widows multiplying cake and oil pointed to communion also. It was a miracle supply of God for daily living during the 3½ years of famine under Elijah and the prophets of Baal worship. All point to that time in Revelation when the saints will be miraculously preserved with communion of the Lord in 3½ years of Great Tribulation (I Kings 17; Revelation 12).

e.   Elijah also was miraculously preserved for 40 days in the strength of the bread and water that the angel brought him (I Kings 19:48). At the end of this time he was translated into the glory world. How much so of the real communion of the body and blood of Christ? God will bless our bread and water (Exodus 23:25).

f.   The Passover Lamb with its body and blood is undoubtedly the greatest shadow of the Communion. For, it was at Passover Supper, the Lord's Supper was brought in. This itself is of great significance indeed.

We note some of the important points of this Passover Supper which were replaced in the Lord's Supper, especially after His death, burial and resurrection.

1)   Christ desired to eat this PASSOVER with the disciples before He suffered (Luke 22:13-26; Matthew 26:26-29; Mark 14:22-25).

He would be THE LAMB to which every other lamb (and animal sacrifice) pointed. (John 1:29, 36; Exodus 12; Revelation 4:12; 13:8; 17:8). He was the original Lamb slain from the foundation of the world.

2)   It was at New Covenant time, even as that Passover Lamb was to a Covenant people. The Communion is for a covenantal people, a people in covenantal relationship with God and with each other (Matthew 26:26-28; Jeremiah 31:31-34; Hebrews 8).

3)   The Lamb was without spot, wrinkle, or blemish and it was to be a male of the first year. It was to be shared in the household meal. So Christ fulfills all in Himself at Passover time on Calvary.

Many are the truths in the Passover Feast (Refer to "*The Feasts of Israel*" for fuller exposition of these things).

4)   Not one feeble member was among Israel when they came forth (Psalms 105:37).

5) What happened to the *body AND blood* of the Lamb was important to God. So Jesus takes the bread, His Body, and the cup, His Blood, and tells them to eat and drink of the same in memorial of Him (I Corinthians 5:7).

Animal body and blood could never deal with sin. His body and blood can and does (Leviticus 17:11; Ephesians 1:7; Hebrews 9:14; I John 1:7; Revelation 1:5).

6) Passover was the great deliverance for Israel. It made possible many miracles in the provision for Israel (Exodus 12-13-14-15-16-17; Nehemiah 9:11-21).

Christ is our Passover and so the Old Testament supper was fulfilled in Christ and replaced in the New Covenant community in the Lord's supper.

6. New Testament Breaking of Bread

There are a number of examples of ''bread'' in the New Testament which can be used to point to the Lord's Table, the Communion.

a. The breaking of the five loaves and two fishes was miracle communion for the multitude (Mark 6:41; Hebrews 7:5-9). The bread/fish multiplied in the 12 apostles' hands (Mark 8:6).

b. The miracle of feeding the five thousand was followed by the profound teaching on eating His flesh and drinking His blood (John 6).

c. On the first day of the week the disciples broke bread together (Acts 20:7-11).

d. The early believers continued stedfastly in the apostles doctrine, fellowship, breaking of bread and prayers (Acts 2:42-47).

e. Paul broke bread with friends (Acts 27:34, 35).

f. Christ was known in the breaking of bread. Their eyes were opened at the covenant table (Luke 24:30-34).

g. Paul taught the Corinthians the revelation of the table (I Corinthians 11:23-34).

h. Most every time Jesus appeared to His disciples in the 40 days post-resurrection ministry He had ate and drank with them (Acts 10:40-41 with Luke 22:16-18).

i. At least six times Jesus spoke of ''eating and drinking'' His body and blood (John 6). The secret was ''the Spirit quickens . . . His words are spirit and life.'' The Jews could not handle this. The Old Testament forbad drinking of blood. Life was not available under Old Covenant sacrifices. Life is in Jesus. Spiritual truths must be for spiritual minds (I Corinthians 2:13; 10:1-6).

j. The communion involves covenant. The New Covenant came into force after the death and resurrection of Christ (Hebrews 9:15-17; Matthew 26:26-28). No covenant could be ratified without the body and blood of the sacrifice. So Christ's body and blood are the ratification of the NEW Covenant (Jeremiah 31:31-34; Hebrews 8 with Matthew 26:26-28).

The communion is not meant to be a formal, lifeless thing, but that which the Spirit quickens and makes alive to all who partake. Formalism has robbed the Church today of its reality and impartation.

7. What Attitudes should we have in coming to the Lord's Table?

a. Come to the table with a desire to participate, even as Christ did (Luke 22:14, 15).

b. Come in faith believing (Hebrews 4:2; 11:6; Romans 14:23).

c. Come in remembrance (memorial) (I Corinthians 11:24, 25). Israel remembered sins; we remember Him.

d. Come with thanksgiving (Eucharist), as Jesus did (Luke 22:17).

e. Come discerning the body and blood of Christ, both physically (His body), and spiritually (The Church, His Body) (I Corinthians 11:27-30).

f.   Come examining our hearts (I Corinthians 11:28), making sure we are in right standing with God and our brother (I Corinthians 11:27; Exodus 12:43-49; Psalms 24:3-5).

g.   Come in unity as a Body (I Corinthians 10:17).

h.   Come partaking together, waiting for each other (I Corinthians 11:33).

It is the bread which *we* break, and the cup which *we* bless (I Corinthians 10:16).

Christ is our great High Priest and we as believer-priests partake together (Acts 2:46, 47, Amplified New Testament).

i.   Come worthily (I Corinthians 11:27-30). Judge ourselves and we will not be judged of the Lord. Receive life and blessing and health and strength as we discern the body of Christ. Otherwise judgment is self-inflicted.

j.   Come with a threefold look to Christ.

1)   A backward look to Calvary — His death, His sufferings for us.

2)   A upward look to heaven — His resurrection and ascension, sitting at the right-hand of the Father interceding as our great High Priest.

3)   A forward look to His second coming when we meet Him, "until He come".

k.   Come in Supper time. The Passover Supper pointed to the Lord's Supper and the Lord's Supper points to the Marriage Supper.

l.   Come to know Him in the breaking of the bread (Luke 24:35).

m.   Come to receive life in right eating. Adam and Eve received death in wrong eating in Eden. The bread of life = the tree of eternal life (John 6).

n.   Come receiving, healing, health, life, strength (I Peter 2:24; II Chronicles 30:15-21; Psalms 105:37; I Kings 19:4-8; Deuteronomy 34:7).

God often used things in Scripture as a point of contact and faith for healing:—

1)   He used Elijah's mantle to open Jordan (I Kings 19:19-21; II Kings 2:11-15).

2)   He used Peter's shadow in healing (Acts 5:15).

3)   He used Elisha's dead bones to resurrect a person (II Kings 13:14-21).

4)   He used the Manna and the Waters of the Rock as literal/spiritual meat and drink (I Corinthians 10:1-4 with Exodus 16-17).

5)   He used Paul's handkerchiefs to exorcise demons and heal the sick (Acts 19:12).

6)   He used the serpent of brass for healing of Israel (Numbers 21 with John 3:14-16).

7)   He used the river Jordan in Naaman's healing of leprosy (II Kings 5).

8)   He used the hem of His garment for virtue to flow (Matthew 9:20-22; Luke 8:43-48).

9)   He used five loaves and two fish to feed thousands (Matthew 14-15).

10) He can use the bread and cup for weakness, sickness and death or strength, healing and life (I Corinthians 11:27-34). Blessing or judgment.

11) The bread and the cup is the communion of the body and blood of Christ (I Corinthians 10:16, 17).
It is the "children's bread" (Matthew 15:26).
It is the "three measures of meal" (Genesis 18; Luke 11:5).
It is the "table of the Lord, His meat" (Malachi 1:6-8).
It is "eating and drinking anew in the kingdom" (Luke 22:16-22).

If the Lord's presence was associated with these things in faith, so it can be in the table of the Lord. If His presence is not there, then all things can degenerate into mere witchcraft and idolatry of things!

Israel partook of the sacrifices of the altar and were holy (Exodus 29:36, 37; I Corinthians 10:18-21; Leviticus 1-7). The body and blood of all Old Testament sacrifices are fulfilled and abolished and now symbolized in the broken body and shed blood of Jesus Christ.

His body and blood are both in heaven for us now. He lives in the power of an endless life, and, by the Spirit, quickens the symbols of His body and blood in the Church, in the bread and the cup. It is this heaven/earth connection that makes the communion real and effectual in our lives!

8. **Practical Procedures in Ministering Communion**

    Following are some of the practical procedures which may be taken in ministering the Communion in the local Church. These are gathered from various references in the Scriptures and brought together here.

    a. **The Place**

        The original Passover took place in the houses of the Israelites. The Lord's Supper originated in a private house. The believers broke bread from house to house (Acts 2:46). Paul broke bread in an upper room (Acts 20:8) where they no doubt had a love-feast also. Early believers had to break bread wherever they could as the Romans forbad Christians to own property in time of persecution. The place is "where two or three gather in My Name" (Matthew 18:15-20).

    b. **The Time**

        The Lord's Supper was originated at Passover Supper. This was an evening meal. The Passover family festival was eaten in various homes of the redeemed. They did this in remembrance of deliverance from Egypt, so Christ asks them to remember His as the Lamb and the deliverance He brought from sin's bondage. At Corinth they had a love-feast, then the Lord's supper (I Corinthians 11:20, 21, 23-34). He had to correct their disorders here. Taking communion at home prevented a clerical and priestcraft from arising, and making communion idolatous.

        Undoubtedly it does not have to be an *evening* time, though it can be. Numerous Churches find that Sunday morning service is the more suitable for the most believers.

    c. **The Day**

        The Lord's Supper was not originated on the first day of the week, or on a Sabbath, but during an evening in the week. Hence any day can be proper. It would be impossible for thousands of believers in Jerusalem to have such on the same day except in homes where they broke bread (Acts 2:46).

        Under the Old Covenant, the priests had the Shewbread every Sabbath; that is, weekly (Leviticus 24).

        Under the New Covenant, it seems that the believers gradually moved to communion on the first day of the week, the Lord's day (Acts 20:7, 8). It does not give this day any pre-eminence, but it certainly was appropriate to have the Lord's supper on the day of His resurrection and the outpouring of the Spirit. It seems that Christ was known in the breaking of the bread on this first day of the week also (Luke 24).

    d. **How Often?**

        The above suggests that communion may be had *weekly*. "As *often* as ye eat this bread and drink this cup" does not say how often. But, if the Old Covenant priests had the Shewbread weekly, and New Testament believers had communion the first day of the week, then weekly celebration of communion would indeed be suitable.

e. **Instruction in the Word**

It is evident even under the Passover that this was a time of instruction in the Word of God (Exodus 12-13). As the children asked what it all meant, then the head of the house was to explain the feast to them.

In John 13-14-15-16 we have the Lord's instructions in truth during the time of the Communion. There are many truths noted in these chapters concerning the Holy Spirit, joy, love, serving one another, tribulation, the Father and Son relationship, vine-life, priesthood prayer, etc.

Paul gave instruction relative to the Lord's table (I Corinthians 11:20).
There should be adequate time for ministry of the Word at a communion service.

f. **Fellowship**

There was "koinonea" between Christ and His disciples in this time (John 13-14-15-16-17). Paul dialogued all night with the disciples (Acts 20:7, 9). So there can be fellowship, sharing together at communion of the Body of Christ.

g. **Hymn Singing**

At communion there was hymn singing also (Matthew 26:26-30). They sang a Hymn or Psalm, possibly The Hallel (Psalms 118). This permits congregational singing at communion time also (Colossians 3:16; Ephesians 5:18). Singing with Psalms, Hymns and Spiritual Songs. Speaking and admonishing one another in these things.

Early Church believers also had solo singing of spiritual songs, others would join in as they could. Tertullian in AD197 speaks of Christian love-feasts, where "every one was invited to sing, either from Scripture, or prompting of his own spirit, some song of praise to God for common edification." (Apology Chapter 39).

It is worthy to note that "*the singers*" prepared the Shewbread in the Temple order (I Chronicles 9:32-33).

h. **Foot-Washing**

Christ ordained the Table at a time of foot-washing. So there could be such a type of service at communion, sharing with each other, washing one another's feet, physically and spiritually (John 13).

i. **Serving Each Other**

Other practical things also can be noted here:

1) Time of examination of the heart before partaking.

2) Exhortation from the Word. The Gospel is here. (The Minister could and should study the Word and prepare 52 Sunday Communion talks for a year).

3) Remember it is a Covenant meal. Sometimes a love-feast could be held.

4) The people should be taught it is an act of faith. It is not magical or ritualistic, or "nothing in it". Beware of extremes of Romanism and Protestantism.

5) The Deacons and Deaconesses can serve the people as being symbolic of their service to the Body members.

6) Bread and wine taken together, waiting until all are served (I Corinthians 11:23-34).

7) Prayer of thanksgiving (Matthew 26:26-28).

8) Suitable time for prophetic word, song of the Lord relative to Table and the body and blood of Christ.

9) Suitable time for members to "discern the body" and receive each other in the bread and the cup, at times can exchange with each other as the symbol of such.

10) Maintain reverent, yet joyful order at the table.

11) Close with suitable hymn or song (Matthew 26:30).

True remembrance is bringing the power of the past into the present. The Holy Spirit makes it real as He was at Calvary!

j. **Receiving from The Communion**

1) For the worthy partaker there is (1) Healing and health (Matthew 15:25, 26; Psalms 105:37; Deuteronomy 29:5; I Corinthians 11:29, 30); (2) Life and quickening (John 6:54-57), and (3) Confirmation of covenantal relationship.

2) For the unworthy partaker there is (1) Guiltiness of the body and blood of the Lord, and (2) Eating and drinking of judgment, and (3) Weakness, sickness and death (I Corinthians 11:27-30).

In Conclusion:

There are three levels of approach to the Table of the Lord, as has been said;

1. **Ritual** — The Communion is only a ceremony or ritual. Many remain at this level and thus never receive anything from it.

2. **Revelation** — The Word revealed by the Spirit brings deeper understanding thereby producing faith to receive the benefits of the broken body and shed blood in healing, deliverance, Divine health, life and strength.

3. **Relationship** — Here it becomes more than just receiving, but a sharing, a fellowship and giving one to another as members of the Body of Christ, as well as ministering to the Lord.

The word ''Communion'' comes from the Greek word ''Koinonia'' meaning ''partnership, participation, communion, fellowship.'' This involves the act of sharing both with God and with the members of the Body of Christ.

It is a Table of Blessing, and a Table of Fellowship. It is in the Table that we express our UNITY with God through Christ and with one another as members of the Body of Christ (John 17).

CHAPTER 33

THE PURPOSE OF THE CHURCH'S EXISTENCE

Introductory:

We conclude our studies on The Church in the the New Testament and ask ourselves "What is the purpose of the Church's existence?"

We will find that the reason for the existence of the Church is basically fourfold. God had an eternal purpose in mind when He planned creation and redemption. This purpose was manifested in Christ and it is an "eternal purpose". This great purpose is THE CHURCH. Nothing will frustrate the eternal purposes of God in Christ and His Church (Ephesians 3). All things work together for good to them that are called according to this purpose (Romans 8:26-28).

Let us consider the fourfold purpose for the existence of the New Testament Church.

A. **Ministry unto the Lord**

The chief purpose for the Church's existence is to glorify and worship God. All things were created by God and for Him and for His pleasure (Revelation 4:11).

The Church is redeemed to be a worshipping community (Psalms 29:1-2). Redeemed to worship Him, then to serve Him (Matthew 4:10). It is first upward, then outward; it is first God, then Man. Worship always precedes service. Study these Scriptures (Deuteronomy 4:19; 5:9; 6:13; 8:19; 11:16; 12:32; 17:3; 26:20; 29:26; 30:17; Joshua 24:14-24).

Man was created to be a worshipper. Sinners cannot worship God. Only the redeemed can. Worship must be in spirit and in truth. John 4:20-24 is the major passage in the New Testament concerning worship and the word "worship" is mentioned here ten times.

John is told "to measure the worshippers" (Revelation 11:1-2). The redeemed must worship God by the energy of the Holy Spirit and according to His Word of truth (John 17:17).

The Westminister Catechism answers the question: "What is the chief end or purpose of man?" by saying: "The chief end of man is to glorify God and to enjoy Him forever."

Let us consider in outline form some of the major points in Scripture concerning the subject of worship in the redeemed community.

1. **WHO to worship**

Man does not know of himself how to worship God and thus creates various forms, liturgy, ritual, etc. and then asks God to bless his program. The great danger is formalism, deadness, monotony, and lack of the life of the Spirit (Jeremiah 3:16, 17; 7:8-16; Psalms 63:1-4).

There is no specific form of worship or order of service laid down in Old or New Testaments. However, the following ingredients are scattered throughout the Old and New Testaments. These things show that one, or more, any or all may be used at any given period of time when the redeemed community meets for worship.

The key is availability, flexibility and adjustability. "To everything there is a time . . ." (Ecclesiastes 3:1-11).

Men worship according to traditions and nullify God's Word so often (Mark 7:1-10).

It is GOD who is SPIRIT who must be worshipped (John 4:20-24). NOT God through any images, relics, priests or ministers, or God of our own concept, but the God of the Bible who reveals Himself as SPIRIT! Any other worship is actually idolatry!

2. **HOW to worship**

John 4:20-24 tells us that we are to worship "in spirit and in truth." This is what the Father God is seeking for? How much does He really find in the Church throughout the earth?

Worship is honour, reverence, homage in thought, feeling and act. The Hebrew word means "to prostrate, render homage, venerate, hold in awe, serve religiously."

a. Worship in spirit means that the Holy Spirit is moving upon, energizing and quickening our redeemed spirit to worship God who is Spirit. True worship begins in the spirit of man quickened by the Holy Spirit (John 3:1-5 with John 4:20-24). How can one not "born of the Spirit", "worship God who is Spirit in spirit and in truth?" There is no possible way to do this!

b. Worship in truth means to worship according to the way God has set out in His Word. His Word is truth, so to worship in truth is to worship according to the Word of God.

The Word of the Lord gives such variety in expression of worship (Psalms 149-150). (The Student is referred to "The Tabernacle of David" which deals more fully with this subject).

Singing and speaking praise to God, lifting hands, kneeling, prostration, and clapping of hands, lifted heads, silence, worship, etc. are involved in the various expressions of worship in truth. Musical instruments also are included (Hebrews 4:15; 12:1; 13:15; I Timothy 2:8; Psalms 3:3; 19:14; 22:22, 25; 28:2; 34:1; 42:5, 9; 49:1-3; 63:4, 5; 95:6; 121:1; 134:2; 141:1; 143:6; Lamentations 3:40, 41; Isaiah 45:23; Luke 11:21; 22:41; 24:50; John 11:41; 17:1).

3. **Old Testament Order of Worship**

In the Old Testament we see WHO (The Person), and HOW and WHEN (The Times), and WHERE (The Place) and the ingredients of worship set out here which ingredients follow in principle into the New Testament Church.

Israel was "The Church in the Wilderness" (Acts 7:38). They were the redeemed community and become a type of the New Covenant Church (I Corinthians 10:6, 11).

a. Weekly Sabbath day was set aside for rest and worship (Psalms 41:4; 81:1-3; Psalms 92, Title; Exodus 31:12-17; 20:8-11).

b. Freewill occasions and gatherings at the Tabernacle of the Lord took place (I Samuel 1-2; Psalms 119:164).

c. Festival seasons of the year (Deuteronomy 16; Leviticus 23). These were three:

1) Passover — Celebration of Paschal Lamb and deliverance from Egypt (Exodus 12).

2) Pentecost — Celebration of giving of Law and Corn Harvest (Leviticus 23).

3) Tabernacles — Celebration of fruit harvest, rains, atonement, booths, etc. (Leviticus 16; 23; Psalms 81:3).

d. The Place where all gathered was where His Name was recorded. i.e. Tabernacle of Moses, Tabernacle of David, Temple of Solomon. The place of the altar and ark (Deuteronomy 12; 16 with Matthew 18:20). Patriarchal Altars were also symbolic.

4. **New Testament Order of Worship**

The New Covenant community follows the basic principles typified in the Old Covenant Church.

a. First day of the week assembling together (Acts 20:8; I Corinthians 16:1).
The resurrection of Christ took place the first day of the week (Matthew 28:1).
The Holy Spirit Pentecost took place the first day of the week (Acts 2:1-4).
The disciples broke bread the first day of the week (Cf. John 20 with Acts 20:8).
Collections were laid aside the first day of the week (I Corinthians 16:1).

b. Believers seek the Lord individually as New Covenant priests.

c. Festival occasions of the year, i.e., Camp Meetings, Special times and seasons of the year.

d.   The Person and Place — Christ Jesus (John 1:14-18; 2:19-21), and then the Local Church (Matthew 18:20; Hebrews 10:25; John 4:20-24; Ezekiel 11:16; I Peter 2:5-9; Revelation 1:6; 5:9-10).

5.   **Old and New Testament Ingredients of a Worship Service**

The basic ingredients of a worshipping service of the priestly body are seen in these things. These things are the WHAT and the HOW of worship in truth.

a.   **Ministry of Music**

Colossians 3:16; Ephesians 5:17-18. Tabernacle of David order. Psalms, Hymns, Spiritual Songs. Good melodies and words for congregational singing. Psalms 100; 150. Instruments of music, however, never to replace the instruments of the believers, individually and corporately. Music to the Lord, to the saint, and also to the sinner. Song leader must have ministry in this area. (Refer to Guidelines for ''*The Service of Song*''.)

b.   **Prayers, Thanksgivings, Intercessions**

I Timothy 2:1. Prayer for kings, rulers, authorities. His house to be a house of prayer for all nations. Includes adoration, thanksgiving, petition and praise (Isaiah 56:7; Matthew 21:13).

c.   **Tithes and Offerings**

Malachi 3:6-10. An act of worship. Not to be belittled or apologized for.

d.   **Ministry of Word**

Psalms 40:9; 138:1-2; Deuteronomy 6:3-15; 11:13-21; Malachi 2:1-7. Priests and Levites teach the Word. The Word is above all things. It is the HUB of the service. All that precedes and follows relates to it as the spokes of a wheel to the hub. The meeting falls apart without this hub; the preaching, teaching and exhorting the Word, the sword of the Spirit. Note the ministry of the Word in the Book of Acts.

e.   **Ministry of Members of Body**

I Corinthians 12-13-14. Testimony, sharing, items, exhortations, Scripture readings, etc. (I Corinthians 14:26).

f.   **Gifts or Charisma**

Gifts of the Spirit should be evidenced (I Corinthians 12-13-14). Fellowship.

g.   **Ordinances**

Water Baptism, Laying on of Hands, Confirmation, Communion, etc.

h.   **Announcements** — Bulletin or brief announcements time.

i.   **Benediction**

Worship is judged as to its final analysis whether it (1) Glorifies the Lord, and (2) Edifies the worshipper in the most holy faith to minister to the world. The Church is called first to minister to THE LORD. All other ministry will only be as effective as this ministry is (Psalms 50:23; John 15:8; Titus 2:10; I Peter 2:9; 4:11; Romans 15:6, 9; Ephesians 1:5, 6, 12, 14, 18; 3:21; II Thessalonians 1:12). Read also I Chronicles 16:5; 23:30; II Chronicles 5:12-14; I Chronicles 16:4-6; 25:1; concerning instruments of music and the singers.

The Book of Revelation shows the redeemed WORSHIPPING God and the Lamb (Revelation 4:4-11; 5:1-14). As we present our bodies a living sacrifice then we can move in priestly ministration and service (Romans 12:1-2).

6.   **Practical Guidelines for Leadership**

a.   The Service should be one unified and harmonious whole. God has a purpose for each meeting. Move from part to whole, whole to part. Seek the guidance of the Holy Spirit. Should lead the people out to meet God (Exodus 19:17; I Corinthians 11:17).

b. The Service should flow like a river, not a flood, not a jerky river. River cuts it own path. The Holy Spirit is a river (John 7:37-39).

c. Ministry of the Word is the hub of the service. All else flows to and from the Word ministry.

d. Edification of the saints is key to all (I Corinthians 14). Does it edify? Does it build up or tear down?

e. Glorification of God and Christ by the Spirit. The Spirit comes to point to the Father and the Son (John 14, 15-16).

f. Variety of the Spirit. Not stereotyped, forms, ritualistic, stiff and starchy. Living Presence of Christ to be there. Not just emotional climax without spiritual and Biblical climax. Not old wineskin with new wine, old garment patched up with new patches.

   Revelation is a Book of worship connecting heaven and earth (Hebrews 12:22-24). Allow for the creativity of the Holy Spirit, and His variety.

g. Beware of sacerdotalism, allowing the leadership to do the priestly ministrations for the people instead of the priesthood of all believers. The persons who lead the service should be the most spiritual, not the carnal ones!

h. Beware of ''me'' centred services. Beware of over subjectivity and not objectivity. Need balance in both, Spirit needs to quicken each area of the service.

i. Types of Ministry can be:

   1) Praise and worship meetings.
   2) Prayer and intercessory meetings.
   3) Communion services.
   4) Foot-washing services.
   5) Ministry of the Word meetings.
   6) Presbytery meetings.
   7) Body members ministry meetings.
   8) Choir and orchestra meetings.

B. Ministry to the Saints

The second purpose for the Church's existence is to edify itself, this being done by the saints ministering to one another. This is the ministry of the Body edifying and increasing itself in love (Ephesians 4:9-16; I Corinthians 12).

Enough has been dealt with in this text to confirm this fact. We note some of the major points in connection with this area of ministry.

1. The saints are to be built up in the most holy faith (Jude 1-4). God has given various ministries for this purpose (Ephesians 4:9-16; Colossians 2:7; I Corinthians 3:10-15; 14:26; Jude 20).

   The fivefold ministries are to educate the members of the Body of Christ with the Divine doctrines of the Word (Matthew 28:18-20).

2. The saints are to be built up as to holiness of character and conformity to the image of Christ. It is the Lord's will that the Church be holy, without spot, blemish, or wrinkle or any such things. He desires to present to Himself a glorious Church as His bride (Ephesians 5:23-33; John 15:2; Hebrews 12:10; I John 3:2; Revelation 19:7; I Corinthians 11:28-32; II Corinthians 7:1).

3. The saints are to be brought into the work of their ministry as functioning members of the Body of Christ also (Ephesians 4:9-16).

4. The Church is also to be a covering and protection for the saints of God. It is the house of the Lord and all that a natural home provides, so should the house of the Lord (Isaiah 2:1-4).

5. The saints will minister one to another (John 13:34, 35; Galatians 6:2; Ephesians 1:22, 23; 5:21), even as the members of the natural body minister one to another.

    a. Love one another (John 13:34, 35; 15:12, 17; I Peter 1:22; I Thessalonians 3:12; 4:9; I John 4:7, 11-12). Love in word and in deed (I John 3:18).

    b. Comfort one another. Help, call alongside (I Thessalonians 4:18).

    c. Consider one another (Hebrews 10:24).

    d. Exhort one another, call near (Hebrews 3:13; 10:25).

    e. Edify one another, build up (Romans 14:19; I Thessalonians 5:11).

    f. Admonish one another (Romans 15:14; Colossians 3:16).

    g. Minister to one another, serve, as deacon (I Peter 4:10).

    h. Forbear one another, hold self back or up (Colossians 3:13; Ephesians 4:2).

    i. Forgive one another, graciousness (Colossians 3:13; Ephesians 4:32).

    j. Submit to one another, set in array under (Ephesians 5:21).

    k. Subject to one another, as submitting (I Peter 5:5).

    l. Teaching one another, instruct, show lessons (Colossians 3:16).

    m. Prefer one another, set above in estimation (Romans 12:10).

    n. Pray for one another, supplicate, petition (James 5:16).

    o. Hospitality to one another, lover of strangers (I Peter 4:9).

    p. Greet one another, salute, welcome, embrace (I Peter 5:14; Romans 16:16).

    q. Fellowship one another, partnership (I John 1:7).

    r. Have the same care one for another (I Corinthians 12:25; Ephesians 4:25).

The human body, with its millions of cells and members, all working in harmony, unity, and life show what can be in the members of the Church, the Body of Christ!

C. Ministry to the Sinner

The third purpose for the Church's existence is to minister the Gospel to the sinner. The more effective our ministry is to the Lord, the more effective ministry is to the saints, then the more effective should be our ministry to the world, to the unsaved. When the saints are built up they should multiply themselves. The Church is to preach the Gospel of the Kingdom to the world before the end of this age comes (Matthew 24:14; 28:18-20).

1. God's promise to Abraham included blessing on all the families of the earth (Genesis 12:1-3). This is the Abrahamic Covenant.

2. God called Israel to bless the nations of the earth as a kingdom of priests also (Exodus 19:1-6).

3. The inheritance of Christ is the salvation of the heathen (Psalms 2:8; 11:6). The world's population in 1982 is almost 4 billion and possibly 8 billion by AD 2000. And 94% of ordained ministry ministers to 10% English speaking people, and 6% speak to the 90% non-English speaking world.

    We are to scatter the seed and win souls (Proverbs 11:23, 24, 30; 13:17; 19:17; 21:13; 22:9; 24:27; 28:27; 31:8-9).

    We are to be a light in the world (Matthew 5:14-16).

    Signs and wonders are to follow the preaching of the Gospel (Mark 16:15-20).

4. The Church is to fulfil the Great Commission and make disciples of all nations in this present age (Matthew 28:18-20; Acts 1:5-8; Luke 4:18-21; John 20:20-22).

5. This is the age for the coming in of the Gentiles to be grafted into the good olive tree with believing Jews (Romans 9-10-11). Here the Gentiles, with the Jews gather into the Tabernacle of David (Acts 13:1-4; 15:15-18; Romans 11:25).

The Church is to be God's arm of salvation to a lost and dying world (John 3:16). He sent His disciples out to continue His ministry until out of every kindred, tongue, tribe and nation there will be those who are the redeemed (Revelation 5:9-10). The Lamb will see the fruit of His sufferings. The Church is to minister the evangel!

D. Ministry of Conquering Satan and His Kingdom

The Church is to finally bring about the downfall and casting out of Satan and his evil hosts. We see this in the following points.

1. The Church is Militant and Triumphant (Matthew 16:15-20).

The type of Church Christ will build is a victorious Church. The Gates of Hades will not prevail against it (Genesis 22:17). It will be militant and come in conflict and warfare in the spiritual realm with the Gates of Hades (Genesis 24:10). It will prevail and go forth conquering and to conquer.

The Church will be clothed with the armour of God and the spiritual weapons of warfare for battle (Ephesians 6:10-20; II Corinthians 10:1-5). The weapons will be mighty through God; not a miliant spirit as in the Dark Ages and the Crusades and so-called "holy wars" against flesh and blood. Our kingdom is not of the world system, thus not a physical battle. The warfare is with principalities and powers and the rulers of the darkness of this world, and wicked spirits in heavenly places (John 18:36, 37; Revelation 12:10, 11; Acts 12:10; Psalms 9:13; Isaiah 38:10; Matthew 7:13; Genesis 28:17; Isaiah 26:2).

The Gates are symbolical of the places where the ancients held their business transactions, Council, Law-Courts and entrance to the cities. The Gates of Hades have to be stormed (Genesis 3:15). The enemy will be bruised by the seed of the woman, the Church militant and triumphant.

2. The Church and The Keys of the Kingdom

The Church will have the keys of the kingdom (Matthew 16:19); the key of knowledge (Luke 11:51); the key of David (Revelation 3:7; Isaiah 22:21-22); and the Lord who holds the keys of death and hades, and the key of the bottomless pit will be working with it (Revelation 1:18; 9:1; 20:1).

The key is always significant of authority and power. The key is an opener. It opens and shuts doors, letting people in or locking them out. Peter at Pentecost opened the door to the Jews and then in Acts 10-11 opened the door of faith to the Gentiles (Acts 2).

The four keys in Acts were The Word, The Spirit, The Name and The Prayers of the Church and of all the saints working together.

The kingdom is the rule and reign of Christ. The kingdoms of this world are subject to His kingdom (Revelation 12:13, 17). The Church is to preach and demonstrate the power of the kingdom (Matthew 24:14).

The message of the kingdom is repentance, faith and baptism (Matthew 4:16; 3:2). The early Church taught and demonstrated the kingdom (Acts 8:12; 19:8; 20:25; 28:28-31). This kingdom is entered by new birth (John 3:1-5; Colossians 1:13, 14). The law and the prophets were until John, since then the kingdom is preached and all men press into it (Luke 16:16; Matthew 5:17, 18; 11:13).

Old Testament Israel was God's Church AND Kingdom (Exodus 19:1-6 with Acts 7:38). The kingdom in its present form has mixture of good and evil, but all evil will be taken out at Christ's advent (Matthew 13).

3. **The Church in Binding and Loosing Ministry**

a. Binding Ministry — Greek "*Deo*" = "to bind, to knit, to wind." It relates to the Gates of Hades in conflict against the Church. The Church is to have power to bind those who oppose; Principalities, powers, wicked spirits (Matthew 12:29). First bind the strong man. The tares are bound into bundles first (Matthew 13:30). Those who are cast out of the Church are bound (Matthew 18:15-20). The Word of God is not bound. Satan is to be bound eternally (Revelation 20:2 with Psalms 105:22-26; 149:8; Mark 5:3; II Timothy 2:9).

b. Loosing Ministry — Greek "*Luo*" = "to loosen, break up, destroy, dissolve, melt." It relates to the keys of the kingdom. The Church is also to have a loosing ministry. Jesus loosed a daughter of Abraham who had been bound by Satan (Luke 13:16). Satan has bound his captives and the Church has to loose these powers that bind (John 11:44; Psalms 102:20; Mark 7:35). Whatsoever ye bind shall be bound . . . whatsoever ye loose on earth shall be loosed (is already loosed in heaven).

c. Heaven and Earth.

"Bound . . . loosed in earth . . . bound, loosed in heaven." The Church is the Body of Christ in the earth, yet joined to her risen Head in heaven.

All power is given to Him in heaven and earth (Matthew 28:19-20). After the ascension of Christ to heaven the disciples went everywhere preaching the Gospel, the Lord working with them from heaven, confirming the Word with signs following (Mark 16:15-20).

He is the possessor of heaven and earth (Genesis 14:18). His will is to be done in earth as it is in heaven (Matthew 6:9). The earth totally depends on heaven for all blessings. Otherwise earth will become dry, empty, a waste and a ruin without heaven's blessings (Deuteronomy 11:1-21).

The New Testament Church is redeemed to minister to the Lord, to the saints, to the sinner and finally be used to judge Satan and his evil kingdom. This is the fourfold purpose of the Church's existence. No wonder Paul said "Unto HIM be glory in THE CHURCH both now and ever more" (Ephesians 3:21).

- - - - - AMEN - - - - -

SUPPLEMENTAL CHAPTER

LOCAL CHURCH CONSTITUTION

> THIS CONSTITUTION IS PRESENTED AS
> AN EXAMPLE WHICH MAY BE
> ADAPTED BY ANY CHURCH THAT
> DESIRES TO BE AN AUTONOMOUS
> AND LOCALLY GOVERNED CHURCH

Introductory:

Relative to any Local Church Constitution, a sample of which is presented here, the following comments need to be made.

Because the believer is a citizen of "two worlds", that of a heavenly country and earthly country, he is therefore required by the authority of the Scriptures to live accordingly as a Christian citizen. This involves the Government of the nation both Scripturally and Legally.

A. Scriptural Constitution

As far as the Christian citizen is concerned, THE SCRIPTURES ALONE are the one and only Constitution by which he lives and submits to as a believer. God's laws and by-laws and His form of government for His Church are laid out therein.

God's government of the Church is that of Elders and Deacons (Philippians 1:1), and these together rule and serve the congregation, the Church. The Bible therefore is the final court of appeal for all matters of Christian Faith and Conduct.

B. Legal Constitution

However, these same Scriptures teach the Christian citizen that he is to obey the powers that be which are ordained of God. This involves Civil Government (Romans 13). These government rulers are the ministers of God also. Therefore, a Christian is called to submit himself to the ordinances of his government as long as they do not violate the government and law of the Kingdom of God (I Peter 2:13-17).

Jesus told us to "render to Caesar the things that are Caesar's" (Matthew 22:17-21). Paul also confirmed this and told us to render to all their dues; tribute to whom tribute is due; custom to whom custom; fear to whom fear; honour to whom honour" (Romans 13:7, 8).

The Australian Government requires that NON-PROFIT and Religious Corporations have a Constitution, and more especially to protect the interests of those members who give funds and invest their interests in the purchase of lands and/or buildings.

Following are the basic requirements by Government for the existence and function of a Non-Profit Organization (or Congregation), and should be covered in its Articles and By-Laws.

1. Name of Corporation or Congregation.
2. Purpose of Existence.
3. Governing Principles.
4. Articles of Faith.
5. Registered Offices, etc.
6. Board of Directors; Number, Election, Removal, Replacement, Powers, Duties, etc.
7. Officers of the Church; Committees, Councils, Powers, Duties, etc.

8. Members — Legal requirements to have membership and records of such. Such should cover qualifications, privileges, rights, discipline. Certificate or Fellowship Card is suitable.

9. Accounts, Records, Auditing of Books, Yearly Business Meetings for the Church.

10. By-Laws that amplify but do not violate the Articles of Constitution.

11. Dissolution of Corporation (or Congregation), Payment of Debts, Disbursement of Funds.

12. Constitution lodged with the Australian Registrar of Non-Profit Organizations.

BECAUSE we are citizens of "two worlds" it is necessary to use language suitable for both Scriptural and Legal purposes.

Scriptural Language	**Legal Language**
The Local Church (Name of Christian Fellowship)	— Corporation/Congregation
Local Church Government	— Autonomy
Elders and Deacons	— Board of Directors: Treasurer, Secretary
Pastor, Minister of the Church	— Senior Minister
Senior Minister	— President
Elders and Deacons	— Directors/Trustees
Church Officers, including the Elders, Deacons, Deaconesses, Heads of various departments such as Young People, Music, Sunday School, Bible School, Women's Meetings, etc.	— Officers
Those above in charge of some department of the Church	— Committee
All Church Officers, together with the Elders and Deacons	— Church Council
Those who count "Christian Fellowship" their Church home and hold Card or Certificate of Baptism and Fellowship and are in good standing	— Membership
Church Membership records for legal purposes	— Records

This Constitution has been designed in such a way as to be suitable and adaptable for any Local Church that desires to be completely autonomous.

The Constitution has also been designed to provide "checks and balances" for all involved in the Local Church Government.

Church History has proven the problems that arise from various forms of Government having no "checks and balances", as seen in the following:

★ **Autocracy** — The rule of the one man, without checks and balances.

★ **Bureaucracy** — The rule of the few, and "hire and fire" system in the Church.

★ **Democracy** — The rule of the people, mass rule, controlling the oversight.

★ **Theocracy** — The rule of Christ through His appointed ministries, having Divine checks and balances in the government of His Church.

Thus:

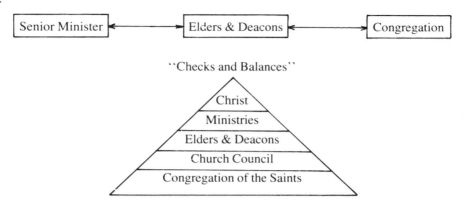

NOTE — The above comments are **NOT** a part of the legal constitution, only introductory remarks for members of that Local Church.

THE CONSTITUTION AND BY-LAW OF "LOCAL CHRISTIAN FELLOWSHIP"
PREAMBLE

WHEREAS, It is the express purpose of God, our heavenly Father, to call out of the world a saved people, who shall constitute the Body or Church of Jesus Christ, built and established upon the foundations of the apostles and prophets, Jesus Christ Himself being the chief cornerstone; and

WHEREAS, The members of the Body, the Church of Jesus Christ, are enjoined to assemble themselves together for worship, fellowship, counsel and instruction in the Word of God and for the exercise of those spiritual gifts and offices set forth in the New Testament;

BE IT RESOLVED, That we recognize ourselves as a body of Christian believers according to the Scriptural plan for the local assembly, in order that we may worship God as a united body, exercising all our inalienable rights and privileges granted to a religious body by the Constitution of Australia and do hereby adopt the Articles of Constitution and By-Laws and agree to be governed by them.

Article I — Name

The name of this Congregation is "CHRISTIAN FELLOWSHIP"; a non-profit Congregation (hereinafter spoken of as the Congregation, Fellowship or Church) as constituted under the Laws of the Commonwealth of Australia, and its duration shall be perpetual.

Article II — Purpose

1. To propagate the Christian Faith and to spread the Gospel of Jesus Christ as revealed through the Holy Scriptures by all means of communication, whether visual, verbal or written.

2. To provide for preaching, teaching and fostering the growth of the Christian Religion in all places; and to licence and ordain ministers; to carry on the work of evangelism; to promote missionary work in all places; to carry on the organization of churches and foster their development and local sovereignty and independence according to this Constitution and its By-Laws.

3. To erect and maintain Church buildings, social halls, business offices, school buildings recreational facilities, parsonages, and such other structures as are deemed necessary, and to

organize and promote such activities as deemed necessary for the upkeep and continuance of said buildings and facilities.

4. To collect, solicit and accept funds, gifts and other subscriptions; to hold in trust, use, mortgage, lease, sell, or otherwise acquire or dispose of property, real or chattel, in keeping with the recited purposes of this Church, and it shall have and exercise all powers that are necessary or convenient to effect any and all of the purposes for which this Congregation is organized.

Article III — Principle of Autonomy

We hold as Scriptural and fundamental the principle of local Church government by qualified men called elders, and in conjunction with the elders are qualified men called deacons, who serve both the eldership and the congregation (Philippians 1:1). These men must qualify according to the qualifications laid down in the Scriptures (I Timothy 3; Titus 1:5-9).

That is, the local Church is sovereign under Christ's headship, and all ecclesiastical power is exercised by each local Church assembled as a congregation and decisions thus made shall not be subject to change or reversal by any other ecclesiastical body. This Church is autonomous, but advice and counsel from qualified ministers of other bodies of like principles and faith may be sought.

Article IV — Faith

The fundamental teachings of this Congregation are reflected in the following clear statements of faith:

1. We believe in the plenary-verbal inspiration of the accepted canon of Scriptures as originally given. The Scriptures are infallible, inerrant, and the sole and final authority for all matters of faith and conduct (II Timothy 3:16; I Corinthians 2:13).

2. We believe in the Eternal Godhead who has revealed Himself as One God existing in Three Persons, Father, Son and Holy Spirit, distinguishable but indivisible (Matthew 28:19; II Corinthians 13:14).

3. We believe in the creation, test and fall of man as recorded in Genesis; his total spiritual depravity and inability to attain to Divine righteousness (Romans 5:12, 18).

4. We believe in the Lord Jesus Christ, the Saviour of men, conceived of the Holy Spirit, born of the Virgin Mary, very God and very Man (Luke 1:26-35; John 1:14-18; Isaiah 7:14; 9:6).

5. We believe Christ died for our sins, was buried and rose again the third day, and personally appeared unto His disciples (I Corinthians 15:1-4; Romans 4:25).

6. We believe in the bodily ascension of Jesus to heaven, His exaltation, and personal, literal and bodily coming again the second time for His Church (John 14:2, 3; and I Thessalonians 4:13-18).

7. We believe in the salvation of sinners by grace, through repentance and faith in the perfect and sufficient work of the cross of Calvary by which we obtain remission of sins (Ephesians 2:8, 9; Hebrews 9:12, 22; Romans 5:11).

8. We believe in the necessity of water baptism by immersion in the Name of the Eternal Godhead in order to fulfil the command of the Lord Jesus Christ (Matthew 28:19; Acts 2:34-36; 19:1-6).

9. We believe in the baptism of the Holy Spirit as a real experience at or subsequent to salvation, with the Scriptural evidence, namely, speaking in other tongues as the Spirit gives utterance (Acts 2:1-4; 8:14-17; 10:44-46; Galatians 3:14-15).

10. We believe in the operation of the Gifts of the Spirit as enumerated in I Corinthians 12-14, as manifested in the Early Church.

11. We believe in the Spirit-filled life, a life of separation from the world and perfecting of holiness

in the fear of God as expressing the true Christian faith (Ephesians 5:18; II Corinthians 6:14; 7:1).

12. We believe in the healing of the body by Divine power, or Divine healing in its varied aspects as practiced in the Early Church (Acts 4:30; Romans 8:11; I Corinthians 12:9; James 5:14).

13. We believe in the table of the Lord, commonly called the Communion or the Lord's Supper, for believers (I Corinthians 11:28-32; Matthew 26:26-28).

14. We believe in the reality and personality of the Devil and eternal judgment in the Lake of Fire for the Devil and his angels (Matthew 25:41; Revelation 20:14, 15).

15. We believe in eternal life for believers (John 5:24; 3:16), and eternal punishment for the unbelievers (Mark 9:43-48; II Thessalonians 1:9; Revelation 20:10-15).

16. We believe that there is one true universal Church, made up of genuine believers, but this one universal Church is also composed of many local Churches in given localities. These Churches are under the sovereign Headship of the Lord Jesus Christ, exercising autonomous government under Him, administering all its local affairs and ministry, as well as the propagation of the Gospel (Acts 15:22; with Matthew 16:18; 18:15-20).

17. We believe that Government is ordained of God, and the powers that be are ordained as ministers of God to us for good. To resist the powers and the ordinances is to resist the ordinance of God. We are subject not only for wrath sake but for conscience sake, rendering to all their dues, custom to whom custom, fear to whom fear, honour to whom honour. We declare out loyalty to our Government and its leaders and will assist in every way possible consistent with our faith in the Scriptures as Christian citizens (Romans 13).

Article V-Board of Directors

1. Board of Directors

This Church, as to its business affairs, shall be fully controlled, governed and operated by its Board of Directors, which shall consist of a minimum of three(3) members or of five(5) members, but the number may be increased as the need arises, these being taken from qualified Elders and/or Deacons. Should the Board of Directors be three(3), there shall be the President, Secretary or Secretary/Treasurer and Advisory Member. Should it consist of five(5), there shall be the President, Vice-President, Secretary/Treasurer and two Advisory Members. Further, this Board of Directors shall consist of Scripturally qualified Elders.

a. Duties of Secretary

It shall be the duty of the Secretary to keep an accurate record of the proceedings of the meetings of the Board and of the Yearly or Special Congregational meetings of business, and all such other duties as pertain to this office as may be prescribed by the Board.

b. Duties of Treasurer

The Treasurer shall have the care and custody of all funds and securities of the Church and shall deposit the same in the name of the Church in such Bank or Banks as the Board of Directors may select.

The Board shall, by resolution, fix all matters of signatures at the time of his taking office, which shall continue during the tenure of office, or until changed by the Board.

The Treasurer shall at all reasonable time exhibit his books or accounts to any member of the Board or Committee appointed by the President for that purpose where such inspection has been requested by the majority vote of the Board on that subject.

2. Directors

The Board of Directors at this period of time consists of the following:

The President, Pastor and Senior Minister.
The Vice-President and Minister.

Advisory Member and Minister.
Secretary/Treasurer and Elder (or Deacon).
Advisory Member and Elder (or Deacon).

3. **New Members**

    New members of the Board shall be appointed by the existing Board as the need arises. All Board members must be chosen and accepted on the basis of the Scriptural qualifications laid down in I Timothy 3 and Titus 1 and must be official members of the Church. No person, other than an Elder (or Deacon), shall be eligible for election or appointment to the Board of Directors.

4. **Term of Office**

    All Board members will maintain their position for life but are subject to removal at any time when they cease to qualify under the original qualifications by which they were appointed.

5. **Replacement**

    The Board of Directors will determine on the basis of the majority vote of two Elders and one Deacon, being the quorum of its constituency, when any member of the Board is no longer fulfilling the necessary qualifications for office, and also his replacement. Board members may also withdraw voluntarily at their own request.

6. **Senior Minister**

    Although Board members can be removed by the majority vote of the Board, the Senior Minister, upon Scriptural qualifications, can only be removed by the majority vote of the Board, but must also have a confirmation by three-fifths of the Voting Church Membership for his removal and replacement.

7. **Successor Senior Minister**

    The Senior Minister shall have the authority to name his successor in counsel with the Board of Directors.

8. **Powers and Duties of the Board of Directors**

    The Board of Directors shall have the powers and duties and the authority to implement such powers and duties as follows:

    a. To exercise the power and business of the Congregation.

    b. To apply to the proper authorities for permission to carry on the business of the Congregation wherever they may be situated in country or state.

    c. To appoint an attorney but only with the consent of the all members of the Board of Directors to do any acts and execute any documents for and on behalf of the Board of Directors or any of them.

    d. To manage and control gifts, legacies and beneficiaries of any kind.

    e. To manage and control investments.

    f. To meet any costs, expenses and liabilities from such funds as may be needed by the Church.

    g. To insure, build, repair and maintain property.

    h. To employ such staff as may be required in the functioning of the Church and to discuss such staff.

    i. To properly attend to accounts and audit and keep records of all payments; the treasurer being appointed to prepare a proper balance sheet of the Church business as at the 30th day of June in each year.

    j. To call for the General Assembly of the Church for an Annual (or Special) Meeting, the date of same to be advised in the Church-News and notice of such Meeting must be given at least two weeks prior to the date of such Meeting.

k. The powers more fully described in the Schedule hereto.

In the event of the dissolution of the Church, no financial requirement will be made on the property of any of the Board Members, but payment of debts and liabilities will be met from the sale of assets and disbursements of funds in Bank deposits and securities.

Artible Vi — The Trustees

1. The Trustees

For the purposes of the Religious Successory and Charitable Trusts Act 1958 the Board of Directors from time to time will also constitute the Trustees. The Senior Minister shall automatically be the President of the Trustees.

2. Powers and Duties of Trustees

The powers and business of the Congregation insofaras they relate to dealings with real or personal property of the Congregation shall be exercised, conducted and controlled by the Trustees for the promotion of the purpose of the Church as set forth in Article II.

The powers and business of the Trustees shall include:

a. To buy, sell, lease or otherwise deal in real and personal property being trust property in the name of the Congregation.

b. To hold trust property and manage trust funds in trust for the Congregation.

c. To sell, mortgage, charge or pledge trust property as affirmed by a three-fifths majority of the voting members of the Church present at a General or Special Meeting of the Church held to approve such sale, mortgage, charge or pledge.

d. To exercise all the powers and duties of the Board of Directors as described in Article V.8 and implied by law insofaras they relate to any dealing with trust property.

In the event of the absence of the President or Vice-President from any Meeting of the Trustees, it shall be for the remaining Trustees to make decisions regarding matters other than in the areas of Spiritual Oversight.

In respect of matters of financial decisions, no authority is vested in these members for payment of sums in excess of five-thousand ($5,000.00) dollars (or a determined upon amount).

Article VII — Committees

1. Number of Officers

The officers of the Congregation shall consist of a President, Secretary or Secretary/Treasurer and Senior Minister. These officers may be derived solely from the Board of Directors.

2. Committees

The Board of Directors may appoint and dismiss one or more committees consisting of officers and assistant officers, as may be deemed necessary. Any officer may serve for an unlimited number of consecutive terms in office.

These officers may include Elders, Deacons, Deaconesses and Heads of various departments of the Church and such additional members as may be deemed advisable.

3. Church Council

Together the officers of all these Committees, with the Board of Directors, constitutes the Church Council.

The officers of each department of the Church shall constitute the standing Committees of the Church. All standing Committees shall be auxiliary and subject to the Board of Directors, and shall have and exercise only the delegated and limited authority given to them by the said Board.

4. **Senior Minister**

   The Senior Minister, who is automatically a member of the Board of Directors, is also an ex-officio member of all Committees designated by the Board of Directors. The position of the Senior Minister is a perpetual position and he can only be removed or be replaced according to the provisions of Article V,6.

   The Senior Minister shall not take action independently in matters not having the approval of the Board of Directors, neither shall the Board seek to take action without the approval of the Senior Minister.

5. **Replacement**

   Any member of the Board, the Committees, or Church Council may voluntarily resign, or be removed by the Board of Directors whenever in their judgment the Scriptural standard or best interests of the Congregation will be served thereby. A vacancy in any office because of death, resignation, removal for disqualification or otherwise shall then be replaced by the choice of the Board of Directors.

Article VII — Membership

1. **Qualifications**

   The Membership of "Christian Fellowship" shall consist of those persons who meet the following qualifications:

   a.   Personal faith in the Lord Jesus Christ as their Lord and Saviour, and a desire to obey the requirements laid down in Acts 2:36-47.

   b.   Agreement with the Doctrines of Faith as stated under Article IV.

   c.   A lifestyle that is consistent with Christian conduct and doctrine.

   d.   Regular attendance at the activities of the Church.

   e.   Financial support of the Church by tithes and freewill offerings.

   f.   Voluntary submission to the spiritual oversight of the Church.

   g.   Application for membership to the Senior Minister and Board of Directors.

   h.   All members are encouraged to complete The Principles of Church Life Class.

2. **Membership**

   Membership shall be limited to those who fulfill the above requirements and have expressed their desire for membership and a willingness to co-operate with the purposes of the Church.

   There shall be three classes of membership of this Church designated, Active Members, Associate Members (who are temporarily in other locations but desire to maintain membership), and Juniors, who are under 18 years of age. Membership may be denied if the Board of Directors decide that this person would be detrimental to the Church.

3. **Certificate**

   Individuals accepted for membership will be received by the right hand of fellowship (Galatians 2:9) and receive a membership certificate or fellowship card which indicates the same. This certificate needs never to be renewed but it may be revoked by the Board of Directors if they unanimously decide that the individual would be a detriment to the Church. When a certificate is thus terminated the person holding the same will be given notice at the last known address that their certificate or fellowship card is invalidated.

   This fellowship certificate may be given at or after baptism.

4. **Voting Members**

   Voting Church Members are adults of 18 years of age and above and have attended regular services of the Church over three months; such have voting rights. Voting members shall be entitled to one vote at any of the General (or Special) Meetings of the local Church provided such vote shall be made personally.

5. **Voting Limits**

Members of this Church having voting privileges shall have such only in the following areas: the removal of the Senior Minister, and replacement of the Senior Minister in conjunction with Article V,6; confirmation of major building constructions and/or extensions, purchase of lands and properties, and the disposition of funds in the event of the dissolution of the Congregation as presented in Article XI. Members in good standing have the privilege of information of the Church records at the Annual Business Meeting.

6. **Discipline of Members**

Conduct contrary to the Scripture as determined by the eldership shall be sufficient grounds upon which any person may be disqualified as a member. Some Scriptures which support such disciplinary action are Romans 16:17, 18; I Corinthians 5:11-12; Galatians 1:18; II Thessalonians 3:6-15; Titus 3:10; II John 9-11.

The steps of the discipline of members shall always be consistent with the instructions given in Matthew 18:16-20 and Galatians 6:1.

The purpose of discipline is restorative, and remedial. However, if a person is separated from the Fellowship, they may not be re-instated until there has been genuine repentance of the offence and reconciliation, which will be attested to by the Senior Minister and confirmed by the elders of the Church.

7. **Records**

The Board of Directors will periodically update the active membership rolls in accordance with its requirements for membership. Absence from attendance of regular Church meetings for three(3) months without reasonable excuse will constitute being removed from membership. This excludes those Associate Members who are temporarily in other locations and desire to maintain membership. Persons withdrawing from membership, persons moving to distant localities, and entering into affiliation with other religious bodies should notify the Senior Minister or the Eldership of the Church of such intention.

Article IX — By-Laws

1. **By-Laws**

This Article is to provide for the making and adoption of a set of By-Laws which shall be in union with and continguous to the Constitution.

2. **Amendments**

The power to alter, amend, or repeal any by-laws, or adopt new by-laws shall be vested in the Board of Directors, and such amendments or alterations shall be approved by the full membership of the Board of Directors.

Article X-Amendment of the Constitution

This Constitution may be amended or altered with the approval of the full membership of the Board of Directors and a three-fifths majority of voting members of the Church present at a General (or Special) Meeting of the Church held to approve such amendment or alteration.

Article XI — Dissolution of Congregation

1. **Dissolution**

Dissolution of the Congregation will be determined by a unanimous decision of the Board of Directors and confirmed by the majority vote of the voting membership of the Church.

2. **Debts**

In the event of the dissolution of the said Congregation the Board of Directors shall pay or make provisions for the payment of all liabilities of the Congregation from the assets of the same.

3. **Distribution of Funds**

Upon such conditions as above all remaining assets of the Congregation shall be given or distributed to other like Religious or Charitable institutions in a manner consistent with this provision and the purpose of the Congregation and at the direction of the Board of Directors.

IN WITNESS WHEREOF we hereunto set our hands and affix our signatures this Sixteenth Day of December in the year A.D. 1981.
(Signatures affixed)

Structural Diagram

Board of Directors/Trustees (Elders & Deacons)			
Officers Committees	Officers Committees	Officers Committees	Officers Committees
Church Council (Inclusive of all above)			
Congregation of Christian Fellowship			

Schedule

Additional Powers of the Board of Directors

1. On behalf of the Congregation to alone or jointly with other persons guarantee the contracts or liabilities of any person or persons, firms or corporations with or without security.

2. To act as agent for any person, firm or company.

3. To open bank accounts and discuss, make, accept, endorse, discount, execute and issue cheque, promissory notes, bills of exchange, bills of lading warrants, debentures and other negotiable or transferrable instruments.

4. To conduct and carry on the business of a School or Schools of any kind whatsoever and be constituted as the School authority and in this respect:—

   a. All monies and properties received or derived in connection with the School will be applied solely for the purposes of the School and no portion thereof shall be paid or transferred directly or indirectly by any means whatsoever to members of the School authority, provided that nothing contained in that provision shall prevent payment in good faith to any person, including a member or employee of the School authority:—

      i) for services rendered in respect of the School;

      ii) for goods supplied in the ordinary and usual conduct of the School;

      iii) of interest rates not exceeding those for the time being prevailing in the community on money borrowed for the purposes of the School from any such member or employee;

iv) of reasonable rent for premises demised or let by any such member or person for the purpose of the School.

b   If upon the winding up or dissolution of the School authority there remains after satisfaction of its debts and liabilities any surplus property, the same shall not be paid or distributed among the members but shall be given or transferred to such School or Schools having objects similar to those of the School authority and by its or their constituents rules prohibiting the distribution of its or their income and property among members to an extent at least as great as it imposed on the School authority, as is determined by the members, by majority vote at or before the winding up, or, in default of such determination, by a judge of the Supreme Court of the State where the School is located who may have or acquire jurisdiction in the matter.

c.   Proper accounts and records of the financial administration of the School shall be kept. The accounts and records shall be separated from the accounts and records of other institutions or undertaking which the School authority conducts or to which it is related and shall show monies received and expended by the School, the manner in which such receipt or expenditure takes place and the property credits and liabilities of the School.

d.   The accounts and records relating to the School shall be available for inspection by authorised officials and agents of the Schools Commission.

e.   The conduct and management of the School shall be entrusted to the Church Committee provided for and appointed in accordance with this Constitution.

5.   The powers more particularly described in the Third Schedule of the Companies Acts 1961 (Australia) insofaras they do not conflict with any of the power expressed in this constitution and insofaras they can be adopted as powers of the Board of Directors of the Congregation.

BIBLIOGRAPHY

1. Beall, James Lee; *Your Pastor, Your Shepherd*, Plainfield, New Jersey, U.S.A., Logos International, 1977.

2. Benjamin, Dick; *Finding Your Place in the Body of Christ*, Anchorage, Alaska, U.S.A., Abbott Loop Community Chapel Inc., 1980.

3. Booth, Mrs William; *Female Ministry* or *Women's Right to Preach the Gospel*, Salvation Army, London.

4. Dresselhaus, Richard L.; *The Deacon and His Ministry*, Springfield, Missouri, U.S.A., Gospel Publishing House, 1978.

5. Ferris, A. J.; *What is wrong with the Churches? And the Remedy*, London, The Marshall Press Ltd., 1946.

6. Hay, Alex Rattray; *The New Testament Order for Church and Missionary*, Audubon, New Jersey, U.S.A., New Testament Missionary Union, 1947.

7. Howell, R. B. C.; *The Deaconship*, Valley Forge, PA, U.S.A., The Judson Press, 1946.

8. Lindsay, Thomas N.; *The Church and the Ministry in the Early Centuries*, Minneapolis, Minnesota, U.S.A., James Family Publishing, 1977.

9. Nee, Watchman; *The Normal Christian Church Life*, Washington 8, D.C., U.S.A., International Studnets Press, 1962.

10. Scheidler, Bill; *The New Testament Church and its Ministries*, Portland, Oregon, U.S.A., Bible Press, Bible Temple, 1980.

11. Williams, Don; *The Apostle Paul & Women in the Church*, Glendale, California, U.S.A., Regal Books, 1977.

PUBLICATIONS
BY KEVIN J. CONNER AND/OR KEN MALMIN

THE BOOK OF ACTS

This new one volume commentary on the Book of Acts provides a fresh approach to this key book of the New Testament, showing its relevance for today as a pattern-book for the operation of the Holy Spirit through the Church.

THE CHURCH OF THE FIRSTBORN AND THE BIRTHRIGHT

The Church of the Firstborn & The Birthright is a fascinating exploration of "The Firstborn" theme that runs from Genesis through to the Book of Revelation. Hebrews 12:14-29, as a base, is used to open many Old and New Testament Scriptures bringing them together in a fresh and exciting manner which shows the great significance of the Church of the Lord Jesus Christ.

THE CHURCH IN THE NEW TESTAMENT

The Church in the New Testament is a very comprehensive textbook. There are some unique features in it dealing with The Church and The Kingdom, The Church in the Old Testament, The Church as the New Ethnic, Church Government, Ascension-Gift Ministries, Elders and Deacons, The Ministry of Women in the Bible, Church Discipline, Stewardship and the Purpose of the Church's Existence are also dealt with. Christ as the Wise Master-Builder can only fill that Church with His glory which is "built according to the pattern".

THE COVENANTS

Undoubtedly one of the master keys to Biblical interpretation is that which is found in The Divine Covenants. The Bible itself is a Covenant Book. The Covenants of Creation and Redemption are considered in a very unique approach. The text-book is a 'must' for all real Bible students.

THE DEATH-RESURRECTION ROUTE

This booklet is actually a Soliloquy, a "talking with oneself." It follows in the steps of Jesus on the Calvary road from His incarnation to His Ascension and Glorification. The believer also is called to "follow in His steps."

TO DRINK OR NOT TO DRINK

This excellent book presents a unique approach to the great and universal problem of drink and alcoholism. It deals with the subject Statistically, Medicinally and Scripturally. What do the Scriptures teach? Do the Scriptures advocate teetotalism? This is a most comprehensive booklet printed as a result of much research.

THE FEASTS OF ISRAEL

A long-awaited study of the three Feasts of the Lord in Israel, this book will be of very great value to the student, the pastor, the teacher and the layman alike. It unlocks some of the greatest truths of God's progressive dealings with His own people, both then and now.

THE FOUNDATIONS OF CHRISTIAN DOCTRINE

This text deals with the foundations of all the Systematic Theology as taught in Portland Bible College, Oregon, U.S.A. The author believes that a person's theology affects their whole interpretation of the Scriptures: hence its importance.

INTERPRETING THE SCRIPTURES

Recognizing that one's beliefs arise out of one's interpretation of Scripture, the authors have produced a comprehensive textbook of how to discover the meaning of Scripture.

INTERPRETING THE SYMBOLS AND TYPES

How often have we all wondered at the use of so many symbols throughout the Bible! In this book we have laid out for us, the clear interpretation of them, including a list of all the symbols in the Book of Revelation and their interpretation.

METHODS & PRINCIPLES OF BIBLE RESEARCH

This text, along with *Interpreting the Scriptures*, is especially designed for use in "*The Key of Knowledge*" Seminars authored and conducted by Kevin J. Conner. Numerous students graduate from various Theological Colleges but many fail to have the necessary "*keys*" and "*How To's*" for their own personal Bible Study. This text lists some of the major "*Tools For Research*" plus some of the major "*Methods of Research*". They include Word, Character, Place, Textual, Topical, Passage and Book Studies. The Seminars especially follow a twofold approach of "teaching the keys" (instruction) and "using the keys" (practical workshop by the student). Here the student finds the joy of discovery for themselves, each using and developing these methods according to their distinctive calling in God and in the body of Christ. The book is designed in such a way that a diligent student may set their own pace as they work through the text assignments.

THE MINISTRY OF WOMEN
(Or, Divine Order)

Kevin and Joyce Conner, in this booklet, set out what they believe is the Divine and Biblical Order for men and women. The Table of Contents sets forth Order in Creation, Order in the Fall, Order in Divine Judgement, Order in Redemption, Order in the Christian Home and Order in the Church for both men and women. This chapter is actually an enlarged chapter taken from The Church in the New Testament. It will help on the controversial subject of Women's Role in the Church.

THE NAME OF GOD

In Proverbs 30:4 Agur asked this prophetic question concerning God, "What is His name, and what is His Son's name, if thou canst tell?" This volume answers the question by presenting a unique approach to the triune name of the eternal Godhead. Its insights are provocative especially in the area of the application of 'The Name' in Water Baptism.

NEW TESTAMENT SURVEY

This text is a companion volume of Old Testament Survey, using the same patterned approach. It also contains additional helps to understand the New Testament as a whole and is easy to use by student and non-student alike.

OLD TESTAMENT SURVEY

This text gives a patterned glimpse of each book in the Old Testament along with additional helps in relating each book to the others. Its fresh outlined approach makes it easy to use by student and non-student alike.

THE SEVENTY WEEKS PROPHE

The author believes this vital prophe to the subject of Eschatology. Whateve The Seventy Weeks is determines then tion of the Books of Daniel and Revelation. author looks at the Dispensational, A-Millenial an Christian Millennial viewpoints.

THE TABERNACLE OF DAVID

The author in designing this book to be used as textbook has opened up a vast area of neglected truth concerning this little known subject. It is also companion book to the Tabernacle of Moses.

THE TABERNACLE OF MOSES

The author has combined a lifetime of research an thought with his God-given ability to make the Bibl come alive in writing this comprehensive volume. is a rather complete work on this subject and it ha excellent pictures and diagrams.

WATER BAPTISM

This is a thesis written for one of his degrees. Her the author treats thoroughly the Bible view c Water Baptism with a very interesting and challeng ing section on the Name of God and its involvemen in baptism.

THIS WE BELIEVE

This simple booklet sets forth the most importan theological statements of faith as seen in the body o Scripture. Fuller development of these statement are seen in The Foundations of Christian Doctrine

Direct enquiries to:

PUBLICATIONS

K.J. & M. J. CONNER
P.O. Box 7
Blackburn South, 3130
Victoria, Australia.